THE MUSIC OF JAMES BOND

THE MUSIC OF
JAMES BOND

JON
BURLINGAME

OXFORD
UNIVERSITY PRESS

OXFORD
UNIVERSITY PRESS

Oxford University Press is a department of the University of Oxford. It furthers the University's objective of excellence in research, scholarship, and education by publishing worldwide.

Oxford   New York
Auckland   Cape Town   Dar es Salaam   Hong Kong   Karachi
Kuala Lumpur   Madrid   Melbourne   Mexico City   Nairobi
New Delhi   Shanghai   Taipei   Toronto

With offices in
Argentina   Austria   Brazil   Chile   Czech Republic   France   Greece
Guatemala   Hungary   Italy   Japan   Poland   Portugal   Singapore
South Korea   Switzerland   Thailand   Turkey   Ukraine   Vietnam

Oxford is a registered trade mark of Oxford University Press in the UK and certain other countries.

Published in the United States of America by
Oxford University Press
198 Madison Avenue, New York, NY 10016

Library of Congress Cataloging-in-Publication Data
Burlingame, Jon.
The music of James Bond / Jon Burlingame.
    pages   cm
Includes bibliographical references and index.
ISBN 978-0-19-986330-3 (alk. paper); 978-0-19-935885-4 (paperback)
1. Motion picture music—History and criticism.   2. James Bond films—History and criticism.   I. Title.
ML2075.B87 2012
781.5'42—dc23   2012006979

Contents

Acknowledgments

Although I am the sole author of this book, I am also the first to say that I have had a lot of help—in fact, more than in any of my three previous books. I am enormously grateful to all of those who agreed to interviews (whose words you will read throughout the book, and who are cited throughout the endnotes) and the many others who have assisted me with research, photographs, contacts and favors. Among them:

Geoff Leonard, coauthor of the definitive John Barry biography, keeper of the http://www.johnbarry.org.uk website, and perhaps the world's leading expert on the life and career of the composer. His generosity is boundless, and he shared with me his time, knowledge and collection of Barry material throughout the process of writing this book.

Craig Henderson, one of the nation's leading experts on spy movies and TV, who first engaged me to write about this subject more than 40 years ago and whose website http://www.for-your-eyes-only.com is an oasis of intelligent cultural and historical insight on the web.

Laurie Barry, widow of John, who supported this project from the start and whose kindness (dating back nearly 25 years) allowed me to interview her very private husband often and visit their Oyster Bay, New York, home on two memorable occasions.

David Arnold, who not only wrote the last five Bond scores but shares my passion for the music of John Barry, and who was kind enough to put me in touch with Sir George Martin and several of his Bond collaborators of the 1990s and beyond.

John Cork, Steven Jay Rubin, Lee Pfeiffer, Graham Rye, Ajay Chowdhury and Danny Biederman, all widely published and internationally renowned 007 authorities who offered assistance and in some cases supplied obscure or unpublished interviews that were immensely helpful. Their books and articles are cited in the endnotes and bibliography, and I encourage readers to seek out their work as the trustworthy chroniclers of the filmed adventures of James Bond.

Greg Bechtloff, who is the senior project manager in the awards department of the National Academy of Recording Arts and Sciences and also happens to be a leading expert on Ian Fleming's creation; he was a partner throughout, making suggestions and helping me track down music, people and relevant articles.

Andrea Chin, my invaluable student assistant, whose knowledge of, and enthusiasm for, the espionage films and television of the 1960s and beyond made her the perfect research associate.

Sandra Garcia-Myers, Steve Hanson and Ned Comstock of the University of Southern California's Cinematic Arts Library, whose holdings include a substantial cache of Bond-related materials and who generously permitted me access to materials that I could not have found anywhere else in America.

Lukas Kendall, publisher of *Film Score Monthly* and producer of the 2003 series of Capitol/EMI CD reissues of many of the Bond scores; and Neil S. Bulk, his Bond-aficionado producer associate, for numerous music-related favors.

Cary Anning, library manager at Abbey Road; Michael Sweeney of the Musicians Union in London; Gordon Carmadelle at Local 47 of the American Federation of Musicians in Los Angeles; Scott Shea, producer of the 30th-anniversary Bond album; London orchestra "fixer" Isobel Griffiths; and musicians Mo Foster and Janet Brittle, all of whom helped me track down recording dates for the Bond scores.

Stephane Lerouge, who generously agreed to interview Michel Legrand for me in France, and Michelle Guy, who translated for me here in Los Angeles; and, for favors too numerous to mention, Legrand's manager Jim DiGiovanni.

My colleagues at *Variety*, especially editors Timothy M. Gray, Steven Gaydos, Steve Chagollan and Andrew Barker, who have allowed me to write about film music in their pages for 15 years, including, on several occasions, Bond and Bond music. I hasten to add that the *Variety* archives proved an invaluable asset in pinpointing details about the lives and careers of the people and films discussed herein.

Friends at the Margaret Herrick Library of the Academy of Motion Picture Arts and Sciences in Los Angeles, especially Stacey Behlmer, Warren Sherk and Faye Thompson.

Robert Vaughn, librarian at the Louis B. Mayer Library of the American Film Institute, who generously allowed me access to the Charles K. Feldman Collection; and Raul Perez at the Sony music library, who made possible a look at Burt Bacharach's music.

Daniel Goldmark, who first suggested the idea, and Norman Hirschy, my editor at Oxford, whose enthusiasm and support for this unusual project has earned my lasting gratitude.

For photographic research and assistance, Hanna Bolte, Julie Edwards, Geoff Leonard, Philip Masheter, Ginger Mason, Joe Sikoryak, Gay Goodwin Wallin, Stephen Woolston, Dave Worrall and The Film Music Society.

Friends and colleagues who aided me in a variety of ways, including Lori Barth, Jeff Bond, Bruce Broughton, Ray Costa, Bill Desowitz, Didier Deutsch,

Lisa Edmondson, Jeff Eldridge, Harry Forbes, Dan Goldwasser, Chuck Granata, Mark Kaproff, Julie Kirgo, Richard Kraft, Beth Krakower, Mike Matessino, Mark Minett, Steve Mitchell, Chris Neel, Melinda Newman, Steve Oxenrider, Ricky Riccardi, Doreen Ringer Ross, Jeff Sanderson, Robert Short, Jeff Smith, Jerry Steinholtz, Amy Stone, Ford A. Thaxton, Gina Vadnais, and two dear friends who have left us: Robert Urband and Ronni Chasen. And friends in the U.K. and on the Continent, including Gareth Bramley, Kenny Clayton, James Fitzpatrick, Anders Frejdh, Chris Malone, Dave Norris, Tommy Pearson, Paul Place, Paul Ryan and Pete Walker.

And finally, to longtime friends Steven Smith, Bruce Babcock and Nick Redman, who patiently listened to me prattle on about this subject for months on end, reviewed the manuscript and offered valuable insight; and to my remarkable wife Marilee Bradford, who enthusiastically agreed to my decision to walk down the aisle at our wedding to "We Have All the Time in the World": my heartfelt thanks. Even the greatest Bond experts probably don't realize that it was Marilee who, while she was a music executive at MGM in 1994, licensed the song to Guinness and enabled it, 25 years after its creation, to become the hit it always deserved to be. As Hal David said to me, "Bless your wife." I do.

J.B., February 2012

Introduction

When Ian Fleming sat down to write *Casino Royale* in 1952, he could hardly have imagined the billion-dollar industry that would result from his novel about the exploits of a British secret agent. Other authors would pen spy novels, to be sure, and many of the best of them would—like Fleming's James Bond novels—be turned into movies and television shows.

A significant part of the multimedia Bond world that would blossom after Fleming's death in 1964 was the music of those films. It all began in 1962 with *Dr. No*, where a chance connection between a songwriter and an arranger would turn the "James Bond Theme" into an unlikely hit and one of the most famous movie themes in history. It would extend two years later to *Goldfinger*, which found even greater commercial success as a popular song and a soundtrack album. Thereafter, the style of music heard in the Bond films would become the de facto sound of international espionage on screen.

"Spy music," as the lounge movement of the late 20th century would come to call it, had a cool, slinky vibe and was rooted as much in jazz and pop as in classical music. Hitchcock films like *The Man Who Knew Too Much* (1956) and *North by Northwest* (1959) sported fine Bernard Herrmann scores, but Herrmann's conservatory training resulted in a fairly traditional symphonic sound for both. As the Bond series was gaining steam, other composers offered fresh musical ideas, notably Henry Mancini with the lighthearted score for *Charade* (1963), Jerry Goldsmith's exciting work on *The Prize* (1963) and

Bond score architect John Barry himself with a moody, cimbalom-infused ambiance in *The Ipcress File* (1965).

The Bond "sound" was an accident, really: Monty Norman had a tune in mind that John Barry arranged into something that would suit a dangerous spy and also work as a pop instrumental record with both rock and jazz elements (highly unusual in 1962). Editor Peter Hunt liked it so much he kept repeating the piece throughout that first film. The success of the "James Bond Theme," both dramatically and commercially, led to future Bond movie assignments for Barry—11 in all.

"It was a mix of all kinds of things," Barry explained many years later, "jazz, classics, pop. I just found myself doing it—I looked at it and said, 'That's working.' That became the Bond style." The approach was as much practical as it was creative: "If you had a car chase, the damned car was right in your face; even the fistfights were noisy, so you had to come up with an orchestrational palette that would cut through all that. Big strong brass chords, sustained strings to retain the tension, and percussion, of course. It was the only thing that worked. You couldn't put soft violins in there. It was an overall mood, all minor keys, very sinister. It was distinctive, and it really set the tone for those Bond movies."

The enormous popularity of the 1960s Bond films made that approach de rigueur for all future Bond installments, and also for the many spy adventures that would follow in their wake. Composers Jerry Goldsmith (in the Derek Flint films and TV's *The Man from U.N.C.L.E.*), Elmer Bernstein (*The Silencers*, first of the Matt Helm movies), Lalo Schifrin (*The Liquidator*, TV's *Mission: Impossible*), Earle Hagen (TV's *I Spy*), Edwin Astley (TV's *Secret Agent*), Laurie Johnson (TV's *The Avengers*) and Quincy Jones (*The Deadly Affair*) were obliged to follow, to varying degrees, Barry's lead. Even Burt Bacharach and Michel Legrand, who would score the two "unofficial" Bond films, found they needed to write lively, jazz-oriented orchestral scores with pop elements in order to compete with the "official" cinematic Bond. And those who followed Barry on the official films—George Martin, Marvin Hamlisch, Bill Conti, Michael Kamen, Eric Serra and David Arnold—understood that they were expected to follow this new style of action-adventure scoring.

"John Barry was one of the few people that created a genre of film music: He uniquely, single-handedly, created the spy genre," says David Arnold, who has scored the last five Bond films. "You have the bebop swing vibe that he created in his initial arrangement of the 'James Bond Theme' coupled with that vicious, distorted electric guitar, which was definitely an instrument of rock 'n' roll. You hadn't really heard that combination before. It represented everything about that character, soundwise, that you would want: it was cocky, swaggering, confident, dark and dangerous. It was suggestive, sexy and unstoppable—all in two minutes."

As for the scores, Arnold explains the innovative mix of musical arenas: "The blueprint of what became the Bond sound are his chordal use of brass; having the entire string section play the melody, and then play it again an

John Barry conducting the orchestra in the score for *You Only Live Twice* in April 1967 at CTS Bayswater

octave up; the dark cello counterpoints, the sharp trumpet and trombone stabs, the use of vibes and brushes, electric bass and electric guitar. It's a very contemporary cross between rock 'n' roll, jazz, swing and to a certain extent classical music."

That style, Arnold argues, "so defined the tone of the films and the character. I still use those ideas. You can go away from it to a certain extent, but I embrace it because I know it's the right sound and the right approach and always will be."

Monty Norman's credit as composer of the "James Bond Theme" graces every Bond movie, and that piece is probably one of the dozen or so most-recognized musical signatures of all time. Even actor Sean Connery, the first to play 007 on the big screen, acknowledges its power: "That theme gives the audience a direct connection to Bond. It's an instant recognition."

As for the Bond songs—especially the classics such as "Goldfinger," "Thunderball," "You Only Live Twice" and "Diamonds Are Forever," but also such later hits as "Live and Let Die," "Nobody Does It Better," "A View to a Kill" and "Die Another Day"—have proven hugely popular among cinema-goers and record buyers alike. Matt Monro, Shirley Bassey, Tom Jones, Nancy Sinatra, Carly Simon, even Louis Armstrong have left their mark on the Bond series as vocalists; and in later years, the contributions of Duran Duran, a-ha, Tina Turner, Sheryl Crow, Madonna, Chris Cornell and Adele have demonstrated the Bond company can shift and change with the times, helping to keep 007 relevant into the 21st century.

This volume marks the first attempt to chronicle the entire 50-year saga of Bond music making with all of its ups and downs, surprises and disappointments, disasters and triumphs. In addition to the film-by-film history of Bond songs and scores, every chapter looks in detail at the music within a film to help fans pinpoint specific themes and musical highlights, enabling them to match up the music from the film with their favorite tracks on the soundtrack albums (an important commercial by-product of the film scores, also examined in detail).

James Bond songs and scores—like diamonds—are forever, and this book celebrates that remarkable legacy.

"... come watch for de moon ..."

Dr. No

Monty Norman wanted a Caribbean vacation.

The singer-turned-songwriter, who had recently enjoyed a huge West End success with the musical *Irma La Douce*, had just been offered a job by movie producers Albert R. ("Cubby") Broccoli and Harry Saltzman: the chance to write the songs and underscore for the first movie to be based on the exploits of James Bond, the globetrotting British Secret Service agent created by author Ian Fleming.

It was the fall of 1961, and they were sitting in the South Audley Street, Mayfair, offices of Eon Productions Ltd., the company that American-born Broccoli and Canadian-born Saltzman had jointly established to produce what they hoped would be a series of action-adventure films based on Fleming's popular novels. United Artists was already on board to finance and distribute them.

The call came from Broccoli, who had recently invested in Norman's short-lived musical *Belle*, a dark comedy based on the true story of a physician who murdered his music-hall singer wife. "Cubby was one of our main backers and he loved the show," Norman recalled. *Belle*, which opened in early May and closed less than six weeks later, had a book by writer Wolf Mankowitz, who had also been called to work on this new film, co-writing (with Richard Maibaum) the first draft of the script that would become *Dr. No*.

Norman didn't know much about James Bond. He had heard of the books, of course—they were already very popular in England—but hadn't read any of them. And besides, he was busy with multiple projects, mostly in the theater: his *Irma La Douce* had made a successful transition to Broadway, his *Expresso Bongo* had been made into a movie with rock 'n' roll star Cliff Richard and he had other musicals in various stages of development.

"I was just about to say, 'Give me a few days to think about it,'" Norman said, when Saltzman offered this: "We're doing all the locations in Jamaica. Why don't you come out to Jamaica, get the atmosphere of the place, write some of the Jamaican music. Bring your wife, all expenses paid." Plus a fee of five hundred pounds.

Norman thought: "Sun, sea and sand . . . and a little bit of work. Great!"

It was an offer that Norman couldn't refuse, and a trip that would change his life.

Ian Fleming was an ex-Naval Intelligence officer and newspaperman whose first novel, *Casino Royale*, introduced British Secret Service agent James Bond and met with immediate success on publication in 1953. He wrote a Bond novel every year thereafter, and when *Life* magazine reported in 1961 that *From Russia with Love* was among President John F. Kennedy's favorite books, the news helped to generate massive American sales too.

Dr. No, the sixth of Fleming's novels, takes agent James Bond, code number 007, to Jamaica to investigate the disappearance of a Secret Service officer. He eventually discovers, and thwarts, a larger plot involving a mysterious German-Chinese scientist who seeks to sabotage American space flights. The film, as Norman saw it, would need "natural songs, rather than studio ones." The trip would allow him to soak up the local atmosphere and, hopefully, provide the film with a touch of musical authenticity.

Norman and his wife, actress-singer Diana Coupland, joined the *Dr. No* team and flew into Kingston, Jamaica on Sunday, January 14, 1962. As the Kingston newspaper, the *Daily Gleaner*, reported two days later: "Monty Norman, who is to write the music for the film, will use local bands as far as possible."

In a stroke of remarkable fortune, the company had already hired London-born, Jamaica-raised Chris Blackwell as location scout and production assistant. Blackwell was the founder of Island Records and would later be acclaimed as the man most responsible for introducing reggae (via such artists as Jimmy Cliff and Bob Marley) to a world audience. Norman immediately asked Blackwell for a "room with a piano and preferably no windows, but certainly a darkened room because," as he later recalled, "I couldn't work in that wonderful lotus-life sunshine."

Shooting began on January 16, but Norman could waste no time because just a week later, on the 23rd, the crew was set to shoot a nightclub sequence that would require original music—meaning it would have to be written and

Monty Norman on the *Dr. No*
set in Jamaica

recorded in order to be played back on the set so the musicians could accurately mime to it.

As a later press release put it: "Norman arrived when shooting first started and, hiding himself away in a small room with a piano, spent his days tinkering with melodic ideas and his nights exploring the vivid and varied nocturnal activities of Kingston." He absorbed the sounds and colors of Jamaican music. Equally important, Blackwell introduced him to Byron Lee, the local bandleader whose group, the Dragonaires, was among the island's most popular, and who would ultimately be seen performing in the film.

Norman worked quickly and wrote three songs: "Kingston Calypso," "Jump Up" and "Under the Mango Tree." The first would accompany the trio of assassins we meet as the film begins; the second would serve as "source music," that is, music actually seen and heard being performed in a local nightspot; and the third would be a folk tune sung by the film's female lead, Honey Ryder, as she searches for shells on Dr. No's off-limits Crab Key.

"Kingston Calypso" was inspired by the opening scene of three "blind" beggars who turn out to be armed killers. Norman watched as the scene was being shot. "I suddenly thought, why not do something that couldn't be more Jamaican—the calypso?" Norman said. "So I took the original 'Three Blind Mice' [tune] and turned that into a calypso."

"Jump Up" was the result of Norman's visits to dance halls on the outskirts of Kingston. "They did all the Jamaican dances," he said, including one called a "jump-up, literally jumping up and putting your hands in the air. And

I thought, this is good, I'll do this as a number." "Jump Up" would become the song that Lee and the Dragonaires perform on camera.

"Under the Mango Tree" was conceived, according to Norman, as something for Honey to sing as she emerges from the water in that now-legendary scene in *Dr. No*. The idea originated in the novel, as Honey whistles the popular calypso tune "Marianne" (also known as "Mary Ann," although Fleming spells it "Marion") on the beach and 007 answers by whistling it himself. Or, as transformed in the film script: "The sun beats down on Bond as he sleeps. In the distance, as if in his dreams, he can hear a woman singing." As he awakens, Honey is said to be "singing softly" and, in the scene, Bond "takes up the calypso refrain."

Norman wanted to write something that would feel like an authentic folk song and so decided to do a little homework. A local theatrical group asked him to speak about working in the London theater, and he took the opportunity to ask them about the local vernacular. "I need patois," he told them, "the best of greenery and grocery and trees"—and especially what the locals might say when referring to lovemaking.

So the lines "mango, banana and tangerine / sugar and akee and cocoa bean" emerged from the flora aspect of his queries, while "me honey and me make boo-loo-loops soon" was a fairly obvious reference to making love. Years later, Norman decided that the locals were having a bit of fun with him, because "boo-loo-loops" (regardless of how one spells it) doesn't seem to appear anywhere else.

Norman didn't have to look far for singers for his "demos." He himself had been a popular singer with the jazz bands of Britain in the 1950s, among them Cyril Stapleton, Stanley Black and Ted Heath. His wife Diana had regularly performed at London's Dorchester and Savoy Hotels (she would later become well known for her role as Jean Abbott in the 1970s sitcom *Bless This House*).

Norman and Coupland went into Kingston's Federal recording studio, recorded the number and gave demo discs to the film's two stars, Sean Connery (as Bond) and Ursula Andress (as Honey). It was a technique that Norman had recently used in the theater, to help teach actors new songs to perform. "I worked with them on the number," Norman recalled. "They learned the melody quite quickly and Sean, I must say, was very good." (The original Coupland and Norman performances would later be preserved on the United Artists soundtrack album.)

Norman, while in Jamaica, began to think about Connery as the male lead opposite Vivien Leigh in a musical that he and Wolf Mankowitz were considering. The subject, ironically, was another classic spy: Mata Hari. It never came to fruition and, as Norman later reflected, it would have been difficult to cast Connery in a stage musical after his screen success as 007.

Byron Lee and his Dragonaires performed "Jump Up" and other Norman-written jazz-rock numbers at Federal. Lee later said, "They gave me a whole soundtrack to be done in two weeks. I don't know how we did that," adding that "they didn't use all our stuff," meaning some music was left on the cutting-room

Ursula Andress and Sean Connery on the beach, just after the two of them sing "Under the Mango Tree"

floor. As Kingston's *Daily Gleaner* reported while the Eon crew completed filming: "Local entertainers and musicians also were employed, among them the currently popular dance band, Byron Lee and the Dragonaires, whose Federal recording of five calypsos will be used in the film. These calypsos were written by London musical director Monty Norman."

The production call sheets for January 23, 24 and 25, 1962, specify Norman's presence on the set at Morgan's Harbour Hotel, where he supervised the musical elements of the scenes at Puss Feller's, the nightspot where Bond, Felix Leiter (Jack Lord) and Quarrel (John Kitzmiller) have a run-in with a female photographer (Margaret LeWars). Lee's band is seen and heard performing "Jump Up" to a happy crowd of dancers.

Lee wasn't the only notable Kingston musician to contribute to the soundtrack of *Dr. No*. Guitarist Ernest Ranglin—another find of Chris Blackwell's—was the featured soloist on many of the Jamaica-recorded tracks, including the electric guitar backing Coupland on "Under the Mango Tree." Trombonist-percussionist Carlos Malcolm, whose Afro-Jamaican Rhythms band would later become world-famous, also played on the Jamaican tracks: "With those wonderful Jamaican musicians, I was able to do quite a lot of the West Indian music," Norman said. (Both musicians later sued Eon for more than £1,000, Malcolm claiming he had been hired to "compose and write musical scores and supervise recordings," Ranglin for arranging duties; less than two weeks later, they settled for a reported £200 and withdrew the legal action. Malcolm's band performed at the *Dr. No* premiere in Kingston the following year.)

A few days before director Terence Young was planning to shoot the arrival of Honey on the beach, Norman visited author Fleming at his home, Goldeneye, located in Oracabessa, on the island's northeastern coast. "He was very interested in 'Under the Mango Tree,'" Norman recalled. Fleming apparently liked Jamaican music; six years earlier, while writing the treatment for his unrealized television series *Commander Jamaica*, he had suggested a calypso as the theme music ("a haunting melody suitable for playing at varying tempos," he wrote).

Having schooled the actors in the song, Norman was on the Laughing Waters beach on February 8 for the filming of Andress's emergence from the water in that unforgettable two-piece swimsuit. "I was a bit worried about Ursula's accent," Norman said. "It gave too much stiffness to what obviously is a loose, easygoing song. I remember thinking, 'This isn't the moment to worry about that because we'll obviously get into the studio back in England and dub this.' I think she did more [of the song] than is left in the film."

Swiss-born, German-speaking Andress's entire dialogue would ultimately be dubbed by another actress, as would her brief singing on the beach; Young and editor Peter Hunt initially used one of Diana Coupland's performance tracks. Norman and Coupland were never informed of this, and according to Norman it became "a slight bone of contention. [Later that year] I saw an almost complete film and there, out of the sea, comes Ursula, and in her mouth is Diana's voice. They didn't tell me anything, and if she hadn't been my wife,

she could have caused an enormous rumpus, because they had no right to do
that and they never paid for it."

Norman struggled to come up with a main theme for the film. He had been
thinking about it even before the Jamaica trip, recalling that an assistant to
Broccoli and Saltzman had remarked, while ushering him out of their London
offices, "See if you can come up with a good theme, because I think we'll get
two films and a television series out of this!"

The piece, which is not heard in the film but appears on the soundtrack
album as "Dr. No's Fantasy," is tuneful and somewhat lighthearted, often
played on electric guitar by Ranglin and the other Jamaican musicians. "That
was my first stab at a Bond theme," Norman said. "I liked it but it didn't have
enough of the mood, the ambiance or the character of James Bond. I thought
I could do better."

Their location work completed in about four weeks, the Normans left Jamaica
and flew to New York for meetings with United Artists executives ("they seemed
to like what we had done so far") as well as with Broadway people on unrelated
projects before returning home to London.

UA's publicity department had been thinking of music in terms of promotional possibilities even before filming began. At a January 9, 1962, meeting,
publicists urged the writing of "a calypso song about the exploits of James
Bond" and suggested "a Scottish theme be written into the score . . . to distin-
guish James Bond throughout the series," the latter apparently referring
more to Scottish actor Sean Connery (who had just been cast as Bond) rather
than that of Bond himself, whose half-Scottish heritage would not be revealed
until *You Only Live Twice* was published in 1964. One UA publicist, having
heard the Jamaica tapes, reported on March 23 that "the music of *Dr. No* is
really exciting, particularly the variation of the theme on 'Three Blind Mice.'
I think that we have a chance for a really successful soundtrack album on this
film."

Back in London, Norman began work on the dramatic music that would be
required. "I had a couple of meetings with Harry and Cubby and Terence
Young," Norman said, "but they weren't ready for music. I didn't get the music
[timing] sheets until quite late," he said, "it may have been April or May,"
with June recording dates looming. "I didn't wait for them, of course. What I
did was write all of the dramatic scenes that I knew were coming up, and developed them."

Norman was essentially a songwriter from a vocal-performance background,
not a trained composer of orchestral music. (*Dr. No* would be his second original film score, following the 1960 Hammer horror film *The Two Faces of Dr.
Jekyll*, a joint effort with his frequent theater collaborator David Heneker.)
"Nevertheless, the development of a tune into what you would call a piece of
underscoring was something I felt I could do, although I always worked with
an orchestrator on those things." So he enlisted Burt Rhodes, with whom he
had worked since *Expresso Bongo* in 1958, to help turn his melodies into fully

fleshed-out pieces for small orchestra. (He would ultimately give Rhodes half of his £500 fee and insist on screen credit for him.)

Norman came up with new musical material that he felt would suit the film's various moods, especially such key sequences as Crab Key, the tarantula in 007's bed, the arrival of the British Navy and the final scene of Bond and Honey in the boat. A key theme would turn out to be one he conceived in Jamaica: a 12-note phrase whose vaguely Chinese feel might represent the villainous Dr. No.

But time was getting short. Recording was set for mid-June, and there was still no musical theme to appropriately characterize James Bond.

Norman recalled talking with Broccoli and Saltzman about the idea. Saltzman was happy enough with "Under the Mango Tree" as the film's opening theme, while Broccoli wanted something "dramatic and atmospheric." Norman began thinking about tunes he had already written, but not yet used, that might be suitable.

"Bad Sign, Good Sign" came to mind. It was what musicians often call a "trunk song," something written, deemed unsuitable or unusable for whatever reasons and then put away in a bottom drawer somewhere for later use in another project.

"Bad Sign, Good Sign" was from an unproduced musical that Norman and his *Irma La Douce* collaborators, lyricist Julian More and director Peter Brook, were working on during the summer of 1961. They were thinking of turning V. S. Naipaul's acclaimed novel *A House for Mr. Biswas* into a West End production. "I did the music, Julian wrote the lyrics and together we did the book [adapted from Naipaul]. We did probably 10 or 12 numbers," Norman guessed. Set in the Hindu immigrant community of Trinidad and focusing on an ambitious but unlucky young man, it was finally deemed too expensive and difficult to cast, and abandoned.

A key early number in the show, "Bad Sign, Good Sign" explained something of Mohun Biswas's character: "I-I was born with this unlu-u-cky sneeze / And what is wo-orse I came into the wo-orld the wrong way round. . . ." As Biswas was born to parents of Indian origin, the accompaniment was to have been sitar and tabla. Norman's inspiration, as he later explained, was to "set aside the lyrics, split the notes of the first melody, and it became dum-di-di-dum-dum, dum dum dum. . . ."

It is at this point that the various stories told by the participants through the years begin to diverge. Editor Peter Hunt maintained, into the 1990s, that during postproduction he was beginning to feel that Norman's music "just doesn't seem to fit the picture somehow. . . . I don't think it's working. Monty had used the Jamaican sound and it was very good in its own right but just not appropriate for the film as we saw it." He quoted director Terence Young as disparaging the Norman score, referring to it as "mining disaster music" and feeling that "we've got to bring someone else in on this." Later on, Young him-

Monty Norman's original manuscript, in his hand, for the "James Bond Theme," written in 1962 but only recently discovered among the composer's papers

self was quoted as saying that "although the score was all right, we didn't have anything exciting for the title music."

Norman said that Hunt "was always very pleasant" and never indicated any dissatisfaction with the music, and that Young, "very much of the old-school type, would rather William Walton had written the score," referring to the renowned English composer of the grand-scale symphonic music for Laurence Olivier's *Henry V*, *Hamlet* and *Richard III*.

In any case, several key personnel on *Dr. No*, including editor and composer, agreed that a fresh voice was needed to ratchet up the excitement level, especially over the opening credits sequence (called, in film parlance, the "main title"). According to Norman, three people—United Artists Music publishing executive Noel Rogers, EMI Records producer John Burgess and his old collaborator Wolf Mankowitz—all suggested the same pop arranger-producer: John Barry. (Hunt claimed that a young assistant had mentioned Barry and that he was the one who urged Saltzman to contact the pop producer. Burgess later denied that he had ever talked with Norman about Barry.)

John Barry was one of the hottest names in British rock 'n' roll. He had had more than a dozen chart hits in less than three years, both as the leader of the John Barry Seven instrumental jazz-rock group and as arranger-producer for the popular vocalist Adam Faith (including number-one singles "What Do You Want" and "Poor Me"). He had written the theme for Britain's *Juke Box Jury* TV series and had begun a film-scoring career with the low-budget *Beat Girl* (1959) and the Peter Sellers drama *Never Let Go* (1960).

The John Barry Seven in the early 1960s. Barry holds the trumpet; guitarist Vic Flick is second from right.

"Noel Rogers, who was the head of United Artists Music at that time, called me on a Friday night," Barry told fellow composer Fred Karlin in 1990. "He said, 'Listen, these two guys, Saltzman and Broccoli, have made this James Bond movie.' And he said that Monty Norman had done the score, but that they weren't all that pleased with it and were in a real bind." Barry had never read the Fleming novels, but he remembered reading the comic-strip adaptations that had run in London's *Daily Express*.

Barry, Rogers and Norman met on a Saturday; whether it was June 9, as Norman contended, or June 16, as Barry believed, is still in debate. Barry's recollection was that everyone was in a hurry and he had only a few days to turn Norman's brief sketch into a fully realized two-minute piece. "I didn't see any film. I worked on the weekend. I'd written 'Bees Knees' which was a twangy-guitar-type thing, and it was almost the Bond theme. . . . Then, of course, it breaks into a swing tempo and goes almost bebop, you know, it was like a Dizzy Gillespie lick. So I did this theme, went into the studio, recorded it and that was it. No strings, just five saxes, nine brass, solo guitar, and rhythm section. I got paid £200 and that was that."

Whether there was one meeting (Barry's story) or four (Norman's), Barry did concede, in a November 1962 interview, that "the composer, Monty Norman, and I got our heads together and discussed the various aspects of the picture and the central character."

Many years later, Norman asserted: "What I needed was a pop orchestrator. I knew that it would help the film if [the theme] could be as contemporary as possible." The two met, discussed Norman's proposed theme and, said Norman, "we got on pretty well. Mainly because both he and I wanted guitar; it was obvious that the main theme was going to be guitar."

Barry often said that, apart from the familiar guitar notes of the opening bars, he found little to work with in Norman's material and just made up the rest, including the bass line, the countermelody and the jazz-oriented bridge. (He had, in the early 1950s, studied via correspondence course with Stan Kenton arranger Bill Russo, and the "bebop" portion of the Bond theme reflects that influence.) Norman insisted that he always "wanted a big-band sound and that's what we got in the middle."

Although Barry cited "Bees Knees," a 1958 John Barry Seven recording that was guitar-driven with a similarly dark tone, it was really his theme for the film *Beat Girl* to which the "James Bond Theme" owes the biggest debt: low, sinister twangy guitar, insistent beat and high, blaring brass—an early and surprising combination of jazz and rock elements for a film about juvenile delinquents in London. Issued as a soundtrack album in 1960, Barry's catchy, hip *Beat Girl* music became England's first long-playing record devoted to a single movie score.

What *Beat Girl* and the "James Bond Theme" also had in common was guitarist Vic Flick. Flick was a key member of the John Barry Seven, his instrument featured prominently in many of their hits, as well as on television (via the BBC's popular *Drumbeat* variety series) and in live stage appearances. A couple of days prior to the scheduled recording, Barry called Flick to confer about the guitar part.

"That sort of heavy guitar sound made him very happy," Flick recalled. "It had an edge to it, sort of a dynamic sound. I went to his apartment, we talked about it and worked out what to do. I overplayed it—I leaned into those thick low strings with the very hard plectrum, played it slightly ahead of the beat, and it came out exciting, almost 'attacking,' which fit the James Bond image."

Surprisingly, Flick did not play the Bond theme on an electric guitar. Instead, he played it on a Clifford Essex Paragon deLuxe acoustic guitar with a DeArmond pickup, as he explained, "gripped by its supporting plates to the strings behind the bridge, and held away from the body of the guitar by a carefully folded Senior Service cigarette packet." He used a Vox 15 amplifier, which the John Barry Seven had been routinely using at the time. Adding to the unique sound, Flick said, "some of my guitar sound was picked up on the many open microphones placed about the studio for the other musicians. This gave a 'room' effect that added to the general ambiance."

Flick was paid all of 7 pounds, 10 shillings for his work ("and I've spent that now," he quipped). He was part of the Barry orchestra on the first five Bond films and then returned for *Licence to Kill* in 1989. And despite rumors that the guitar was "cracked" and thrown away, the original Bond guitar survives, undamaged. It has been on display at museums such as the Rock and Roll Hall of Fame in Cleveland, Ohio.

In the late 1970s, John Barry began hinting—or, at the very least, did not discourage rumors—that he wrote the Bond theme. "Well, if I didn't, I don't know why I got to do all the others," he said in 1992. Noel Rogers had tantalized him with the promise of future work on the Bond films if the first one was successful; it was part of the reason he agreed to the rush job on the theme. And sure enough, the Bond producers did call him for their next film, *From Russia with Love*, and 10 more after that.

Though there can be little doubt that the familiar guitar riff is derived directly from Norman's trunk song "Bad Sign, Good Sign," what about the rest? The dark bass line, the driving rhythm, the jazzy midsection? Both Norman and his orchestrator, Burt Rhodes, insisted that Barry served only as an arranger and orchestrator for the theme recording and that the essential elements of the theme were already present when Barry was hired in June 1962. Rhodes, a veteran music director (notably for London's Talk of the Town theater restaurant, where many famous singers performed), said that he had added harmony and a countermelody to Norman's basic sketch before it was handed over to Barry for orchestration. He even recalled writing it in A minor but said that it was probably Barry who changed it to E minor for the recording.

The "James Bond Theme" was recorded for the first time on Thursday, June 21, 1962, at Cine-Tele Sound (CTS) studios, in Kensington Gardens Square in London's Bayswater district. Norman remembers the session: "I was absolutely thrilled. Whatever differences I had with John Barry, I've never said anything other than, his orchestration is the definitive orchestration. Nobody has bettered it."

Flick summed it up this way: "I would say it's part Monty Norman's talent, John Barry's and mine, all put together. When you're hearing it, you know it's a James Bond movie."

The remainder of the score was recorded the following week, on June 25 and 26, not at CTS but rather at London's Denham Film Studios. Rhodes orchestrated Norman's dramatic cues, and Eric Rogers conducted the orchestra, which Norman recalled consisted of 20 to 30 musicians. Rogers, who would go on to score many of the bawdy *Carry On* comedies of the '60s and '70s, would unfortunately see his name misspelled "Rodgers" in the film's credits. (Editor Hunt's contention that there was an earlier recording session that led to those claims of dissatisfaction with the Norman score, has never been corroborated, and no Musicians Union records from the era survive.)

Over those two days, Norman recalled, "lots of moody strings and woodwind sounds" offered a musical contrast to the lively, on-location Jamaican source-music recordings.

Once again, however, there were creative disagreements about Norman's handling of the dramatic music. When Bond discovers a deadly tarantula crawling on him in the middle of the night, producer Broccoli felt that Norman's music was "too melodic. There was no strong identification with what was happening on the screen. As the tarantula crawled close to Sean's face, the music was too low-key. When he finally dislodges the creature and starts pounding it with the heel of his shoe, I asked for the music to pound—crash . . . crash . . . crash!—in unison."

Later on, when audiences laughed at the end of this scene, Broccoli said the director blamed him: "You made me score it that way, and it's awful," Young told him. But Broccoli disagreed, recognizing that the laughter marked a release of audience tension, and that the musical rewrite had worked.

Over the next three months, as postproduction continued, Hunt made many decisions about where to place the various musical cues, and how loud or soft they should be, while he finished editing the film to its 110-minute running time. Norman was not consulted on any of them.

He was consulted, however, on the use of music over the film's animated title sequence, directed by Maurice Binder. They clashed over his musical reorganization of the Bond theme (using only a minute and 15 seconds but starting with the big-band midsection and crossfading into a Jamaican bongo track). As Norman wrote Broccoli and Saltzman on August 22, 1962: "After spending a day with Maurice Binder at Pinewood, I still wasn't able to convince him that the 'James Bond Theme' would have more impact and subtlety played as per the John Barry record instead of the disjointed, unmusical version he has made of it. I am looking at this purely from its commercial impact and publicity values to the film and not as the composer. Let us hope that EMI do not take umbrage and consequently withdraw the record and/or their support."

Norman was referring to the second recording of the "James Bond Theme" that Barry made on July 23, a somewhat more polished, two-minute version (again with Vic Flick on guitar) that would, in fact, be released on the Columbia

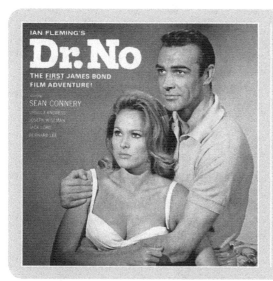

SCORE HIGHLIGHTS

After 17 seconds' worth of sound effects accompanying the "Harry Saltzman and Albert R. Broccoli Present" card and the original gun-barrel sequence in which a shadowy figure shoots at the camera, drawing blood, *Dr. No* opens with the John Barry Orchestra's performance of the "James Bond Theme" (unfortunately truncated and re-edited by title designer Maurice Binder).

Surprisingly, despite all the effort that went into creating a dynamic, exciting arrangement of the signature piece, and all the controversy that followed—from Norman's objections to the main-title version to Barry's annoyance that his piece was "all over the film"—the "James Bond Theme" (running only a minute and 45 seconds) is never heard in its complete form anywhere in the film.

label as a single in September 1962. Saltzman and Broccoli sided with Binder, and the titles remained as Binder had designed them.

Dr. No opened at the London Pavilion on October 5, 1962. It opened in America on May 8, 1963, and a handful of critics mentioned the music: "a jazzy score by Monty Norman" (*Los Angeles Times*), "Monty Norman's music is a solid asset" (*The Hollywood Reporter*), "music composed by Monty Norman is provocative" (*The Film Daily*).

Within weeks, the music community was abuzz about the movie's theme. London's *Daily Mirror* liked it even before the film opened: "It sums up Bond musically . . . rugged, dramatic and slick." "What may turn out to be a major copyright has been commissioned by United Artists Music," wrote *Billboard* in an especially prescient story on October 20. "It is the theme for a series of films based on Ian Fleming's James Bond novels. . . . The theme was written by Monty Norman and was scored for the film by John Barry." On November 1, Barry's EMI-Columbia single charted in the U.K. and it rose to number 13, Barry's most successful single in more than two years.

In the United States, *Billboard* declared the UA release of Barry's "Bond Theme" a "four-star single" on April 27, 1963, and reviewed the UA soundtrack album as deserving "pop special merit" on June 22: "some good tracks on the set, including 'The James Bond Theme' . . . could make good programming." And although the "Bond Theme" single never charted in the United States, the album did on July 27, reaching number 82 on *Billboard*'s Top LPs chart on August 17, 1963.

But, as happened with the film, no one at the record label consulted the composer about the marketing of his score on records. Some producer or artists-and-repertoire (A&R) executive assembled 17 of the Jamaican tracks and the Barry recording of the Bond theme into an "original motion picture

The Barry arrangement resurfaces seven more times, most memorably a little over eight minutes into the film, as Sylvia Trench asks the handsome man across the chemin de fer table at a private London club to identify himself. His now-famous response—"Bond, James Bond"—is accompanied by 20 seconds of the theme. Editor Peter Hunt, who made all the musical choices, fades it in and out, often abruptly and often with little musicality.

"I was very fortunate, in the end, of getting this marvelous James Bond theme," Hunt later said. "So every time James Bond was about to do something, or something was about to happen, I inserted this music." Hunt plays just under a minute of the theme as Bond flirts with Sylvia and departs the club. It's heard again as Bond arrives at the Kingston airport (almost 17 minutes into the film), as he returns to his hotel (41 minutes), drives to the rendezvous with Miss Taro (49-plus minutes) and when he shows up at her door unexpectedly (nearly 52 minutes). It doesn't appear again until the end titles, and then only for 16 seconds during the cast roll.

But what an impression that theme makes. It was the perfect signature for a ruthless secret agent with a license to kill: a sinister opening; a very modern '60s sound via that twangy, amplified and slightly echoing guitar; brass that builds and builds into a jazzy, swinging midsection that harks back slightly to the '50s but, at the same time, suggests a confident, sexy man of the world. No wonder it became the most famous spy music ever written.

Norman's entire *Dr. No* score totals less than 30 minutes, surprisingly sparse by modern standards.

soundtrack album," completely eliminating all of the dramatic underscore Norman had written and recorded in London. Norman thought that the unexpected box-office success of *Dr. No* in America caught UA executives by surprise, and that they threw the album together in a hurry to get it released and into the marketplace. "They just thought it was going to be a Limey spy story. I was very annoyed," he said, because none of his dramatic music—notably the tarantula scene, his music for the fight scene on the beach and his march for the Royal Navy near the end of the film—was included. And, except for the songs, none of the titles on the album were Norman's either. Asked who he thought might have assembled the album, Norman said, "I don't know, but I should think he was sacked afterwards."

Norman's theory may be correct. UA's prerelease "exploitation manual" for *Dr. No* indicates that the 45 rpm single ("Dr. No theme," as it's referred to) would be released in April but makes no mention of a full 33 rpm album. (It also recommends that American exhibitors visit disc jockeys "using a lovely lady as 'Bond's woman' as your planter.")

Hunt's musical choices throughout the film precipitated another problem: John Barry was furious, too, for a different reason. His arrangement and recording of the Bond theme "was supposed to be just the Main Title," he recalled in 1990. "The movie opened on a Friday in London, and on a Sunday afternoon I went in and saw the movie. Now the goddamn theme is all over the movie. I phoned Noel [Rogers] on Monday and I said, 'What is this?' He said, 'Uh-oh, I've been waiting for this phone call. I knew this was going to happen.'"

Hunt had so liked the Barry arrangement of the Bond theme, with its hints of danger and action, that he simply dropped it into the film wherever he deemed it appropriate. "Look, they know what your contribution is," Rogers told Barry, referring to Broccoli and Saltzman, and implied there would be

"Under the Mango Tree" appears almost as often as the Bond theme. It's first heard (about 28½ minutes into the film) as source music, presumably from a radio, when Bond follows Quarrel into a local bar; in fact, it's Norman himself singing on the demo recording he made to teach Connery the song. Diana Coupland's vocal version is heard (at 56½ minutes) when Bond decides to play a phonograph record at Miss Taro's while awaiting Professor Dent's arrival. But its most memorable rendition is the one heard when Honey makes her first appearance (just after the 1 hour, 2 minute mark); Ursula Andress appears to be singing, but it is actually the voice of actress Nikki van der Zyl, who dubbed Andress throughout the film. Connery responds with his own brief rendition of the first line. And it's heard one final time, briefly, as Bond and Honey snuggle in the boat at the end of the movie.

Two of the other tunes that Norman wrote in Jamaica are prominently featured. "Kingston Calypso" actually begins during the main title, as Binder begins his transition from the silhouetted trio of blind beggars to the actual film of the three, who aren't really blind and are about to commit two murders. Norman's notion was to do "Three Blind Mice" as a calypso, to help establish the Jamaican setting, but also, he said, to "make sure that Bond wasn't taken too seriously. Three assassins, about to kill somebody, you could have done in a really dramatic way. But instead, 'Three Blind Mice' changed the whole atmosphere," thus presaging the lighter, more tongue-in-cheek nature of what the Bond films would become.

"Jump Up" is heard (31½ minutes into the film) as Byron Lee and his Dragonaires appear, perform-

future work for him on the Bond films. Broccoli acknowledged this in his autobiography: "Monty Norman composed the original 007 theme for us. This has become a Bond trademark now. To do the scoring, I brought in the brilliant John Barry, whose soundtracks for this and the other Bond films—he has worked on 12 of them—are some of the best in cinema music."

Norman was immediately hired again by Broccoli and Saltzman for their next film, *Call Me Bwana*, a Bob Hope comedy that began shooting in October 1962. Norman penned a title song for Hope to sing, and while "it wasn't easy working with him, nevertheless I enjoyed it," the composer said. In addition, he wrote a piece, "The Big Safari," for the film's African setting that was arranged and recorded by John Barry in April 1963 and released as a single in the U.K.

Norman worked for months without a contract, and when he was finished, he called Saltzman for a meeting. "Isn't it time we talked money?" Norman asked. And in a response worthy of the great Sam Goldwyn, Saltzman replied, "Monty, if you want to talk money, we can't do business."

Ultimately, Norman said, he was paid, but he never worked for Eon again. He won an Ivor Novello Award from England's Performing Rights Society (PRS) for the Bond theme in 1977. But, he said, neither Broccoli nor Saltzman ever thanked him for his contribution to the James Bond films.

Said the composer: "I'm very proud to have done *Dr. No*. I have, in that first film, two iconic moments: 'Underneath the Mango Tree,' when Ursula comes out of the water, and of course, when Sean lights his cigarette and says, 'Bond, James Bond.' I never felt that they owed me the next film or the film after that. I think once they found that Barry was good in *From Russia with Love*, that was it, and quite rightly so. And there's no question that Barry was one of the best film score writers ever. My path has always been much more in the theatre than in films. So I have no complaints."

(SCORE HIGHLIGHTS, CONT.)

ing at Puss Feller's nightclub in a scene where Bond, Leiter and Quarrel discuss the mystery of Crab Key and confront a nasty female photographer. Although it turns up four times on the *Dr. No* soundtrack, it's actually heard only once in the film.

The Bond theme—not the Barry recording but the first few notes (the so-called guitar riff) realized orchestrally within the dramatic cues—recurs five more times in Norman's underscore: first (at 14 minutes into the film) when Bond discovers Sylvia Trench in his apartment; then (at 20 minutes in) when he interrogates and beats his cab driver outside of Kingston; in an interesting variation as No's security detail threatens them on the beach (at an hour and 5 minutes); as they battle the guards on the beach (1 hour, 9 minutes); and during the final battle in No's laboratory (1 hour, 44 minutes).

Of equal importance is Norman's "Dr. No" theme, which first surfaces right after the murder of Strangways's secretary (just five minutes into the film) as the killers discover the "Crab Key" and "Dr. No" files; it's a series of seven ascending notes, usually followed by five descending notes, that hint at the villain's presence, or power. It's heard when the assassins target Bond (nearly 36 minutes in); as Bond, Leiter and Quarrel approach Crab Key by boat (59½ minutes); as the security guards threaten Bond and Honey on the beach (an hour and 5 minutes); when No visits the drugged Bond and Honey (1 hour, 24 minutes); when he addresses Bond (1 hour, 27 minutes); and finally when Bond battles No to the death (1 hour, 44 minutes).

Other notable musical moments involve the tarantula in Bond's bed (43 minutes in), which ends in

In the November 1997 issue of the British music magazine *Mojo*, new Bond composer David Arnold did a Q&A with his famous predecessor, John Barry, in part to promote Arnold's new collection of 007 themes, *Shaken and Stirred*. In it, Arnold stated: "Everyone assumes you wrote the original Bond theme, yet it's credited to Monty Norman."

Barry's response, probably ill-advised, included the following: "If I didn't do it, why the hell did they not continue to employ Mr. Norman for the following 14 Bond movies? Name another two scores that Mr. Norman has composed. He was contracted to do it, but they had problems, so I got brought in. . . . I didn't care that Norman took the credit . . . in those days I'd write for anything that moved on celluloid."

An arts writer at London's *Sunday Times* followed up on the allegation and, in an October 12, 1997, story headlined "Theme Tune Wrangle Has 007 Shaken and Stirred," wrote that John Barry "is claiming that he wrote 007's most familiar tune" instead of Norman, who was described as "a little-known London musician [who] appears content to live quietly and collect his royalties through the Performing Rights Society (PRS)."

Norman sued *The Sunday Times* for libel. This was not the first time he had taken legal action against a publication that claimed he didn't write the Bond theme: he sued *Melody Maker*, another British music magazine, in 1988 after it claimed he purchased the tune from a Jamaican for $100; and in 1993 he demanded and got an apology from *Vox* magazine, which went even farther out on a limb by claiming that Barry had written the theme "only days" before *Dr. No*'s premiere.

The *Mojo* piece was also not the first time that Barry had taken credit for the Bond theme. As far back as 1978, he told *The James Bond Films* author

five synchronized orchestral "hits" as Bond uses his shoe to crush the little beast; and the arrival of a British naval boat (nearly 1 hour, 48 minutes) to rescue Bond and Honey, which begins with a patriotic march and ends with "Under the Mango Tree" as they let the rope run out and linger alone in the Caribbean.

Only seven of the soundtrack album's 18 tracks are actually in the film: the Bond theme, the original versions of "Kingston Calypso" and "Jump Up," both vocal versions of "Under the Mango Tree," "The Island Speaks" (the "Dr. No" theme, as the boat approaches Crab Key) and "Love at Last" (a source-music backdrop for Bond's conversations with Strangways's card-playing friends, 26 minutes into the film). None of the four versions of Norman's original attempt at a Bond theme ("Twisting with James," "Dr. No's Fantasy," "The Boy's Chase" and the album's penultimate track, interestingly titled "James Bond Theme") are in the film. "Twisting with James" may have been conceived as one of the numbers for the band in Puss Feller's restaurant, as the script specifies "a particularly Jamaican type of Twist." "Audio Bongo" is one of the most audacious tracks on the album, and it's a shame it never found a place in the film score. It's the "Dr. No" theme for organ, flute and electric guitars (and no bongos).

Steven Jay Rubin he had written it, and then for interviews in Fred Karlin's film-scoring textbook *On the Track* in 1990 and for the American classical-music magazine *Fanfare* in 1993. All took him at his word.

The highly charged, widely publicized case finally reached the High Court in March 2001. Over seven days, testimony was heard from Norman, Barry, Burt Rhodes, Vic Flick, musicologist Stanley Sadie, conductor Guy Protheroe and others. Norman said that *The Sunday Times* had "rubbished my career" and that he felt that only by suing could he clear his name and reputation.

The 60 bars of the "James Bond Theme" were broken down and analyzed in depth, including discussion of the "vamp" (the opening bass line, similar to that heard in the opening bars of Kurt Weill's "Lonely House" or Artie Shaw's "Nightmare"), the "guitar riff" (the familiar guitar line) and a pair of "bebop phrases" (the big-band midsection). Sadie, editor of the respected *Grove Dictionary of Music and Musicians*, concluded that Barry's arrangement was "extreme" but that most of the tune derived from Norman's "Bad Sign, Good Sign" song.

The *Times* attorney contended that the theme "was composed by John Barry with some input from an idea by Monty Norman," while Barry pointed out that he had never challenged the songwriting credit or demanded royalties for it (and Norman's royalties, testimony indicated, were often in the hundreds of thousands of pounds per year).

A jury deliberated for four hours and decided in Norman's favor on March 19, 2001, awarding him £30,000 in libel damages and costs (estimated at £500,000) against the Times Newspapers. Norman said afterwards he felt "delighted and vindicated. *The Sunday Times* always said that they were only interested in the truth. Well, now they've got the truth."

"... but oh, you haunted me so ..."

From Russia with Love

John Barry's irritation at seeing his work all over the film of *Dr. No* would soon turn to elation. He had proven himself with his dynamic—and commercially valuable—recording of the "James Bond Theme," and Peter Hunt's application of it at several key moments had clearly demonstrated its viability as dramatic music.

He wasn't sitting around waiting for Broccoli and Saltzman to call. He had, in the meantime, scored the comedy *The Amorous Prawn* (based on the long-running British play) and, more significantly, written a pair of jazz numbers for the Leslie Caron drama *The L-Shaped Room* (which would launch a long and satisfying multifilm collaboration with director Bryan Forbes). Barry's long-desired film scoring career was quietly gaining momentum.

With *Dr. No* now a box-office success, Noel Rogers—who ran United Artists Music's London operation and had essentially brokered the Bond-theme deal between Barry and Eon—set up a meeting. "That was the first time I met Cubby Broccoli, Harry Saltzman and Peter Hunt," Barry later recalled.

The filmmakers were in preproduction on the second James Bond film, *From Russia with Love*. And, perhaps because Barry had engineered a chart hit in the "James Bond Theme," they were starting to think about music in a more serious way—not only its role in the film but as a means of promoting the film outside of the cinema world. "And, although I'd had instrumental hits, I hadn't actually written a hit song," Barry admitted.

So they began a procedure that continues to this day. They sought out the biggest names in music to supply a title song that could help them market their movie: songwriter Lionel Bart, whose musical *Oliver!* was already a hit on London's West End and which had just opened (in January 1963) to rave reviews on Broadway. (Vocalist Matt Monro would sign on later.)

Director Terence Young, too, was impressed with what Barry had done with the title music on *Dr. No*. But, he later recalled, Saltzman and Broccoli "were awfully wary about him. They thought he was too young and inexperienced in film music, and I had a little bit to do with his finally doing *From Russia with Love*. Somebody wanted Lionel Bart to do the music . . . and I said that if John Barry was inexperienced, then so was Lionel, and I think we owe it to John to give him a chance."

According to Young, it was Saltzman who had committed to Bart for the title song, but Broccoli and Young were eager for Barry to take on the scoring chores. Sid Margo, the violinist who became Barry's orchestral contractor (or "fixer" as they were known in London), recalled Barry's excitement at the news: "He called me up straight away and said, 'I've got the Bond film, Sid! I can't believe it!'"

Barry and Bart were part of the March 1963 press party to announce the film and its cast at London's Connaught Hotel. It was there that Barry met Fleming for the first and only time. "He was a very tall gentleman, very, very

(left to right) Harry Saltzman, Lionel Bart, Cubby Broccoli, John Barry at the March 1963 press party for *From Russia with Love*

English, and very reserved," Barry said many years later. "I never saw him again after that. I was never aware of him being involved, other than selling the rights. I think he came down that one day and that was the end of his fascination with the movie business." (In fact, Fleming visited the locations of *Dr. No*, *Russia* and *Goldfinger*, before his untimely death on August 12, 1964.)

And, as with Monty Norman on *Dr. No*, Barry was invited to join the company on their foreign travels in order to soak up the atmosphere and gain a little musical inspiration. So, in late April 1963, Barry flew to Turkey along with UA's Noel Rogers. "I became a part of the team," he recalled in 1993. "It was like a family. There was Cubby and Harry and Sean; we all got on the same plane, we all flew to Istanbul, and we all stayed at the same hotel."

Much of the story of *From Russia with Love* takes place in Turkey: Bond is sent there to try to obtain a Lektor, the latest Soviet cipher machine that could enable the British to decode top-secret Soviet signals. Supposedly a cipher clerk named Tatiana Romanova (Daniela Bianchi) has fallen in love with 007 and is offering to defect. Bond works with Istanbul station head Kerim Bay (Pedro Armendariz); what neither of them know is that Tatiana is a pawn of Rosa Klebb (Lotte Lenya), a former high-level Soviet colonel who has joined the international criminal organization SPECTRE and has recruited a ruthless killer named Grant (Robert Shaw) to murder 007.

Recalling his visit to Istanbul, Barry said, "It was like no place I'd ever been in my life. [The trip] was supposedly to seep up the music, so Noel Rogers and I used to go 'round to these nightclubs and listen to all this stuff. We had the strangest week, and really came away with nothing, except a lot of ridiculous stories. We went back, talked to Lionel, and then he wrote 'From Russia with Love.'"

Barry would later regale friends with tales of "the biggest, hottest star in Istanbul . . . the Elvis Presley of Turkey" doing a wildly popular drag act for a diverse crowd that ranged from farmers and shepherds to patrons in evening attire; drinking for hours at an old oaken bar with a 50-foot-long brass rail that simply collapsed when Barry leaned on it; and cab rides with old women carrying live chickens. "I could write a book on that week in Istanbul. It was out of Kafka," Barry laughed. "We were quite happy when we got on that plane to fly back to London."

Despite his enthusiasm for the project, time was not on Barry's side. He was already occupied by his new role as A&R director at Jeffrey Kruger's Ember Records (where he produced, in the summer of 1963, an Annie Ross album of jazz standards, the banned-by-the-BBC single "Christine" and the Chad and Jeremy hit "Yesterday's Gone"); and a prestigious assignment to score a high-profile American television special in which Elizabeth Taylor tours London while sharing its storied history.

Meanwhile, Young had fallen behind in shooting *Russia*, with various crises including actor Armendariz's terminal illness, a helicopter accident in which Young nearly drowned, a car accident involving Bianchi that delayed shooting for two weeks, and the need to reshoot numerous scenes because of script changes throughout the production. Editor Peter Hunt was racing to keep up while Young was finishing principal photography, and all of this meant that postproduction—and the availability of something for Barry to view, and then compose for—was falling farther and farther behind.

With the deadline for the *Elizabeth Taylor in London* special approaching, Barry composed key themes and turned the job of arranging and conducting specific scenes over to the talented Johnnie Spence, whom Barry had known for years on the London recording scene. Barry supervised the recording on August 12 (and, a few months later, received his first major show-business award recognition, an Emmy nomination for his original score).

Musically speaking, *From Russia with Love* was to be quite different from *Dr. No.* The musical emphasis of the first film was on the songs that Monty Norman had written (and, at the last minute, a theme for Bond). For *Russia*, the primary need would be the dramatic underscore—more than 45 minutes of it—with the title song coming at the end of the film.

There was, however, one scene in which music plays a pivotal role: that of the gypsy camp where Kerim Bay takes Bond for a night out and they are entertained by a beautiful belly dancer (played by Leila Guiraut). Shot at the Pinewood Paddock during the evenings of June 4–7, 1963, the scene called for musical playback (and five "musicians" pretending to play instruments including a violin, clarinet and tambourine visible in the film). For more than two minutes, she dances to an authentic gypsy-music track with wild clarinet licks, probably a real recording obtained while the crew was on location. Although Barry later composed music to replace it (titled "Leila Dances" on the album), for unknown reasons the substitution never took place. Thus the movie contains the real gypsy music (although it is credited to Barry on the film's official cue sheet, as is an earlier gypsy-camp piece), complete with the finger cymbals that Leila is wearing and clicking during her dance.

Barry took up the challenge of creating colorful material for the locale, even if all of it wasn't used. "The actual content of the music was not based on Turkish scales, it's based on Western musical structure, if you like," he later explained. "It's the instrumentation that gave it the slightly exotic feel of Istanbul, finger cymbals and things like that. It was really the salt and pepper, the dressing and condiments, of the orchestra—a full-blooded, traditional English orchestra, with these colors added to it that gave it a Turkish feeling. But it really was no more than that."

The camp sequence is one that guitarist Vic Flick (who had so memorably played the original Bond theme) vividly recalled. He was sitting in the orchestra looking at his music, which had just a single chord symbol and the instruction "solo" written on it. Flick remembers asking Barry what he was looking for. "It's a gypsy encampment," Barry replied. "We need some gypsy guitar music."

Flick asked to see the specific scene and then, he recalled, "I played a little standard Spanish guitar-type music. The next time we did a take, and that was it. So whether it was going to be good or bad was kind of down to me,

Eunice Gayson and Sean Connery, moments after hearing "From Russia With Love" sung via transistor radio

which is what the session business is all about." The "Gypsy Camp" cue remains a highlight of the score, and the centerpiece is Flick's completely improvised, but entirely appropriate, acoustic guitar solo.

Although postproduction was running late, Barry did have an advantage in that he already had the film's two primary musical themes in hand: Bart's title song and the "James Bond Theme," which had been established (in no small part due to his own thrilling arrangement) in *Dr. No*. And a brand new theme he decided to contribute to the Bond canon: "007."

"That was a product of leaning slightly more to the sense of fun in the Bond movies," Barry later explained. "The audience caught on so quick. The style had been set in *Dr. No* [so] when they went into *From Russia with Love* they knew they were in for a good time. So I wanted a lighter, adventuresome sound, so the audience could sit and relax."

"007"—first heard during the battle in the gypsy camp—offered a military-style drumbeat with staccato brass underpinning a melodic line, taken first by the horns, then by the strings. It combined the drama with a more lighthearted feeling, unlike the exciting but all-business "James Bond Theme." "It was a lighter, more airy, uplifting kind of theme. It had a great, driving sense, too. And then I just wrote this big, 16-bar open melody, like a feel-good adventure theme, with the trumpets and the horns, that staccato accompaniment." "007" would resurface in four more Bond films: *Thunderball*, *You Only Live Twice*, *Diamonds Are Forever* and *Moonraker*.

Young was effusive in his praise of Barry on this film: "At various times, I've wanted something different, but he said, 'Would you let me try it this way; if you don't like it, I'll do what you want,' and with one or two exceptions, I've always been able to say, 'Look, I'm completely wrong and you're completely right, John.' Sometimes I've said, 'No, I want to change it,' and he goes [and alters the cue] straight away because he knows that I'm not doing it for any ego trip.

SCORE HIGHLIGHTS

From Russia with Love established a Bond tradition: the precredits sequence, usually a few minutes long, filled with action and designed to whet moviegoers' appetites for the high adventure to follow. The producers retained the gun-barrel opening, so John Barry begins his score with the "James Bond Theme" featuring Vic Flick playing the tune even faster than in the original recording. In the scene, Bond and Grant stalk each other through a statue-filled park at night to ominous variations on the Bond theme, punctuated by frightening brass shouts. (Barry did not title his cues, but the soundtrack album refers to this as "Stalking.")

For the main title sequence, Barry invented a machine-gun effect for brass and percussion that underscores "Harry Saltzman and Albert R. Broccoli

"John is a very gifted film musician . . . and I think this is one of his very best scores. Very often [music] can be distracting. But in John's case, nearly all of his [cues] are helpful; they add to the mood, to the excitement of a sequence. They certainly did in the gypsy sequence and that battle. It was enormously effective, a long stretch of music running about eight minutes on the go. Very, very effective."

Bart had actually finished the song by early July, but—although vocalist Johnny De Little (who would go on to record Barry's theme for *The Knack . . . and How to Get It*) had recorded a demo version of the theme—there was still no final decision on who should sing it for the film.

Enter Don Black, a 25-year-old ex-standup comedian, song plugger and would-be lyricist who was then managing singer Matt Monro. Barry and Black already knew each other from the London music world, and it was Black who suggested to Barry that he should consider Monro as singer of the Bart tune. "Matt was doing well; he had a couple of hits," Black remembered, among them the top-five "Portrait of My Love" and "My Kind of Girl" and, more recently, the top-10 hit "Softly As I Leave You." Monro was a crooner in the Sinatra mold. As George Martin, a producer at EMI's Parlophone, Monro's label, pointed out: "Matt Monro had one of the best pop voices I've ever worked with. He was a little guy, but he could produce the most wonderful note and hang onto it for ages. The fact that he smoked 60 to 80 cigarettes a day, and drank about a bottle of brandy a night, made no difference. He was able to produce this glorious sound."

Johnnie Spence, who had handled Barry's Elizabeth Taylor TV special, also happened to be Monro's musical director. It was Spence who arranged and conducted Monro's vocal for the film and the album. Martin produced the sessions at Abbey Road (orchestra on September 1, vocal track two days later). And to give it a little "Russian" flavor, Martin came up with a musical

Present" and serves as an intro to the title song, which is heard instrumentally over Robert Brownjohn's clever credits (the words projected over various parts of a scantily clad belly dancer, foreshadowing Leila's act later in the film). Spicing up Barry's arrangement of the Lionel Bart tune are the organ improvisations of Alan Haven, who was then playing at Annie Ross's London jazz club (and whose organ would be prominently featured throughout Barry's 1965 score for *The Knack . . . and How to Get It*). Interestingly, Barry chose a different track for the album, omitting Haven's jazzy embellishment. The last 45 seconds of the main title is the Bond theme, not the guitar portion but rather the jazz-based midsection, followed by a reprise of his rat-a-tat opening. The combination of music and image is arresting, with Barry making a confident splash as James Bond's new composer.

Barry uses four main themes throughout the score. Bart's song serves nicely as a love theme and occasionally as a scene-setting piece; the Bond theme resurfaces whenever 007's cool persona or man-of-action needs reinforcement; Barry's new "007" offers a more lighthearted adventure theme for Bond's field work; and the delicate, ascending harp-vibraphone duet for the villains of SPECTRE that is first heard about eight minutes into the film, as Kronsteen wins the chess tournament and is summoned to meet with Blofeld and Rosa Klebb ("SPECTRE Island" on the album).

At just over 14 minutes into the film, variations on the "From Russia with Love" tune help introduce us to Tatiana (Tania) Romanova, SPECTRE's Russian-born pawn, as she gets her assignment from Klebb. The song itself makes its first appearance as a vocal

(left to right) Lyricist Don Black, vocalist Matt Monro, composer John Barry

trick: Spence's tack piano was recorded at half speed and down an octave, so that when it was played back at normal speed it sounded like an Eastern European instrument, perhaps a zither or cimbalom.

Black remembered talking with Bart about "how brilliant that song was," specifically the internal rhyme of "tongue-tied young pride"—"he was very proud of that," Black recalled. "He liked the idea that he could be so versa-

(SCORE HIGHLIGHTS, CONT.)

(18 minutes) as we dissolve to a peaceful English-countryside scene where Bond is romancing Sylvia Trench; a punt floats by and the Monro vocal is heard coming from a radio.

Barry scores Bond's arrival in Istanbul and chauffeured trip to meet Kerim Bay (24 minutes) with the Bond theme, this time marked by jazzy new brass phrases and a duet for string bass and bongo drums (on the album, "James Bond with Bongos"). Ironically, although Barry's original recording of the "James Bond Theme" is never heard in its entirely in *Dr. No*, that same recording is played in full in *Russia* (at 29 minutes) as Bond searches his hotel room for listening devices.

The limpet-mine attack on Kerim's office and its aftermath is met with high-brass alarms, pounding timpani and a quieter variation on "From Russia with Love" (this forms the first minute of the "Death of Grant" track on the LP), but Kerim and Bond's underground boat trip to the Soviet consulate is left unscored.

Two pieces that Barry composed for the gypsy-camp sequence (on the album, "Leila Dances" and "Guitar Lament") are not used, but two obviously authentic pieces of ethnic music are (as they enter the camp, and as Leila dances). A few minutes later (43 minutes), Bond and Kerim witness a fight between gypsy girls that inspired one of Barry's most dramatic pieces ("Girl Trouble" on the LP): repeated notes in the basses and percussion providing a consistent rhythm topped by an unusual strings-and-xylophone combination.

Asked many years later about the use of xylophone (which will return in later Bond films), Barry

tile, and have such a range. People were surprised that he wrote it." (Barry said, in later years, that it might be a nice idea to use "From Russia with Love" as background for a scene set in Russia. It never happened.)

Monro's wife Mickie remembered seeing the film for the first time and being disappointed that it wasn't over the opening credits, and when first heard in the film it was for only half a minute as a transistor-radio broadcast in a passing boat. "Matt loved the Bond films and was avidly watching the action," she said. "He seemed immersed in the movie so I didn't voice my upset, but knew he must have felt disappointed himself. Then right at the very end, at the closing credits, his voice filled the cinema and in the space of seconds I went from feeling decidedly dejected to euphoric."

Bart was so pleased about how Barry handled his music in the film that they agreed to collaborate on *The Winston Affair* (later retitled *Man in the Middle*, a 1964 release), with Bart writing a military march and Barry using it as the basis for his score. Also that summer, Bart backed out of his commission to write the score for producer Stanley Baker's upcoming African epic *Zulu* and recommended Barry for the job; it became, along with *Russia*, one of the young composer's most prestigious early scoring assignments.

From Russia with Love opened in London October 10, 1963 (and in the United States on April 8, 1964) and this time the title sequence featured the prominent credits "title song by Lionel Bart" and "orchestral music composed and conducted by John Barry." And this time, UA publicity trumpeted the music more prominently than even the screenwriters:

In all of the James Bond films, the background music is given special consideration by the producers, who feel that the proper score will always add to the atmosphere of suspense and fast-paced action that typifies the Bond stories. Last year, composer Monte [sic] Norman's theme

said: "You can get wiped out by the sound-effects guys, so I found a very high flute-xylophone-string figure and then a heavy, low end—those big, low brass chords—and then a middle, penetrating horn and trumpet. The style was developed out of the necessity of what those movies were throwing at me. If you write a middle-range, cluster kind of orchestral score and put a heavyweight sound track against it, you're dead."

The catfight is interrupted by the attack of the Bulgars on the gypsies, and here (44 minutes) we hear "007" for the first time. It's a full-scale guns-and-knives battle, and Barry treats it accordingly, with a strong rhythm section anchored by the timpani, brass and piccolos adding color and musical interest (the album version, slower and with strings playing the melody, is not in the film).

Bond's initial encounter with Tania (54 minutes) is treated at first with a romantic version of "From Russia with Love" but ends with the SPECTRE theme as she seduces him. Another dramatic moment occurs (57 minutes) when Bond and Tania visit St. Sophia, an ancient mosque; Barry's score, with its dark percussion, religioso chimes and muted brass, has both dignity and suspense within its brief minute-long running time. ("The Golden Horn," which is on the album but not in the film, refers to an estuary near the historic center of Istanbul and was probably written for a scene that was later cut.)

"007" returns (at 1 hour, 4 minutes) when Bond steals the Lektor decoding unit from the Soviet consulate and escapes with Tania and Kerim through the underground tunnels; this time, the lighter, up-beat melody signals a victory of sorts. (At 1 hour,

John Barry conducting *From Russia with Love* at CTS Studios

(SCORE HIGHLIGHTS, CONT.)

7 minutes, as the Orient Express is leaving Istanbul with Bond, Tania and Grant on board, there is a dramatic brass-and-percussion cue which presages Barry's opening of *Zulu*, his next score.)

Kerim's death (at nearly 1 hour, 14 minutes) is another moment of high drama, as Barry begins with his moving-train motif (a "Russia" variation), segues into a more pure version of "Russia" for a romantic moment with Tania, acknowledges the crisis with timpani and then segues into the SPECTRE theme to suggest who was responsible for Kerim's murder.

Two of the film's most memorable sequences are left unscored: the brutal fight to the death between Bond and Grant (about 1 hour, 34 minutes in) and the helicopter chase a few minutes later. The Grant sequence is especially interesting because Barry clearly wrote music for it. Barry apparently in-

tended the middle portion of the album's "Death of Grant" track (from 1:01 to 1:24, delicate suspense music featuring violins and xylophone) to accompany Grant's opening of the booby-trapped attaché case, and the rest (from 1:25 to 2:00, high-tension music featuring pounding percussion and brass) to underscore the end of the fight, as Grant is about to garrote Bond but Bond kills him instead.

Yet, oddly, Hunt—after complaining about Monty Norman's melodramatic music in *Dr. No*—twice reprises its climactic finale music: first, for about 15 seconds as Bond shoots the helicopter co-pilot and it explodes; and then after the speedboat chase (1 hour, 48 minutes), as Bond has set the sea and his pursuers on fire.

Just before the (otherwise unscored) speedboat chase, Bond throws his captive overboard and

music for Dr. No was lauded almost as much as the film itself and, as a LP record, remained among the top 10 of the British Hit Parade for 14 weeks. For *From Russia With Love*, the producers were fortunate enough to sign Lionel Bart, Britain's leading theater composer, to write the title song. Yorkshireman John Barry composed and conducted the orchestral music for *From Russia With Love*. Barry also has a current LP hit with his theme score of *The Human Jungle* TV series.

The misspelling of Norman's first name was not just in the press release; it also appeared that way in the film itself. (UA's publicity people also seemed confused about the difference between a 33-rpm LP and a 45-rpm single and were prone to exaggeration. There was no "British Hit Parade," the single never hit the top 10 and it charted for 11 weeks, not 14; *The Human Jungle* theme was released as a single in the U.K. but never charted at all.)

Few film critics noticed—*Daily Variety* begrudgingly granted that "Lionel Bart's title song is apt though unlikely to hit the Top 10, but John Barry's background music is pleasantly unobtrusive." *Weekly Variety* praised the soundtrack album: "A good title pop song, written by Lionel Bart and delivered in fine style by Matt Monro. . . . John Barry has furnished some arresting melodies and orchestral effects." Monro's single charted on November 14 and reached number 20 on the U.K. charts, while John Barry's instrumental of the title tune reached number 39 in December. In America, the soundtrack was cited as a "breakout album" by *Billboard* on April 25, 1964, charted on May 2, reached number 27 on August 22 and remained on the *Billboard* charts for a surprising 34 weeks.

And as *Variety* reported in early May, the title tune was popular with numerous groups, including the Dixieland combo the Village Stompers, whose single (using a banjo for a pseudo-balalaika sound) managed to reach number 81 on

Blofeld confronts Klebb and Kronsteen about their failures (1 hour, 43 minutes)—lively variations on the Bond theme followed by an extended version of the SPECTRE theme. Bond and Tania are in a Venice gondola as the Monro vocal is heard in its entirety.

The film's vocal was also released as a single, and on Monro's own Liberty LP; a different take is heard on the United Artists soundtrack. Both, intriguingly, suffer from a flaw that few heard in 1963 but that is obvious to close listeners in the CD era: speeded-up voices talking at about 1:04 into the track (as Monro is singing "but oh, you haunted me so"). It's studio chatter behind Spence's slowed-down tack piano which was later played back at normal speed; the voices remained on the track when it was overdubbed and apparently no one noticed.

Bart's lyric, like that in "Under the Mango Tree" in *Dr. No*, was about love; and in the case of "Russia," about discovering what one has lost and hopes to recover. For the next film, *Goldfinger*, the songwriters would dispense with the warm and fuzzy altogether and just go for the jugular.

Billboard's Hot 100 chart in May 1964. Monro issued an album titled *From Russia with Love* on the Liberty label in the United States, but the quieter side of the music business (that is, music publishing) was quietly hauling its receipts off to the bank.

"The scores were done by the producers and John Barry," recalled David V. Picker, the longtime United Artists executive who was in charge of the company's record division. "It was obviously beneficial to the pictures and to the [record] label to get a hit song, if we could, to carry the album. The real value was in the music publishing. Publishing is always lucrative; it's a license to make money if you have the right artists. We were able to capitalize on our soundtracks, because we started to focus on them instead of giving them away."

For Saltzman and Broccoli, *From Russia with Love* cost twice as much as *Dr. No* ($2.2 million) but also made twice as much: $12.5 million. The Bond series was now firmly established, and John Barry had proven himself as a talented dramatic composer; for the first time, a soundtrack album would bear the credit "Music Composed, Arranged and Conducted by John Barry." He would go on to score 10 more 007 films.

"... the Midas touch—a spider's touch ..."

Goldfinger

In the spring of 1964, actors Michael Caine and Terence Stamp were thrown out of their apartment ("for rent arrears," according to Caine; "a little too much traffic going through there, the ladies, you know," suggested John Barry).

Stamp found other accommodations. Caine asked Barry if he could temporarily sleep in his spare bedroom. As they were all friends and regular lunchmates at songwriter Leslie Bricusse's Pickwick Club in Great Newport Street, Barry couldn't say no. So for months, Barry and Caine were roommates in the composer's Cadogan Square apartment.

Caine recalled one particular night: "He bloody played the piano all night. I was upstairs trying to get to sleep, and when I came down in the morning to breakfast, he was sitting there. He hadn't been to sleep either. He looked at me and said, 'Listen to this,' and played me a tune. I knew he was working on a Bond film, but I didn't know what he was writing. I was the first person to hear 'Goldfinger.'"

Barry said it took him more than one night to write the most iconic song in the history of Bond movies. But regardless of how long it took, it was *Goldfinger*, both music and movie, that truly defined the James Bond cinema experience. "Everything came together," said Barry, "the song, the score, the style."

John Barry, 1964

Barry had not been idle since the end of *From Russia with Love*. He had demonstrated an increasing compositional depth with his powerful score for the African epic *Zulu*, a lively one for the black comedy *A Jolly Bad Fellow*, and an eerie and suspenseful one for the thriller *Seance on a Wet Afternoon*. His growing body of work, and his personal confidence in his own abilities as a dramatic composer, convinced Cubby Broccoli and Harry Saltzman to let him write the title song as well as score the next film. For the first time, there would be a unifying consistency of musical material throughout—and indeed, most of the *Goldfinger* score is related thematically to the song heard over the main title.

In the story, M sends 007 to Miami to look into the activities of wealthy international gold dealer Auric Goldfinger (Gert Frobe), who is suspected of illegal trade activities. When Jill Masterson (Shirley Eaton) is bizarrely murdered by being painted gold, Bond moves closer to the rotund industrialist, first on an English golf course—where he meets the villain's Korean-born, mute manservant Oddjob (Harold Sakata)—and then at his plant in Switzerland, where Bond is captured. Bond is taken to Goldfinger's stud horse farm in Kentucky, where he learns that the madman plans, with the aid of pilot Pussy Galore (Honor Blackman), to break into the federal bullion depository at nearby Fort Knox.

Guy Hamilton, who was offered the chance to direct *Dr. No* but turned it down, said yes to directing *Goldfinger*. He and Barry had worked together previously (on the controversial, unreleased *The Party's Over*, and on *Man in the Middle*). "I'd got a recording of 'Mack the Knife' that seemed to me dirty

(left to right) Sean Connery, Shirley Eaton, Bond author Ian Fleming on the *Goldfinger* set

and gritty and sort of Goldfinger-ish," Hamilton said. "He came up to my apartment, I played this for him, and I think it cued him in."

"'From Russia with Love'" was a great song title," Barry remembered, "and it was a very lyrical song. The movie lent itself to that. But Goldfinger was the name of the villain—a guy that painted nude bodies in gold to suffocate them—so it's kind of a weird thing to have to write a song about. So I sat down and wrote this rather strange, angular thing which, for me, was right. It couldn't be a free-wheeling, open melody. It had to have angles."

It also had to have lyrics, and they would not be easily arrived at. Having finished the melody, Barry turned to an old colleague, actor-writer Trevor Peacock, with whom he had written songs for *Beat Girl*. Peacock admitted to a Liverpool newspaper in early March 1964 that he was working on it ("it's rather like 007 at the moment, terribly hush-hush," he said). But he struggled with the idea—"Goldfinger . . . mustn't linger . . . right-winger . . ."—and finally confessed to Barry that he was unable to come up with anything useful.

Barry turned to two other old friends: Bricusse, whom he saw every Friday for lunch at the Pickwick, and Bricusse's writing partner, Anthony Newley, who had just had a huge international stage hit in *Stop the World, I Want to Get Off* (resulting in the top-40 hit "What Kind of Fool Am I" for Newley). And Barry, as A&R man at Ember Records, had overseen the release of the Newley-Bricusse comedy album *Fool Britannia*, which poked fun at the 1963 Profumo scandal.

"So," said Bricusse, "we went over to his apartment in Cadogan Square, number 65, went upstairs and schmoozed for a bit. And then he sat down at the piano and played dah-DAH-dah [the opening three notes] and Newley and I both went, 'wider than a mile . . .' without even looking at each other." They were pointing out, somewhat sarcastically, that Barry's opening three notes were identical to those of Henry Mancini's popular, and Oscar-winning, song "Moon River."

"John was not amused," Newley later remembered, but they quickly got on with the task; Barry played through the rest of the song and gave them a tape of his piano demo. "John was a very good songwriter," Bricusse said. "John's

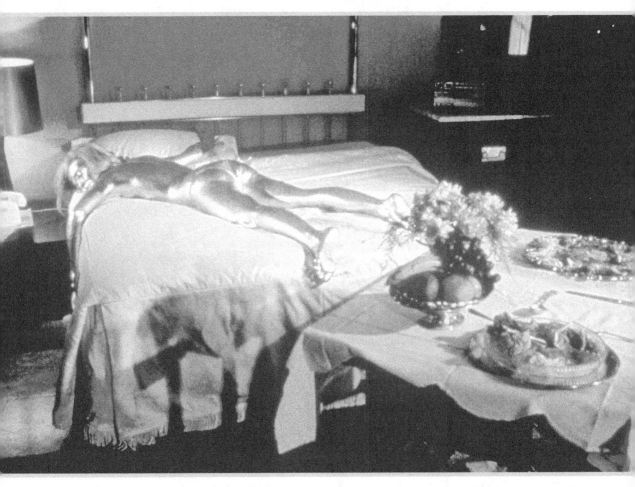

". . . for a golden girl knows when he's kissed her"

music was as identifiable as a Van Gogh painting, because he used chord structures that nobody else ever used. Nobody wrote like John."

Bricusse was already a Fleming fan. "I read the books from the day they came out," he said, and eventually he acquired rare first editions of all the novels. There were no scripts or screenings of footage, but they weren't necessary; they consulted Broccoli and found out about Eaton being painted gold, which became another clue to writing the lyric ("for a golden girl knows when he's kissed her / it's the kiss of death from mister Goldfinger").

According to Bricusse, the key to the lyric was the phrase "the Midas touch"; once they found that, and began rhyming it, they quickly finished the words. No one remembers just how long it took, but Bricusse said it would not have been more than a couple of days at most: "You needed to know the character. The song is really advice to a girl: look out. . . ."

Newley sang two versions of it in a demo session conducted by Barry on May 14, 1964. "It was terrific," Barry said. "Tony sang it in a very creepy way. He didn't want to sing it in the movie because they thought it was a bit weird." There were no rewrites or changes requested; "You always know when you've got it right," said Bricusse. And with that, Newley and Bricusse departed for the Italian fishing village of Portofino to spend the summer writing *The Roar of the Greasepaint, The Smell of the Crowd*, their next stage show.

The Welsh-born, 27-year-old singer Shirley Bassey was chosen to sing "Goldfinger." "She was firmly established as a big singing star in England," Bricusse pointed out. "John probably said, 'No one will sing this better than Shirley,' and they didn't argue with him." They had worked together recently, Barry having been conductor of a 23-piece orchestra for her December 1963 concert tour. (And, according to biographers of both, they enjoyed a brief affair around this time.)

Not long after the end of the tour, Bassey recalled, Barry called and asked her to listen to the theme he had written for the latest Bond film. It didn't have words yet, she said, but "I just got goose pimples" and she promised to sing it regardless of the lyric.

Choosing a singer, Barry said, was like casting a movie. "Shirley was great casting for *Goldfinger*. Nobody could have sung it like her; she had that great dramatic sense. When it came to the studio, she didn't know what the hell the song was about, but she sang it with such total conviction that she convinced the rest of the world."

They recorded on August 20, 1964, at CTS studios. Eric Tomlinson, who engineered the scores for *From Russia with Love*, *Goldfinger* and *Thunderball*, remembered Barry asking for take after take, which eventually frustrated the singer. Explained Bassey: "I had to do it over and over again, because something went wrong with the musicians, or there was something technically wrong, or I went wrong. It was an all-night session."

And, according to guitarist Vic Flick, who was sitting just 10 feet from Bassey's vocal booth, it took a wardrobe modification to get the vocal just

(left to right) Leslie Bricusse, singer Shirley Bassey, Anthony Newley celebrate their gold record for the hit song "Goldfinger"

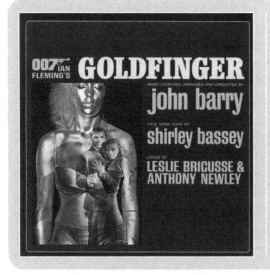

007 IAN FLEMING'S **GOLDFINGER**

MUSIC COMPOSED ARRANGED AND CONDUCTED BY

john barry

TITLE SONG SUNG BY

shirley bassey

LYRICS BY

LESLIE BRICUSSE & ANTHONY NEWLEY

SCORE HIGHLIGHTS

The history of the Bond soundtrack albums is almost as interesting as the films themselves. *Goldfinger* had two distinctively different LPs, and if you liked the music you needed to own both. The American album totaled just over 30 minutes of music (which was the norm for U.S. movie soundtracks in that era) and included Barry's powerful rock version of the theme. The British edition was much longer, at 38 minutes, including four tracks not available on the American LP (but not Barry's instrumental). All were finally brought together nearly 40 years later on the remastered Capitol-EMI CD.

But the 41-plus minutes from the two 1964 LPs contain all of the score's highlights, beginning with one of the best Bond pre-title sequences ever filmed, called on the album "Bond Back in Action

right. "Barry wanted this long note held. He said to do it again, and she said she couldn't. But then there was a rustling noise and suddenly this bra comes over the top of the vocal booth. And then she really let it go." Bassey, surprisingly, confirmed the story: "I had this restricting bustier on, and so I let it all hang out," she said with a laugh. (Added Flick: "Some of the string players shouted, 'Take it up a tone!' so she'd have to take more off.")

"And then came the end with that note," Bassey remembered. "I was holding it, and holding it. I was looking at John and I was going blue in the face—and he's going, hold it just one more second. When it finished I nearly passed out. But anyway, it was exciting. And I never thought it would be a hit."

One other classic moment in Bond musical history happened by accident the same night. Barry had written the opening two-note phrase, which repeats, without its now-familiar sassy muted-trumpet embellishment. "The wah-wah-wah-wah figure was not in the original orchestration," Barry noted. "We'd been rehearsing with Shirley and the orchestras for about an hour and a half, I guess. They broke for a 20-minute tea break or whatever it was.

"And I just heard that by-yah-yah-yah-yah, I don't know why. I went to the piano and I put it down. I got the copyist to put it on the trumpet parts with the wah-wah mute. And when they came back from their tea, I'd written this figure in. And thank God, because it was the hook, the thing that really grabbed you."

Derek Watkins, one of the trumpet players on that session (and on nearly every Bond film since), remembers discussion taking place about whether to use a hand, or the plunger mute. Once the plunger mute was decided on, Watkins said, Barry wanted the players to "make it even more dirty," so some

Again." As we watch a wetsuited 007 emerge from the water, break into a drug kingpin's laboratory and prepare to blow it up, we hear the "James Bond Theme" in an alternately suspenseful and exciting new arrangement—with our first glimmer of the new *Goldfinger* theme in the harp—and a sense of humor, as when Bond sheds his wetsuit to reveal a tux and Barry subtly highlights 007 adding a red carnation to his elegant wardrobe with a final high note in the violins.

The main-title sequence (just after five minutes into the film), justifiably famous for Robert Brownjohn's golden-girl titles, introduces the "Goldfinger" song and thus the main thematic material for the entire score. Nearly all 48 minutes of the score is based in some way on the theme, or a variant of it. *Goldfinger*, as Barry often said, set the style for all

future Bond scores, with a heady mixture of jazz figures, a pop sensibility and traditional orchestral scoring that was unlike any other score of its time. "I just found myself doing it," Barry said later. "That became the Bond style. That's why there's a similarity in all the Bond songs. It's not the melody, it's an attitude towards a piece of music. The beginning was so important." Thus Barry blasts those opening two notes, and their sassy answering trumpets, and "Goldfinger" is off and running. Also of note: Barry incorporates the familiar bass line of the Bond theme (right after Bassey sings "but don't go in"), ensuring a degree of musical continuity from previous films.

Aerial shots of Miami Beach (about eight minutes into the film) are accompanied by big-band swing (called "Into Miami" on the album) with John Scott's raucous alto sax solo. All of the cues are

of them added a throaty growl as they played the notes, "really kind of earthy. It just grew more and more, each time we played it. 'Oh, yeah, that's it! Give us more of that!'"

As so often happens, it's a combination of factors that make movie magic. It wasn't just the song, or the singer, or the sassy brass; it was also the imagery that accompanied all of them. Robert Brownjohn's title sequence—projecting scenes from the film (and previous Bond films) onto a gold-painted, bikini-clad girl—was a brilliant addition. Some are hilarious, as when Bassey sings "it's the kiss of death from Mr. Goldfinger" for the first time and the revolving license plate from Bond's Aston Martin appears directly over the girl's mouth; and when the golf ball putts right into her cleavage. "The mixture of his images and the song was irresistible," Barry said.

The song was only two and a half minutes out of a 48-minute score. This time, Barry didn't make it to any foreign locations, and with Hamilton falling behind schedule on the shoot he used the time to plan out what the film would need, musically. There had been only one scene that required musical playback on the set: Connery's first day of shooting, March 19, 1964, for the Central American El Scorpio nightclub, where Bonita (Nadja Regin, who played Kerim's girl in *From Russia with Love*) is dancing for patrons when Bond's bomb blows up a nearby heroin operation. She probably danced to a Latin recording that Barry later replaced with less than half a minute of guitar, bass and tambourine.

Barry's concept, from *Goldfinger* on, was to use the Bond theme as necessary (and sometimes "007") but to write a song that would be specific to the story as well as dramatically flexible. "I wanted to use the thematic music dramatically throughout the movie. A lot of writers in the thirties would write a theme for a movie and repeat it throughout—perhaps not as expansively as

(SCORE HIGHLIGHTS, CONT.)

fairly short—a touch of "Goldfinger" when we first glimpse the man, a bit of "Bond Theme" when he meets Jill—until Oddjob arrives on the scene (16 minutes), knocks out Bond and murders Jill by painting her entire body gold. Here, for the first time, we hear metallic percussion sounds suggesting the shiny precious metal and the nefarious use to which it's been put (the U.K. album track is called "Golden Girl"). This sound will return often, especially when Oddjob is involved.

Bond's golf game with Goldfinger is unscored until the very end (31 minutes) when the music chuckles at Goldfinger's defeat with pizzicato strings. More substantial cues begin when Bond flies to Switzerland and, on the road in his new Aston Martin DB5, encounters Jill's sister Tilly (34 minutes). This time, the main theme has a much more pleasant, subdued tone, perhaps reflecting the beauty of the countryside and the relative lack of action (the album calls this "Alpine Drive"). The very next cue (40 minutes) occurs as Bond infiltrates Goldfinger's factory and discovers his smuggling secrets accompanied by short bursts of brass amid high strings and timpani, all very suspenseful until he interrupts Tilly's latest attempt to shoot Goldfinger ("Auric's Factory" on the LP). Barry leaves the subsequent car chase unscored until Oddjob arrives, kills Tilly with his deadly flying bowler (46 minutes, "Death of Tilly" on the British LP) and captures Bond.

A favorite scene for many Bond fans is the exchange between Goldfinger and Bond while the latter is restrained and about to be cut in half by a high-powered laser ("choose your next witticism carefully, Mr. Bond, it may be your last"). This scene,

I did, but this was the classical way of scoring movies. My main themes were in the songs, and this was the Bond style." Moviegoers may have been wowed by the title song, but by the time they left the theater they had also heard the tune again and again in varying orchestral arrangements, and it would have been impossible to forget. It was a formula that worked.

He further explained his concept in a 1965 British magazine piece: "Consider the scene in *Goldfinger* where Bond is captured. He is taken off to Goldfinger's headquarters and it would appear that he's had it. But the audience is not at all convinced that it is the end for Bond; they know there is a button. So what do you do when writing music for this scene? Do you relax the music? No—you keep the edge on it. . . . You keep the tension in the music all the time. Then, when Bond presses the button and all hell breaks loose on the screen, you increase the tension and let every man in a 60-piece orchestra give his everything to produce a vast tumult of sound."

Barry explained that he read the script, visited the shooting stage and consulted with director and editor. At the rough-cut stage, they "spot" the film, deciding where music will go and what its precise timing and specific function will be. "I may need long sequences lasting several minutes or I may have to deal with action lasting as little as 10 seconds. But whatever I do, my timing must be right to within a third of a second," he said, giving a sense of the technical side of film composition.

But, as he also told the Associated Press in 1966: "You don't write a tailor-made score until they have a fine cut. From the fine-cut stage to the recording date is three to five weeks, depending on when the distributors are screaming they want the release date. On Bond movies, the time is murderously short. They measure the first two reels and then send it to me as they go along. On *Goldfinger*, I didn't get the final measurements of the last two reels until Friday tea-time and they were recording Monday. You just burn the midnight oil."

too, is scored (51 minutes, called "The Laser Beam" on the British LP), and the combination of Peter Hunt's editing and Barry's score makes it an edge-of-the-seat experience; again, it's an adaptation of the theme, with a new, repeated figure for strings and a slow build of low brass underneath.

Yet another variation on the main theme is the briefly fanfarish music for Galore's team of women pilots (one hour in, called "Pussy Galore's Flying Circus" on the U.K. LP), briefly interrupted by Oddjob's metallic motif and augmented by a sexy saxophone for the beautiful quintet. Flick's banjo piece follows immediately (1 hour, 3 minutes) as Barry suggests Americana for a brief moment on Goldfinger's Kentucky horse farm.

All four of the next cues are clearly heard in the film and all were on both LPs: "Teasing the Korean" (1 hour, 8 minutes), in which 007 entices his Korean guard to enter the cell and disarms him; "Gassing the Gangsters" (1 hour, 14 minutes), in which Goldfinger kills all his criminal cohorts to the tune of pounding timpani and those telltale metallic chiming sounds; and "Oddjob's Pressing Engagement," which is actually two cues. The first (1 hour, 16 minutes) opens with the midsection of the Bond theme but quickly segues to a loud, brassy rendition of "Goldfinger" as Oddjob kills the American gangster Solo and drives to a car-crushing operation where his Lincoln Continental is destroyed; and the second (1 hour, 20 minutes) as Leiter is mystified by the loss of signal from Bond's homing device and Oddjob returns home in another car.

"Goldfinger" turns briefly romantic (1 hour, 25 minutes) as Pussy escorts Bond to the stables and

Indeed, it must have been a panic getting everything written, orchestrated and recorded. Principal photography didn't finish until July 21, and "by the time the picture was done," Hamilton later recalled, "Peter Hunt and I were frantically putting it together imagining that the producers in their wisdom would delay the opening date." They didn't.

Barry also orchestrated everything himself, as was the practice in England at the time, meaning he not only composed the themes but arranged them (deciding what the overall sound and style of each cue, or individual piece of music, would be) and wrote out the full score (specifying every note that every instrument would play in every cue). Only in the most severe cases of time crunch would he rely on an outside orchestrator, and that was usually Bobby Richards, an ex-drummer from Barry's early rock 'n' roll days. It is possible that Richards made a contribution to *Goldfinger*; John Scott, who played the alto saxophone solo on "Into Miami," the memorable big-band jazz piece heard right after the title song, said he believed that Richards arranged it.

But Barry himself was always the architect of the specific sound of each score. When conceptualizing *Goldfinger*, he sought a metallic sound that might remind listeners of the shiny gold bricks that the villain loved and that were filling the corridors of Fort Knox. "I used the sound of finger cymbals," Barry later revealed. "You hear it the first time you see Oddjob. I wanted the sound of metal, and finger cymbals are very small but they have a distinctive 'ting' sound—it was the whole idea of metal, of gold and the hardness of it. You can hear this, too, in the use of brass at the beginning—the trombones and horns in the introduction to the song."

Once again, Barry turned to his old bandmate Vic Flick for a colorful solo, this time on the banjo, for the scenes on Goldfinger's Kentucky horse farm. "Banjo solo, bluegrass style" was the only direction on his music; Flick man-

(SCORE HIGHLIGHTS, CONT.)

they engage in a judo duel where high, light strings accentuate their falls into the hay; Barry offers a fresh twist on the theme as they kiss and Pussy succumbs to 007's charms. One of the highlights of the score immediately follows: "Dawn Raid on Fort Knox" (nearly 1 hour, 28 minutes), a seven-minute tour de force in which Barry puts a military spin on the main theme with snare drums, trumpet calls and cymbal crashes for Pussy's planes spraying gas around the installation to put the Army to sleep while Goldfinger's task force moves in and destroys the main gate.

Placement of the atomic device (1 hour, 35 minutes) again relies on the "Goldfinger" theme for material (specifically the "he's the man" portion of the song); on both U.S. and U.K. albums this is combined with the highly dramatic "Goldfinger"

variations (1 hour, 42 minutes) that underscore Bond's desperate, last-minute attempts to stop the A-bomb from detonating ("The Arrival of the Bomb and Countdown" on LP). There is no music for the firefight outside or Bond's final battle with Oddjob except for the moment when Bond grabs and throws Oddjob's lethal hat, and this offers a final opportunity for the metallic sounds we associate with the Korean killer.

Barry supplies near-comical piccolos for a lighthearted march (1 hour, 45 minutes) as Bond climbs aboard a jet supposedly headed for Washington, but the mood doesn't last as Goldfinger returns (1 hour, 47 minutes) to battle Bond one final time, and the aircraft crashes into the sea; again Barry turns the main theme into a tension-filled, high-strings and screaming-brass climax. This cue, plus

aged to come up with something appropriate on the spot. Also on at least one of the *Goldfinger* recording sessions: guitarist Jimmy Page, well before his rock 'n' roll stardom as part of the Yardbirds and Led Zeppelin.

One sequence failed to please director Hamilton, but how Barry handled it impressed him: "There was one bit of music which was for the part when Goldfinger's troops are turning up at Fort Knox, and for some reason it didn't work. It was overorchestrated or there was something wrong, and I went to John, who was on the podium conducting. . . . I was convinced that John was going to have to work all night because we'd got another music session the next day. . . . But he just listened, took the point and then suddenly turned and said to the orchestra, "Right, the violins are tacet, the brass will repeat the next six bars from G, the drums will do so-and-so," and off we went again. And it was a totally different piece. He'd reorchestrated it there and then and it worked magnificently."

Harry Saltzman, however, hated the title song. Barry recalled getting a late-August phone call from the producer, berating him for writing "the worst song I've ever heard in my goddamn life. It's terrible. If we weren't opening in three weeks time, I'd take it out," Barry quoted him as saying.

The joke was on Saltzman. Within days of the film's September 17 London premiere, Bassey's single was in stores and getting airplay. In England, it charted on October 15 and reached number 21. In America, the *Billboard* review on November 14 said "already a hit abroad, will draw much attention here"—and it did, after the film's New York opening December 21. Her single charted in the United States on February 27, 1965, and went all the way to number 8, the best showing yet for a Bond song. (Bassey's single version, incidentally, used a different take from that on the album.)

Barry's mostly unused end-title music, were combined into the "Death of Goldfinger / End Titles" track on both LPs. In the film, an edited version of Bassey's vocal is heard.

More significantly, the public seemed to be paying equal attention to *Gold-finger*'s bold, brassy Barry score. "The musical soundtrack is slickly furnished by John Barry, who also composed the title song," noted *Variety*'s film critic; its music critic later praised the album as "the strongest Bond film score to date." In the United Kingdom, the soundtrack album made the charts on October 31 and reached number 14. But in America, it appeared on December 12 and rocketed up the charts, reaching number 1 on March 20, 1965. It edged out the *Mary Poppins* soundtrack (which in turn had displaced *Beatles '65* at the top) and remained the most popular album in America for three weeks.

Goldfinger would be the only Bond soundtrack album to reach the top of the charts. Barry was nominated for a Grammy Award, and although there was no Oscar attention—for Barry, that would come later, and not for James Bond—there was the satisfaction of worldwide commercial success. United Artists Records released Barry's driving rock instrumental of *Goldfinger* (with Flick on guitar) and, a few months later, an LP titled *John Barry Plays Goldfinger* (a compilation of his arrangements from the first three Bond films plus a handful of easy-listening tunes).

Bricusse, who had been away with Newley writing *Roar of the Greasepaint*, remembered his astonishment at the call from United Artists to come and pick up their gold record, signifying $1 million in sales. "We had not seen the film, we didn't know the record was out, we knew nothing about it," he said. "It was amazing, a total surprise to us."

As for Saltzman, after the album hit the top of the American charts, he ran into Barry one day having his usual lunch at the Pickwick with Michael Caine and Terence Stamp. Saltzman paused briefly at the table, said a curt "thank you" and walked away.

". . . he looks at this world and wants it all . . ."

Thunderball

When filmgoers went to see *Thunderball*, few of them were aware of the behind-the-scenes intrigue that had gone on for years prior to its release. Ian Fleming's 1960 novel, written just before his deal with Bond producers Harry Saltzman and Albert R. Broccoli, drew on material that he, screenwriter Jack Whittingham and producer Kevin McClory had created in 1959 for a Bond movie that was never made. McClory's subsequent lawsuit resulted in his acquisition of rights to a *Thunderball* movie, which ultimately led to McClory becoming a producing partner with Broccoli and Saltzman for that single film.

Just as the screenplay issues had to be settled (both in and out of court) before production could begin, the music of *Thunderball* would also be embroiled in intrigue, uncertainty, hurt feelings and last-minute rewrites; it too would end up in a London courtroom before the film reached theaters in December 1965.

It began innocently enough. Given John Barry's enormous creative and commercial success with the music of *Goldfinger*, there was no doubt that he would remain 007's musical muse. He had demonstrated, working in different capacities on all three previous Bond films, that he could effectively score them regardless of locale and turn Bond themes into hit recordings as well.

And he was generating considerable new publicity himself. He was the subject of profiles in both *Billboard* and *Variety* in January and February 1965 (the latter, in classic *Variety* style, was headlined "007's B.O. Click Tunes Deals for Composer Barry," B.O. being *Variety* slang for "box office"). Since finishing *Goldfinger*, he had written fresh, innovative scores for Richard Lester's stylish *The Knack . . . and How to Get It* (which would win top honors at the Cannes film festival) and his former flatmate Michael Caine's starring turn in a more low-key spy film, the Saltzman-produced *The Ipcress File*. Topping it all off, in the week the *Goldfinger* album hit the top of the American charts, it was announced that Barry had signed a three-year deal with CBS Records (Columbia in the U.S.) as both artist and producer.

But he was already thinking ahead to *Thunderball*. As Barry later recalled, on a flight from London to the States, "I picked up a newspaper. The Bond thing was in full stride by then, and in one article it said that the Italians called Bond 'Mr. Kiss Kiss Bang Bang.' All I knew was that 'Thunderball' was the most horrendous title for a song." He remembered joking about it with Anthony Newley, when they were talking about what they could do with "Thunderball" as a title, and the clever Newley immediately responded, "Thunderball, marvelous, you should care for me," taking his cue from a George and Ira Gershwin song.

"We can redefine Bond through the lyrics, through that title," Barry thought; he would write a song called "Mr. Kiss Kiss Bang Bang." He won approval from Broccoli and Saltzman and, with shooting already under way in the Bahamas, director Terence Young decided to incorporate the song title into one of the Nassau locations. The script referred to the Jump Jump Club, where Bond would end up while trying to elude his SPECTRE pursuers; and although the call sheet for April 5, 1965, refers to the Jump Jump Club, the schedule for April 6 renames the nightspot as the Kiss Kiss Club. This is the title seen on screen.

In *Thunderball*, SPECTRE decides to hijack a NATO jet armed with two atomic warheads and then demand £100 million in ransom money or face the possibility of a major city being destroyed. Bond's investigation leads him first to an English health farm and then to the Bahamas, where he meets SPECTRE operative Emilio Largo (Adolfo Celi) and his beautiful ward Domino (Claudine Auger).

The film's most memorable musical moment takes place there, in the specially built Paradise Island set. In the script, Bond is dancing with Largo's henchwoman Fiona (Luciana Paluzzi) when "the drummer breaks into a frantic solo" and 007 wheels Fiona around just in time to make sure she takes the bullet meant for him. That wild conga-and-bongo solo was played by 23-year-old percussionist King Errisson (billed as "King Erison" on screen), and those featured 22 seconds helped to propel him to fame.

Errisson was discovered by Connery and McClory, who, along with other members of the *Thunderball* crew, would seek late-night revelry at the Conch Shell Club, "over the hill on the ghetto side of town. After a couple of weeks

"The music is going to go on all night anyhow," says Luciana Paluzzi to Sean Connery during their love scene—one of few moments in the film when "Thunderball" is actually played as underscore.

of coming in every night, they decided I was the guy to do the part," Errisson recalled. For the scene, Errisson actually played a composition of his own, "where I would play a certain tempo and raise it and raise it until I get to the crescendo that you see. What they wanted was for me to go crazy when I see the gun coming out of the curtain, in order to make Bond look at me." That piece was eventually replaced, to Errisson's disappointment, by a Barry original. Another song that Errisson performed, his Nassau hit "Wings of a Dove," was recorded for potential use (and even teased in an August 1965 *Billboard* article as a featured number in the film) but ultimately discarded over music-rights issues. Errisson went on to become Neil Diamond's conga player for more than 40 years.

Having finished recording *King Rat* in Los Angeles, Barry flew to the film's Nassau location on April 20, 1965. The idea, *Variety* reported, was "to dig up native musical ideas for his fourth James Bond film assignment."

"I spent a week down there and listened to calypsos and things, none of it really very useful in terms of the dramatic context of the movie," Barry said.

"We would go out to these restaurants in the evenings and whoop it up a lot. Harry and Cubby used to have maybe 20 people in a restaurant, with Sean and everybody. The actual goodies that wound up on the screen from these adventures was very minimal. But it was fun."

When Barry returned to London, he began crafting the melody for "Mr. Kiss Kiss Bang Bang." True to form, Barry wrote something fresh and vital, a jazz waltz that could be applied dramatically in many contexts, from warmly romantic to darkly suspenseful. And once again, and as he had recently done with *The Knack*, he turned to Bricusse for a lyric.

"John called me to say that Cubby and Harry were very taken with the nickname 'Mr. Kiss Kiss Bang Bang,'" Bricusse recalled. "It came very quickly, too. It was dead easy, that one. I loved the tune. I just think there's an excitement in jazz waltzes, and the fact that it was jazzy suited the character of the man and the piece."

As with *Goldfinger*, Bricusse didn't see any footage or read a script; he simply worked from the title and Barry's music. "John was one of that rare breed," Bricusse reflected. "There are not many really good film composers who are really good songwriters. Hank Mancini was one, John Barry was one, John Williams is another. The gift of melody, in terms of songwriting structure, eludes a lot of top film composers." Barry's tunes, Bricusse added, "took enormous thought, planning and work."

Bricusse's lyrics were smart and witty: "He's tall and he's dark / and like a shark, he looks for trouble / that's why the zero's double . . ." and although it might have seemed a natural for Shirley Bassey to belt out, à la *Goldfinger*, she would not wind up getting the first call on the song.

For the next three months, while *Thunderball* continued shooting in Nassau and at Pinewood, Barry shifted attention to his first stage musical, *Passion Flower Hotel*, which opened August 24, 1965, at the Prince of Wales Theatre (after a three-week tryout in Manchester). His collaborators were old show-biz cronies: Trevor Peacock, the *Beat Girl* lyricist who struck out trying to put words to *Goldfinger*; and Wolf Mankowitz, the man who introduced Cubby Broccoli to Harry Saltzman and who had penned the book for Monty Norman's first musical *Expresso Bongo*. (Barry wound up marrying one of the girls in the *Passion Flower Hotel* cast, a young Jane Birkin, and for a while they were one of the hottest couples in Swinging Sixties London.)

By September, it was back to Bond. *Thunderball* was an even greater challenge than *Goldfinger*, not only because it required far more music (nearly 80 minutes in the film, even more recorded and not used) but also because large sections of the film take place underwater. To create a feeling of suspension, he decided to make extensive use of harp, vibraphone, flutes and strings, often in adaptations of "Kiss Kiss Bang Bang" or the jazzy midsection of the Bond theme—and recorded in such a way that the music seemed distant, or echoing. "Lots of echo, and no bass," he later explained. "It was just melodies and lines floating. It wasn't rooted, which is what you feel when you swim underwater; you're not attached to anything. I just removed all that low end and did it in a strange, linear scale of overtones with alto flutes and vibraphones to create the effect."

In terms of basic musical material, he already had three themes to draw from: "Mr. Kiss Kiss Bang Bang," the Bond theme and "007," which he had written for *From Russia with Love* but which could (with new variations) cover some of the action sequences.

First to be recorded would be "Mr. Kiss Kiss Bang Bang," on September 4. Rising American star Dionne Warwick was chosen to sing. She had had four top-40 hits in 1964, and she was doing a European tour in late August and early September that made her available for a London recording. "Dionne's was marvelous," Barry later said. "It was a three-four kind of thing with a whole section of cowbells doing the rhythm. It was a strange kind of a song, but I liked it," he added. Warwick's vocal had a warmth and an ease about it, and it dovetailed nicely with Maurice Binder's title sequence of underwater nudes—although it needed a seemingly interminable 48-second intro, apparently because nobody wanted the vocal to begin until after the title *Thunderball* appeared on screen. "John made a marvelous recording with Dionne," Bricusse later remarked, "and we were convinced we had a big hit."

And then, while Barry was in the midst of writing and orchestrating a score based on this very melody, the unexpected happened. Broccoli and Saltzman told the composer that "Mr. Kiss Kiss Bang Bang" had to be jettisoned from the film. "We've got to have a song called 'Thunderball,'" Barry quoted Broccoli as saying, "because that's the title of the movie and United Artists wants that title on the radio. 'Kiss Kiss Bang Bang' doesn't mean a thing."

With deadlines approaching, both in terms of finishing the film and getting a finished soundtrack album to United Artists Records, the pressure was on. Bricusse was unavailable, having left to write the songs for 20th Century-Fox's film musical *Dr. Dolittle*. So Barry decided to take a chance on Matt Monro's manager Don Black, whose lyric-writing career had taken off with "Walk Away," a hit for Monro in late 1964. "Do you fancy having a go at the new Bond song?" Black remembered Barry asking.

Barry said nothing of "Mr. Kiss Kiss Bang Bang," only that the producers were in a hurry to do this. In a day or so, the composer wrote a new melody (with an intro drawn from the bebop midsection of the Bond theme) that ended with three notes that might say "Thunderball." Black, excited about the opportunity, accepted immediately; but he still had to write a lyric around a word that made no sense. He checked the dictionary and found no "thunderball." And there was no time for script readings or film screenings.

"So I used it as a kind of code word," Black remembered. "I thought the opening line was good—'he always runs while others walk'—I thought, well, that's Bond, isn't it? I just kept going like that. I've always found that if the lyric hugs the contours of the melody and doesn't offend what the composer's written, you're in pretty good shape. When I wrote it, I thought of two things:

(left to right) John Barry, singer Tom Jones and lyricist Don Black listen to a playback of "Thunderball"

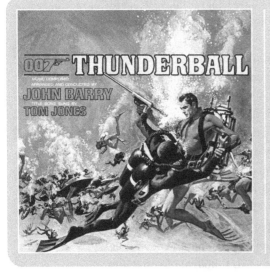

John Barry initially approached *Thunderball* with three themes in hand: "Mr. Kiss Kiss Bang Bang" would become the main theme, with help from the "James Bond Theme" (in particular, its jazzy mid-section) and "007," the lighthearted adventure theme he first introduced in *From Russia with Love*. When the song "Thunderball" was added to the mix late in the game, Barry quickly modified a few cues to incorporate the new theme and make it seem more a part of the entire tapestry.

The precredits sequence features one of Barry's all-time great developments of the Bond theme (called, on the album, "Chateau Flight"), a high-energy piece for Bond's unmasking of Col. Bouvar, their fight and his aerial departure via conveniently placed jetpack. The "Thunderball" song featuring

James Bond and Shirley Bassey, that kind of full-throated, powerful voice. It's a Bond thing—'any woman he wants, he'll get / he will break any heart without regret'—it's a summation of that lifestyle."

The whole song was written over a mid-September weekend. And Welsh-born singer Tom Jones, an old friend of Black's who had already had two top-10 hits earlier that year ("It's Not Unusual" and "What's New Pussycat?"), quickly agreed to sing it. Black liked his "steely, manly voice." Britain's *New Musical Express* announced Jones's signing on September 24, and they went into the studio on October 11 to lay down the track.

"I was thrilled to bits when they asked me to do *Thunderball*," Jones remembered many years later. "There was a connection, because Les Reed, who wrote a lot of my big songs, was John Barry's pianist. The most memorable thing about the session was hitting that note at the end. John told me to hold on to this very high note for as long as possible."

Jones's now-legendary final note lasts nine full seconds, and in the isolated vocal recording he can be heard running out of breath, although that last part is buried in the final mix with the orchestra. "I closed my eyes, hit the note and held on," Jones said on another occasion. "When I opened my eyes the room was spinning. I had to grab hold of the booth I was in to steady myself. If I hadn't, I would not have passed out, but maybe fallen down. But it paid off, because it is a long note and it's high."

But, when the lyric says "he looks at this world and wants it all," is the song about the villain or the hero? "It's not about the villain in the film, it's a song unto itself," Jones said. "It's a fictitious character that Don Black wrote about that's not really in the film. I was so thrilled to do it, I didn't question it." Black insisted that the song was about Bond. Barry just wanted to get a great performance: "Tom sings with great conviction. He doesn't ask any questions."

Tom Jones's vocal (five minutes into the film) is notable for its heavy application of that same brassy portion of the Bond theme, and it is so prevalent throughout the score that it gives credence to the idea that Barry always believed this portion of the Bond theme to be his own work (something Monty Norman always denied). "Thunderball" would also mark the last time Barry incorporated the bass line of the Bond theme into his title song (right after "he looks at this world and wants it all").

Largo reveals his plan to hijack a NATO Vulcan jet with two atomic warheads, and the scene switches from SPECTRE headquarters to a health farm in England, where Bond meets Count Lippe; these two suspense cues (starting at 10½ minutes into the film), the latter based specifically on "Mr. Kiss Kiss Bang Bang," show up on the LP as "The Spa." Bond discovers the dead NATO pilot (23 minutes in) to a suspense cue ("Switching the Body") that, intriguingly, opens with a variation on the late-composed "Thunderball" theme but segues into suspense with a repeated passage for alto flute and harpsichord; it then ends with a quote from "KKBB."

One of the score's highlights is "The Bomb" (31 minutes in), which is actually three cues totaling nearly six minutes for a tension-filled sequence in which the Vulcan's SPECTRE pilot is murdered underwater and Largo's minions steal the atomic bombs aboard, all set to an elaborate series of variations on the midsection of the Bond theme; here, and often in later underwater sequences, Barry deploys flute, strings, vibraphone and piano in repeating patterns. The complete piece is on the album; in the film only about 4½ minutes remain, probably

(left to right) John Barry, singer Shirley Bassey and manager Kenneth Hume discuss her vocal of "Mr. Kiss Kiss Bang Bang" in October 1965

because of last-minute edits. (Another piece largely lost in the film is the music for the car chase, at 37 minutes into the film, as Lippe's car is destroyed by a rocket-firing motorcycle as Bond watches; the screaming-brass Bond theme survives on the expanded *Thunderball* CD.)

Bond travels to the Bahamas to find Domino Derval, the sister of the dead NATO pilot. Two delightful lounge-music versions of the main themes are heard back to back: "Thunderball" (nearly 49 minutes in) with a jazzy piano solo (slightly different from the album version, which adds a nice alto sax solo), and "Mr. Kiss Kiss Bang Bang" (52 minutes), which becomes "Cafe Martinique" on the album, the name of the restaurant where Bond and Domino dine and dance.

Bond goes diving beneath Largo's yacht (1 hour, 3 minutes into the film), and again Barry turns to Bond theme variations, but with far more urgency and what would later become a Barry-Bond trademark, strings and xylophone together; vibraphone and strings play repeating phrases while shrill brass figures denote hand-grenade tosses into the water (this cue, too, is truncated but plays in full, as "Bond Below Disco Volante," on the LP). Bond and Leiter's helicopter search for the missing NATO jet (at 1 hour, 9 minutes) also takes its cue from "KKBB" ("Search for Vulcan" on the LP) and once again features dramatic harpsichord and high, muted, wah-wah trumpets.

"007" makes its first appearance in the film (1 hour, 26 minutes) as Bond runs into the Junkaroo

With a new title song firmly in place, Barry worked overtime to incorporate the new theme into the score so that it wouldn't look like the kind of pasted-on song he loathed. "I like to get a song that is the basis for my thematic approach for everything," he told the Associated Press, "instead of just a song stuck on the front. I know a lot of people write a song and the rest of the music is unrelated. I think it's important to relate."

So, in another last-minute move, he recorded "Thunderball" in a handful of instrumental versions spread throughout the film, all designed to give the impression that it wasn't "just a song stuck on the front."

"Mr. Kiss Kiss Bang Bang" wasn't dead, however. On September 30, Eon agreed to hire Shirley Bassey to sing it, for possible use under the end titles. She recorded at CTS on October 12, the day after Jones had recorded the title song. The arrangement was classic Bond and Barry, too: trumpets playing at the top of their registers, with flutes and cowbells providing a surprising rhythmic beat and a sensuous muted-trumpet solo under the "damoiselles and danger" line; it seemed an irresistible combination.

By the end of the month, Bassey's involvement with *Thunderball* was news in the music world; when United Artists confirmed that Bassey would be included in the new Bond film (as *Variety* reported, "to sing a different ditty over the pic's finale"), it looked as if *Thunderball* would have not one but two great songs.

By October 26, Barry—recording in film order, starting with reel one—had recorded more than half the film's score. At some point within the next several days, however, another fateful decision was made: to drop the Bassey recording of "Mr. Kiss Kiss Bang Bang." As the public would soon find out, her performance had been problematic. Over eleven takes, Bassey didn't always

parade to escape Fiona and Largo's henchmen; but instead of its usual lighthearted tone (as in the album version) this contains much more urgency and continuously shifts keys upward. In 2003, an alternate version of this cue (10M1, "Street Chase" on the CD) was discovered in tapes found in the EMI vaults at London's Abbey Road: "Barry originally scored the street chase not with the '007' theme but with a variation of the KKBB theme (the four-note introductory motive that leads off the song versions), escalating sequentially as the '007' theme does in the finished version ... with the same squealing piccolos that cap each musical 'sentence' as in the film version, and then ratchets up to the next key," wrote album producer Lukas Kendall. But there were "performance problems"

and "the concept was apparently abandoned before a master take could be made."

Music for the fire dancer at the Kiss Kiss Club presages the "Death of Fiona" scene, in which Bond is caught on the dance floor by the malevolent Fiona (1 hour, 29 minutes) and, during an intense conga-and-bongo-drum solo by local bandleader King Errisson, Fiona is shot and killed. Barry's music (again based on "KKBB") is a brilliant example of a single piece of music that starts as source music, becomes dramatic underscore (as we see the gun in the curtain, the music reaches a pitch of frenzy as Fiona is shot) and then returns to its original mode as source. Bond's line as he puts Fiona's lifeless body into a chair is also a classic: "Do you mind if my friend sits this one out? She's just dead."

hit the notes properly, and she kept singing "ban ban" instead of "bang bang." The final version was good, but not great, Bassey.

When Bassey learned that she had been tossed out of *Thunderball*, she was "furious," according to her biographer, and attempted to have her vocal reinstated. When the Bond producers refused, Bassey's company filed suit, demanding that the film's release be halted unless her song was reinserted into the film and she got a prominent screen credit. A UA attorney's November 12 memo referred to Bassey's action as a "sticky wicket" and, by November 18, it was news in the legal pages of *The Times*.

Broccoli submitted an affidavit detailing the imminent release dates (the first being in South Africa on December 10) and the potential financial impact even if the song were to be reinstated, which the producers declined to do. Broccoli's statement suggested that even though it was technically possible, it not only would be expensive but might actually damage her reputation because the recording was "artistically unmeritorious." In addition, the nature of the song made it inappropriate to follow the film's "whimsical ending," it was said, making "both the arrangement of the song and her rendition of it . . . dramatically inapposite." The court declined to stop distribution of the film and recommended that Bassey seek damages instead. The case was eventually settled, but the inevitable rift between Saltzman and Bassey's manager (and ex-husband) Kenneth Hume took her off the Bond market until after Hume's death in 1967. She would return in the 1970s with memorable performances in *Diamonds Are Forever* and *Moonraker*.

Barry finished recording *Thunderball* on November 17, 1965. As for the troublesome song, Bricusse was surprised that "Mr. Kiss Kiss Bang Bang" didn't show up in a later Bond movie because, he said, "it was a theme for all the Bonds; it's about him." In fact, he said, "I would love to have written every Bond song that's ever been."

(A few seconds of Errisson's original drumming, which was replaced by Barry's "Death of Fiona" music, could be heard in *The Incredible World of James Bond* television special which aired Nov. 26, 1965 on NBC.)

No music from the film's final 39 minutes made it onto the original LP; UA Records needed to finalize the contents of the soundtrack album and assembled it on the basis of what had been recorded to that point, presumably late October 1965. Bond finds the hidden Vulcan (1 hour, 32 minutes) and Barry reprises material from the "Search for Vulcan" and "Bomb" sequences for Bond's search. A brief romantic interlude for Bond and Domino underwater (1 hour, 37 minutes) is among the most beautiful in the score, a Debussy-style impressionistic passage for harps, flutes, strings and vibraphone.

A few moments later (1 hour, 41 minutes), the intro to "007" returns as Bond dons a wetsuit and joins Largo and his SPECTRE divers; and when they reach the secret underwater location of the stolen bombs, the "KKBB" brass is heard again. Curiously, editor Peter Hunt uses the Bond-theme variations of "Chateau Flight" for Bond's discovery and fight with a Largo lackey.

Barry's "Bomb" motif returns, with a heroic spin and swirling strings, as NATO divers plunge into the sea (1 hour, 53 minutes) and the underwater battle begins. Although the first minute and a half is unscored, music returns when Bond reenters the water (1 hour, 56 minutes) and "007," along with its shrieking piccolos and escalating-key variations, dominates much of the sequence ("Bond Joins Underwater Battle" on the expanded CD). Bond and

Because of all the last-minute changes to song and score, assembly of the *Thunderball* soundtrack album was rushed, and inevitably, mistakes were made. The final track on the American album was different depending on whether you bought the monaural or stereo version: both were "Mr. Kiss Kiss Bang Bang," but the mono version was a middle-of-the-road, radio-friendly arrangement, while the stereo version was the orchestral backing track for the original main title, with an alto sax solo replacing the Warwick vocal.

Few critics bothered to mention the music. The *Los Angeles Times* referred to its "raucous theme song," while *The Hollywood Reporter* said "the music has the frantic quality of Bond's superheated adventures and sets a note of excitement from the opening titles." The music industry, however, took notice: *Billboard*'s lead story on December 4 was headlined "Record Men Roll 007s in 'Thunderball' Game," noting that UA Records had shipped 350,000 copies of the album, that Parrot Records had the Tom Jones single and that cover versions had already been recorded by numerous other artists from pianist Peter Nero and guitarist Billy Strange to bandleader Roland Shaw.

Jones's "Thunderball" single, touted by *Billboard* as "a slow driving powerhouse of blues material," charted on December 11 and reached a high of number 25 on January 22, 1966. The album, too, charted on December 11 and reached number 10 on March 5, 1966—another big seller for UA Records and for composer Barry. In England, the Jones single reached number 35. "Mr. Kiss Kiss Bang Bang," meanwhile, was not entirely forgotten: singers Glenda Grainger, Buddy Greco and Ann-Margret recorded it, although the original Warwick and Bassey vocals did not surface until a 30th-anniversary Bond music retrospective was issued on compact disc in 1992.

As he was finishing his work on *Thunderball*, Barry gave an interview to a London magazine in which he referred to the Bond scores as "super-colossal Mickey Mouse music. A Bond film is geared to give entertainment—in terms

Largo battle underwater briefly to "KKBB" as NATO forces rout the SPECTRE operatives; Bond manages to board the Disco Volante as it speeds toward Miami, and those "007" variations return (2 hours, 5 minutes in) for much of the final three-minute action sequence as Bond battles Largo to the death. And the original recording of the "James Bond Theme" returns for the finale.

Additional pop-oriented versions of "Thunderball" and "Mr. Kiss Kiss Bang Bang" were recorded by Barry during the sessions but were never released.

of color, thrills, laughs—on a giant scale, and I have to write music to match what is happening on screen." A few weeks later, in a profile headlined "Aboard the Bondwagon" in America's widely read and prestigious *Time* magazine, he referred to it as "million-dollar Mickey Mouse music."

He didn't mean it in a pejorative way, as he was forced to explain to a fuming Harry Saltzman. Rather, the films demanded over-the-top, mock-Wagnerian musical gestures: "The films put forth a kind of simple, almost endearing comic-strip attitude toward danger, intrigue and romance. The main thing is to carry it off with style; don't belittle the subject matter or make it cheap. Just give it a whole lot of style and make it sound like a million dollars."

5

". . . well, it takes my breath away . . ."

Casino Royale (1967)

When Broccoli and Saltzman acquired the rights to Fleming's novels in 1961, one was missing: *Casino Royale*, the author's first, published in 1953. In 1954, CBS Television produced an adaptation of *Casino Royale* for its weekly dramatic anthology series *Climax!* starring Barry Nelson as an American Bond and Peter Lorre as the villain Le Chiffre. Their high-stakes baccarat game was the centerpiece of this live, one-hour drama. It had no original music, just a few brief transitional and climactic cues drawn from the generic dramatic music in the network's Los Angeles music library.

Over the years, the rights had passed from actor-director Gregory Ratoff to his widow to agent-producer Charles K. Feldman (who had produced *A Streetcar Named Desire* and *The Seven Year Itch* and was once Broccoli's boss at the Famous Artists Agency). Feldman, aware that he was now competing with a global phenomenon in the Bond movie series, decided the only way to proceed was to create a big-budget, all-star Bond sendup. He managed to recruit David Niven, Peter Sellers, Woody Allen, Orson Welles, Deborah Kerr and former Bond girl Ursula Andress, and he hired five directors (including the venerable John Huston) and multiple screenwriters (including Wolf Mankowitz, who had declined credit for co-writing *Dr. No*) for what would wind up as a $12-million extravaganza bankrolled by Columbia Pictures and shot in London.

The "plot" is virtually incomprehensible: Niven plays a retired, knighted James Bond who is summoned back to duty; Sellers plays a baccarat expert, Welles is Le Chiffre, Allen one "Jimmy Bond" who turns out to be the real villain, and Andress is a millionaire ex-spy. Joanna Pettet plays the love child of Bond and Mata Hari! By the end of the movie there are flying saucers over London, cowboys and Indians dropping out of the sky, threats of biological warfare and nuclear destruction.

Burt Bacharach and Hal David—the brilliant songwriters who had already enjoyed huge success in the pop market with such hits as "Don't Make Me Over," "Anyone Who Had a Heart" and "Walk on By"—were Feldman's first choice for songs and score for *Casino Royale*. Although they had written movie

Vesper Lynd (Ursula Andress) begins her seduction of Evelyn Tremble (Peter Sellers) while "The Look of Love" plays in the background of *Casino Royale*

songs before (including "Wives and Lovers" and "Alfie"), it was Feldman who had given Bacharach his first chance to write a complete film score, with the comedy *What's New, Pussycat?* in 1965 (yielding, not incidentally, a top-five hit for the wacky title song sung by Tom Jones).

"Charlie Feldman was the nicest guy I ever worked for," said lyricist Hal David. "Charlie asked us if we had an agent. We didn't have one at the time. He saw to it that we did OK."

David's involvement with *Casino Royale* would span only a few months. Bacharach's odyssey with this mad carnival of a movie would take nearly two years.

According to Feldman's diaries and datebooks, the producer gave the composer a script for *Casino Royale* at a dinner (that also included Woody Allen) on August 21, 1965, just two months after the *Pussycat* premiere. He formally announced Bacharach as composer on September 27; dinners, meetings and various discussions about music continued off and on for the entire next year. During that time Bacharach also scored *After the Fox* but, because production on *Casino Royale* dragged on, he had to drop out of the Jack Lemmon comedy *Luv*.

In April 1966, *Variety* reported that Bacharach and David would "collaborate on a half-dozen ditties" for the film. "We wrote a group of songs, I don't know how many, but more than we wound up with," David recalled. "Everything we wrote in New York, except maybe for the title song—and I'm not sure of that—didn't fit with the new movie. The script had changed."

In the meantime, Feldman interviewed 19-year-old singer Kiki Dee and talked to casting director Maude Spector about singers Cilla Black and Lulu. They were just three of the many possibilities for performers that would come and go before the end of scoring in January 1967.

Bacharach and David were scheduled to fly to London to see an early cut in July 1966, but the lack of sufficient completed scenes led them to cancel the trip and reschedule for October. Just four days before their arrival in London on October 17, Henry Mancini—then Hollywood's best-known composer, coming off such hits as *Charade* and *The Pink Panther*—called Feldman to say he was "anxious to do the film," according to Feldman's diary, although Feldman remained committed to Bacharach.

The songwriters spent a week in London. They screened a rough cut of the film on their first day and then met regularly with Feldman (along with at least two of the directors, and Columbia music executive Jonie Taps) throughout the week. Bacharach stressed to Feldman the need for 10 weeks to write the necessary music but, despite Feldman's pleas, declined to return to London before the new year. (He and wife Angie Dickinson had a new daughter, Nikki, born three months prematurely and suffering from health problems.)

So Bacharach and David did much of their work in New York and L.A. in late 1966, conferring via phone with Feldman in London. Feldman conceded to Columbia executives in late November that there were "problems, primarily music." On December 12, Feldman informed Bacharach that he wanted a "comedic song for the opening of the picture." They responded with a song that Feldman referred to as "Little French Girl, Little French Boy."

The songwriters arrived in London on January 3, 1967, and the next day sang and played through much of what they had written. Feldman said he "made many suggestions of changes to them," including the replacement of "Little French Girl" with what he referred to as "the baroque number" to which David would pen new lyrics. On January 8, Feldman reported, he heard "the baroque number theme song and liked it." And at that point they started discussing possible singers, including Johnny Rivers (who had just had a top-10 hit with the television theme "Secret Agent Man"), Dusty Springfield (who Bacharach considered the best pop singer in England) and the Animals (the rock 'n' roll group that had enjoyed a string of top-10 hits in the U.K.).

The "baroque number" Feldman referred to was what would become the "Casino Royale" theme, with parody lyrics ("they've got us on the run / with guns and knives / we're fighting for our lives / Have no fear, Bond is here . . ."). Bacharach found a singer, 27-year-old Mike Redway—who, unbeknownst to the composer, sang the "demo" of "What's New, Pussycat?" for a music publisher two years earlier—to impart a nostalgic, period flavor to the song.

"Burt wanted somebody who could do a Noel Coward impersonation," Redway recalled. "The more eccentric I could do it, the better for Burt. He wanted that real over-the-top thing. I think even Noel Coward would have had

Burt Bacharach and Hal David in the late 1960s

Singer Mike Redway in a publicity pose for *Casino Royale*

a job singing it, because it's such a rangey song. But it wasn't difficult, because that's what I do. I'm a tenor. We did about two takes and it was in the bag."

Redway said he wasn't certain where it would finally end up in the movie. "I didn't know at the time that it was [for] the closing titles, but I didn't mind." He also received no screen credit.

In the meantime, Bacharach and David needed to write another song. Director Joseph McGrath—who handled all of the scenes involving Peter Sellers—had shot a romantic sequence with Sellers and Andress (including slow-motion scenes shot through a fish tank). Feldman hated it: "Take that arty-farty shit out, I want Sellers to be funny," he said, according to McGrath.

McGrath thought the scene could be romantic with the right music. He had used the Stan Getz–Astrud Gilberto bossa nova hit "The Girl from Ipanema" for playback on the set, and "Peter and Ursula, consciously or unconsciously, moved in tempo to that tune," McGrath recalled. Bacharach told Feldman to leave the sequence in; he would "write a tune to cover it."

The tune, written in London, turned out to be "The Look of Love."

"That song was established off what Ursula Andress looked like," Bacharach explained a few years later, "for her specific character and situation." "It started out as an instrumental theme, a sensual piece of music that would kind of underline Ursula Andress. . . . It wasn't really a love theme as much as a kind of very understated sexual theme written for her body and her face," he added in later interviews. With "Girl from Ipanema" as the model, Bacharach came up with a warm, lovely bossa, to which David added words appropriate to the seduction of Sellers's character ("the look of love / it's on your face . . .") but also applicable to anyone in love ("so much more than just words could ever say / and what my heart has heard, well, it takes my breath away . . .").

CHARLES K. FELDMAN'S
CASINO ROYALE

Music Composed and Conducted by
BURT BACHARACH
"Casino Royale Theme" played by
HERB ALPERT
& the
TIJUANA BRASS
"The Look of Love" song by
DUSTY SPRINGFIELD

SCORE HIGHLIGHTS

Without question, the best part of *Casino Royale* is Burt Bacharach's lively, endlessly tuneful score. It's not just the glue that holds this crazy concoction together, its energy and sheer joy keeps us interested even when we have no idea what's happening in the story or why.

The composer undoubtedly benefited from having written several songs that were jettisoned along the way; the melodies from "Little French Girl, Little French Boy" and "Let Your Love Come Through," for example, show up as motifs in the final score. And when it proved difficult to find a major artist to sing the parody song "Casino Royale," the late addition of "The Look of Love" with its indelible Dusty Springfield vocal made a "Casino Royale" instrumental— with Herb Alpert's trumpet atop the London orches-

"I wrote the lyric in, maybe, a couple of days," David said years later. Dusty Springfield was summoned to perform the song. "We were crazy about the way she did our songs," David said. "Dusty was a lovely person. She was one of the great singers in the popular idiom."

Bacharach brought in veteran Hollywood orchestrators Leo Shuken and Jack Hayes to assist and asked New York–based engineer-producer Phil Ramone to supervise the London recording. "At the time, I was doing quite a few singles," Ramone recalled, "and Burt and I loved working with each other." Ramone remembered the origins of "Look of Love": "Burt was in the throes of fleshing out a melody that he'd devised . . . a pretty, Brazilian-influenced melody that he believed could be expanded into a song. . . . Hal wrote the lyrics on the spot."

With more than 60 minutes of music in the score, recording took eight full days at CTS starting on January 21 and ending on January 29. English union rules precluded Ramone from doing the actual engineering; that was handled by CTS mixer Jack Clegg. Ramone was in the booth listening and offering suggestions to Bacharach, who was on the podium conducting an orchestra that Redway estimated at "between 50 and 60" musicians.

Johnny Rivers emerged as the first choice to sing "Casino Royale" over the opening titles. Rivers and Bacharach had met at Steve McQueen's party for the opening of his movie *The Sand Pebbles* in December. "Burt spoke to Rivers yesterday and he [is] most interested, apparently," Feldman cabled Columbia music executive Jonie Taps on January 9. Rivers flew to London on January 18 and was even formally announced by Columbia the next day as the film's title-song performer. But Rivers declined at the last minute. As he later told an interviewer, "I turned it down. I just didn't like the song. It was terrible." As late as February 17, the trades and wire services were still reporting Rivers as having recorded "Casino Royale."

tral track—a more sensible creative choice. (And they wound up with two top-40 song hits instead of one, a feat no Bond film has ever duplicated.)

There are more than 100 individual cues in the score, many lasting only a few seconds; some of Bacharach's score went unused, some was repeated, some shifted to new spots as the film was recut and a number of cues were truncated from the original recorded versions.

The main title, or what Feldman referred to as "the baroque number," is an instrumental version of the song "Casino Royale" that will surface in vocal form much later in the film. A happy, fanfarish theme written for four Bach trumpets and such Bacharach signature instruments as tack piano and harpsichord (Alpert's own trumpet, overdubbing himself, was added later), its lighthearted fun is perfectly complemented by Richard Williams's amusing animated titles (including lots of naked women blowing horns). ("Little French Girl, Little French Boy," originally penned for the opening, may have been inspired by an earlier cut of the film, as French children are seen marching by singing "Frère Jacques" when we first see Peter Sellers.)

The opening shot of cars converging (3 minutes in, the first 50 seconds of "The Venerable Sir James Bond" on the LP) offers the first of many delightful secondary motifs, this one featuring flugelhorn and a harpsichord ending that again harks back to Feldman's "baroque" comment. The first musical joke in the film is the use of Bond composer John Barry's *Born Free* theme (5 minutes in) when M's Rolls-Royce encounters lions en route to Bond's retirement home. Sir James (David Niven) plays Debussy's

The Animals also came in, either to audition or possibly to record a song, the night of January 25; their short-lived participation was never publicized. Springfield recorded her "Look of Love" vocal on the evening of January 29, but at the Philips London studio, not at CTS. Director McGrath attended the session: "She was incredibly shy, but what an amazing voice." Added Bacharach: "She was delivering great vocals. But when it came time to listen to a playback, she didn't want me or the engineer or anybody else to be in the control room with her."

As for the title track, Bacharach had recorded the orchestra but, with the abrupt departure of Rivers, had no performer. Redway's vocals were slotted for the end titles and scenes elsewhere in the film. Bacharach and Feldman met for dinner on January 30 and then, according to Feldman's diaries, made calls to the managers of both Tom Jones and Herb Alpert about participating in the film—Jones as possible vocalist, Alpert to augment the theme with his own, then wildly popular, Tijuana Brass sound. The idea of an instrumental main title won out.

"Burt called me from London," Alpert recalled. "Apparently another artist took a stab at that *Casino Royale* song, and he wasn't happy with it. I don't know if it was a vocal or an instrumental; I didn't really probe him on that. He called and asked me if I would consider putting my trumpet on it."

Alpert asked him to play the track over the phone. "He started singing it," Alpert said. "He had this really interesting interpretation of the melody, which I kind of adapted when I finally recorded it." Bacharach sent the multitrack recording from London. "I put a couple of trumpets on and added some light percussion, sent it back to him, and it was inserted into the movie."

The Tijuana Brass was an ensemble of studio musicians that, under Alpert's direction, had enjoyed 10 top-10 hits since 1962, including "The Lonely Bull"

(SCORE HIGHLIGHTS, CONT.)

"Clair de Lune" at the piano (10 minutes); his visit to Scotland is accompanied by bagpipes (12 minutes) playing a traditional lament; more bagpipe music follows for M's wake (20 minutes). The wassail ceremony (24 minutes) alternates between Sir James' flugelhorn theme and various silly trumpet calls played by SMERSH agent Mimi (Deborah Kerr).

Mimi's confinement merits sad violins (28 minutes), specified in Bacharach's score as "very deliberate, high satire . . . melodrama style," but her escape gets the first reprise of the main theme with, as Bacharach put it, "high screeching effect on trumpets" (first 1:32 of "Sir James' Trip to Find Mata" on the LP). "Little French Boy," as it's called on Bacharach's score (and on the LP), makes its first appearance during the Bentley-Jaguar car chase back to London (34 minutes); the phrase "little French girl, little French boy" fits nicely into the contours of the jaunty melody, with its old-fashioned alto sax and trombone duet perhaps reflecting Bond's traditional values.

Moneypenny's (Barbara Bouchet) nighttime assignment to find a suitable young agent begins with military snare drums (40 minutes) but quickly segues into a sexy number ("very exaggerated, sell sex" was the composer's direction for the alto sax); the same theme gets a stronger treatment as the new Bond (Terence Cooper) goes through his training (titled "Moneypenny Goes for Broke" on the LP).

"The Look of Love" is first heard as an instrumental (46 minutes) when Vesper (Ursula Andress) meets Evelyn Tremble (Peter Sellers); this time it's a tenor sax that plays over the sensual bossa rhythm ("free Brazilian feel," Bacharach instructed the gui-

and "A Taste of Honey." Most of their hits were light, catchy, fun numbers that had a slightly Mexican mariachi flavor.

American Federation of Musicians union contracts indicate that members of the Tijuana Brass recorded "Casino Royale" in Los Angeles on February 22 and 28, but it is unlikely that those tracks became part of the final film mix. Surviving members of the band remembered recording it, but the film track most prominently featured Alpert's signature-sound trumpet (overdubbing himself) along with a touch of marimba (possibly Julius Wechter, who regularly played percussion on Tijuana Brass recordings). It may be that the full-band takes were deemed unsatisfactory or unusable for contractual reasons and were shelved.

"This was just a matter of adding trumpets," Alpert said. "There was already a full orchestra with a rhythm section. It was super-fast. Three days after I received it, it was back in London. It was a rush deal."

The addition of Alpert permitted Feldman to promote the music in an even greater way. Advertising not only had Bacharach in the credit block as composer, there was also an entire separate line devoted to the theme: "Hear the CASINO ROYALE theme music played in the film by HERB ALPERT and the TIJUANA BRASS and on the Colgems LP soundtrack album."

Feldman seemed pleased by Bacharach's contribution, calling it "dynamic and completely unique. His sense of humor comes through in the music and gives a further sense of unity to the entire film. I think it is the very best job he has done yet."

Casino Royale had its world premiere in London on April 13, 1967, and its American premiere in New York on April 28. And while reviewers were generally unkind to the wild Bond spoof, an astute few noted the composer's efforts at unifying the disparate elements into a more amusing whole: "Bacharach's

---

tarist). The Dusty Springfield vocal of "Look" underscores a slow-motion scene of Vesper seducing Tremble in her apartment (48 minutes, also considerably longer on the LP); the sax solo underscores their dialogue. (In another movie-music joke, Sellers briefly dresses as Toulouse-Lautrec and Bacharach plays Georges Auric's theme from *Moulin Rouge*.)

Sir James treks to Siam to find his daughter Mata (Joanna Pettet) dancing in a temple (1 hour, 2 minutes); sitar and finger cymbals open the scene, but Mata's exotic dance—choreographed by Norwegian actor-dancer Tutte Lemkow—is scored for 53-piece orchestra and is among the score's highlights, with its swaying, yearning string section, powerful brass and dramatic, balletic percussion (on the LP, this is the last minute and a half of the "Sir James' Trip to Find Mata" track).

On Mata's arrival in Berlin (1 hour, 9 minutes), Bacharach plays "Let Your Love Come Through" as an instrumental—the score direction is "funky and raunchy"—and alternates with mandolin doubling balalaika for the brief shots of Communist-controlled East Berlin (on the album this is called "First Stop Berlin"). Mata's theft of valuable film (1 hour, 18 minutes) gets a lighthearted treatment with a "German, 1920s-style, small circus brass band" and Bacharach ups the slapstick quotient with the same tune a minute later as she escapes; saxes and organ are directed to play "very funky" (on the album the track is titled "Home James, Don't Spare the Horses"; the last minute, expanded, became Bacharach's "Bond Street" single). Yet another musical joke occurs when Mata lifts a manhole cover and hears a girl trio singing Bacharach's theme from *What's New, Pussycat?*

score is thoroughly mod, bright and cheerful, the most consistently happy note in the film," wrote the critic from the *Los Angeles Times*. "One of the most consistently good elements in the film . . . an infectious title theme," said *The Hollywood Reporter*; "a sufficiently jaunty lilt," noted *Variety*, although its film critic was clearly no judge of popular songs, dismissing "The Look of Love" as "a so-so song."

Music critics were a little sharper: "An exceptionally exciting score . . . the music is alive and thoroughly vivid," said *Billboard*. "A surefire winner," added *Variety*'s music writer. "Herb Alpert's Tijuana Brass should be enough to put it over the top. . . . Bossa nova 'The Look of Love' is an excellent ballad. . . ."

At virtually the same time, Alpert signed Bacharach to his A&M label, which allowed the composer to record and release as his first single one of the film's secondary melodies, the catchy, brassy "Bond Street"; it was in stores before the end of March. (It became part of Bacharach's first A&M album, *Reach Out*, released in the fall of 1967; the LP also included Bacharach's own take on "The Look of Love.")

The other commercial releases were the most complicated yet for a Bond film. The soundtrack album, on the RCA Victor–distributed Colgems label (which handled many Columbia movie soundtracks) coupled the Alpert-performed main theme and the Springfield "Look of Love" vocal with highlights from Bacharach's score. It hit *Billboard*'s album chart on May 13, 1967, and reached all the way to number 22 on July 15. (Two decades later, the LP became a highly sought-after collector's item, when audiophiles acclaimed it as the greatest-sounding, finest-engineered vinyl album in history.)

The "Casino Royale" single, however, was on Alpert's own A&M label, and it was the first of the two songs to become a hit. It charted on April 8, 1967, and reached number 27 on *Billboard*'s Hot 100 charts May 27, but

(SCORE HIGHLIGHTS, CONT.)

"The Look of Love" returns (1 hour, 23 minutes for Vesper, but Bacharach reprises his earlier Moneypenny-seduction theme for Miss Goodthighs (Jacqueline Bisset) and asked his tenor and alto sax players to play "very sexy and sneaky" (1 hour, 25 minutes, on the LP titled "Hi There Miss Goodthighs"). The drugged Tremble dreams of women and cards (1 hour, 26 minutes) while we hear the first vocal of "Casino Royale" sung, Noel Coward–style, by Mike Redway. The composer asked for the singer to sing "through a megaphone" and wanted the three saxophones to play "Guy Lombardo style, with nostalgic vibrato" before seguing back to "The Look of Love" (on the LP titled "Dream On James, You're Winning").

Tremble's baccarat game with Le Chiffre goes unscored. Vesper's kidnapping (1 hour, 41 minutes) is scored with a briefly action-oriented "Look of Love,"

while Le Chiffre's beauty-pageant mind-torture (1 hour, 44 minutes) gets what the composer termed a "1920s nostalgic" sax sound, followed by a bagpipes-and-drums cue that Bacharach titled "Sellers and the 11,000 Pipers" (both are combined on the LP as "Le Chiffre's Torture of the Mind").

Bacharach reprises the title theme, with the wildest flourishes yet, for Mata's kidnapping and the landing of a flying saucer in Trafalgar Square (1 hour, 47 minutes, called simply "Flying Saucer" on the LP). At Casino Royale, Sir James and Moneypenny enter the inner sanctum of the evil Dr. Noah (Woody Allen) to electronic sounds, specified in the score as being produced by a "wavelength generator" (1 hour, 52 minutes).

Bacharach's lighthearted approach to the insane finale, involving American cowboys and Indians bat-

number 1 on the adult contemporary chart on June 3. (It rounded out the Tijuana Brass' *Sounds Like . . .* LP, which reached number 1 on June 17, the group's fourth number 1 album in two years.) In England, the stories were similar: "Casino Royale" charted on April 27 and reached number 27, while the album (on RCA) charted on July 22 and reached number 35.

And though the Dusty Springfield vocal from the film was on the Colgems soundtrack, it was a slightly different arrangement that became the hit single on her home label of Philips—and, even stranger, it wasn't the A side of the single ("Give Me Time" was). Disc jockeys flipped the disc and made the Bond tune the hit, although much later in the year, reaching number 22 on November 4. Shockingly, considering Springfield's popularity in the U.K., her "Look of Love" never charted.

Also in April, English singer Shani Wallis—who was about to go before the cameras as Nancy in the screen version of *Oliver!*—released a Kapp Records single of the dramatic "Let Your Love Come Through," another of the early, discarded Bacharach-David songs (the melody of which remained in the score, however). Both the single and her album *Look to Love* (released in June) were spotlighted as potential hits by *Billboard*, but neither managed to make the charts.

"The Look of Love" fared somewhat better in the larger scheme of 1960s popular music. It received the film's only Oscar nomination and, as such, merited full-page color trade advertisements ("The Look of Love Is the Sound of Excitement, From *Casino Royale*! Burt Bacharach and Hal David's 'The Look of Love' Is the Love Song of the Year!") featuring the film's key art, a naked, long-haired woman covered with playing-card-design tattoos, wearing "007" earrings and wielding matching pistols.

The A&M single of "Casino Royale" and the Colgems soundtrack album received a total of four Grammy nominations (Instrumental Theme, Instrumental

tling SMERSH agents in the casino (2 hours, 4 minutes), leaves no doubt it was all intended as a giant lark: his soprano saxes and organ solo, his brass-band waltz for Sir James, the silent-movie piano for the black-and-white Keystone Kops footage and the final Indian war dance (titled by the composer, tongue-in-cheek, "the final, thank goodness, fight sequence"). On the LP, this music (titled "The Big Cowboys and Indians Fight at Casino Royale") is condensed into a suite that leads into a reprise of the title theme. But in the film, instead of the Tijuana Brass overlay, we hear the complete Mike Redway vocal with Hal David's parody lyrics ("the formula is safe with old 007 / he's got a redhead in his arms!") playing under the end titles (2 hours, 8 minutes).

Performance, Instrumental Arrangement and Original Score) but lost them all at the Grammy Awards on February 29, 1968.

Springfield had planned to sing her song at the Oscar ceremony on April 8, 1968, until the production schedule for her BBC television series intervened. Instead, a group on Alpert's A&M label, Sergio Mendes and Brasil '66, was announced to pinch-hit for her. Mendes and his group had performed "Look of Love" on an Alpert-hosted episode of ABC's *Hollywood Palace* variety show on December 12, 1967 (which also featured Bacharach at the piano and Alpert miming to the "Casino Royale" track).

The Academy Awards were postponed by two days, until April 10, because Dr. Martin Luther King, Jr., was assassinated on April 4 and his funeral was held on April 9. Although the mood was inevitably somber, the Mendes performance of "Look of Love"—complete with psychedelic lighting effects— was cited by one critic as the show's "brightest entertainment moment." The large audience tune-in undoubtedly helped to propel sales of the group's "Look of Love" single, which reached number 4 on July 6, 1968.

Unfortunately, the song, widely predicted to win as the best of the lot, lost the Oscar to "Talk to the Animals" from the musical *Dr. Dolittle*, by past-and-future Bond songwriter Leslie Bricusse. It was the third successive loss for Bacharach and David, although they would win two years later for "Raindrops Keep Falling on My Head" from *Butch Cassidy and the Sundance Kid*.

Bricusse was unable to attend. But years later he remembered telling Bacharach that "The Look of Love" should have won. "Talk to the Animals," Bricusse said, "is not even one of my three favorite songs in *Dr. Dolittle*, let alone of the year. 'The Look of Love' is 10 times better."

"... make one dream come true ..."

You Only Live Twice

As Sean Connery was losing interest in playing Bond, John Barry's music for the character only grew more memorable and compelling.

By mid-1966, as filming got under way on *You Only Live Twice*, the fifth official 007 film, it was apparent that Connery was tired of the role and had no intention of continuing beyond his five-picture contract. For Barry, however, Bond was just one facet of a diverse musical career that was now embracing all kinds of movies (not to mention television and the theater).

The composer used the excitement, and high grosses, surrounding *Thunderball* to launch his own series of albums on CBS/Columbia: a new arrangement of the title tune led off his *Great Movie Sounds of John Barry*, released in May 1966. The album met with raves: "Haunting, intriguing, terrific stereo masterpiece by British arranger-composer-conductor John Barry," said *Billboard*; "shows how complex, varied and successful his film music can be . . . convincing proof that Barry now ranks high indeed in this demanding split-second art form," added the *Los Angeles Times*.

In fact, show business in general was abuzz with the new sound of secret agentry as created and developed by Barry. "Everybody wants a new beat in background music," *Variety* quoted a music executive as saying in late 1966. "The trade calls it 'James Bond music.'" Indeed, the practically patented Barry hybrid of pop, jazz and traditional orchestral elements was finding its way into the music of TV spies (*The Man from U.N.C.L.E.*, *Danger Man*, *I Spy*,

John Barry conducting the orchestra at the *You Only Live Twice* recording sessions in April 1967

Mission: Impossible) as well as big-screen espionage tales (*Our Man Flint*, *The Silencers*, even Barry's own *The Ipcress File* with its distinctive, Eastern European cimbalom sound). Bandleaders such as Roland Shaw even managed to hit the charts with covers of Bond and other spy music, and United Artists' own compilation *Music to Read James Bond By* successfully competed.

It would be more than a year after finishing *Thunderball* before Barry would be called back into service with Bond. In the meantime, he had written the music for the Southern potboiler *The Chase*, the African-lion adventure *Born Free*, the comedy *The Wrong Box* and another spy film, the Harold Pinter–scripted *The Quiller Memorandum*, not to mention themes for the BBC's new TV series *Vendetta* and a Sunsilk shampoo commercial.

The new 007 adventure was set almost entirely in Japan. After the Secret Service fakes Bond's death in Hong Kong, M sends Bond to Japan, which appears to be the location of a secret rocket base that may be responsible for a diabolical plot involving the in-space hijacking of manned Soviet and American spacecraft. Bond meets Tiger Tanaka (Tetsuro Tamba), head of the Japanese Secret Service, and they eventually discover that SPECTRE head Blofeld

Sean Connery and Mie Hama as James Bond and Kissy Suzuki during the wedding scene in *You Only Live Twice*

(Donald Pleasence) is attempting to pit the two superpowers against each other and start World War III. Along the way Bond gets a Japanese makeover and marries agent Kissy Suzuki (Mie Hama).

Unlike *Thunderball*, *You Only Live Twice* offered a workable song title that could lend itself to all kinds of lyrical treatments. And, as he had done with his last Bond brainstorm, "Mr. Kiss Kiss Bang Bang," Barry started early and sought out his old friend Leslie Bricusse for lyrics. They ultimately wrote two songs; their first attempt was quickly forgotten and shelved as an unsuccessful demo. It resurfaced only in 1992 when EMI issued a 30th Anniversary James Bond music collection.

Bricusse lived in Beverly Hills, across the street from entertainer Danny Kaye and his wife Sylvia Fine. "He was a wonderful cook of Chinese food," Bricusse recalled. "He would cook these 10-course dinners, and we met everybody in Hollywood at that table. Kirk Douglas was one of those people. Kirk invited us down to Palm Springs the week that John asked me to write the song." In his autobiography, he remembered penning the original on an autumn Sunday morning: "I remember smugly thinking as I sat there, how good can it get? I was being handsomely paid to spend the weekend in the home of one of my favorite movie stars, writing the title song for a movie of one of my favorite heroes of fiction. I was the houseguest of Spartacus, writing for James Bond."

The first "You Only Live Twice" had a more pronounced Oriental feel than its successor, opening and closing with the sound of a gong and featuring, throughout the song, a marimba beating out a vaguely Eastern rhythm. The initial Bricusse lyric, about life and death being a game of dice, had some intriguing lines ("you gamble with danger, you gamble with love / each one is a stranger in a black velvet glove")—and, like "Mr. Kiss Kiss Bang Bang," the song was about Bond and his edgy lifestyle.

It was written in late 1966, and Julie Rogers was chosen to perform it. She had had a big 1964 hit in both the United States and the U.K. with "The Wedding" and two other top-40 songs in the U.K. since then. "It was never presented to me as a demo record," Rogers later said. "It was presented to me as, 'Will you do the Bond theme?'" She recalled a 40-to-50-piece orchestra, with Barry conducting, and only later was she told that "there were politics involved [and] they wanted a bigger name," so her Bond theme was jettisoned. "It was such a wonderful opportunity that just fizzled away," she said.

Bricusse's story was that he and Barry simply felt they could do better. Barry came up with a new, more sophisticated melody and met with Bricusse during a two-week stay in Hollywood in January 1967, whereupon Bricusse went back to work.

Once again, there was no script reading, and with the film still being edited back in England, no screenings. Bricusse already knew the book, but it wasn't all that relevant. The object was to write a song with this title that worked for the film but might get on the radio too. This time, Bricusse's approach was more philosophical. "You live two lives: the life that you actually live, and the life you dream about," he explained. "That's really what it is: 'one life for yourself, and one for your dreams,' whether or not they come true.

"John made it easy for the lyric writer in that the music said what it was meant to be. Remember, you go in (a) knowing the context, (b) you've got the melody, and (c) you're given the title of the song. So it's fill in the blanks."

Recently asked if he ever considered using Fleming's original line, modeled after 17th-century Haiku master Basho's poetry ("you only live twice: once when you are born, and once when you look death in the face"), Bricusse responded: "No. Who wants to sing that?!"

Saltzman, who hated "Goldfinger" and concurred with UA's notion to kill "Mr. Kiss Kiss Bang Bang," came up with a notion that further irritated Bond's composer: he hired a "music supervisor" to advise on song issues. "I don't know where Harry came up with this idea," Barry later said (although the concept was years ahead of its time, and today music supervisors are major players on all studio films). "I used to refer to him as Jiminy Cricket. He used to suggest certain things and we used to try and overcome his suggestions. He didn't last for long." One of his notions was to try an up-and-coming soul singer named Aretha Franklin, but Barry didn't feel she was right for the song. (An earlier report that the Walker Brothers, a U.K. trio, were "tentatively approached" for the honor proved unfounded.)

Cubby Broccoli and Frank Sinatra were old friends, and the Broccolis and Sinatras often socialized together. So Broccoli watched Sinatra's daughter Nancy grow up and, in the mid-1960s, begin a singing career of her own. In 1966 alone she had had four top-40 hits in America—three of which were also in the top 40 in Great Britain—including the top-selling "These Boots Are Made for Walkin'" and the more recent "Sugar Town." And because "You

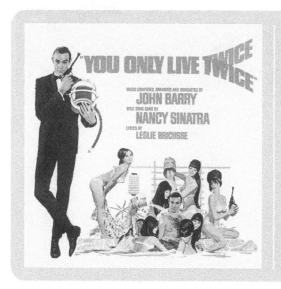

SCORE HIGHLIGHTS

The Far Eastern locale and the space sequences of *You Only Live Twice* inspired some of John Barry's most compelling James Bond music. Most of the score is built around three themes: the title tune, a dramatic march for the space hijackings and a secondary romantic theme for Bond's entanglements with Japanese women.

After a shrill new version of the Bond-theme gun-barrel opening featuring piccolos, Barry offers his first outer-space music in the Bond canon: dark and mysterious, with delicate flute and shimmering strings over a circular piano figure. Building brass and more insistent percussion signal the impending danger, as an unknown ship overtakes and swallows up the American capsule, killing a spacewalking astronaut. The scene ranks among the most terrifying

John Barry consults with singer Nancy Sinatra during the recording session for her "You Only Live Twice" vocal

Only Live Twice" in its second incarnation was a love song that needed a more delicate touch—"a more lyrical style," as Barry put it—Nancy Sinatra was asked to lend her voice to the next Bond theme.

Sinatra made the trip from Los Angeles to London with her sister Tina in late April 1967. "I remember being so nervous," she recalled many years later. "First of all, I hate to fly. I dragged my sister along—she wanted to go to London—so I wasn't by myself, at least. But I was really scared going there because I knew this was nitty-gritty hardcore singing. This wasn't pretend singing, personality-on-record and silliness the way I was doing some of the songs. . . . When I walked into the studio itself, there must have been, it felt like 200 musicians . . . it was like a symphony orchestra. You know how John Barry works with that gorgeous, huge sound that he has."

It only seemed like 200; in fact, there were 60 musicians on May 2 at the CTS studios. UA's publicity department invited numerous reporters and photographers to attend, and Sinatra's discomfort was duly reported. "Nancy, an accomplished singer of both ballads and pop songs, spent a nerve-racking evening at the Cine-Tele Sound studios in Bayswater trying to perfect her voice on the soundtrack of John Barry's beautiful title music," wrote one reporter. Sinatra was quoted as saying, "Oh, dear, I shouldn't have come all this way. You've got a problem child on your hands, John."

As Sinatra later recalled: "By the time I was actually standing behind the three-sided baffle—to protect the sounds from my mic from the other sounds of the orchestra—I was a wreck, a total wreck. Cubby was sitting in that booth, and I've known him since I was born. John finally noticed my nerves. I think I tried to squeak out two or three takes; I sounded like Minnie Mouse."

One reporter estimated that "she must have sung the song about 30 times" as the evening wore on; "sometimes she broke off halfway through." Photographs of the session depict a worried or unhappy 26-year-old; one even

(SCORE HIGHLIGHTS, CONT.)

in the 1960s Bonds, and Barry's "Capsule in Space" (as it was labeled on the soundtrack album) was a major factor.

Nancy Sinatra's vocal of the title song (6 minutes into the picture) plays out against Maurice Binder's images of volcanic eruptions, portraits and silhouettes of Asian beauties. Barry refined the sound of the orchestra over a series of nine takes, with the electric guitar scaled back from a more prominent pop sound at first to a fun, almost synthesizer-like color for the final version; he added marimba on take six.

Bond's funeral, burial at sea and recovery (9 minutes in) is accompanied by variations on the Bond theme and gentle flutes, while his arrival in Tokyo (15 minutes) marks the first use of "You Only Live Twice" as scene-setting underscore. The Bond theme resurfaces as 007 impersonates Henderson's assassin (22 minutes), but the fight that ensues at Osato's office building is unscored.

Aki (Akiko Wakabayashi) rescues Bond, and although Barry wrote music for their fast-car escape and her running off into the dark (part of the "Aki, Tiger and Osato" track on the expanded 2003 album), little of it was used; similarly, Barry introduced a secondary, Japanese motif for the scene in which Bond meets Tanaka (30 minutes in), but it wasn't used in the final cut. (Called "Tanaka's World" on the LP, it's a gentle, quizzical piece relying mostly on flutes and strings and is reminiscent of some of Barry's wistful music for The Whisperers, written just a few months earlier.)

The Japanese love theme is first heard as background for Tanaka introducing Bond to the pleasures of the bathing ritual (33 minutes). Aki's second

shows her seated on Broccoli's lap as he appears to be reassuring her. Despite her belief that Barry really wanted "the unpolished singing style that I had . . . it was one of the scariest times of my whole life." But, she added, "it's the most beautiful of the Bond songs, and it makes the most sense away from the movie."

"That was painful," engineer John Richards recalled. Richards, who had been a tape operator and assistant engineer at CTS starting in 1962, began recording the Bond scores with *You Only Live Twice*, as Eric Tomlinson (who had recorded *From Russia with Love*, *Goldfinger* and *Thunderball*) had left CTS for Anvil in Denham in 1966. "She was one that we had to sit and work with long after the orchestra had gone. She just didn't have the voice. It was evident from take one. I remember John pulling the talk-back key at the end of every take—'it's coming, it's coming, just do one more,' over and over again."

Luckily, among all those takes, many of them incomplete, Barry had a whole song. "The final thing was, I think, bits from like 25 different takes," Barry recalled. "That's how we wound up finishing the actual record. 'I love that bit. Can we take that bit from there?' It's a common practice in the record world." Richards remembered a three-track mix of the orchestra and an isolated vocal track, and it was the latter that was cut and reassembled into a seamless audio mix.

Sinatra's American producer Lee Hazlewood produced a different, Billy Strange–arranged version that became the U.S. single. Less vocally demanding, with double-tracking on her voice, backup singers and rock guitar, it was the one that American radio listeners heard, peaking at number 44 the week of July 29, 1967. It was even more popular in the U.K., charting on July 5 and reaching number 11.

(SCORE HIGHLIGHTS, CONT.)

rescue of 007 comes as he leaves Osato's office, and a car chase ensues; this sequence (41 minutes in, called "A Drop in the Ocean" on the LP) features a staccato-brass action motif that transitions unexpectedly into waltz time as the mystified gunmen find themselves airborne over Tokyo and literally dumped into the Pacific.

"Fight at Kobe Dock" (45 minutes) is one of the score's highlights, as it features a surprisingly bold statement of the "You Only Live Twice" theme, as Aki runs off and 007 eludes his pursuers during a memorable aerial shot of the fight sequence; the rhythm combination of harpsichord, tambourine and electric bass is reminiscent of Barry's theme for the BBC Mafia drama *Vendetta*, which debuted just a few months before he wrote *You Only Live Twice*. Helga (Karin Dor) interrogates, then romances, him to

the title tune (47 minutes), which offers the score's first sexy muted-trumpet solo.

Barry lightens the mood further when Q arrives with Little Nellie, the autogyro—a one-man miniature helicopter—whose assembly (52 minutes in) merits a fresh arrangement of Barry's "007" theme, which gets a more elegant, and then urgent, treatment as he surveys the countryside. The attack by four full-sized helicopters (56 minutes) is scored with Barry's original 1962 recording of the "James Bond Theme," a creative music-editing choice by Peter Hunt that irritated the composer.

"Peter Hunt loved that 'James Bond Theme,'" Barry said in 1978. "If we had discussed it at the time, I could have used [the Bond theme] there, but it would most certainly have been orchestrated and treated in a totally different and more appropriate

This time, Barry didn't visit the locations during filming (which began in July 1966). His ideas about Japanese music—or at least what would sound Japanese to Western ears in the context of an action-adventure story—would be the product of his own imagination. "That was more melodic and more subtle," Barry conceded years later. "I tried to intertwine the whole Japanese thing, the elegance, the Oriental feel, into the story." He did employ two of his favorite soloists for key scenes involving Bond's romantic adventures: John Leach, who had played the Hungarian cimbalom on Barry's *The Ipcress File*, played koto, the 13-stringed national instrument of Japan; and Hugo D'Alton, perhaps England's greatest mandolin player.

The other unique musical aspect of *You Only Live Twice* was the necessity to aurally depict the beauty and terror of space. Barry described it as being similar to writing music for the underwater scenes in *Thunderball*: "a similar phenomenon of that floating feeling, to create an otherworldliness. Except when the action started in space; then it became more war-like, and we brought in the big guns [orchestrally speaking]."

The music for *You Only Live Twice* was recorded over six days between April 10 and May 2, 1967. By comparison with the *Thunderball* chaos of last-minute changes and legal challenges, this was much easier going; plus, the film was shorter and required much less music, about 65 minutes in all.

Apart from the song, which had to be finalized early in order to become a key element in the underscore, Barry spent all of March and part of April writing the music. He was too busy to travel to Hollywood for the Academy Awards, even though he had just been nominated for the first time—twice, in fact, for Best Song and Best Original Score for *Born Free*. The competition was fierce, including Burt Bacharach's "Alfie" in the song category and the massive symphonic scores for *Hawaii* and *The Sand Pebbles*, by American composers Elmer Bernstein and Jerry Goldsmith, in the score field.

manner. There's no intrigue, dramatically. [As used in the film] it had that 'record feel,' it doesn't draw you into the picture."

Barry reprises "Capsule in Space" for SPECTRE's identical attack on a Soviet spacecraft (59 minutes). The dark martial material for the cosmonauts being removed from the ship and incarcerated (1 hour, 5 minutes) wound up on the album as the first minute and a half of the track titled "James Bond—Astronaut?"

The single longest cue in the score (more than 4 minutes), and certainly one of its high points, is the music for Bond's "becoming Japanese," taking Aki to bed and her accidental poisoning by one of Osato's men (1 hour, 12 minutes). It begins simply, with mandolin (emulating koto), harp and triangle reprising the Japanese love theme, then broadens

to strings and oboe; it turns melancholy, foreshadowing Aki's death and finally reflecting 007's genuine sorrow over the girl (on the album, "The Death of Aki"). The Japanese love theme returns, in a similar orchestration, as Bond sees Kissy (Mie Hama) for the first time (1 hour, 17 minutes) and they are married (on the LP, "The Wedding"); they pose as humble fishermen to reach the island where SPECTRE's base is located.

Barry revisits his title theme (1 hour, 24 minutes) for scenes of the island at daybreak; there is a brief sense of danger, as Bond smells gas and they jump into the water; the tune returns as they climb the side of the volcano ("Mountains and Sunsets" on the LP).

The film's final half-hour is filled with action, and more than half of it is scored. It begins (1 hour, 29

On top of all this, Barry's wife Jane Birkin gave birth to a daughter, Kate, on April 8. *You Only Live Twice* began recording on April 10 and the Oscar ceremony was that evening. During the early morning hours of April 11—which would be the second day of recording *Twice*—actor Michael Crawford called Barry to tell him he had just won two Academy Awards. (Crawford had starred in *The Knack*, which sported a jazzy Barry score; he would later star in Barry's West End musical *Billy*.) Lyricist Don Black did attend, however, and accepted the song award for both of them. *Born Free* producer Paul Radin accepted the score award on Barry's behalf.

You Only Live Twice was the first 007 movie to open in the summer (June 13 in the United States), and this time UA and its music companies were fully prepared to blitz the record-buying public. Sinatra's vocal performance was formally announced on May 5; 10 days later, UA executives announced that the soundtrack album would be in stores May 22. Still another press release touted the "all-out campaign on behalf of the music," listing numerous recordings of the song and instrumental versions of themes from the score. All of them capitalized on Barry's new status as an "Academy Award winner."

Trade reviewers, by now educated in the Barry-Bond sound, took greater notice: "John Barry's score is more subdued and romantic than his past 007 music . . . title song could catch on," opined *Variety*; "John Barry's score is tops," noted the *Hollywood Reporter*, which also referred to "the sensuous title song . . . performed well by Nancy Sinatra."

The movie's box-office success, and Barry's own fame as a (now Oscar-winning) film composer who consistently delivered melodic and powerful scores, wound up selling hundreds of thousands of albums, at least in America. The soundtrack charted on July 15, peaked at number 27 on September 16 and remained on the charts through the first week of 1968. The album

(SCORE HIGHLIGHTS, CONT.)

minutes) with heavy music as Bond discovers the base and sneaks inside; "Capsule in Space" variations, with plenty of alto flute and low-brass suspense, follow as Bond frees the captive astronauts and cosmonauts (1 hour, 33 minutes). And it returns, in the original arrangement, as Bond impersonates one of the SPECTRE astronauts and nearly gets aboard (1 hour, 35 minutes; "James Bond—Astronaut?" on the LP).

Barry builds suspense with the dramatic last half of his powerful space march as Bond meets Blofeld for the first time and the SPECTRE craft nears launch (1 hour, 38 minutes; "Countdown to Blofeld" on the LP). Bond kills a control-room technician, accompanied briefly by action music, but most of the five-minute, stunt- and explosion-filled battle between Tanaka's ninjas and Blofeld's personnel is unscored. Music returns for Bond's desperate attempt to reach the control room and explode the SPECTRE ship (1 hour, 49 minutes, "Bond Averts World War III" on the LP): this high-energy piece is mostly based on the space march, punctuated with staccato bursts of percussion and high flutes.

The title tune provides a softer finale after the volcano explodes (1 hour, 53 minutes)—a solo trumpet signals the arrival of a British submarine, just in time—and the Sinatra vocal is reprised over the end titles. Barry also provided an instrumental conclusion ("Twice Is the Only Way to Live" on some international pressings of the LP) that went unheard in the movie.

failed to chart in Barry's own country, though, as if to prove a point he made in an April profile in which he complained that the British still associated him with the John Barry Seven rather than his more recent orchestral achievements. "Natives cannot shake their pop-oriented conception of him," the piece said. "[The] film industry, however, is savvy to his commercial quill and companies are eager to hitch onto the Barrywagon."

"... we have all the time in the world ..."

On Her Majesty's Secret Service

When Sean Connery decided that he was through playing James Bond, and Broccoli and Saltzman cast an unknown as 007, the pressure was not only on Australian model George Lazenby to prove he was Ian Fleming's indomitable secret agent; it was also on John Barry to musically reinforce the idea in the minds of moviegoers.

The sixth Bond film was to be *On Her Majesty's Secret Service*, the long-postponed filming of Ian Fleming's 10th Bond novel, published in 1963. (It had once been intended to come after *Goldfinger*, then after *Thunderball*. With the completion of *You Only Live Twice*, it was finally on the schedule.) In the story, Bond meets and falls in love with Tracy (Diana Rigg), the beautiful daughter of a Corsican crime lord (Gabriele Ferzetti). Bond finds Blofeld (Telly Savalas) in Switzerland and halts his biological warfare plot, but Blofeld manages to take his revenge: moments after Bond and Tracy marry, she is murdered.

Peter Hunt, who earned his stripes editing the previous five Bonds, was promoted to the director's chair. He urged regular Bond screenwriter Richard Maibaum to forego the overabundance of gadgets from the last two films and hew closely to the novel. The result was the last of the Bond films that would do so, the longest of all the Bond films to date, one that took longer to recoup its investment than any other, and paradoxically one of the most respected and admired Bond films ever made.

Between finishing *You Only Live Twice* in mid-1967 and starting *On Her Majesty's Secret Service* in August 1969, Barry's fame and respect within the show-business community had grown even greater. He had written a single-movement guitar concerto for Bryan Forbes's heist film *Deadfall*; scored Richard Lester's ultra-hip Julie Christie drama *Petulia*; received the advertising world's highest honor, the Clio, for his two-minute Eastern Airlines commercial "Second Summer"; and won a third Academy Award for his stunning choral-and-orchestral score for the 12th-century English historical drama *The Lion in Winter*. He also began work on a musical of *The Great Gatsby* that bandleader Artie Shaw hoped to mount on Broadway, launched a company to begin producing films of his own, and served as "musical supervisor" as well as composer on the acclaimed John Schlesinger film *Midnight Cowboy*.

But his loyalty to the Bond producers, who had done so much to launch him on this path, was unwavering. And, in return, he was given a completely free hand with the music of *On Her Majesty's Secret Service*, which would lead to radical choices about the sound of the score, the nature of the song and the surprising vocalist he would choose to sing it.

Tracy and Bond (Diana Rigg, George Lazenby) at their wedding in *On Her Majesty's Secret Service*

"Even if things didn't work out with Lazenby," director Hunt said many years later, "I knew that come what may, John Barry would deliver the goods. 'Cause otherwise, if he didn't, I told him I would kill him!" Barry agreed that the score was even more critical than usual because of the new leading man— "to make the audience forget that they don't have Sean," as he later said. "What I did was to overemphasize everything that I'd done in the first few movies, just go over the top to try and make the soundtrack strong. To do Bondian beyond Bondian."

While the film was in production in early 1969, Lazenby suggested to the producers that they consider the hot new jazz-rock group Blood, Sweat & Tears for a song. Apparently no one took him seriously.

Also not taken seriously was the idea of a song called "On Her Majesty's Secret Service." "A title song should have the title of the film," said Hunt, "that's the benefit of it. But you can hardly have an 'On Her Majesty's Secret Service' song; it would have to be some sort of march, and I wasn't really keen on that idea." Barry agreed that it wouldn't work "unless we're going to do it like Gilbert and Sullivan."

Lyricist Leslie Bricusse claimed, years later, to have written "a good lyric called 'On Her Majesty's Secret Service,' and it really was the title of the song, it wasn't just a line like 'the spy who loved me' [in "Nobody Does It Better"]; I wrote a song based on the idea of Her Majesty's Secret Service. One of the things that appeals to me in bizarre titles is making them work." (In later years, Barry professed to be unaware of it.)

So Barry got the go-ahead to write an instrumental piece over the main-title sequence for the first time in a Bond film since *Dr. No*, and to write a song, based on a different melody, for use elsewhere in the picture. For his main theme, Barry followed Hunt's notion of a march (this was, after all, for "Her Majesty's Secret Service") but the most contemporary march imaginable, with a Moog synthesizer, electric bass and tambourine providing a fast-moving rhythmic figure beneath a heroic, fanfare-like melody for brass (which, on its second verse, added plunger mutes for that classic Bond sound).

Barry's choice of Moog synthesizer was an especially daring one. The modular synthesizer—developed by New York electronic-music pioneer Robert A. Moog—used oscillators, keyboards, filters and modulators to generate unusual musical sounds. In 1967 and 1968 it became popular with rock musicians (including George Harrison and the Doors), but the enormous commercial success of the album *Switched-on Bach* made it famous. *Switched-on Bach*, a collection of classical pieces performed entirely on the Moog, became the biggest-selling classical record of its time and even reached, in April 1969, the top 10 of *Billboard*'s pop charts.

Barry had experimented with the Moog on two earlier films, both noteworthy: for a deep bass sound in the main title of *The Lion in Winter* (1968) and as musical spice for a light moment in *Midnight Cowboy* (early 1969). In *On Her Majesty's Secret Service*, however, Moog sounds are incorporated throughout the score. The film's release in December 1969 marked the first time any major studio film had featured the synthesizer so prominently, and at the same time fully integrated within the traditional orchestra. It wasn't just trendy; it was a groundbreaking application of electronic music that would presage decades of synthesizer use by film composers everywhere.

Recording engineer and record producer Phil Ramone had collaborated with Barry on *Midnight Cowboy* earlier in the year; together they assembled the landmark pop-rock soundtrack, and Ramone engineered the recording of Barry's score (which would win a Grammy for Best Instrumental Theme) in New York.

"John gave me my first credit as a producer," Ramone noted, referring to the film scores he produced for Barry, including *On Her Majesty's Secret Service*, *Monte Walsh*, *Walkabout* and *The Last Valley*. In the case of the Bond film, Barry alerted Ramone that he intended to use the Moog extensively—and that he wanted the synths to play "live" with the orchestra, not overdub later, which is how most Moog sounds were handled at the time.

Ramone, sensing that the synthesizer could potentially transform the music business, had already trained with Robert Moog and others who understood the technical complexities of the machine. But synthesizers in that era were not polyphonic—they could play only one tone at a time. When Barry told him of his ideas for the Bond film, Ramone recalled: "I called Robert and said, 'This is what I've got to do. How do I do it all live?' Most people overdubbed everything. Robert gave me the clue: he said to get three keyboards and three sets of oscillators, which is how you make the sounds. It was hard to keep them in tune. You needed three keyboards so that you could actually have the full range of an 88-note keyboard."

Barry brought Ramone to London and gave him three weeks—before recording was to begin—to experiment with the Moog, discover its sonic possibilities, and figure out how to program them so that they could be played live with the orchestra. "I literally programmed all of the things that I felt would work, from the score as he was writing. I wrote down everything that I was trying, every sound that was different or unusual. John was as curious as I was."

When recording began in late September 1969 at CTS, John Richards again served as mixing engineer but Ramone was in charge of the synthesizers. "We had double or triple keyboards, doubling each set of sounds," Ramone said. "I could switch keyboards while a cue was going on, and inside the cue might be two different sounds. It was crude, but you could switch. The keyboard players played right along with the orchestra."

Editor John Glen recalled being at the sessions: "John [Barry] was always keen to introduce new sounds in the music. He came up with this Moog synthesizer, which had this resonant bass that made the whole room tremble. It was quite unique at the time, very much a new toy. Later on it became generally used, but old John was the pioneer."

Added Ramone: "Bond films always sounded incredible in the theater. I think that was due to John's beautiful spread in writing, plus the engineers he

Trade advertisement promoting the *On Her Majesty's Secret Service* song and score for Oscar consideration in December 1969

had over there. He loved the orchestra to be large and slow underneath a high-speed chase. And, so typical of John, those soaring melodies."

There was plenty of action requiring music, particularly during the ski chase sequences filmed in Switzerland, and the main theme would serve those scenes well. But the love story, too, would require a theme, and that, Barry decided, would be the place for a song. It would be based on a key line that is spoken by Bond three times in Fleming's book—in fact, it's the last line he says in the aftermath of his wife's murder: "We've got all the time in the world." In Maibaum's film script, it's altered slightly to read, "We have all the time in the world." It would become one of the most memorable and important songs in the history of the Bond franchise.

Hal David was in London in August and September 1969 as the early-October West End opening of his stage musical *Promises, Promises* neared. Barry and David met and, David later recalled, "became great friends immediately. We did a lot of pub-hopping, which was our wont in those days. I think I knew every pub on a main street or a mews in the middle of London."

David signed on to write the words for two songs in *On Her Majesty's Secret Service*: "We Have All the Time in the World" and a Christmas song that would be needed as source music. As usual with the composer, in the case of the love song, the tune came first. The melody was classic Barry: something wistful, something hopeful, a touch of melancholy—just right for two damaged souls finding each other, seeking a promising future but aware of the wreckage of their past lives. It was a love song for adults who are past starry-eyed notions of romance (written by a composer who was about to embark on his third marriage).

David took his initial cue from Fleming and expanded from there: "time enough for life to unfold / all the precious things love has in store . . . every step of the way will find us / with the cares of the world far behind us. . . ."

On Her Majesty's Secret Service

007
JAMES BOND

Music composed and conducted by John Barry
Lyrics by Hal David

"We have all the time in the world" sung by Louis Armstrong
"Do you know how Christmas trees are grown?" sung by Nina

SCORE HIGHLIGHTS

From the start of the gun-barrel sequence of *On Her Majesty's Secret Service*, moviegoers were reminded that this was James Bond, and also told at the same time—via the sounds of the Moog synthesizer replacing the old guitar on the "James Bond Theme"—that this was very much *today's* James Bond. This is echoed almost immediately (just over a minute into the film) by the use of the Bond theme, with Moog, as Tracy speeds past Bond in a hurry to get to the beach. This music, along with the action music to follow, is called "This Never Happened to the Other Feller" on the LP.

Underscoring Maurice Binder's main-title visuals (almost 7 minutes into the film) is Barry's title theme. Befitting Fleming's phrase "On Her Majesty's Secret Service," he wrote a march—but a very modern one,

John Barry and vocalist Louis Armstrong at the October 1969 recording session for "We Have All the Time in the World"

with Moog chords, electric bass and tambourine beating out a contemporary rhythm while the brass offers a fanfare that will serve as the key music for the later action sequences. Binder's titles are clever, starting with an hourglass (representing the passage of time) that becomes a coat of arms (relating to the plot device of Bond impersonating a genealogist) containing the Union Jack, a crown and the inevitable silhouettes of naked girls. The clock arms swing around and the "sands" of the hourglass depict scenes from the five previous Bond films. Surprisingly, however, this theme will not reappear for almost an hour and a half.

"We Have All the Time in the World" is really the main theme of the film. Most often played for Tracy, sometimes for Bond, it is first heard (17 minutes in) on flute, then strings, as Tracy appears in Bond's hotel room; then (20 minutes in) in a lighthearted martial form as he's abducted by the men of Tracy's father Draco, head of one of Europe's biggest criminal syndicates. "We Have . . ." returns in a beautiful, all-strings arrangement (23 minutes) as Draco explains Tracy's troubled past and then, in even slower form (28 minutes) as Bond resigns from the service. (Then, as he packs up his desk, themes from *Dr. No*, *From Russia with Love* and *Thunderball* briefly play; as the janitor outside Draco's office was whistling the *Goldfinger* theme a few minutes earlier, that's music from four of the five previous Bonds heard in the sixth.)

Louis Armstrong sings "We Have All the Time in the World" as Bond and Tracy embrace (35 minutes in) and a two-minute montage of their love affair (riding horseback, walking through statued gardens,

And in a stroke of genius, Barry thought of Louis Armstrong as a possible vocalist. He had always been fond of "September Song," the Kurt Weill–Maxwell Anderson tune from *Knickerbocker Holiday* that actor Walter Huston had turned into an unlikely hit in 1939, "where, as an older character, he sang about his life in a kind of reflective vein. I always thought that very poignant. I started thinking, who had the kind of personality that could carry that off? What about Louis Armstrong?" The New Orleans jazzman had performed at Barry's father's theater in York back in the mid-1930s, and Barry still had photographs of the occasion. Both Broccoli and Hunt agreed, despite the fact that the choice was purely an artistic one and decidedly uncommercial.

Barry recorded more than 80 minutes of music over five days, spread out from September 23 to October 18, 1969, at CTS in Bayswater. Ultimately about 75 minutes would be used in the final version of the film.

In the meantime, Louis Armstrong agreed to record "We Have All the Time in the World." Armstrong, then 69, had been in ill health for much of the previous year, in and out of hospitals and unable to perform. But he liked the demo he had heard and, on Thursday, October 23, appeared at New York's legendary A&R Studios at 799 Seventh Avenue, where Barry would conduct an American orchestra for the first time in music for a James Bond film.

"Louis was a guy that I idolized," Ramone said. "He was not in great shape by then. He certainly knew the song, which I wasn't expecting; I expected him to ad lib a lot. But that gentility was what I noticed immediately—the charm, the warmth, and the 'hello, guys,' talking to the band."

Barry conducted, Ramone engineered and Hal David was present. "He was so frail," David recalled, "and I thought, my goodness, can he do it? But I remember the thrill I felt the moment that first line came out. It was so wonderful. He was so human, and so humble. He did two or three takes and that

shopping, running on the beach) plays out. Soon Bond is using high-tech methods to crack a safe in Switzerland (38 minutes), and Barry scores the next four minutes with a slowly building, Moog-accented, basses-and-timpani piece ("Gumbold's Safe" on the expanded 2003 CD) that, when strings and brass are finally added, ratchets up the tension to an almost unbearable degree.

Barry plays the gorgeous scenery for the first time (50 minutes in) as Bond travels via helicopter across the Alps ("Journey to Blofeld's Hideaway," truncated on the LP but complete on the expanded CD). And he adds a new voice when Bond encounters the bevy of women (57 minutes) at the "allergy research" clinic run by Blofeld: sexy saxophone and flutes. The lighter, even comic, tone returns for each of Bond's romantic adventures, almost like a siren call.

His tryst with Ruby (1 hour, 8 minutes) is accompanied by a new theme, a lyrical interlude for flute and strings that Barry later turned into an instrumental theme called "Who Will Buy My Yesterdays" and included on his 1970 Columbia album, *Ready When You Are, J.B.*, interestingly without any mention of its origins in the Bond film. The Bond-Ruby romance is interrupted by Blofeld's hypnosis treatment (1 hour, 10 minutes), which is dominated by the pings and bongs of the Moog synthesizer, heard again (1 hour, 26 minutes) as the girls undergo their final hypnosis.

Barry's title tune returns for the first time since the opening credits (1 hour, 33 minutes) for Bond's nighttime escape from Piz Gloria, skiing down the mountain and immediately pursued by Blofeld's minions. "On Her Majesty's Secret Service" becomes

was it. He asked us if it was all right!" Said the composer, reminiscing in 1978: "Louis Armstrong was the sweetest man alive, but having been laid up for over a year, he had no energy left. And still he summoned the energy to do our song. At the end of the recording session, he came up to me and said, 'Thank you for this job.' He was such a marvelous man. He died soon after that."

In fact, he died about a year and half later, in July 1971. Armstrong's biographer later wrote that "the extra rawness and fragility of his health made him connect even deeper with the song's emotions. Armstrong was truly in his September years, just thankful to be alive, and the joy and love in his voice is contagious throughout the performance." Armstrong did not play his trumpet—that's a studio musician's flugelhorn on the track—although he did play on "Pretty Little Missy," the B-side tune that was recorded that same afternoon at A&R.

David's other contribution to *On Her Majesty's Secret Service* was the song "Do You Know How Christmas Trees Are Grown?" Much of the film takes place in snowy Switzerland in December, so a Christmas song seemed natural for "source music" that would be heard emanating from the speakers at the train station and elsewhere in the town below Blofeld's Piz Gloria hideaway.

According to David, Barry departed from his usual practice and set the lyricist's holiday poem about Christmas trees, Santa's travels and Christmas cards to music. "I think it's the only time, with John, that I wrote the lyric first," he said. Barry imagined it sung by a favorite past collaborator, Danish singer-actress Nina van Pallandt, to a group of children who would sing their responses.

Barry had served as her musical director in the early 1960s, when, as half of the singing duo Nina and Frederik, she performed in concert and cabaret venues in London. He arranged and conducted their performance of four tra-

(SCORE HIGHLIGHTS, CONT.)

the action theme for the rest of the film, its swirling strings and brushes on drums suggesting some of the swooshing sounds of skis on snow.

The holiday song "Do You Know How Christmas Trees Are Grown?" is heard three times in the film. The first, the vocal with Nina and children's chorus, comes over loudspeakers at the train station (47 minutes) when Bond arrives in Mürren; much later, instrumentally, it is on synth (1 hour, 23 minutes) as Blofeld's girls are opening their Christmas gifts. And finally (1 hour, 40 minutes) there is a reprise of the vocal by Nina and the children's choir as Bond is trying to escape Bunt at the skating rink in the village and runs into Tracy.

"OHMSS" returns for the nighttime car chase (1 hour, 44 minutes) as Tracy races away from Bunt and winds up on an icy stock-car track. Sound ef-

fects dominate for the next few minutes, and when Bond and Tracy find a barn for an overnight stay (1 hour, 49 minutes) he proposes, to an exquisite string arrangement of "We Have All the Time. . . ."

Bond and Tracy are chased down another mountain by Blofeld and his men on skis (1 hour, 53 minutes) to a version of "OHMSS" (titled "Ski Chase" on the original LP) notable for the slight echo in the brass; the flute at the end coincides with the avalanche that swamps hero and heroine.

As Bond and Draco fly phony Red Cross helicopters to Piz Gloria (2 hours in), Blofeld attempts to charm Tracy to a light-textured version of "OHMSS" (called "Over and Out" on the LP) spiced with synthesizer. Their attack on Blofeld's sanctuary is, at first, unscored, but director Hunt once more, to Barry's chagrin, insisted on applying the original

ditional holiday songs, including "White Christmas" and "Silent Night," for a 1962 Columbia recording. (Van Pallandt later co-starred in three Robert Altman films, including *The Long Goodbye*, and gained notoriety for her role in author Clifford Irving's infamous attempt to create a fake Howard Hughes autobiography in the early 1970s.)

Van Pallandt sang another Barry-David song, "The More Things Change," as the flip side of a "Do You Know How Christmas Trees Are Grown?" single that CBS Records issued in the U.K. in late 1969. And she performed "Christmas Trees" on the BBC's family-entertainment show *Morecambe & Wise*, which aired on Christmas Day.

On Her Majesty's Secret Service premiered in London on December 18, 1969, and, although the critics generally savaged Lazenby's first (and last) appearance as 007, the savvy ones also mentioned Barry's alternately touching and powerful score: "John Barry's music is always intelligent," wrote the *Los Angeles Times*, "and this time has a chance to be extensively lyrical as well as adventurous." England's *Films & Filming* began its review by talking about the music: "John Barry's strident brass section heralds the fact that Bond is back. . . ." And *Variety* even cited Barry's new synthesizer sounds, albeit in a crude way: "In one suspense sequence where Bond is opening a safe with a special computer, a bleeper beat counterpointing the full orchestration creates a palpably electric tension."

Broccoli and United Artists were sufficiently proud of the music of *On Her Majesty's Secret Service* that, for the first time in the Bond series, they promoted the song and score for Academy Award consideration, taking out specially designed full-page advertisements in the trade papers with the film's music credits superimposed over the movie poster art. Unfortunately, music-branch members of the Academy of Motion Picture Arts and Sciences did not take the Bond films seriously; *Goldfinger* and *Thunderball* won Oscars for

1962 recording of the "James Bond Theme" (2 hours, 6 minutes) under much of it. A fast-paced "OHMSS" returns (2 hours, 9 minutes) as Bond pursues Blofeld, the entire installation is about to explode ("Battle at Piz Gloria" on the LP) and they escape via bobsled.

Most of the bobsled chase is unscored—again, sound effects rule—until Blofeld drops a hand grenade and tries to retrieve it (2 hours, 12 minutes) to action music derived from "This Never Happened to the Other Feller" more than 2 hours earlier, with the addition of a strange new Moog sound. As Blofeld seems to meet his end hanging from a tree, Bond is met by a Saint Bernard to the lighthearted "We Have All . . ." march from earlier in the film.

Bond and Tracy marry to the sound of pealing church bells and, as Bond tells her moments later,

"We have all the time in the world." Blofeld and Bunt speed by, riddling the car with bullets. Bond holds the murdered Tracy in his arms (2 hours, 18 minutes) as a lone flute and strings quietly play "We Have All the Time in the World" and the camera lingers on the bullet hole in the windshield. Barry brings back the fast-paced, Moog-driven "James Bond Theme" for the end credits.

sound effects and visual effects, respectively, but Barry's "million-dollar Mickey Mouse music" was generally dismissed as not award-worthy.

United Artists Records issued a soundtrack album, as usual, along with a single featuring the Armstrong vocal in both the United States and U.K. (in Britain, it was a gatefold album featuring a giant painting of Lazenby with skis, a gun and a drink). The U.S. album charted in early February 1970 but only managed to reach number 103 on the pop charts; the Armstrong single, sadly, didn't chart at all and, despite his appreciation of the tune, Armstrong never sang the song in public. It seemed for a long time to be the least recognized Bond song ever.

That is, until 1994, when advertising agency Ogilvy & Mather licensed "We Have All the Time in the World" for use in, of all things, a television commercial for Guinness beer. The spot, which played the Armstrong vocal under a visual tour de force of sailing-through-the-universe imagery, led to a re-release of the single and a stunning number 3 spot on the U.K. singles chart. As Barry later observed: "It's ironic in a way that somebody's selling ale and you get a hit out of it. But that's the way of the world." The final image, as Armstrong sings the final words "only love," is of a pint of Guinness and the words "pure genius"—a description of the song and its performer as much as the product.

8

"... touch it, stroke it and undress it ..."

Diamonds Are Forever

Once again, Broccoli and Saltzman went looking for a new James Bond, and so once again a sense of musical continuity was critical. John Barry's services would be required as they prepared *Diamonds Are Forever*.

On the casting side, there was briefly a notion that maybe the new Bond should be American, so actor John Gavin was temporarily signed as 007—until Sean Connery agreed to return in exchange for a $1.25 million donation toward his new charity, the Scottish International Education Trust. So Connery was back, but the film itself would be mostly American, much of it shot on location in the desert gambling mecca of Las Vegas, Nevada.

Although Barry hadn't visited the Japanese or Swiss locations for *You Only Live Twice* or *On Her Majesty's Secret Service*, he did visit Las Vegas during the April–May 1971 shoot. "Back then, it was a hard-nosed gambling town," he reminisced. "It was Frank Sinatra and Dean Martin, this adult entertainment thing. You never saw a child in Las Vegas," he added with a laugh. "They gambled all the way through the night. Five o'clock in the morning, they were down there. They never closed."

Barry's Vegas experience paid dividends when he began thinking about music for *Diamonds*, especially the source music that would be required for the hotels and casinos. It would be his most "American" score since *The Chase* five years earlier. "It had that particularly American thing about it that, hopefully, is in the score," he said. "There's a certain vibration that rubs off

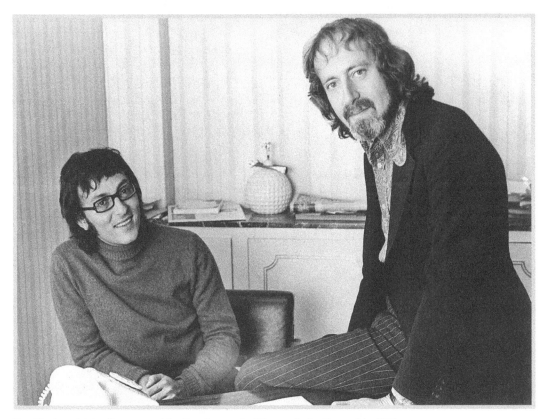

Don Black and John Barry around the time they wrote "Diamonds Are Forever" in 1971

from all that activity. You just get the smell and the feel of it, and it comes out in the notes."

Barry thrived on change, especially when it came to film assignments. In the two years since he had finished *On Her Majesty's Secret Service*, he had composed and conducted four major orchestral scores, three of them featuring choir (*The Last Valley*; *Walkabout*; *Mary, Queen of Scots*) and written a musical with famed lyricist Alan Jay Lerner (*Lolita, My Love* which, too daring for American theater audiences, closed during its pre-Broadway run).

Diamonds uses only a bit of the original Fleming story. In the film, Bond investigates a plot to smuggle South African diamonds into Holland and then into the United States, specifically Las Vegas. There it turns out Blofeld (Charles Gray) has usurped the vast business empire of reclusive billionaire Willard Whyte (Jimmy Dean) and employed his resources to launch a formidable space-based laser weapon into orbit. Bond recruits smuggler Tiffany Case (Jill St. John) but finds himself repeatedly menaced by gay killers Wint and Kidd (Bruce Glover, Putter Smith).

The casting was particularly interesting from a musical standpoint, considering that Dean was a major country star of the 1960s ("Big Bad John") and Smith was one of the West Coast's top jazz bassists. Neither got to apply their musical skills, however. For Barry, the first order of business was the title song. Of the seven prior Bond songs, five dealt with love ("Under the Mango

Tree," "From Russia with Love," "You Only Live Twice," "The Look of Love" and "We Have All the Time in the World"), one was about the villain ("Gold-finger") and one ("Thunderball") was either about Bond or another villain, depending on your point of view.

Barry conceived the song as opening with the title phrase; but perhaps of equal importance, its underpinning would be a repeating series of eight notes, suggesting the eight sides of the gem. For lyrics, he turned to his old "Thun-derball" and "Born Free" collaborator, Don Black.

Eighteen years earlier, Marilyn Monroe had sung "Diamonds Are a Girl's Best Friend" to iconic status in *Gentlemen Prefer Blondes*. Black's words would make a Bond song equally famous. "Diamonds Are Forever" is more about fleeting relationships and less about the permanence of those shiny jewels that are often the remnant of a love affair—although one phrase in particular would result in the song becoming slightly infamous, and possibly costing it an Academy Award nomination.

It's in the second verse: "hold one up and then caress it / touch it, stroke it and undress it." "Seediness was what we wanted," Black would later ex-plain. "Sleaziness, theatrical vulgarity. It had to be over the top." Or, as Barry himself would reveal in numerous interviews 20 years later, that particular verse was more about male genitalia than about precious stones: "Write it as though she's thinking about a penis," had been Barry's advice to Black.

It was all a great lark—except to Harry Saltzman. "I remember a very dodgy meeting at John's apartment," Black later recalled, where Barry, Black and a pianist were to demonstrate their "Diamonds" song for Broccoli and Saltzman. "I remember Harry getting red in the face. 'I don't like it, it's just not right. The lyric, it's dirty,'" Black remembered Saltzman saying. Black attempted to reason with him: "It's not dirty, it's provocative, it's Bond, it's sexy, sensual, inviting." But Barry—who, Black reminded, "has got a much

John Barry's *Diamonds Are Forever* score con-tained a broader range of musical material than any Bond film to date: from Vegas lounge music and a choral requiem for Bond, to a delicately sinister theme for effeminate killers and one of the greatest title songs yet.

Notably, after Barry's extensive use of the Moog synthesizer in *On Her Majesty's Secret Service*, the cutting-edge electronic instrument appears nowhere in his next Bond score. So as the gun-barrel logo appears at the start of the film—and again as 007 accosts the French bikinied beauty in his search for Blofeld—the Bond theme is again played by an am-plified guitar.

Maurice Binder's colorful titles feature the usual naked women (and, this time, cats) wearing the

shorter fuse than I have"—responded with a much sharper, "What the hell would you know about it?!"

Saltzman stormed out of the apartment, slamming the door. Then after a minute of silence, Broccoli spoke up: "Do you have any Jack Daniels?" "So we all hit the Jack Daniels," Barry recalled with a laugh. Broccoli approved the song.

Black later conceded that "there is a kind of striptease nakedness about it all" but pointed out that Barry's music was always inspirational. "The intros are wonderful," he added, singing that eight-note opening to "Diamonds." "You're in that world from the first bar of music, which is very, very clever. Deceptively brilliant, really."

As for choosing a performer, by 1971 all was forgiven with Shirley Bassey. It was nearly six years since the "Kiss Kiss Bang Bang" lawsuit, and she was invited back to sing "Diamonds Are Forever." Black was thrilled: "I write with Shirley Bassey in mind, that outrageous, marvelous, provocative style she has. Shirley Bassey is one of the great storytellers of a lyric."

Yet Barry was facing another schedule crunch. Legendary producer Hal B. Wallis had hired him to score the historical drama *Mary, Queen of Scots*, and the music had to be written in August for a September recording. So he got a head start on *Diamonds*: he scheduled his first recording session on July 31, including Bassey's vocal and parts of reels one, two and five which had already been edited.

As he had done before, Barry refined his arrangement in the studio during the recording of the title song. Early takes have a more mysterious opening, and an additional verse that was discarded halfway through the session. The missing verse: "Diamonds are forever / I can taste the satisfaction / flawless physical attraction / bitter cold, icy fresh, till they rest on the flesh they crave

sparkling gems while Shirley Bassey sings. The instrument that plays the indelible eight-note pattern beneath the melody was an electronic organ owned by CTS, the recording studio for all the early Bond films.

"John used just one facet of that organ," recalled engineer John Richards, who recorded *Diamonds*, "that tinkly bright sound that you couldn't get on anything else. It was a very unique sound of that particular instrument. It might have been a Yamaha, and it was their biggest showpiece that they made at the time, a multicolored, bells-and-whistles console." Barry would go on to apply the sound in his very next score, for *The Public Eye* (1972).

Barry uses a variation on the eight-note pattern to underline his secondary theme, for gay killers Wint and Kidd, who are first seen stealing diamonds in South Africa (10 minutes into the film). Its melody is a fun little motif for saxophone and flute. Heard again (13 minutes) for their transferal of the gems to an old lady and again when they kill her (15 minutes), it will return for all of their screen appearances.

Barry gets "composed, conducted and arranged" credit on *Diamonds*, and he arranged two source-music versions of his title song, one of which is prominently heard (17 minutes) when Bond visits his Amsterdam contact, Tiffany Case; another warm piece, called "Tiffany Case" on the LP, follows immediately as Bond tries to make time with her. Though Barry leaves most of Bond's fight in the elevator unscored, he does apply a five-note action theme (23 minutes) for the climax and murder.

for." Black later said this verse was discarded simply because the song was running long.

Much of *Diamonds Are Forever* takes place in the hotels and casinos of Las Vegas, requiring considerable "source music" appropriate to such venues. In fact, nearly a third of the film's 67 minutes of music is background source, and only two of those 12 pieces are adaptations of the title song. All the rest are one-of-a-kind background tunes: Casino jazz, music for Las Vegas attractions, hotel and airport Muzak, even mortuary music—and as a result the *Diamonds* score was in many ways the most musically diverse Bond film yet.

Barry's sharp ears and even sharper pencil caught the unique Vegas ambiance: the sleazy gambling jazz of "The Whyte House" and "Q's Trick," the cocktail-piano rendition of "Diamonds Are Forever," the lighter-than-air waltz of "Circus, Circus," for example. Being British wasn't a handicap in discerning and reproducing the music of America, as Barry had demonstrated on earlier occasions—the Southern twang of *The Chase*, the cool San Francisco sophistication of *Petulia*, the lonely harmonica of *Midnight Cowboy*.

In terms of the dramatic score, Barry quickly found that his title song would be perfectly functional for romantic scenes and a handful of mystery and transitional moments, but more themes would clearly be needed. The film's other main theme was written for assassins Wint and Kidd; he begins with another eight-note accompaniment, a slow and deliberate stroll topped by a slinky, even amusing tune played by flute and saxophone with a memorable falloff.

The sole piece of music mentioned in the script was something Barry didn't have to worry about: an audiocassette of "World's Greatest Marches" that Bond inserts into a control panel to try to destroy Blofeld's rogue satellite. The script suggested that "The Marine Hymn" be played, but it's actually

Among the score's highlights is the music for Slumber Inc., the Las Vegas funeral home, site of Bond's early encounters with American gangsters. After some nondescript chapel organ, the late Peter Franks is incinerated (29 minutes) to a brief choral piece. But when Bond is knocked unconscious, put into a coffin and nearly burned to death, Barry offers a melodramatic, orchestral-and-choral "Requiem for Bond" (32 minutes) that—like "Death of Fiona" in *Thunderball*—brilliantly serves as both source music and score.

For Bond's arrival in the United States, Barry supplies a series of jazz pieces appropriate to the various venues: a sax-driven one for Los Angeles International Airport (26 minutes); a string-drenched one for his Las Vegas hotel (34 minutes); a brassy big-band number for dancing girls in the casino (34 minutes, called "The Whyte House" on the expanded CD), reprised when Bond meets Plenty O'Toole (Lana Wood); a more sedate jazz number (36 minutes, called "Q's Trick" on the LP) that returns when Bond wins $50,000 at the craps tables; an elegant waltz for aerial acrobatics at "Circus, Circus" (44 minutes, on the LP); a Dixieland jazz number for another casino scene with Tiffany (45 minutes); and exotic drumming for the gorilla-girl attraction (48 minutes).

Plenty visits Bond's hotel room (39 minutes) to a sexy muted trumpet and strings, and then Tiffany arrives (41 minutes) to a rich string version of the "Diamonds" theme. The "Diamonds" theme recurs in many forms, not just romantic but in dramatic variations for traveling (54 minutes).

Bond's adventures in Whyte's Tectronics labs and the Nevada desert merited new music: staccato

"The British Grenadiers"; Blofeld plays a brief excerpt and remarks, "I do so hate martial music." The track was licensed from the Boosey & Hawkes music library.

All of the remaining source music and the entire dramatic score were recorded over five consecutive days during the last week of October 1971 at CTS. Stephen Pickard, then working as a sound editor at Pinewood, wrangled an invitation to sit in on the sessions. "The tone was very relaxed," he recalled. "John was businesslike, very confident, but also very pleasant. He sat down a lot while he was conducting. The musicians didn't need a lot of rehearsal; they were so professional, there was never any difficulty with anything."

Director Guy Hamilton returned to the Bond series for the first time since his triumph with *Goldfinger*, and even though he and Barry had enjoyed a good and profitable collaboration there, on *Diamonds* there would be a few bumps along the way. The new film's tone was much lighter than any previous Eon-produced Bond, and this led to a difference of opinion on how the film's "Moon Buggy Chase" should be handled musically.

In the film, Bond escapes the Blofeld-controlled Whyte Tectronics complex by sneaking onto a moonwalk-simulation set, stealing a prototype lunar transport vehicle and piloting it into the Nevada desert. The outlandish nature of the scene led Hamilton to suggest a comic touch, as Barry told budding Bond screenwriter Cary Bates in 1972. "Wrong, said Barry," Bates later reported; "you can't spoof a spoof. His theory is the music must play straight and pull in the audience, not play games with them. Hamilton wanted some fluffy, whimsical music; Barry wanted to give it a throbbing, exciting backdrop." So the original version of cue 6M3, which can be heard on the expanded 2003 CD, stresses the action for the full two minutes, while the rewritten 6M3A (the final film version) represented a compromise that opened with the feathery strings-and-xylophone as Bond tooled around the desert evading

brass bursts for Bond's theft of a moon-buggy prototype, which is at first dramatic (59 minutes), but then as Bond is pursued by all-terrain vehicles (1 hour, 1 minute) the comic nature of the chase is emphasized with strings doubling xylophone at first, and finally a return to the sharper, brass-driven material as he escapes with Tiffany.

Most of the car chase down the Vegas Strip is unscored until the Mustang-on-its-side stunt (1 hour, 7 minutes), which gets a comic-saxophone post-script that goes directly into another romantic "Diamonds" for strings and organ and a reprise of the "Diamonds" we first heard at Tiffany's Amsterdam apartment. Bond's entry into the mysterious Willard Whyte's penthouse begins a series of memorable cues, including "Death at the Whyte House" (1 hour, 16 minutes), in which Bond kills one of Blofeld's

doubles to a "Diamonds" variation and segues to the Wint-Kidd theme when the pair dump his unconscious body in the desert at night; "Bond Smells a Rat" (1 hour, 20 minutes), dramatic music for 007 being buried in an underground pipe; and "Bond Meets Bambi and Thumper" (1 hour, 24 minutes), which cleverly intertwines the Bond Theme bass line with the "Diamonds" melody and adds the Bond Theme itself (electric guitar over organ, then flutes answering brass). Barry originally used "Diamonds" in the piece but, apparently at the insistence of the filmmakers, rescored it with the Bond Theme.

Barry, who wrote such a memorable "Space March" for *You Only Live Twice*, returns to the milieu with another (1 hour, 33 minutes), titled "007 and Counting" on the LP, for the revelation that Whyte's satellite has been commandeered by Blofeld and

Sean Connery as James Bond in action mode during the "Moon Buggy Ride" sequence that underwent musical changes in *Diamonds Are Forever*

incompetent security men in cars, then segued into the original, stronger action material halfway through. Stories persisted over the next few years of a "rift" between Hamilton and Barry.

Film and score, however, were highly successful. *Diamonds Are Forever* opened December 17, 1971, to huge grosses, although Connery would not return to the role for another 12 years and then not in an officially sanctioned Eon production.

Critics were by now so accustomed to Barry's "million-dollar Mickey Mouse music" that there seemed to be little to add to prior raves. The best that *Variety* could do was "John Barry's music score is of the proper Bond genre" while the *Los Angeles Times* managed "John Barry did the music as before, including a title song for the splendid Shirley Bassey."

And, although the studio's initial Bond music campaign—to try to have "We Have All the Time in the World" nominated for an Oscar—had failed in 1970, United Artists tried again, and harder, with a better-designed full-page advertisement in the Hollywood trades, the names of Barry and Black presented more prominently, and a long list of the artists who had already recorded the title song. The film's own advertising campaign subtly incorporated the title song lyric by repeating "Forever" multiple times, just as Bassey did in her vocal. Unfortunately, the Academy of Motion Picture Arts and Sciences, which had consistently refused to nominate any Bond score or song for its highest honor, declined even to include "Diamonds" on its list of 10 finalists for the five Best Song nominees.

Perhaps because the *On Her Majesty's Secret Service* soundtrack album failed to match the high sales of *Goldfinger*, *Thunderball*, or *You Only Live Twice*, United Artists Records was said to be "holding off on pressing huge amounts of *Diamonds Are Forever* product until early consumer reactions to the film and album are in," although executives also professed to be "ready to jump in with massive shipments" if its marketing campaign paid off.

(SCORE HIGHLIGHTS, CONT.)

turned into a powerful new weapon. Like the 1967 piece, this one is a very deliberate march with the "Diamonds" organ offering shimmering sounds and dark brass colors for Blofeld's explosive demonstration of this new power.

The climax, which takes place on an oil rig off Baja California, begins with a fanfare for the aerial shots (1 hour, 37 minutes), another (1 hour, 45 minutes) for the weather balloon that signals the start of the helicopter attack, and the return of Barry's now-venerable "007" theme as a lighthearted treatment of the Bond-torments-Blofeld scene (1 hour, 51 minutes) and a reminder that he's saving the day again. The Wint-Kidd theme returns (1 hour, 54 minutes) for their final attempt to kill him aboard a cruise ship with Tiffany, and the Bassey vocal underscores the end titles (1 hour, 58 minutes).

Trade ad promoting the song and score of *Diamonds Are Forever* for Oscar consideration in December 1971

The soundtrack album, which over the years became the object of fan deri-sion because it failed to include many significant dramatic cues, was not orig-inally designed that way. Barry's album concept included many of the best dramatic cues. But United Artists Records overruled him and dropped much of that material in favor of middle-of-the-road lounge music that was thought to play better with American record buyers.

To a degree, it did. The Bassey single reached number 57 on the *Billboard* pop charts, while the album charted on January 8, 1972, and reached number 74—better than *On Her Majesty's Secret Service* but failing to match the much higher ranking for *You Only Live Twice*. The news was somewhat better in England, where the Bassey single reached number 38, although the album didn't make it onto charts. Instead of *Diamonds Are Forever*, the hit John Barry album in the U.K. in early 1972 was *The Persuaders!* a collection fea-turing his new theme from the ITC television series starring Tony Curtis and Roger Moore. It hit the U.K. top 20.

Curiously, in January 1972 ex-Beatle Paul McCartney asked his old Apple Records pal Ron Kass, who was then working for Harry Saltzman, to set up a screening of *Diamonds Are Forever* for him and Ringo Starr. Afterwards, *Vari-ety* columnist Army Archerd reported, "Paul said he wished he had penned the score."

"... you gotta give the other fellow hell ..."

Live and Let Die

John Barry spent much of 1972 and 1973 writing musicals, all with his friend and now regular collaborator Don Black: a lavish, all-star screen adaptation of *Alice's Adventures in Wonderland* with Peter Sellers, Dudley Moore and others; an ill-fated version of *Gulliver's Travels*, filmed with Richard Harris but then shelved for years; and *Billy*, a stage musical based on the play and film *Billy Liar*, which opened on the West End in May 1974 and made a singing and dancing star of Michael Crawford (who would go on to greater fame in *The Phantom of the Opera*).

Barry was through with Bond for now. First there was Harry Saltzman's door-slamming incident over the "Diamonds Are Forever" song; then disagreements with Guy Hamilton over the tone of parts of the *Diamonds* score; and finally, the films themselves, with Connery departing the role for good and a new emphasis on jokes and silliness instead of suspense and danger.

And even though the Oscars again ignored his smart and memorable work as a songwriter on the Bonds, he had been nominated for a 1971 Academy Award for *Mary, Queen of Scots*. The projects that lay ahead for him were ones where the music would take center stage, not remain as unappreciated background.

"The Bond pictures are technically very difficult," he told composer Michael Perilstein at the time, "because they are right down to split-second timing, which is really kind of an old-time movie-scoring attitude. Each one gets more and more difficult to write, because it's a kind of formula. Trying to move around within that same formula gets more difficult. My least favorite scores are the recent Bond scores, because they are really like second-hand *Goldfinger*s. It's a trap, and I don't know how to get out of it, really."

The next film was to be *Live and Let Die*, which would cash in on the new blaxploitation film craze with a black villain, a plot involving voodoo, and settings in Harlem, New Orleans and the Caribbean. Roger Moore, once *The Saint* and more recently Lord Brett Sinclair of *The Persuaders!* was announced as the new James Bond in August 1972, and Guy Hamilton was once again recruited to direct. Saltzman, who by now was alternating with Broccoli as primary producer on the Bonds, would be in charge of *Live and Let Die*; this was another likely factor in the apparently mutual decision for Barry to leave the franchise. As Barry told writer Cary Bates in 1972: "You know, I'm not doing them anymore." He didn't sound bitter, Bates said; "he just sounded like it was a fait accompli."

Enter Ron Kass. In 1968 the American-born music executive ran the Beatles's label Apple Records; in 1969 he took over as president of MGM Records and its publishing subsidiary; and in 1970, he became vice president of Edgar Bronfman's Sagittarius Productions. In the summer of 1971, Harry Saltzman named him managing director of CDF Ltd., Saltzman's non-Bond film production company; later he also ran Hilary Music, Saltzman's music-publishing company (named after the producer's daughter). Kass also happened to be married to Joan Collins, who was not only *Goldfinger* lyricist Anthony Newley's ex-wife but also very close with the new 007, Roger Moore.

With Barry unavailable for *Live and Let Die*, Kass pulled off a major musical coup using his long-established London music connections: he asked his old Apple Records pal Paul McCartney if he'd like to take a shot at writing the theme for the next Bond film.

"If you're the kind of writer I am," McCartney later said, "it's always one of those little ambitions: do the Bond song."

McCartney, who was then in the midst of recording *Red Rose Speedway*, the second album from his band Wings, got a copy of the Fleming novel and reportedly read it on a Saturday, probably in late September or early October 1972. "It's a very fast read," McCartney later told England's *Mojo* magazine. "On the Sunday, I sat down and thought, OK, the hardest thing to do here is to work in that title. . . . So I thought, 'live and let die,' really what they mean is 'live and let live' and there's the switch. So I came at it from the very obvious angle. I just thought, 'when you were younger you used to say that, but now you say this.'"

McCartney's wife Linda came up with the midsection of the tune, the reggae-style "what does it matter to you . . ." but Paul made the most critical call of all: to George Martin, his former Beatles producer and a veteran of tailoring rock songs for film. Not only had Martin received an Oscar nomination for adapting the Beatles songs into the score for *A Hard Day's Night* (1964) but he had also done the lion's share of the work on *The Family Way* (1966), a

Linda and Paul McCartney at the governor's ball following the Academy Awards at which their "Live and Let Die" was performed

drama with Hayley Mills for which McCartney, in a rare non-Beatles assignment at the time, had written the theme. Martin adapted McCartney's ideas into a full score for the Boulting Brothers film.

"Paul contacted me to say he wanted to make a demo of a song he had in mind for a Bond film," Sir George Martin later recalled. "I went to his house in St. John's Wood and he played me his ideas on the piano, but when he described what he wanted it was obvious that a large orchestra would be necessary. In those days synthesizers and computer effects were in their infancy, and nothing could beat the sound of a large orchestra."

At Martin's AIR studios, "we started by using Paul's band, and I used Paul, Linda and Eric Stewart to sing backup vocals. I then went away and wrote the score for overlaying, using about 55 musicians. Some demo! That became the final version; I could not make it any better," Martin said. He also double-tracked McCartney's voice although, as Martin later said, "Paul does it so accurately that it almost sounds like a single voice, though it still gives a stronger and better sound."

"Live and Let Die" begins quietly, with just McCartney singing and playing piano, but he demonstrates a flair for the dramatic just over half a minute

Composer George Martin

into the song, not just with the title phrase but with half a minute of instrumental pyrotechnics that might prove useful for the inevitable action
sequences. On October 24, *Daily Variety* announced that "Paul and Linda
McCartney have composed and recorded title theme tune for the James Bond
pic . . . now before cameras in New Orleans."

Kass and Broccoli took Martin to lunch in London, "since they had been
impressed by the orchestration on the record," Martin later remembered.
Lunch, however, was merely a prelude to one of Martin's most memorable and
jaw-dropping producer conversations, as he was then asked to fly to Jamaica,
where Saltzman was overseeing production in November and December.

As Martin recalled, Saltzman professed to like the McCartney song. "Very
nice record. Like the score. Now tell me, who do you think we should get to
sing it?"

Martin was taken "completely aback" by the question. "After all, he was
holding the Paul McCartney recording we had made. . . . But he was clearly
treating it as a demo disc." It was obvious that Saltzman had no idea how
important the ex-Beatle was in the music world and what impact a McCartney
theme might have, both creatively and commercially, on a Bond film.

"What do you think of Thelma Houston?" Saltzman asked Martin, apparently thinking in terms of a black female artist for the film. "Well, she's very
good," Martin replied diplomatically, "but I don't see that it's necessary when
you've got Paul McCartney."

Martin was forced to explain, as gently as possible, that McCartney "was the ideal choice, even if he wasn't a black lady, and that secondly, if Paul's recording wasn't used as the title song, it was very doubtful whether Paul would let him use the song for his film anyway." Ultimately, and to the relief of all concerned, Saltzman finally agreed, perhaps because director Guy Hamilton advised him about McCartney's stature. "Harry said, 'What do you think?' and I said, 'It's not exactly my bag, but coming from Paul McCartney, one would be absolutely idiotic not to use it.'"

Shooting had already begun in New Orleans in mid-October and a key number had already been recorded. In the story, Kananga (Yaphet Kotto), the dictator of the Caribbean island nation San Monique, is also Mr. Big, a drug kingpin; his girlfriend is Solitaire (Jane Seymour), a tarot-card reader whose virginity is the key to her ability to see the future. Bond visits New York, New Orleans and San Monique to investigate, along the way encountering crocodiles, killer snakes and voodoo ceremonies.

The precredits sequence involved a traditional New Orleans funeral, with a brass band playing "Just a Closer Walk with Thee" as the mourners marched through the streets, then breaking into a lively Dixieland number after a bizarre murder is committed (one of the cleverer moments of Tom Mankiewicz's

Roger Moore and Jane Seymour as Bond and Solitaire in *Live and Let Die*

screenplay). Lending an air of authenticity was Harold Dejan's Olympia Brass Band, which regularly played at the legendary Preservation Hall in New Orleans. Their arrangement of "Just a Closer Walk," and the jazzy "New Second Line," were penned by trumpeter Milton Batiste, a fixture on the Big Easy music scene for decades. These scenes were shot on Chartres Street on October 26 and November 9, 1972.

The Jamaica portion of the shoot began on November 14. "I started work on the film when I was with Harry in Jamaica," Martin later recalled. "He asked me to provide a rhythm beat for the voodoo scene with the snake. The crowd needed to move together with a beat that could be enlarged later. So I stayed on for about a week," Martin said. The scene in question, shot on November 25 at Ocho Rios on the island's northern coast, marked a return visit for many of the Bond crew, as that was the site of shooting for *Dr. No* a decade earlier.

With the McCartney song accepted and Martin now on board, it was up to Ron Kass to make the deal for both musicians. Perhaps predictably, it turned out to be more in McCartney's favor than Martin's, even though McCartney's tune was three minutes long and Martin would contribute nearly an hour's worth of music to the final product.

It all hinged on Barry's fee for composing *Diamonds*. An undated memo from Kass to Saltzman, probably from October 1972, specifies "Paul McCartney is to be paid $15,000 for composing the title song. In addition, his father-in-law Lee Eastman has said he would be agreeable to splitting the music publishing with the administration of the publishing in the hands of United Artists. . . . Since John Barry was paid $25,000 for *Diamonds Are Forever*, the $15,000 fee was negotiated in order to leave an amount of $10,000 to pay for the additional scoring necessary, as well as the arranging and conducting services."

ALBERT R. BROCCOLI and HARRY SALTZMAN present
ROGER MOORE as JAMES BOND
IAN FLEMING'S
'LIVE AND LET DIE'
Directed by GUY HAMILTON

Title Song Composed by
PAUL and LINDA McCARTNEY
And Performed by
PAUL McCARTNEY and WINGS
Music Score by
GEORGE MARTIN

SCORE HIGHLIGHTS

More than any James Bond film to that point, *Live and Let Die* reflects something of a modern rock sensibility, partly due to the McCartney theme, but also to George Martin's long history of working with rock artists. There is a harder edge to much of the score, from the rougher, grittier "Bond Theme" sound to the authentic soul sounds of the Fillet of Soul clubs in New Orleans and Harlem.

After the brief United Nations opening, when we meet Kananga and Solitaire for the first time, the scene shifts (at about 2 minutes into the film) to New Orleans for the jazz funeral of one agent ("Just a Closer Walk With Thee" and "New Second Line") and then to the Caribbean island nation of San Monique (4 minutes in) where the insistent rhythms of voodoo drummers is soon enhanced by Martin's

The most interesting aspect of Kass's two-page memo indicates that "The Fifth Dimension will perform a version of the title song in a live performance in the Fillet of Soul scene. Paul McCartney has agreed to produce the Fifth Dimension's performance. The original soundtrack album will be an extremely commercial package composing of Paul McCartney as composer, performer and producer, as well as the Fifth Dimension, who have had many number one records, and Wings, McCartney's musical group."

The Fifth Dimension had actually had two number-one hits in the United States: "Aquarius/Let the Sun Shine In" and "Wedding Bell Blues," both in 1969, and five other top-10 hits, including "Up, Up and Away" and "One Less Bell to Answer." Kass noted that "we are negotiating with Marc Gordon, manager of the Fifth Dimension, for a fee which would include recording as well as the performance on the screen." For either business or creative reasons, the deal fell through and the Fifth Dimension did not perform the song, either in the film or later on records.

Instead, a little-known artist named Brenda Arnau (known professionally at the time as B. J. Arnau) was signed to sing "Live and Let Die" in the New Orleans Fillet of Soul nightclub sequence. She had appeared, uncredited, in the film musical *Finian's Rainbow* and released several singles on various labels that went nowhere. Eventually she wound up in the London cast of *Oh! Calcutta!* and snagged the Bond gig, about the time she also landed an RCA record contract.

Martin, not McCartney, produced and arranged Arnau's version of the title song. He later said he never knew about plans for the Fifth Dimension. "I arranged the Brenda Arnau version later as a matter of course," he said. "Brenda was good, and easy to work with. We did the session pretty quickly without any dramas." Arnau's on-camera scenes, in which she lip-syncs to the track she recorded with Martin, were filmed at Pinewood on January 31 and February 1,

"Day in the Life"-style string section, as a second agent succumbs.

Maurice Binder's colorful title sequence (almost 5 minutes in) is among the most spectacular in the entire Bond series. His crimson-flame torches and naked black women whose heads explode into flaming skulls brilliantly showcase the McCartney theme. Musically, McCartney's style was so radically different from prior 007 themes that, in 1973, it was a jarring listen (the sophomoric "you know you did, you know you did, you know you did," the reggae-style midsection, the naggingly problematic line "in which we live in"). But time has proven its durability—and McCartney still does it in concert, with wild lights and pyrotechnics, to the cheers of a whole new generation of listeners.

Martin introduces Solitaire's theme (12 minutes in), as the mystic predicts Bond's arrival in New York; it's heard again as the opening of the first big action scene (14 minutes), as Bond's driver is killed by Kananga henchman Whisper and a Manhattan car chase ensues. Martin uses the bass line of the Bond theme but otherwise heightens the suspense with the rhythm section and eventually the full orchestra (like Barry, Martin did not title his cues; on the album, the piece is called "Whisper Who Dares").

Martin's arrangement of the "James Bond Theme" appears (20 minutes) as Bond hails a cab and heads for Harlem; it's hard-hitting, with shrill piccolos adding a fresh touch. Inside the Fillet of Soul bar, the Solitaire theme returns (23 minutes) as Bond introduces himself ("Bond Meets Solitaire" on

B. J. ARNAU'S "LIVE AND LET DIE" IS NO COVER.

APBO-0014

She's the only one who sings it and appears in the new James Bond thriller of the same name.

B. J. Arnau. Her first RCA single in America. "Live and Let Die." Written by Paul McCartney and produced by George Martin. Right on target.

RC∧ Records and Tapes

Trade advertisement promoting singer B. J. Arnau and her song in *Live and Let Die*

1973. RCA, which released her version as a single at the end of June, took out trade ads carefully touting Arnau as "the only one who sings it and appears in the new James Bond thriller." Although neither the Arnau single nor album charted, she went on to major success on the London stage that summer with rave reviews for her work in the rock-music version of Shakespeare's *Two Gentlemen of Verona*. (Broccoli was an unabashed fan of Arnau, stating in a May 1973 memo to UA that "she really is a star" and using her sizzling "Live and Let Die" performance in the coming-attraction trailers for the film.)

After Moore finished shooting *Live and Let Die* in March, he invited Kass and wife Joan Collins, as well as fellow show-biz pal (and earlier Bond lyricist) Leslie Bricusse, to vacation with him in Acapulco. That same year, Kass hired Martin to oversee the scoring of the Peter Sellers film *The Optimists*, with songs by Lionel Bart; and in October 1973, a few months after the opening of the Bond film, Kass returned to the record business as managing director of Warner Bros. Records in Great Britain.

As for the score, Martin remembered calling his old EMI colleague John Barry "and kind of apologized for taking over. He was a good friend and had no problems. I heard about the row he had with Saltzman, and his advice to me was, 'Just screw 'em for me, would you?'"

The blaxploitation trend of the time, including the success of such soul-driven soundtracks as *Shaft* and *Superfly*, was not an influence, Martin said: "I just wanted to make as dynamic a sound as I could without losing the Bond feel. It was a long job, and I was given four weeks before I had to start recording. My speed of fitting and scoring for a large orchestra was about two minutes per day, so I had to work it all out to get the job done." He conducted an orchestra of "around 55" at his own AIR studios in the late spring of 1973.

Martin found director Hamilton "a very easy man to work with. . . . He was always very concise in his specifications and his brief. He would tell me

the LP) and meets the hook-wearing, gun-twisting Tee Hee before Mr. Big orders Bond's execution.

The wonderful Geoffrey Holder, as the mysterious white-top-hatted Baron Samedi ("the man who cannot die"), makes his first appearance (28 minutes) as a dancer leading a troupe of entertainers on San Monique (the brassy number "Baron Samedi's Dance of Death"). Jazzy source music in Bond's hotel room (30 minutes, "San Monique" on the LP) quickly gives way to a queasy-sounding string cue as a deadly snake slithers into Bond's bathroom (32 minutes, "Snakes Alive") and the malevolent Whisper enters (the Bond bass line coupled with the Solitaire theme).

The McCartney theme returns (39 minutes) for the first time since the opening titles as a jazzy, Caribbean scene-setting cue, then again (44 minutes)

as CIA agent Rosie spots a voodoo symbol, runs into the jungle and is killed. For Bond's descent via parasail into Kananga's fortress (48 minutes, "Bond Drops In"), Martin offers an appropriately descending string line. Once again, the rhythm section is particularly strong, with a prominent part for harpsichord. Bond seduces Solitaire (50 minutes) to a variation on McCartney's theme. Escaping into the jungle, they encounter Baron Samedi playing a wood flute in a cemetery (55 minutes), which serves as a prelude to a big orchestral buildup ("If He Finds It, Kill Him") when Bond finds the vast poppy fields that are the source of Kananga's ill-gotten wealth.

Bond's double-decker bus chase is unscored until he runs into the low bridge (1 hour), shears off its top half and reaches the boat, for which Martin again uses the McCartney instrumental bridge; this,

exactly where he wanted the music, and the kind of effect he wanted from it."
Few revisions were required at the recording session, Martin said. "I thought
the score held up pretty well," he said many years later, "and I was pleased
with the way it came out. One of my best films, although I still think *Yellow
Submarine* was possibly better."

"Live and Let Die" was unveiled as part of a one-hour television special,
James Paul McCartney, that aired April 16, 1973, in the United States and
May 10, 1973, in the U.K., and featured McCartney and Wings performing the
tune in a studio, along with footage from the movie and a few pyrotechnics at
the end. It was excellent promotion for the film, which would open June 27,
1973, in the United States.

McCartney's lyrics were debated then, and for years to come. In the opening verse, was he singing "in this ever-changing world in which we're living"
or, as it sounds, the more grammatically troubled "in this ever-changing world
in which we live in"? The published sheet music, presumably the official version, uses the latter. More than three decades later, pressed by a *Washington
Post* reporter, McCartney admitted, "I don't think about the lyric when I sing
it. I think it's 'in which we're living.' Or it could be 'in which we live in,' and
that's kind of, sort of, wronger but cuter.'" He finally decided it should be "in
which we're living."

Critics were divided on the new musical direction of Bond. *Variety* was
unimpressed by the McCartney theme: "It is a serviceable melody, lacking
the guts of previous Bond pix themes, but then in harmony with the current
overall concept." *The Hollywood Reporter* shrugged, "The title song . . .
sounds like all the other Bond songs, as does the music by George Martin."
The *Los Angeles Herald-Examiner* critic decided that "the score by George
Martin sounds enough like John Barry's work to keep a sense of continuity,
and there is an excellent title song by Paul and Linda McCartney over the

(SCORE HIGHLIGHTS, CONT.)

plus the lighthearted action music for Bond's escape and theft of a small plane in New Orleans
(1 hour, 4 minutes), are coupled on the expanded
2003 CD as "New Orleans." The comic plane chase
is also unscored. The jazz funeral music returns
(1 hour, 7 minutes) as Bond and Leiter (David Hedison) visit the Fillet of Soul restaurant, where soul
music is being played (1 hour, 9 minutes) just before
B. J. Arnau's onstage performance of "Live and Let
Die."

Solitaire's failure to accurately read the tarot
cards for Kananga, and the return of the perpetually
amused Samedi, leads to another dramatic version
of the Solitaire theme ("Solitaire Gets Her Cards,"
1 hour, 17 minutes). Martin treats the Bond-versus-
crocodiles sequence ("Trespassers Will Be Eaten,"
1 hour, 23 minutes) with appropriate suspense at

first, but his famous dash across the backs of the
crocs is surprisingly unscored; music resumes as
Bond escapes and sets fire to the lab.

The speedboat chase that follows is unscored
(sound effects dominate) for the first eight minutes,
but music resumes briefly (1 hour, 34 minutes) with
another version of the Solitaire theme, and again
(1 hour, 38 minutes) with a reprise of the McCartney
instrumental ("Boat Chase" on the expanded CD).

Back in San Monique, voodoo drums dominate
(1 hour, 40 minutes) in scenes choreographed by
Holder, but when Solitaire emerges as their next
victim (1 hour, 42 minutes, "Sacrifice" on the LP),
Martin heightens the moment with bursts of brass,
those queasy strings for the snakes and a building
orchestral intensity. Bond and Solitaire escape, only
to be captured again and (1 hour, 51 minutes)—to a

lush, stylish, slightly mysterious, sensual title credits." The *Washington Post* critic was a little more succinct: "Paul and Linda McCartney composed the title song, but it takes a resounding back seat to Maurice Binder's titles, once more a flamboyant, erotic triumph."

McCartney's single was issued on Wings's label Apple, although the album (as usual for a Bond score) was on the United Artists label. In the U.K., with a somewhat earlier release, it charted on June 9 and reached number 9. In the United States, it earned a rave from *Billboard*: "A bit of distinctively sweet McCartney melody, a sudden booming uproar of massed symphony orchestra, a snatch of reggae and some more bombast a la '1812 Overture.' The best 007 movie theme of all and one of McCartney's two or three most satisfying records ever." The single charted on July 21 and reached number 2, where it stayed for three weeks. This inevitably helped the album—which charted a week later, spent 15 weeks on the chart and peaked at number 17 (the best showing for a Bond soundtrack since *Thunderball*). The theme would, on March 2, 1974, win the first major industry award given to any Bond song: A well-deserved Grammy for Best Arrangement Accompanying Vocalists, to George Martin. The song was also Grammy-nominated for Best Pop Vocal Performance by a Duo, Group or Chorus, and the soundtrack album was nominated as Best Album of Original Score Written for a Motion Picture or Television Special.

Once again, United Artists promoted the song for Oscar consideration in trade advertisements that not only cited McCartney and Wings but also used the mystical tarot-card theme of the movie itself—despite Broccoli's opposition to such ads, as noted in a December 1973 memo to UA executives by Eon marketing executive Jerry Juroe: "Cubby considers the categories mentioned, cinematography, music, film editing, art direction, costume design and sound, are relatively unimportant. . . . Cubby feels it is not worth the time, effort or

return of McCartney's instrumental theme—about to be dropped into shark-infested waters. After Kananga's demise and their final escape, Bond's train-compartment battle with Tee Hee is unscored, but the unexpected reappearance of Samedi (1 hour, 59 minutes) heralds the end titles and the return of the performance by Wings of the title song, to Binder's flaming skull from the main-title sequence.

money to put forward for Academy member consideration these lesser categories . . . for a James Bond picture."

Ironically, the undesired UA campaign paid off: "Live and Let Die" became the first Bond title song to be nominated for an Academy Award. Whether it was because music-branch voters were starstruck by a former Beatle writing a movie theme, or because they were starting to recognize (after the victory of *Shaft*'s title song two years earlier) the value of rock 'n' roll in movie music, or perhaps because of the effectiveness of the song against Binder's explosive visuals, no one can now say. It was also the only nomination for the film, despite a truly off-the-wall UA campaign to promote Clifton James, as dumb-hick Southern Sheriff J. W. Pepper, for Best Supporting Actor.

The McCartneys flew to Los Angeles to attend the Oscars on April 2, 1974. As he later told a *Los Angeles Times* writer, it might have seemed churlish to skip it. "We didn't really expect to win," McCartney said. "A few people told us it was stupid to go to the Oscars. They said, 'Why go? This man's gonna say you lost and you're gonna have to sit there.' But that's not the point to me. . . . By attending the Oscars, we were just saying hello, glad to be here, we respect what you're doing." He did admit to the reporter, however, that he might have worked a little harder on the song if he had realized it had Academy Award potential.

The Oscar performance was certainly offbeat. Instead of asking Wings to perform it live, the producers played the record and choreographed to it a three-minute dance number featuring B-movie actress and sometime singer-dancer Connie Stevens. Moore himself introduced the number (and got in a plug for the next film, *The Man with the Golden Gun*, along the way). A troupe of orange-, pink- and lavender-clad dancers spun, leapt and scurried up ladders while Stevens—in a skimpy silver-lamé outfit with a bizarre Indian-style headdress—descended from the ceiling, only to be variously lifted and tossed about by her fellow dancers before running away. *Variety* later panned the sequence as "the evening's most ridiculous segment. . . . Pre-hyped as the Academy's all-out spectacular, the production was hilarious on the home screen with Stevens doing little but posing as if she's seen Lana Turner in *The Prodigal* once too often. The cameras, unfortunately, refrained from providing a glimpse of composer Paul McCartney's reaction."

The song lost, perhaps inevitably, to "The Way We Were," a nostalgic ballad for the eponymous Barbra Streisand film (by future Bond composer Marvin Hamlisch and future Bond lyricists Alan and Marilyn Bergman).

". . . an assassin that's second to none . . ."

The Man with the Golden Gun

John Barry didn't leave Bond entirely behind when he decided to skip *Live and Let Die*. For a rare black-tie appearance as conductor of the Filharmonic concert at the Royal Albert Hall on October 7, 1972, he prepared an 18-minute symphonic suite of Bond themes (which included not only his "Goldfinger," "Thunderball," "007," "You Only Live Twice," "On Her Majesty's Secret Service" and "Diamonds Are Forever" but also Monty Norman's "James Bond Theme" and Lionel Bart's "From Russia with Love"). He recorded it as part of *The Concert John Barry*, released under his new contract with Polydor Records, and performed excerpts from it on a BBC television special on December 17, 1972. The following summer, on August 18, he conducted the Los Angeles Philharmonic in the entire "James Bond Suite" at the Hollywood Bowl.

By mid-1974, Barry had a huge West End hit with his musical *Billy*; composed the music for another spy film, *The Tamarind Seed*, for director Blake Edwards; and scored a sailing adventure, *The Dove*, for producer Gregory Peck. He was beginning work on *The Day of the Locust* for director John Schlesinger, as well as on the prestige television film *Love Among the Ruins* for his old friend Katharine Hepburn (and Laurence Olivier, who would briefly sing, on camera, an original song by Barry and Don Black).

But Cubby Broccoli wanted him back on Bond, in part because he and Saltzman were far along on the new film, *The Man with the Golden Gun*. Produc-

Christopher Lee and Roger Moore, as Scaramanga and Bond, about to begin their final duel in *The Man with the Golden Gun*

tion was running late, there would be very little time to write a song and score the film and Broccoli knew that Barry could deliver in a pinch. He always had.

Fleming's novel, published posthumously in 1965, was mostly discarded as a source of ideas. The plot of the film involves Francisco Scaramanga

ALBERT R. BROCCOLI and HARRY SALTZMAN present
ROGER MOORE as JAMES BOND
IAN FLEMING'S
007
"THE MAN WITH THE GOLDEN GUN"
Directed by GUY HAMILTON
Music Composed and Conducted by JOHN BARRY · Lyrics by DON BLACK · Title song performed by LULU

SCORE HIGHLIGHTS

John Barry may have returned to James Bond, but a new lighter tone was immediately noticeable when, during the gun-barrel logo, he gave the melody of the "James Bond Theme" to the strings, a tactic he would repeat throughout the 57-minute score for *The Man with the Golden Gun*.

The opening gun battle between Scaramanga and an American hood (3 minutes into the film) is darkly suspenseful, with low strings, alto flute and the occasional brass punctuation, spiced with tack piano (for the Western gunfighter) and Dixieland (for the 1930s gangsters) versions of the main theme (Barry never named his cues; on the album this is called "Scaramanga's Fun House").

The title song (8 minutes in) is prefaced by a musical machine-gun sound and a surprising electric-

(Christopher Lee), the world's highest-paid assassin, who dispatches his victims with a golden gun and gold bullets, and his involvement with a revolutionary solar cell. His assistant is the diminutive Nick Nack (Herve Villechaize), his mistress the beautiful Andrea Anders (Maud Adams). Helping Bond are novice agent Mary Goodnight (Britt Ekland) and Lt. Hip (Soon-Tek Oh). Once again taking advantage of popular movie trends, the Far East locations (Phuket and Bangkok, Thailand; Hong Kong and Macau) provided an excuse to incorporate martial-arts action into the story.

Only one scene required musical playback on the set, and the crew was already back at Pinewood wrapping up final scenes in mid-August 1974. Carmen Du Sautoy, as the Beirut belly dancer Saida, was moving to music provided by dance adviser Jean Issakoff (and credited to him on the movie's official cue sheet). Matching the soundtrack, three percussionists and a flutist can be seen behind Saida in the film during the scene prior to Bond's romancing her to retrieve the smashed gold bullet from her navel.

Barry found himself in a terrible time crunch. He was knee-deep in work on Schlesinger's ambitious, highly anticipated film of Nathanael West's 1939 novel *The Day of the Locust* (which reunited the *Midnight Cowboy* team of writer Waldo Salt, producer Jerome Hellman, director Schlesinger and composer Barry), set to record in mid-September 1974.

"I used to like to have time on the songs," Barry said years later. "For many of the movies, I'd write two or three until I got the one that felt right. [But on *Golden Gun*] there was no time. It was a crazy rush. I was never happy with it. I don't think anybody was happy with it. I thought the score was very good, actually, but the song just didn't happen."

Lyricist Don Black, on his third Bond song, found himself stuck with another problematic title. "If I had a chance to do that again," he said, "I would tuck the title away in the bridge somewhere and call it something else." Again

guitar solo, the most rock-oriented yet among the Barry scores. Lulu's vocal is set against Maurice Binder's usual naked-girl images, this time as if in rippling water, and of course the occasional golden gun.

Bond's trip to Beirut (15 minutes) marks the first of two instances of authentic, exotic source music: Saida's belly-dancing music (at 15 minutes, credited to Jean Issakoff) and the traditional Thai music (1 hour, 5 minutes, uncredited) when Bond is in Bangkok treating Goodnight to dinner (and Phuyuck wine!). One of Barry's signature sexy saxophone solos signals 007's attempt to retrieve the smashed gold bullet while kissing Saida's belly, and the fight that ensues (17 minutes, titled "Getting the Bullet" on the LP). A unique version of the "Bond Theme" follows (21 minutes), for strings and, apparently, cimbalom, attempting to simulate the sound of an Oriental instrument, as Bond visits Macau.

Bond enters Andrea's hotel room (28 minutes) to the main theme, voiced for strings and delicately echoing keyboard, adding a touch of suspense. Rock source music for the Bottoms Up club (33 minutes) is interrupted by curious woodwinds for Nick Nack and a dramatic Bond-theme bass line as Scaramanga shoots the solar-energy scientist and, in one of the most dramatic and tuneful pieces in the score, Hip whisks 007 away to the sunken *Queen Elizabeth* (36 minutes, called "Hip's Trip" on the LP); the main theme, again for strings, interrupts briefly as Scaramanga returns to Andrea's bed.

Bond visits Hai Fat's Bangkok palace (44 minutes in) to a gong and a bit of colorful Oriental atmosphere as he meets a naked girl swimming in a pool;

Singer Lulu in an early press
appearance to promote her
role as vocalist in the new
Bond film

trying to write "provocative, sensual lyrics," Black admitted years later, "they were a bit on the nose. 'He has a powerful weapon,' that got your attention straight away. It's all just a delicious piece of nonsense, really—a piece of cartoon hokum, if you like."

"The Man with the Golden Gun" became the second villain song in the Bond canon (third if you count "Thunderball," which Black contended is about

(SCORE HIGHLIGHTS, CONT.) a few minutes later (49 minutes), he encounters a pair of sumo wrestlers but is ultimately knocked out by Nick Nack; it's in this cue that Barry produces wah-wah comedy sounds using muted brass. These two pieces form "Chew Me in Grisly Land" on the LP.

Our initial look at Hai Fat's martial-arts school is unscored, but the arrival of Hip and his karate-expert nieces, just in time to save Bond (56 minutes), is again scored with a lighter touch—mostly strings and high flutes with repeated gong strikes—and even their escape uses the main theme, lightened by piccolos. Bond's boat chase through Bangkok's waterways, mostly unscored, begins immediately thereafter.

Bond toasts Goodnight at dinner (1 hour, 6 minutes) to a slow rendition of the main theme with cocktail-piano embellishment. A longer, more sen- sual version begins (1 hour, 8 minutes) when Bond begins to romance Goodnight but is interrupted by Andrea; interestingly, Bond and Andrea make love to music heard earlier (when Bond entered Andrea's hotel room), and Andrea's late arrival back at Scaramanga's (1 hour, 13 minutes) gets more dramatic treatment. Barry scored the entire hotel-room sequence with a single five-minute-plus cue (the long, languorous version of the theme called "Goodnight Goodnight" on the LP) that perfectly fits the sequence and nicely hits its dramatic high points, but only the first 52 seconds and the final 44 seconds remain in the film.

Oddly, Andrea's murder is left unscored. Barry's treatment of Nick Nack is, again, slightly comic (1 hour, 19 minutes), although Goodnight's fall into the car trunk and Bond's concern over the missing

Trade advertisement promoting the song and score for Oscar consideration.

007). And, like "Goldfinger," it was mostly literal ("he charges a million a shot / an assassin second to none . . .") but also, as Black later conceded, "too much about the man with the golden gun, you know, alluding to the male member. It's too on the nose; you've got to have a certain subtlety with this stuff."

Scottish singer Lulu was an old friend of Black's from the 1960s. She had sung "To Sir with Love," from the Sidney Poitier movie (with lyrics by Black), which rose to the number-one spot in America in 1967; in the U.K., she had had six top-10 hits in the previous nine years, including a recent one in "The Man Who Sold the World," produced by David Bowie. As Broccoli said, announcing the choice of singer to the British press on October 7, 1974: "She sings with soul, and besides, she's cute as a button."

Many years later, Lulu reflected: "I jumped at the chance because it meant working with John Barry, who was an incredible writer. I think, musically, I was miscast because it was not my kind of song. The song was more Shirley Bassey than me, but in terms of profile it was huge. My agent and manager nearly jumped out of their skin, but I did it because I wanted to work with him."

On another occasion, she opined: "The only proper way to do a Bond theme was as a Shirley Bassey impression. They wanted that 'he has a POW-ER-FUL WEA-pon!' type of thing. That's not normally how I sing. When I listen to it now, I think, God, it doesn't even sound like me, or Shirley. It's more like Ethel Merman."

The song was recorded September 4 at CTS studios' new location in Wembley. Mixing engineer John Richards recalled Lulu as "a lovely girl. She had a wonderful personality. She was everybody's sweetheart. She was so upset that, when we had our vocal session, she was battling a cold and wasn't sure how it was going to turn out." In fact, the raw quality of her vocal worked in the song's favor.

Solex Agitator get more of a sense of urgency. The first few minutes of Bond's car chase are unscored; music begins (1 hour, 25 minutes) after half a dozen cars are wrecked, and it's a combination of the main theme and the Bond theme, fairly light in tone, complete with piccolos. The car stunt with the comic slide-whistle effect is next, followed by a more serious conclusion as Bond and his unlikely passenger, J. W. Pepper, reach Scaramanga's hangar (on the LP, "Let's Go Get 'Em").

One of the score's best cues may have been inspired by the images of the remote, stunning islands of Phang Nga Bay near Phuket, as Bond does an aerial search for Scaramanga's hideout. Alternately dramatic, urgent and haunting, the 2½ minute piece (1 hour, 32 minutes, called "In Search of

Scaramanga's Island") precedes Bond's final debates with Scaramanga and their beachfront duel. Alto flutes and ominous low piano notes (1 hour, 41 minutes) accompany Scaramanga's weapons demonstration, blowing up Bond's plane.

Their final duel (1 hour, 46 minutes) reprises the "funhouse" music from the precredits sequence: stealthy and sinister, once again adding a tack-piano version of the theme for the Western shootout and, when Bond sees his own wax figure, the Bond-theme bass line. This arrangement is darker and more dramatic than the first one, though, especially as Bond eludes the cameras; the shrill flutes and eerie strings build to the moment of Scaramanga's fall, which is met with silence (on the LP, the six-minute piece is titled "Return to Scaramanga's Fun House").

But Barry could not begin work on the score; he was due back in L.A. "I was here in Los Angeles doing *The Day of the Locust* for John Schlesinger," Barry recalled in a 1979 interview. He finished the score and spent the entire week of September 16 recording with a Hollywood orchestra. "I flew back on a Sunday, went to work on a Monday and had just three weeks to complete that score." On Monday, October 14, Barry began five days of recording on *Man with the Golden Gun.* Barry later said that it was the shortest time he had had to work on a major studio feature to date.

Despite the short time frame, the film offered fresh musical challenges. The Roger Moore Bonds were considerably lighter in tone (sometimes even comedic) than the more serious Connery efforts. Beginning with *The Man with the Golden Gun,* Barry often played the melody of the "James Bond Theme" in the strings, a considerably less intense sound. "Roger played the whole character much lighter, and so we tried to lighten it up a bit," Barry later explained. "It wasn't a big switch, just a little thing in the orchestration. I think it worked better for Roger."

As on *Diamonds,* however, director Hamilton liked an occasional nod to the humor: delicately amusing clarinet for Nick Nack, for example, and wah-wah trumpet sounds for Bond attacking sumo wrestlers' private parts. The worst of them, one that Barry later regretted, was adding a slide whistle to the daring car stunt when Bond and passenger J. W. Pepper do a complete flip in mid-air. "Earlier on, I'd have played it for all it was worth as a really dangerous moment," Barry said. "I just took the liberty of poking fun at it. It made a mockery of Bond, looking back on it. Even Cubby didn't like that. But it was me getting to the end of it. If there were any cracks in the painting, as it were, they were starting to appear then."

Lulu attended the film's London premiere on December 19, 1974, just a few weeks before launching a weekly Saturday-night variety series on the

---

Barry scores Bond's attempts to retrieve the Solar Agitator, despite Goodnight's bungling (1 hour, 54 minutes), with dramatic timpani hits and suspenseful brass and strings. The installation blows up to no music at all, as Bond and Goodnight escape on Scaramanga's junk, and they embrace (1 hour, 59 minutes) to the warmer sounds of the main theme. And after Bond rids them of Nick Nack for a final time, the theme returns (2 hours, 1 minute), with a segue into the end-title vocal, with the altered lyrics ("Goodnight, Goodnight . . .").

Barry recorded another piece that appears only on the LP: a fun, full-out Dixieland arrangement of the theme (called "jazz instrumental" on the album, a broad expansion of the brief gangster music in the funhouse sequences). It, like the string figure in "Re-turn to Scaramanga's Fun House," may have been the result of Barry's musical experiments for *The Day of the Locust,* which he had completed just weeks earlier and which included 1930s-style jazz and microtonal string writing.

BBC. *The Hollywood Reporter* offered an upbeat appraisal: "John Barry keeps his James Bond theme music fresh and adventuresome, with amusing lyrics by Don Black"—perhaps referring, in part, to a first-ever end-title lyric that differed slightly from its main-title counterpart: "Goodnight, Goodnight / sleep well, my dear / no need to fear, James Bond is here. . . . "

Variety was less enthusiastic: "British pop singer Lulu warbles the John Barry–Don Black title theme, less exciting than prior themes but okay in context." *Billboard* loved the score: "Another skillful, ballsy, usual topnotch job from John Barry. Some good jazz-based instrumentals, some powerful big brassy works and some fine low-key material." And at least one British newspaper loved the song: "From the first raucous blast you know this is the latest Bond film theme. Lulu, sounding like a rough-cut Shirley Bassey, gives it the full 007 treatment. A hit."

A mid-January review of the soundtrack album, however, correctly predicted the outcome: "Lulu's handling of the title tune doesn't figure to be anywhere near the big seller Paul McCartney's rendering of 'Live and Let Die' was last year." For the first time in the history of the Bond franchise, neither single nor album charted on either side of the Atlantic. A degree of musical retrenching was in order.

". . . nobody does it better . . ."

The Spy Who Loved Me

James Bond has weathered a lot of changes over the past half-century, but few as tumultuous as those of the three years between *The Man with the Golden Gun* and *The Spy Who Loved Me*. Harry Saltzman, Cubby Broccoli's partner in the Bond business since 1961, sold his interest to United Artists in 1975, making Broccoli the sole producer of all future 007 adventures. And John Barry, who had contributed music to eight of the nine official Bond films, had become a "tax exile" and could no longer work in the United Kingdom.

Barry was just one of many high-earning show-business personalities to flee Britain because of onerous tax burdens. His friends Shirley Bassey and Michael Caine, as well as the Rolling Stones, Rod Stewart and David Bowie, all left during the 1960s and 1970s, although most later settled their tax debts and returned home.

Barry spent much of 1975 at his second home in Majorca, off the coast of Spain, and in the fall of that year began working consistently in the United States, first on the prestige ABC miniseries *Eleanor and Franklin* and then on a jazz-oriented concept album, *Americans*. He stayed on in Los Angeles in 1976 to score *Robin and Marian* (starring ex-007 Sean Connery) and later the big-budget Dino DeLaurentiis remake of *King Kong*.

There may have, briefly, been some thought about finding a way for Barry to stick with Bond. *Spy Who Loved Me* script number 241 had the name "John Barry" written on its cover. In late May he attended a Hollywood fundraising event with his old friend Cubby Broccoli, and although Broccoli's focus was very much on the next Bond film, the fact was that Barry could not return to England, where the music would have to be recorded. Broccoli needed to find another composer.

In 1976, 32-year-old Marvin Hamlisch was the hottest composer in show business. Three years earlier, he was a wunderkind who had taken Hollywood by storm, becoming the first composer to win all three music Oscars in the same year: for Best Song and Best Score for the Barbra Streisand film *The Way We Were*, and Best Adaptation Score for the caper film *The Sting*. "I think we can talk as friends," he quipped to the Academy Awards crowd upon receiving his third Oscar of the night.

He then received four Grammy Awards, including Song of the Year and Best New Artist, and then moved on to the stage and won a Tony Award and a Pulitzer Prize for co-writing *A Chorus Line*, one of the most acclaimed and now most beloved musicals in the history of Broadway. (He eventually completed his sweep of the major show-business awards by winning four Emmys, including three for televised Streisand concerts.)

"John Barry couldn't do this film," Hamlisch later said, "and because he couldn't, they started looking for other composers, and somehow my name came up." Hamlisch met with Broccoli and landed the job in late 1976, while production was under way. He then did his homework by screening every Bond film. "And what I realized was, besides the famous theme, there was this bigger-than-life feeling, always a big symphony orchestra. I decided, basically, to follow that scheme."

But first he had to come up with a song.

Hamlisch had recently begun writing with a new lyricist, Carole Bayer Sager, whose pop hits had included "A Groovy Kind of Love" and "Midnight Blue." One day, as she was leaving Hamlisch's New York City apartment after working on some other songs, "Marvin said, 'Can I play you something? It's something I'm working on for the Bond movie,'" Sager recalled, and Hamlisch, a fine pianist, played her the tune he had been writing. Almost immediately, Sager said, "I have a good title for that: Nobody Does It Better."

Hamlisch liked it. "I think we even wrote the chorus right then and there in his apartment," Sager said. Reflecting later on the inspiration of the moment, she said, "It just came into my mind. It was one of those moments that you're thankful for afterwards." Both songwriters felt it was perfect for James Bond.

The composer's other inspiration was to start small. Since everything in Bond was "bigger than life," he thought, why not go in the opposite direction? "The song should start off anything but bombastic—start very small, and become very big. Starting in a kind of music-box, Mozartian way," as he described it, for just solo piano.

Unfortunately, Hamlisch was running out of time. It was early 1977, and he had to fly to London to begin work on the score. So for the next few weeks,

Carole Bayer Sager and Marvin Hamlisch at the time they wrote "Nobody Does It Better" in 1976–77

Hamlisch and Sager finished the song long-distance. "I had to write the verses completely without him here. I can do that," she said, "but my favorite way of writing is to be in the room with the person I'm collaborating with, so they can immediately go, 'I love that' or 'I don't love that.'" Over the next few weeks, they worked out the song, mostly through transatlantic phone calls. "I took a long time with the lyric," Sager said, "until he said he was out of time. He needed to play it for them" (referring to the film executives).

"Nobody Does It Better" was admittedly a great title, but it would also mark the first time that a song used in the Bond title sequence didn't actually use the Fleming book title. "For that reason," Sager said, "I put in 'like heaven above me, the spy who loved me, is keeping all my secrets safe tonight.' So at least their title was in there. I was a pop songwriter, that's where my roots were, and 'The Spy Who Loved Me' didn't feel like a pop hit."

In addition, the song was about Bond, not a villain or a generic love song—the first to be about the character, if one believes Hamlisch, or the second, if one accepts Don Black's view that "Thunderball" is really about Bond and not about the villain of that film.

As for the vocalist, the stars aligned again for Hamlisch: "This was the only time in my life—except for 'The Way We Were'—in which the artist that I wanted to sing the song, actually sang the song." Hamlisch's first and only choice: Carly Simon.

Simon was one of the 1970s' hottest artists, with six top-20 hits in the previous six years, including "That's the Way I Always Heard It Should Be," "Anticipation" and "You're So Vain." "We felt that we could make a great record with her," Hamlisch said. "Carly is one of the great pop singers of her time, maybe all time," added Sager.

"It was my dream to sing a song for a movie in the first place," Simon reminisced years later, "and a James Bond movie made the whole thing score higher. When I was a child, I was asked what I wanted to be, and my first choice was a spy. It was mainly because of the wardrobe; I wanted to wear a black trench coat and walk around with briefcases and a lot of information. I think I was on to something."

Hamlisch visited Simon in New York to audition the song. "It had the proper sense of humor . . . great musicality, wonderful lyrics," she later said. Hamlisch and Sager agreed that Richard Perry, who had produced several of her hits, should repeat on this song. "We just felt that he could make a hell of a record," Hamlisch said. Perry recorded Simon and the rhythm section in Los Angeles (including Toto's Jeff Porcaro on drums) but insisted on recording the strings in London. Recalled Hamlisch: "That was part of the deal: if he produced the record, he wanted to make sure he could work in London. So we did the string track at Abbey Road. The whole thing was very Bond-like."

"After we'd finished the basic tracks," Simon said, "we decided that it was going to have to be very lushly scored . . . kind of a sneaky, sexy, slightly bad-boy vibe." She later added: "The song sort of grows on you. As long as you realize it's not supposed to be serious. It's kind of tongue-in-cheek."

Both songwriters were enamored of Perry's work, especially the ad-libbed ending in which Simon sings "baby, you're the best . . . sweet baby . . . darling, you're the best. . . ." "Richard Perry was known for his fade-out endings," Hamlisch said. "Carly sang it five or six times, and then he just layered them one after the other. It was just like, wow."

Thus, song finished, Hamlisch went to Pinewood, where the film was still in production, to play it for the producer and director. "I came out there, and I wanted to play it for people, and nobody really had time for me. The only person that was interested in hearing the song was Roger Moore. He's the one who actually said, 'Let's listen to it!' He was really interested in what I was working on." (Bond producer Michael Wilson and director Lewis Gilbert recalled Hamlisch auditioning the song for them. "He came in and played the song for us on the piano, and sang it himself," Wilson said. Added Gilbert: "One sensed that it could be a hit as soon as he played it.")

Hamlisch and Sager fell in love. Playwright Neil Simon was so fascinated by their relationship that he wrote *They're Playing Our Song*, with songs by the duo, about them; it opened on Broadway in 1979 with Robert Klein and Lucie Arnaz and received a Tony nomination as Best Musical. By 1980, however, they had broken up. Sager later married another Bond composer: Burt Bacharach.

Fleming's 1962 novel was something of a departure, being told from a woman's perspective; its critical failure led Fleming to insist that any film made of it could use the title but not the story. So a new, up-to-date scenario was invented that involved a villain named Stromberg (Curt Jurgens) obsessed with the oceans, a supertanker that swallowed nuclear submarines, a steel-toothed giant henchman named Jaws (Richard Kiel) and—in a nod to the then-burgeoning feminist movement—a Soviet spy, Maj. Anya Amasova (Barbara Bach), with rank and stature comparable to those of 007.

Production began in late August 1976, at Pinewood, and among the earliest scenes shot were those in the Mujaba Club, an Egyptian nightspot where Bond and Anya meet. The Egyptian Folklore Group was booked to perform over four days in September, and that would become one of the film's key source-music requirements. Then, in October, the company actually filmed in Egypt, although the Pyramids (site of another cat-and-mouse sequence that would demand elaborate musical treatment) proved impossible to shoot at night and many of the Pyramid shots were inserted later by the effects team.

Most of the film was shot between the beginning of November and the end of January at the newly built "007 Stage" at Pinewood (although second-unit footage continued to be shot in the Bahamas through the end of February). By mid-March, *Variety* reported, Hamlisch was "ensconced at Pinewood" composing the score (although, more accurately, Hamlisch recalled, he was writing in an apartment in London). Maurice Binder's titles were shot to the already recorded song on March 10 and 11.

"I always write from the beginning to the end," Hamlisch said. "I am a big, big believer in pacing. It's almost like architecture. What am I going to write here? Is it going to be fast or slow? [And in a Bond film] you've got to keep moving like a banshee." To start, the composer was lucky enough to get, in *The Spy Who Loved Me*, what may be the greatest pre-title sequence in all of the Bonds: the harrowing ski jump off the side of a mountain (in the script, it's Austria; in reality, a Canadian glacier above the Arctic Circle) that ends with Bond opening a parachute adorned with the Union Jack.

Hamlisch decided to apply the "James Bond Theme" but update it with a more contemporary musical sound, including then-trendy use of synthesizers and a pop rhythm section. "I listened to a lot of contemporary stuff, and to be honest, I stole a little bit from the Bee Gees," he explained, noting that he called Freddie Gershon, lawyer for the popular 1970s group (which enjoyed such disco hits as "Jive Talkin'" and "You Should Be Dancing"), to say "I hope you don't sue me because the basic rhythmic track, I have to tell you, is pure Bee Gees."

There is actually less music in *The Spy Who Loved Me* than in any Bond film since *Dr. No*, only about 46 minutes, and seven minutes of that isn't by Hamlisch. The film contains several musical jokes that, Hamlisch said, weren't his idea but ones he agreed might be funny. Two of them involve Oscar-winning scores by Maurice Jarre: Soviet agents Sergei and Anya are interrupted by a music box playing "Lara's Theme" from *Doctor Zhivago*, and later Bond and Anya hike through the desert to the main theme from *Lawrence of Arabia*. "It was like, well, if we can buy the rights, wouldn't it be a wonderful joke? The difference between working on a Bond film and on any other film is, on every other film you're trying to save money. On a Bond film, it's like, oh, another $200,000, who cares? So I was all for it."

Stromberg is revealed to be a classical-music buff, playing Bach, Mozart and Chopin at various times in his undersea lair. And the faux-Egyptian source music heard when Bond and Anya meet at the Mujaba Club was actually the work of London-born Paul Buckmaster, a composer who had recently worked as an arranger and conductor on a Sager album.

"We tried to get very correct in terms of the music that is played in the Egyptian restaurant. I brought in a writer that understood that kind of Middle Eastern music," Hamlisch said. The script called for "a troupe of whirling dervishes . . . some playing drums and other percussion instruments," and these are seen on screen. Hamlisch found Buckmaster when Sager visited London (with song producer Perry) and all had dinner together. He handed them a copy of an album he had recently produced for an Iranian singer named Shusha, a collection of traditional Persian songs called *From East to West*.

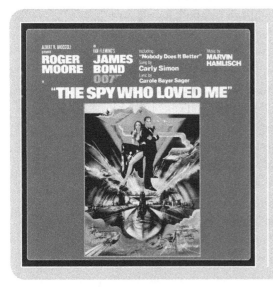

Bond's Lotus under water in *The Spy Who Loved Me*

mountainside pursued by Soviet assassins. Called "Skidoo" on the film's official cue sheet, it surrounds the classic guitar phrase with (ultramodern for 1977) synth-driven rhythm derived, as Hamlisch admitted, from favorite Bee Gees disco tracks. Bond kills the Soviet agent and then skis off the side of the mountain in a stunt that still astounds. Music stops for a full 20 seconds (only the sound of wind is heard)—a great dramatic choice, as is Bond's deployment of a Union Jack parachute to the screaming-brass bebop midsection of the Bond theme, a wink to the audience that this is all just a very expensive lark. (This music, augmented with chase music from elsewhere in the film and newly arranged, became "Bond '77" on the LP.)

The main title (8 minutes) is the first to use Roger Moore's image along with the usual naked-women silhouettes, this time jumping around on trampolines and doing acrobatics on giant guns to Carly Simon's rendition of "Nobody Does It Better."

Interestingly, there is no theme for the villain Stromberg (mastermind behind the theft of the nuclear submarines). He murders his treacherous assistant to music of Bach ("Air on a G String," 16 minutes in), then raises his giant underwater installation Atlantis to Mozart (Piano Concerto no. 21, at 18 minutes). Bond visits Egypt, but as is the case with most fight and action scenes his struggle with Stromberg's henchman Sandor goes unscored.

The Pyramids sequence (27 minutes in) is a fascinating use of source music that sometimes doubles as score. Hamlisch wrote a grand, melodramatic piece for the "Son et Lumiere" nighttime show at the Pyramids (where Bond is to meet contact

"A few days later," Buckmaster recalled, "he called and asked me to compose two pieces in that style, which was a blend of Iranian, North African, Egyptian and Arabic styles, for a couple of nightclub scenes . . . some kind of belly-dancing type of source music. He gave me the tempi, and of course he attended the sessions, made sure he got exactly what he wanted."

He also asked Buckmaster to pen a theme for Anya that would appear not in the film but on the soundtrack album. Hamlisch conducted this exotic-sounding piece for flute, harp and strings. "So there are three pieces by me on the album; two appear in the movie," Buckmaster said. (Oddly, the main source piece is called "Mojave Club," not Mujaba Club, both in the film cue sheet and on the album. Bass player Doni Harvey wrote part of the bridge, Buckmaster said, hence his co-writer credit on that track.)

In addition to the Bond theme and the new song, Hamlisch needed to come up with three more main themes: a large-scale piece for orchestra and choir for the Pyramids "Son et Lumiere" show, which forms the backdrop for Bond's search for the missing microfilm; music for Atlantis and the underwater scenes in Bond's amphibious Lotus Esprit; and grandly villainous music for Stromberg's massive, sub-swallowing supertanker.

"Some of my favorite cues in the film are the underwater sequence," Hamlisch said, "one of the best things I've ever written. 'Atlantis.' I love that cue because it has water, you know, that bubbly sound. That took a while to get.

"The thing about Bond is to hear that big orchestra. If you say to Cubby Broccoli, 'I need a hundred-piece orchestra,' you get a hundred-piece orchestra. On one day, we had 103. I remember we used six French horns. I think it's one of the more contemporary scores; it uses, here and there, a synthesizer, which was just starting out in those days, but it uses the big, big orchestra." Hamlisch estimated that he had "six to seven weeks" to write and, according

Fekkesh), but its dramatic high points coincide with the arrival of the hulking Jaws, his murder of Fekkesh and Bond's first encounter with Anya (which, notably, is accompanied by choir as the piece reaches its climax). This three-minute piece is unfortunately split into two tracks on the album (titled "The Pyramids" and "Conclusion").

Paul Buckmaster's two Near Eastern–flavored source cues accompany the colorfully garbed dancers at the Mujaba Club ("Mojave Club," as it's referred to in the cue sheet and on the album, 33 minutes in; "Eastern Lights," as Bond and Anya meet with Max Kalba just before Jaws kills him and steals the microfilm, 36 minutes). Both are complete on the LP, although only about a third of "Eastern Lights" is used in the film. Doni Harvey is co-credited with writing "Mojave Club," and according to the

album credits Hamlisch played Fender Rhodes on the tracks.

"Nobody Does It Better" is reprised just four times in the score, always as a love theme for Bond and Anya. Its first appearance, featuring electric guitar, is during their truck ride into the desert (39 minutes), as Anya falls asleep on Bond's shoulder. Their fight with Jaws at Luxor and retrieval of the microfilm (41 minutes, called "Pow") features an exotic-sounding oboe, the Bond-theme bass line, and suspenseful strings. Their trip back through the desert in the nearly destroyed van gets a comedic march (46 minutes, called "The We All Make Mistakes March"), and moments later they walk back to the strains of Lawrence of Arabia.

"Nobody Does It Better" returns (49 minutes) as Bond and Anya converse and kiss for the first time

to press reports of the time, he was in London for three months on the project as a whole.

Hamlisch began recording on April 25, 1977, at CTS Wembley (which was now dubbed The Music Centre). But much of the score was in tiny bits and pieces; more than three-quarters of the entire work consists of cues that are less than a minute in duration. So Hamlisch reconceived the score for album purposes, expanding key cues for a better listening experience and re-recording that material over three days in early May at AIR studios.

Hamlisch assembled a suite from the score and debuted it in a concert at the Kennedy Center in Washington, D.C., on June 25. The *Washington Post* critic said the music "seemed to capture, in an almost satirical vein, the electronic sharpness of Ian Fleming's fictional character."

Then, two weeks before the film's July 27 New York opening, Hamlisch made arrangements to screen a finished print for Carly Simon at a private screening room in Manhattan. Present were Hamlisch and Sager plus Simon and her husband, singer James Taylor. As the film neared the eight-minute mark and the titles began, Hamlisch (who has perfect pitch) noticed that the song "sounds to me like it's in the wrong key. That's weird," he thought, "it's like a half tone lower. And in the next few seconds it starts going lower and lower, and then stops. The room goes black. We have no electricity."

It was 9:25 P.M. on July 13, 1977, the night of the famous New York City blackout.

Hamlisch recalled "running on the streets of New York with everybody, trying, number one, to get a cab, and number two, more important, getting votive candles from a store so that we can set Carly up in her home with candles because New York is pitch black. I'll never forget it. Everything about Bond is over the top."

on the boat; once again, Hamlisch employs electric guitar and piano. On the train ride across Europe, Jaws attacks, followed by another romantic interlude (1 hour into the film) in which "Nobody Does It Better" is reprised in more of a lounge-music arrangement featuring sexy saxophone and strings; it finishes with an Italian touch (accordion) for their arrival in Sardinia.

Stromberg's assistant Naomi (Caroline Munro) delivers Bond and Anya to his Atlantis fortress by boat to a new theme, a pleasant combination of orchestral and synthesizer sounds (1 hour, 4 minutes into the film; greatly expanded from 37 seconds in the film to more than three minutes on the LP as "Ride to Atlantis"). Bond finds Stromberg listening to Chopin ("Nocturne," op. 27, no. 2, at 1 hour, 6 minutes) and planning underwater cities.

Hamlisch reprises his "Bond '77" music (1 hour, 12 minutes) for the car chase in which Bond's Lotus is pursued by a car containing Jaws and then Naomi piloting a helicopter. The amphibious Lotus is greeted by warm, floating strings and piano, then a reprise of the "Ride to Atlantis" music as they survey the undersea installation (1 hour, 15 minutes), but the idyll doesn't last long, for Hamlisch returns to the "Bond '77" music (1 hour, 17 minutes) when they are menaced by Stromberg's divers.

Hamlisch does not accentuate Anya's death threat to Bond. But when they are aboard a sub as Stromberg's massive supertanker *Liparus* threatens and then swallows the vessel (1 hour, 25 minutes in), Hamlisch supplies low, heavy, ominous sounds—the most sinister and melodramatic music of the entire score (called "The Tanker" on the LP, again

Trade ad for Carly Simon promoting the song "Nobody Does It Better"

Initial reviews, surprisingly, were mixed:. *The Hollywood Reporter* described "Marvin Hamlisch's witty yet dramatically effective score," while *Variety* dismissed it: "The score by Marvin Hamlisch . . . does nothing for the film, whatever it may achieve on disk." *High Fidelity*, reviewing the album, was especially vicious, complaining about the composer's "nondescript melodies, clumsy orchestrations, trite jazz riffs, and overall dramatic and technical ineptitude."

But the *Los Angeles Times* praised the music as "vivid," and in a surprising departure from its usual practice of ignoring music in its film reviews, Janet Maslin declared in the *New York Times*, "The theme song, sung by Carly Simon, ranks with Paul McCartney's theme from *Live and Let Die* as one of the most delightful surprises the series has had to offer—even if it is accompanied by footage of a naked woman, in silhouette, doing silly calisthenics on the barrel of an enormous gun."

The public agreed, making "Nobody Does It Better" a colossal hit. Simon's single charted on August 27 and climbed all the way to number 2 on the American charts, remaining there for three weeks beginning October 22, 1977. *Billboard* described the song as "the perfect example of a collaboration between a top-of-the-charts artist, producer and writing team." The song also became the first Bond tune to make it to number 1 on the Adult Contemporary chart; that occurred on September 10 and it remained there seven weeks. In the U.K. it charted even earlier, on August 6, and reached number 7. The album also charted August 27 in the States and reached number 40, which, apart from the McCartney hit-fueled *Live and Let Die*, was the best showing for a Bond soundtrack in a decade.

"Nobody Does It Better Than Bond!" even became the new tag line in newspaper advertising a few weeks into the film's summer run, the first time a Bond song title turned out to have value in a larger promotional sense. Then,

expanded from the 1½ minutes of the film cue). Dark, suspenseful strings and brass accompany the departure of two of the subs from the *Liparus* (1 hour, 32 minutes). The "Bond '77" theme returns again (1 hour, 35 minutes) when Bond frees one of the sub crews and the battle begins with Stromberg's men. The battle itself is rife with gunfire and explosions and is unscored.

Hamlisch plays the most complete version of the Bond theme when Bond disables the ship's camera system (1 hour, 43 minutes) and later reprises it for Bond's waterbike ride to Atlantis, with added sassy saxophone. The music for the submarine departure returns (1 hour, 46 minutes) as the two subs launch nuclear missiles at each other. The surviving sub escapes, and the *Liparus* sinks, to more grim and powerful music (1 hour, 50 minutes).

Bond's final battle with Jaws and his rescue of Anya while Atlantis sinks go unscored.

Hamlisch gets in a final musical joke, adding a male choir belting a Broadway-style "Nobody Does It Better" (2 hours, 3 minutes) before reprising Carly Simon's vocal over the end titles.

come Academy Awards campaign time, United Artists took the unprecedented step of placing a giant two-page trade ad—featuring photos of Hamlisch, Sager and Simon—touting "the massive global hit record from *The Spy Who Loved Me*." It followed up with a series of additional ads that were more obviously aimed at Oscar voters. These used illustrator Bob Peak's key art depicting Moore and Bach and, this time, even quoted the critics raving about Hamlisch and Simon. The result was a pair of music nominations: not only was "Nobody Does It Better" nominated for Best Song but—for the first and only time in the 50-year history of Bond music—the film's composer was nominated for Best Original Score.

Equally astounding, the song was nominated for Song of the Year at the Grammys, Hamlisch received two more Grammy nominations (for "Bond '77" as Best Instrumental Composition and for Best Album of Original Score Written for a Motion Picture or TV Special), and Simon was nominated for Best Pop Vocal Performance, Female.

Hamlisch performed at the Academy Awards ceremony on March 28, 1978—but not his Bond song. Instead, the producers hired Aretha Franklin to do a soulful rendition of "Nobody Does It Better," unfortunately as part of a five-minute production number while, one writer complained, "some dancers fiddled around with Hula Hoops." *Variety*, in different reviews, referred to "the smash choreography of 'Nobody Does It Better'" and to "the respectful yelp from the audience" at the end of the number. (For Franklin, it was an ironic postscript to the talk of possibly engaging her to sing "You Only Live Twice" in 1967, which didn't get far.) Hamlisch's performance was, instead, of a new song, "Come Light the Candles," which Sammy Davis, Jr., sang during the "in memoriam" necrology segment. The composer lost in both categories: in Best Song, to "You Light Up My Life," which had spent longer at the top of the charts, and in Original Score, to John Williams for the probably unbeatable *Star Wars*.

Hamlisch remained proud of his work, yet was mystified and disappointed by something else in his Bond experience: "The fact that I was never asked to do another Bond film escapes me. I don't know what more you can do: you can deliver a score. You can deliver an Oscar-nominated song. You can deliver a number-two record, and it still ain't good enough."

". . . that moonlight trail that leads to your side . . ."

Moonraker

John Barry wasn't the only tax exile among the Bond family. After making *The Spy Who Loved Me*, Roger Moore joined Sean Connery, Michael Caine and other leading British actors who didn't want to give the British government 83 percent of their earnings and left the country.

Cubby Broccoli was affected, too. As *The Hollywood Reporter* pointed out after *Spy* opened in 1977: "Broccoli has given up his 25-year residency in London since most of the principals he works with on the Bond films can no longer enter the country for tax reasons. Great Britain stands to lose a substantial amount on each Bond picture as a result." All of this, plus director Lewis Gilbert having a home in France, contributed to the decision to make the next Bond film in Paris.

The original plan was to make *For Your Eyes Only*, but moviegoers' late-1970s fascination with space subjects like *Star Wars* and *Close Encounters of the Third Kind* made *Moonraker*, the sole remaining unused title among Fleming's 11 original Bond novels, a natural. And, as the movie plots had become increasingly outlandish and the stakes ever higher, the idea of sending 007 into space seemed irresistible. So, to help finance the anticipated $30 million cost, Eon joined forces with Les Productions Artistes Associés, making *Moonraker* a British-French co-production, with the bulk of the film to be shot on Paris locations and soundstages and with postproduction done there as well.

This made it possible not only for Moore to continue as Bond but for Barry to resume his role as 007's musical director. Unfortunately, the story of *Moonraker*'s music is one of great plans that crashed and burned, one after another; yet despite endless setbacks and a last-minute dash for a new lyric and singer, it is a score that ranks among the most elegant of all the Bonds.

Barry had visited space before, notably in *You Only Live Twice* (with Blofeld's spacecraft-swallowing ship) and *Diamonds Are Forever* (with Blofeld's lethal, gem-studded satellite), and more recently in the Italian-produced science-fiction film *Starcrash*, which got a limited U.S. release in early 1979.

Fleming's original *Moonraker* plot (destroying London with a nuclear missile) was now too tame, so the film borrowed the name of the villain (Hugo Drax) and jettisoned the rest. In the film, Drax (Michael Lonsdale) plans to destroy all human life and repopulate the globe with a new "master race" from his hidden space-station base. Moonraker is the name of the space shuttle he

Roger Moore and Lois Chiles as Bond and Holly Goodhead, weightless in space

is building; a scientist named Holly Goodhead (Lois Chiles) becomes Bond's partner in thwarting Drax's mad scheme.

Barry's original idea was to write an eight-movement symphonic work and record it with the prestigious Orchestre de Paris while production was still under way. "We know the nature of all the Bond stuff," he told an interviewer in late 1978. "Why don't I use that time in front to make it a more substantial and more important part of the picture?"

He had done this once before, in 1966, with excellent results. British director Bryan Forbes commissioned him to write music for *The Whisperers*, based entirely on the script; after the film was completed, Barry tailored the material into a final score. "By doing it this way, we get all the music that's in the movie plus a little more—but it's in forms that are far more attractive to listen to," Barry said. "We'll have the score finished by the time they finish shooting the movie." He had hoped to turn it into a two-LP set à la the colossally successful *Star Wars* album; Broccoli agreed, Barry said, and was going to talk it over with United Artists.

It was an ambitious, brilliant concept. It went nowhere.

In the meantime, Broccoli's long friendship with Frank Sinatra—which had, six films earlier, led to Frank's daughter Nancy singing "You Only Live Twice"—finally produced an agreement to sing a Bond title song. While production was under way in France, Venice and Rio de Janeiro, Barry began working on the melody. He recorded a demo of the tune, with just a handful of Los Angeles musicians, on January 30, and gave the song to his lyricist of choice, Paul Williams.

Williams was one of Hollywood's top singer-songwriters, having penned several hits including "We've Only Just Begun" for the Carpenters, "Just an Old-Fashioned Love Song" for Three Dog Night and "You and Me Against the World" for Helen Reddy. He won a 1976 Academy Award for co-writing "Evergreen" with Barbra Streisand for *A Star Is Born* (and would go on to write "The Rainbow Connection" and other songs for *The Muppet Movie*, which, like *Moonraker*, would have a summer 1979 release).

Four years earlier, Williams had written a beautiful lyric to Barry's gentle theme for *The Day of the Locust*. "The melody had such an intense loneliness to it that I decided to call it 'Lonely Hearts,' an homage to Nathanael West's other brilliant novel," Williams recalled. Barry called him again for *Moonraker* and Williams wrote the lyrics—as usual, without benefit of script or footage—with Sinatra in mind. (Williams had penned the lyrics to "Dream Away," a John Williams song from *The Man Who Loved Cat Dancing*, which Sinatra sang on his *Ol' Blue Eyes Is Back* album in 1973.) The lyrics, as recalled by Williams many years later:

Moonraker
lift up our dreams
passion and starlight are insep'rable teams. . . .

Original *Moonraker* lyricist Paul
Williams

with later lines (as remembered by Williams) including:

> carry us high
> and with care
> dreams gave the night its worth
> falling in love seldom leads down to earth. . . .

and:

> we'll fly like time
> in the hands of friends
> change spring's mind so she never ends
> Moonraker
> make her mine.

In late February, as he was preparing to fly to France, Barry told an interviewer that *Moonraker* "will have about an hour and a quarter of music . . .
more music in this Bond film than the others, because it's such a big picture."
And he planned "a larger, more symphonic style in terms of orchestration."

Most of the score was written in Paris. Barry spent all of March writing and
began recording in early April. Williams recalled writing the lyric while he
was in London and Paris during this period. "I flew into Paris," Williams
recalled, "and John's [recording] was magnificent. Live strings, the whole ball

of wax. I returned to the States with cassette in hand to play for the man himself."

Williams met with Sinatra and his longtime aide "Sarge" Weiss at Sinatra's office on the old General Services lot in Hollywood. "The amazing thing is, there was nothing there to play the demo on," Williams recalled. "Sarge finally came up with a rusty old portable radio with a cassette player, mono, salty from the beach. And that's what Frank heard the song on. And he loved it. 'Marvelous, Mr. Paulie, marvelous.' This from Music Royalty to me, and I was thrilled," Williams said.

Sinatra opened a briefcase, which contained his datebook (and a .38, Williams noted), and they discussed possible dates for recording. "I left his office walking on air. We were all delighted. Then Frank was out. I don't know what happened but, I was told at the time, Cubby and Frank had a big fight and he was history."

No one remembers for certain why Sinatra ultimately declined to sing "Moonraker." It may be that he had second thoughts, or that his ambitious *Trilogy* album was already in preparation and he preferred to concentrate on that. The story of a falling-out between Sinatra and Broccoli may be apocryphal, because Frank and Barbara Sinatra were all smiles at the New York premiere of *Moonraker* on June 28.

In the meantime, Barry spent a week at Studio Davout recording the *Moonraker* score with an approximately 80-piece orchestra and small choir. Dan Wallin, who was Barry's regular recording engineer from 1975 to 1986, accompanied Barry to Paris to supervise the recording. He recalled: "It was an old movie theater. The room sounded quite good, but the underground [train] ran right underneath it, and every time it ran through, it would vibrate and you'd have to do another take."

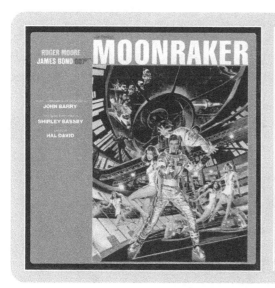

Barry's early guess of about 75 minutes of music in Moonraker turned out to be a substantial overestimate. The film contains just under 50 minutes of music, and less than 44 is actually Barry's own. And Barry's complaints about how his music was used and heard were well founded, with several cues needlessly truncated or dialed out for no good dramatic reason.

Moonraker was the first Bond to be treated to Barry's increasingly sedate symphonic sound, which would be welcomed in such upcoming films as *Somewhere in Time* and *Raise the Titanic* (both 1980) and win him Oscars for *Out of Africa* (1985) and *Dances with Wolves* (1990).

The pre-title sequence is highlighted by a midair hijacking of a space shuttle and the film's first

(left to right) John Barry, Laurie Barry and Dan Wallin in Paris for the *Moonraker* recording sessions

substantive use of the "Bond Theme" when 007 is pushed out of a jet (about 4 minutes into the film), must wrestle another man's parachute away from him while both are in freefall and then fight Jaws as well. (Neither this nor the subsequent use of the "Bond Theme" is represented on the soundtrack album, which is the only Bond soundtrack to omit the theme entirely.)

The title song—set against silhouetted naked women, presumably weightless, in space—is a departure from recent Bond songs in that it is the film's love theme, an elegant, graceful tune with a hint of mystery and melancholy in its lyrics. Bond's arrival at Drax's French-style chateau gets a regal fanfare (13 minutes), and Drax himself is introduced playing Chopin at the piano (Prelude, op. 28 no. 15).

Curiously, despite an album track entitled "Miss Goodhead Meets Bond," there is no music for the first meeting of the two. Most of Bond's centrifuge ride is unscored; only when he disables the spinning machine (at 23 minutes) does Barry offer a touch of musical relief. "Moonraker" returns in a warm string arrangement as Bond romances helicopter pilot Corinne (25 minutes, called "You Presume a Great Deal, Mr. Bond" on the film's official cue sheet) and says goodbye to her (27 minutes, "18 Carat"). These two cues are combined on the soundtrack album as "Miss Goodhead Meets Bond."

The first of several musical jokes occurs (30 minutes) when the pheasant-hunting Drax directs a bugler to play, and it's the first three notes of "Also sprach Zarathustra" (a reference to its use in *2001:*

Wallin, although technically the recording engineer, faced the same problem that Phil Ramone had in London on *On Her Majesty's Secret Service*: as an American, he couldn't touch the console because of union rules. He could only advise the French engineer, which inevitably led to conflict. "I practically moved his hands on the faders, and I finally got it to what you heard in the end. But by the time we got all through it was not a lovefest."

And, Wallin recalled, the musicians were French with the exception of the rhythm section, which came over from England. "It's a good score," Wallin said. "I don't think there's ever been anybody better at spotting a movie—putting the right music in the right place—or at writing a melody, than John Barry. John was absolutely a master of that. His scores were always emotional."

Barry, then newly married to his fourth wife Laurie, enjoyed the Paris night life with Wallin and his wife Gay Goodwin. Broccoli was there too, Wallin remembered: "Cubby was around a lot. He pretty much gave John his head. You couldn't tell John to do much of anything, but what he did was usually right, and who could argue with that?"

As Barry could not return to England, it was Wallin who personally ferried the tapes to London and did some music remixing at Anvil Studios in Denham. Barry, meanwhile, returned to Los Angeles to record the title song. With Sinatra out of the picture, veteran vocalist Johnny Mathis became a surprising and offbeat second choice. Mathis's biggest hits were from two decades earlier ("Chances Are," "The Twelfth of Never"), although he had reached number 1 again in early 1978 with a duet with Deniece Williams, "Too Much, Too Little, Too Late."

Paul Williams recalled: "I was asked to change the lyric. Crafted for Sinatra, it 'no longer worked' or something," he said. Williams refused, on the grounds that "when Sinatra likes a lyric, it's finished. That was the last time I

A Space Odyssey). Drax upbraids Corinne, who runs into the woods pursued by Drax's vicious dogs (32 minutes) to an unsettling, building piece (called "Corrine Put Down" on the album), although director Gilbert replaces the last 15 seconds with church bells pealing.

In Venice, Bond races through the canals in a high-powered gondola to another fast-paced "Bond Theme" (38 minutes) with a postscript of the "Tritsch-Tratsch Polka" of Johann Strauss, Jr., supposedly being played by the on-screen street orchestra while Bond drives his gondola-turned-hovercraft through St. Mark's Square. Yet another musical joke is the use of John Williams's famous five-note theme from *Close Encounters of the Third Kind* as the code to enter Drax's secret laboratory.

The lab itself gets an ominous treatment (43 minutes) as Bond witnesses the death of two scientists from the spilled nerve gas (called "Rat Lab" on the cue sheet, "Bond Smells a Rat" on the LP).

Bond's fight with Drax's martial-arts expert Chang is unscored, but its aftermath, as Chang falls from an upper story into the middle of a cafe orchestra accompanying a singer performing Leoncavallo's "Vesti la giubba" (48 minutes), is another light moment with musical punctuation. "Moonraker" as string-based love theme returns when Bond and Holly kiss (51 minutes, "It Could Have Its Compensations") but then resurfaces in an attractive arrangement with Latin rhythms and female choir when Bond flies into Brazil (56 minutes, "Bond Arrives in Rio" on the album).

heard from John." He later regretted his decision. "My response should have been, 'of course, let's discuss how we can make this better . . . find something for the highest good of all concerned.' I was proud of the work, still am, but it's one of two instances where I dug in when I should have been flexible. It's a collaborative art form and I think I've become a much more civil and considerate collaborator," Williams said.

Mathis recorded the song in Los Angeles, with Barry conducting. Williams was unaware of the Mathis date, and it is not clear whether there were changes made to his lyric, because the vocal was shelved almost immediately. "The following day," Barry later confessed, "we decided this was not working for us, through no fault of his. It was just one of those things. Paul is a fantastic songwriter; Johnny Mathis can sing the hell out of a ballad. It just didn't work."

Twenty-year-old Kate Bush was next in line. Perhaps Britain's hottest young singer at the time, she might have been an ideal choice, having placed three singles in England's top 20 (including the chart-topping "Wuthering Heights") in the previous 15 months, although she had yet to break through in America. Her label, EMI, told the press Bush turned down the offer because she was "too busy." At this point, according to press accounts, the Williams lyric was still in the mix; but time was getting perilously short, with only a month before the film's premiere, and still no recorded title song.

And then a miracle happened. Barry ran into an old friend in the Polo Lounge of the Beverly Hills Hotel. "I was having lunch and who should walk in but Shirley Bassey," he later reminisced. "I didn't even know she was in town. And I said, 'Oh my God, do you want to do another Bond song?' I got Cubby Broccoli on the phone and we were in a studio within a week. It was virtually the same arrangement, everything the same."

Except for the words. Paul Williams's lyrics were discarded when Hal David, Barry's collaborator on *On Her Majesty's Secret Service*, agreed to write

Music recorded on location during Rio's Carnival is heard during Jaws's attack on Manuela (1 hour), although Barry contributes his own "Mardi Gras" music (1 hour, 3 minutes) for a colorfully dressed, on-screen street band. Jaws attacks Bond and Holly atop a Rio cable car (1 hour, 7 minutes) to classic brass-driven Barry action music—only to have the tension completely dissipated by Tchaikovsky's *Romeo and Juliet* ballet music, used to underscore the "romantic" first meeting of Jaws and diminutive Dolly (1 hour, 10 minutes). Yet another musical joke, which one imagines must have been forced on Barry, is the use of Elmer Bernstein's *The Magnificent Seven* as Bond, on horseback, visits M and Q in a Brazilian monastery (1 hour, 13 minutes).

Bond's sleek, high-powered boat is attacked in the Amazon jungle and, though there is no music at first, Barry returned to an old classic, "007," for Bond's escape from multiple pursuers (1 hour, 18 minutes); this arrangement was a bit more sedate and is dialed in and out of the sequence. The full version was on the album as "Boat Chase"; nearly half a minute was dropped from the film.

The first of three highlights from the film's final third occurs when Bond follows a mysterious blonde in a flowing white dress to a ruined pyramid in the jungle (1 hour, 20 minutes), which turns out to be Drax's space base; called "Bond Lured to Pyramid" on the album, it's a warm, seductive, two-minute piece for orchestra and female choir. Moments later, however, Bond is dragged underwater by a mur-

a new lyric in a hurry. Responding to a rather desperate call from Barry ("you've got to come out right away"), David flew from New York on a Friday and they met on Saturday. Unfortunately, the only recording Barry had to play for David was the existing Mathis vocal with the Williams lyric, which David understandably did not want to hear. (He also was never told the identity of his predecessor.)

"John really couldn't play piano to any extent," David recalled. "He could get chords, and a melody, but not together and not in time. He tried to play it, but I think he explained it to me in terms of 'and this is repeated. . . .' Anyway, I'm pretty musical myself, and I was able to get the whole melody. I wrote the lyric over the weekend, because they were going to record on Monday or Tuesday."

David never saw a script, saw no footage, didn't read the novel, and confessed that he had no idea what a "moonraker" was. "It's kind of mystic," he said of the song, "and probably because I didn't see the movie, I couldn't be more specific." The next day ("I think it was a Sunday") Broccoli met Barry and David at Barry's rented home at 912 North Roxbury Drive (a house once occupied by Rita Hayworth and Orson Welles). "He tried to play it, and I tried to sing it," David said with a laugh. "Cubby seemed to like it. He was very enthusiastic. I guess he didn't have much choice. There were musicians waiting the next day."

Barry conducted Bassey and a 57-piece orchestra on May 14 at the Warner Bros. scoring stage, with Wallin once again engineering. Hal David's "Moonraker," not unlike Paul Williams's, was a love song filled with mystery ("I've seen your smile in a thousand dreams . . ."). For the end-title version, however, Bassey sang a more upbeat arrangement with a disco beat, a concession to the commercial market (as Barry had adopted for Donna Summer in *The Deep* in 1977).

derous python to more action music (1 hour, 23 minutes).

Bond and Holly pilot Moonraker 6 into orbit (1 hour, 32 minutes) to one of Barry's longest and most awe-inspiring cues in any of the Bond films—soaringly beautiful, stately and mysterious, military and dramatic—as Drax's hitherto-secret space station is unveiled. Barry adds a full choir to his orchestra for "Flight into Space"; although written as one long 6½ minute cue, director Gilbert unfortunately dialed out about 45 seconds and split it into two pieces.

Bond throws the station into chaos when its artificial gravity is lost (1 hour, 49 minutes, "Emergency Stop"), just before the American forces engage Drax's astronauts in battle around the station

(1 hour, 50 minutes); Barry draws on "Flight into Space." Again, this piece was conceived as one cue of nearly three minutes but is dialed in and out in the film. "Space Laser Battle" (misspelled as "Lazer Battle" on the album jacket) is a grim, stately piece that proceeds slowly, just as the weightless astronauts do in space; orchestra is again accompanied by choir and just a bit of synthesizer (unlike Barry's next score, for Disney's *The Black Hole* later in 1979, which would feature far more synth).

Barry offers the "Moonraker" love theme for the reunited Jaws and Dolly (1 hour, 57 minutes). Shirley Bassey sings it again over the end titles (2 hours, 3 minutes), this time with a disco beat, as Bond and Holly go "around the world" one last time.

Bassey admitted, years later, that John "wanted me to do this song to get him out of trouble. It was not really my song, it was Johnny's song, you know [referring to Mathis]. But I did it for John Barry, my mate, to help him out." Wallin remembered recording Bassey: "She was a great singer. Her dynamic range was unbelievable. I had to stay on my toes for that one."

Bassey attended the New York premiere on June 28, 1979 (with Sinatra, although there is no record of whether the two spoke about title songs and what might have been). Both song and score were noticed by some critics. *The New Yorker* was the biggest surprise, citing "its torchy opening song belted out by Shirley Bassey ('I search for love . . . where are you? . . . take my unfinished life and make it complete") and its lavish John Barry score." *The Hollywood Reporter* referred to "John Barry's effective score," and the *Los Angeles Times* cited "the propulsive music." *Time* magazine disapproved: "The title song, the important kickoff for Bond movies, is no match for 'Nobody Does It Better,' the Carly Simon dazzler of *Spy*."

Billboard chose Bassey's song as its "top single pick" among Adult Contemporary releases, and the score album among its "recommended LPs": "Shirley Bassey provides a sensuous main title—one of the best for an 007 movie—and Barry's score conjures up jarring and soothing counterpoint; lots of dramatic elements here." Unfortunately, the song failed to chart on either side of the Atlantic, although the album briefly made *Billboard*'s album chart (August 18, reaching number 159).

Barry was unhappy with how his music was treated in the film and made no secret of his displeasure, blaming director Gilbert for failing to understand modern technological advances in mixing music, dialogue and sound effects (known in film parlance as the "dub"). In early July, he told a reporter: "I'm very disappointed with the dub of Moonraker. It was done in London where I couldn't be in attendance. For some odd reason, Lewis Gilbert decided to play it in monaural. And if you compare the dub of the picture with the soundtrack album and match the quality of the album against that of the film, there's at least a 50 percent differential in terms of impact. When this occurs, one feels almost violated, as if you've been robbed. Personally, I believe Lewis Gilbert's ears were out to lunch when he made that dub. I think a director should spend a few days familiarizing himself with what Dolby offers and how best to employ these new balances and perspectives in order to get the maximum effect instead of simply going in cold with a traditional mind.

"I think the cinema is the concert hall of the future. I mean, when you think about it—writing, say, an hour's worth of music for a Bond film, the audience you're hitting within a month's time is phenomenal. Nobody's ever had that kind of audience before."

13

For Your Eyes Only

After four increasingly outlandish, jokey adventures with Roger Moore, Broccoli and company decided to take a more grounded, serious approach with the next film, *For Your Eyes Only*. Moore would continue as Bond, but longtime editor and second-unit director John Glen would graduate to the director's chair while veteran screenwriter Richard Maibaum and executive producer Michael Wilson would return to original Ian Fleming material (drawing on the short stories "For Your Eyes Only" and "Risico") for their screenplay.

But John Barry was forced to skip *For Your Eyes Only*. Not only could he not go back to England, where postproduction would return for this film, but he had a full schedule of projects that would take him through late 1980 and early 1981 (including *Inside Moves* for director Richard Donner, *Body Heat* for director Lawrence Kasdan and the beginnings of work on his long-planned Broadway musical *The Little Prince and the Aviator*).

So he recommended American composer Bill Conti, whose music for *Rocky* had not only garnered an Academy Award nomination but helped to propel the underdog-boxer movie to box-office heights in 1976. "My agent called me and said, 'Cubby Broccoli would like to have lunch with you on Friday," Conti recalled, "and I said, 'Fine.' He hung up, called me back, and said, 'Oh, by the way, Cubby's in London.' So in true Hollywood style, the limo came, I flew to London to meet Cubby and John Glen and all the people at

Bill Conti conducting the James Bond tribute at the Academy Awards on March 29, 1982

Pinewood, spent the night at the Dorchester Hotel and then came home the next day."

Conti had a proven ability to write a hit song ("Gonna Fly Now" from *Rocky* had gone to number 1) as well as a muscular, energetic score—a necessity for a Bond composer. The lunch took place just before Christmas 1980. Conti was announced as James Bond's new composer in mid-February, and on March 20, 1981, he flew into London to begin two months' work on *For Your Eyes Only*.

The first order of business was to come up with a title tune. "Before you think about the movie, you have to think about the song," Conti said in 1981. And that meant thinking about the artist. "I wanted Barbra Streisand to write the lyrics, and Donna Summer to sing it," he admitted many years later. "I thought it was a clever idea. I actually talked to Barbra, who was very busy doing *Yentl*. The last person I had in mind was the one United Artists suggested to me, which was Sheena Easton."

Easton, then 21, was a Scottish singer whose meteoric rise had already included three top-10 hits in the U.K., including "Modern Girl" and "9 to 5," the latter of which (retitled "Morning Train") reached number 1 in the United States while Conti was in England working on the Bond film. Conti heard her album and was not convinced that her "poppy" sound, as he put it, was right for a Bond film. But he called her producer, Christopher Neil, and he suggested a meeting.

Easton visited Conti at his London apartment and he quickly decided "she could really sing." Michael (Mick) Leeson was suggested as a lyricist with whom Easton was comfortable, and work began on a possible title song. Their original song used the phrase "for your eyes only" in the chorus but not in the verse. The song began "You can hide your fear / hide your joy and grief / you can hide suspicion and suspend belief . . ." and the chorus added, "for your eyes only could ever see / all of the secrets that once eluded me. . . ."

Conti had a meeting scheduled with Broccoli to audition the song and chose to meet title designer Maurice Binder for lunch beforehand at Pinewood. Binder expressed the hope that Conti's song would open with the phrase so that it could coincide with the appearance of that title on the screen. (In fact, of the 1970s Bonds, the only time the two didn't coincide was in *The Spy Who Loved Me*.)

"I canceled the meeting with Cubby," Conti remembered. "I called Mick, he came over to the house, and I said, 'Listen, this tune begins with "for your eyes only." I don't care what you say after that.'" So a second "For Your Eyes Only" song, with some musical similarities but an entirely new lyric, was written. Easton sang demos of both songs, which eventually began to circulate among Bond buffs, but the second tune was clearly superior. (Even the final version underwent revision, discarding early lyrics including "I'd never, ever lose control unless I wanted to / I'm not afraid to play with fire for you. . . .")

Binder took a greater than usual interest in the five-foot-one-inch-tall Easton. "When he saw Sheena, man, did he fall in love," Conti said with a smile. "She's a slight little girl and he was a short little man. I saw a gleam in his eye. All of a sudden this girl had to be in [the titles]. It was his idea to include her. It wasn't a hustle from her people."

So, months before the debut of MTV and wide public awareness of the growing visual art form of the "music video," Binder decided to incorporate Easton's image into his title sequence—the first and only time the singer of a Bond song is actually seen performing it during the opening titles. The final version of the song was finished and produced on April 21, with Conti himself playing the piano, and Binder photographed Easton lip-syncing to the completed track on April 24 on Pinewood's Stage C.

"Some of the greatest singers had done the Bond themes," Easton later reflected, "and it was always something that you think, oh wow, it's a great honor to be asked. So it was really exciting. It turned out to be a great song." Producer Neil, concerned about Easton's state of mind during the recording process, refused to allow Broccoli or other Bond executives into the recording session. Easton recalled Binder as "wacky [but] really creative," and that shooting the title sequence was trying because although she was "supposed to be perfectly relaxed and sexy and naked and underwater," she was actually

Sheena Easton working with title designer Maurice Binder during the main-title shoot

Bond (Roger Moore) climbs to a mountaintop monastery in *For Your Eyes Only*

"wrapped in a towel and clamped at the back of the neck" during parts of the shoot.

Broccoli encouraged Conti to bring his family to England for the two months it would take to complete the score. "I can't say enough about Cubby Broccoli and the entire production team," Conti said later. "I have a wife and two daughters, and we were just treated royally. No one was nervous, everyone was wonderful, we had a great time, and my girls got to see so much."

The composer's assignment would be to score the most serious Bond adventure in more than a decade: few quips, little sex and a more credible plot. This time Bond joins forces with the grieving daughter (Carole Bouquet) of murdered archaeologists to try to recover a British defense system before a scheming millionaire (Julian Glover) obtains it for likely sale to the Soviets.

Along the way he meets a helpful Greek smuggler (Topol) and a troublesome American skater (Lynn-Holly Johnson).

Conti "spotted" the film (that is, decided where each piece of music would be placed and what its function was) with Broccoli and Glen. "A little apologetically, they said, 'When James goes into action, we've got to play his tune.' And I, as a James Bond fan, said, 'Of course! Naturally.' I couldn't think of using anything but that." Exactly how he would apply the "Bond Theme" was not discussed, Conti said; "they hire people and don't tell them exactly what to do." Conti's bold, brassy style would be welcome.

Reflecting the times, Conti's orchestral score was augmented by synthesizers, which had been making inroads in movie music (notably by European pop artists Giorgio Moroder, in *Midnight Express*, and Vangelis, in the soon-to-be-released *Chariots of Fire*). "The feeling from the 1970s on was, let's include some of the newest synthetic stuff," Conti explained. "You wanted to be the guy who brought it to the public first."

The synthesizers were a contemporary touch that kept Bond's music up-to-date. But one musical experiment failed, Conti recalled: "There is a sequence when James is in the Citroën, going through the olive groves. And at one point we—meaning both John Glen and Cubby Broccoli—thought that it could be a little bit country, just for fun. Then when I recorded it, the three of us looked at each other and said, 'Oh, no, this is not something that James Bond would be involved in, a little country-western music.' So I rewrote the scene. It didn't work, and we knew it immediately."

The ski chase scenes seemed to Conti, "at the time of the writing, endless, but you have to keep the interest up and realize that the film editor is trying to give you shots that are exciting. The composer tries to make a piece of music that makes sense and follows the movie. In all the twisting and turning that the film does, he's trying to make it comprehensible. You want it to make

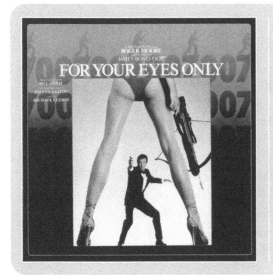

SCORE HIGHLIGHTS

Several factors may have contributed to Bill Conti having to write more music than usual for a Bond film, including the more serious tone than in previous films, along with the number of underwater sequences and their lack of dialogue. Interestingly, for all the attention given to the song "For Your Eyes Only," the tune itself appears only four times in the score (aside from the Sheena Easton vocals under the main- and end-title sequences). What does appear frequently is Conti's two-note intro to the theme, which helps to link parts of the score to the title song and thus give a sense of musical consistency.

Conti opens, naturally, with the "Bond Theme" under the gun-barrel logo, although he uses the brass to play the melody instead of a guitar or strings as in all previous Bond films. That two-note

sense with the movie, and make sense as a piece of music, which is kind of tricky."

At nearly 69 minutes of score, *For Your Eyes Only* contained more music than any Bond since *On Her Majesty's Secret Service*. Conti recorded even more: "Seventy-five minutes of incidental music," he said at the time. "That's not as incidental as you think. Somebody's got to write all that." And with only about six weeks to compose, he called on an old colleague, English composer-arranger Peter Myers, to orchestrate (Myers spent much of the 1980s scoring episodes of television's *Dynasty* and *Falcon Crest*, both of which featured Conti themes). "I prepare a four-to-six-line sketch," Conti explained, referring to the basic musical material he created for each cue. "Pete was invaluable. Someone has to do the laborious task of putting it all down on the big page for the copyist," who then prepares individual parts for each musician to read and play.

Myers recalled arriving in London and "screening five or six of Broccoli's favorite Bond movies" to get a sense of what might be required musically. He told Conti that he thought they would need "rock and roll timpani," as he put it, so he asked the contractor for an "all-world timpani player" who could handle contemporary percussion rhythms.

Conti also put family and friends to work: Early in the film, a piece of rock music was needed for a scene at a Spanish hacienda, and he enlisted his wife Shelby and family friend Chris West (son of author Morris West, who wrote *The Shoes of the Fisherman*) to pen lyrics.

Conti recorded the score over five days in early May 1981 and insisted on Bond's usual engineer and studio: John Richards and The Music Centre in Wembley. Richards recalled "working hard for months on end" and hoping for a break, but Conti really wanted John Barry's English engineer for the classic Bond sound. "I had to cancel a vacation," Richards said, "but Bill was a delight to work with. I admired his professionalism."

"Eyes Only" signature appears almost immediately as Bond visits his wife Tracy's grave (whose headstone, notably, contains the phrase "we have all the time in the world," a nice touch). His helicopter ride is unscored until 007 climbs into the pilot's seat, and Conti breaks into a modified "Bond Theme" (5½ minutes into the film) with fun brass and electric guitar as 007 deposits the wheelchair-bound Blofeld into a London chimney. (Conti wrote another half-minute of music that wasn't used in the film; the entire cue found its way onto the LP as the last three-quarters of the track titled "Melina's Revenge." Conti, like Barry, did not title his cues.)

Maurice Binder's main-title sequence (6½ minutes in) is filled with watery images, but it is Sheena Easton's mesmerizing face (and what Binder referred to as her "70mm lips") that keeps us looking and listening to the title song.

The murder of Melina's parents (16 minutes) gets especially dramatic treatment, with a bit of Greek flavor for the Ionian Sea setting; it became the first 34 seconds of the somewhat misleadingly titled track "Melina's Revenge" on the LP. Conti tries a flamenco touch for Bond's arrival in Madrid (19 minutes) in search of Cuban assassin Gonzales, but he shifts gears completely for a lively action cue as Gonzales is killed and Bond escapes from his compound (22 minutes); a pop rhythm section including electric guitar and synthesizer add an ultramodern feel, with the brief addition of Latin percussion for the destruction of Bond's Lotus and a comic car-horn effect for Melina's yellow Citroën. These two

Conti's work was completed by May 27 and he returned to the States. Easton's was just beginning. On June 12 and 13, she took part in the United Artists–orchestrated press junket in New York City, joining Moore, the film's other stars, Broccoli, Wilson and Glen. With the soundtrack on the Liberty label (the first time that UA didn't have the album rights), UA and Liberty joined forces to screen the film for disc jockeys, record retailers, music press and promotional people in 13 cities around the United States. The album hit stores on June 22, just two days before the film's London royal premiere.

Both film and title song were immediate hits. "Bill Conti's musical score is appropriately versatile, sensual when appropriate or spunky when needed," said *The Hollywood Reporter*. "And Maurice Binder's opening titles, always one of the fancier features of the Bond movies, are still terrific," added the *New York Times*. The single charted on July 25 and reached number 4 on the *Billboard* charts, nearly as high as Carly Simon's "Nobody Does It Better" four years earlier. The album charted on the same date and managed to reach number 84.

The story was similar in the U.K.: the single charted June 27 and reached number 8, Easton's best showing since "Modern Girl" a year earlier, although the album (like other recent Bond soundtracks) didn't chart at all. The song was so popular that United Artists defied the earlier "no trade ads" edict by promoting "For Your Eyes Only" with full-page January 1982 trade ads for a possible Best Song Oscar nomination.

But spending 25 weeks on the *Billboard* charts kept the song in people's ears for the rest of the year and just in time for awards season. Easton received two Grammy nominations, for Best Pop Vocal Performance (Female) and Best New Artist, winning the latter award on February 24, 1982. She sang "For Your Eyes Only" on the live television broadcast of the ceremonies.

And then, on March 29, 1982, James Bond received his biggest-ever tribute at the Academy Awards. Not only was "For Your Eyes Only" nominated as

cues are combined as "Gonzales Takes a Drive" on the LP; this was probably a typographical error, as Gonzales is killed after a dive. Between the two is "Make It Last All Night," a sexy rock song heard at Gonzales's pool (20 minutes) that opened side two of the LP.

The car chase continues (25 minutes) with a rhythm-heavy, guitar-and-synth-dominated accompaniment that includes the Bond theme in brass; titled "A Drive in the Country" on the LP, this mad dash through Spanish olive groves is the piece that Conti originally wrote as a country-flavored tune but rewrote without the picking and fiddling. Bond's arrival in Cortina, in the Italian Alps (34 minutes), is greeted with a beautiful new theme for strings, along with the repeated two-note "Eyes Only" motif. The meeting with Kristatos, and Bond's first encoun-

ter with Bibi, is accompanied only by the tinkly piano and bouncy strings of the outdoor loudspeakers.

"For Your Eyes Only" gets a warm reprise for the sleigh ride by Bond and Melina (41 minutes). The eight-minute ski chase sequence is mostly scored, beginning (47 minutes) with some fascinating Ennio Morricone–style piano, strings and percussion suspense; continuing through the ski jump scene with light percussion and echoing piano (both contained on the expanded 2000 CD in the track titled "Ski . . . Shoot . . . Jump"); and concluding (52 minutes), as Bond is pursued by machine-gunning motorcycles down the Cortina slopes, with signature Conti brass, fast-moving string lines and high-pitched synthesizers as good guys and bad careen down the bobsled run at incredible speed (the "Runaway" track on the LP).

Sheena Easton sings "For Your Eyes Only" during the Oscar telecast

Best Original Song, but Broccoli was named the recipient of the Irving G. Thalberg Award (given to a producer whose work reflects a "consistently high quality of motion picture production") and Conti happened to be serving as the program's musical director. So a 007 extravaganza at the Oscars came as no surprise.

Conti opened the show with a movie-theme medley that included the "James Bond Theme," played "Nobody Does It Better" to introduce Roger Moore, and accompanied Broccoli's entrance with "Goldfinger." But it was the performance of "For Your Eyes Only" that wowed the crowd at the Dorothy Chandler Pavilion.

The elaborate four-minute production number was conceived and choreographed by Walter Painter, whose work that year would be Emmy-nominated. It cast Easton, in a shimmering blue and silver dress, as a Bond girl who needed rescuing between verses of the song. Actors playing Dr. No and Blofeld (with stuffed white cat) appeared at the beginning of the number, but it was the presence of Harold Sakata (Oddjob from *Goldfinger*) and Richard Kiel (Jaws in *The Spy Who Loved Me* and *Moonraker*) that gave the number a touch of Bond authenticity. Both managed to get out of the way when the futuristically clad dancers began dashing around amidst laser beams, explosions and other pyrotechnics, while Conti's Oscar orchestra played his variations on the "James Bond Theme." At the end, Bond (played by L.A. dancer Joseph Malone) unzipped his orange jumpsuit to reveal a white dinner jacket and whisked Easton away on a rocket that lifted off the stage. (Malone was a last-minute replacement for another dancer—tall, handsome Blair Farrington, a dance partner of Juliet Prowse—who badly injured a knee in a fall on the set two days before the show. Farrington never danced again and became a producer-director in Las Vegas.)

(SCORE HIGHLIGHTS, CONT.)

The Greek source music for Bond and Melina's Corfu reunion was licensed. A beautiful version of "For Your Eyes Only" (59 minutes) underlines their emotional talk. Nearly six minutes of lounge music (all Conti's) is heard in the casino scenes, but the evening is capped with Bond taking the Countess home (1 hour, 8 minutes in). This leads to one of the score's most sensuous moments for their romantic fireside chat, complete with flugelhorn solo (by London musician Eddie Blair; the album version, "Take Me Home," is nearly a minute longer).

Conti brings the flugelhorn back for a gorgeous arrangement of "For Your Eyes Only" (1 hour, 20 minutes) as Bond joins Melina during her underwater archaeological dig; longtime Bond trumpeter Derek Watkins plays the solo. Bond and Melina take a two-man submarine down, and Conti brings the

"Bond Theme" back in a synth-driven version (1 hour, 23 minutes); it becomes more dramatic as they sight the sunken St. George's ship and settle on the ocean floor. On the LP, this cue is titled "Submarine."

Their search for the ATAC machine (1 hour, 26 minutes), the fight with one of Kristatos's men who also wants it, and the underwater battle of submarines (1 hour, 33 minutes) are all scored with dark, suspenseful and often intense orchestral combinations, including the pairing of high strings and very low piano. The memorable sequence of Bond and Melina being tied together and dragged through the water is unscored.

Traditional Greek instruments, including bouzouki playing the two-note "Eyes Only" motif, spice the Bond-and-Columbo mission to St. Cyril's 15th-century monastery (1 hour, 45 minutes). The religioso

"You had to see the lavish production numbers, such as 'For Your Eyes Only,' live on stage," *Variety*'s Army Archerd reported the next day, "to feel the excitement of the action and the props." Bond managed to become a punchline later in the evening, however, when Bette Midler presented the Best Song award, lampooning all of the nominees with hilarious one-liners: "'For Your Eyes Only' from *For Your Eyes Only* and they weren't kidding, I couldn't watch a single frame."

As the winner—"Arthur's Theme" from *Arthur*, co-written by two ex-Bond songwriters, Burt Bacharach and Carole Bayer Sager—was announced, Conti later recalled, many of the musicians and singers in the pit felt too bad for his loss to look at him. He was trying to cue them to play "Arthur's Theme" as the winners walked to the stage; a four-second delay ensued. "The director's screaming, 'Music!' I said, 'I can't, nobody's looking at me.' So James Bond was nominated and something else won."

touches, including the woodwind lines for the stained-glass interiors, are interspersed with delicate strings-and-harp for Bond's solo climb up the sheer rock face (although much is also left unscored, heightening the tension as Bond nearly plummets to his death). Bond's arrival at the top (1 hour, 53 minutes) is greeted by the return of the Bond-theme bass line, incorporated here and there into another suspense sequence as Columbo, Melina and men ascend to the top. The first and last of these cues were combined into the "St. Cyril's Monastery" track on the LP.

Almost none of the action in the film's finale, including the hand-to-hand combat, arrival of Gen. Gogol and death of Kristatos, is scored. "For Your Eyes Only" returns (2 hours, 3 minutes) for Bond and Melina sharing a romantic moment, with a more military-style variation and some Elgar-esque material for the concluding bit with Margaret Thatcher (which apparently had British audiences rolling in the aisles; called "The P. M. Gets the Bird" on the LP). Easton's "For Your Eyes Only" is reprised over the end titles.

"... hold on tight, let the flight begin ..."

Octopussy

John Barry settled his tax debt (reported to be £134,000, with interest possibly bringing the total closer to £200,000) with Britain's Inland Revenue department in 1983. Just in time, too, because it allowed him to return to England and rejoin the Bond team for *Octopussy*, which was then facing unexpected competition from an old Bond in new clothing: Sean Connery, who had agreed to star in producer Kevin McClory's *Thunderball* remake *Never Say Never Again* the same year.

As usual, it all began with the song. Lyricist Don Black, who had continued to collaborate with Barry (including the troubled stage musical *The Little Prince and the Aviator* in late 1981 and the television musical *Svengali* in early 1982), was off doing *Merlin* on Broadway with Elmer Bernstein and thus was unavailable for *Octopussy*. So Barry tried out a new wordsmith: Tim Rice.

Rice was hardly new to show business: he had already become famous working with composer Andrew Lloyd Webber on such theatrical smashes as *Jesus Christ Superstar* and *Evita*. "It really was a bit out of the blue," Sir Tim Rice recalled many years later. "I was very surprised, to be honest. My first thought was, obviously, great! My second thought was, what's the film called? And when I was told *Octopussy*, I thought, hmmm, not so great."

In fact, Barry confirmed for Rice, *Octopussy* was so problematic as a title that there was no need to even include it in the lyric. So, in late 1982, Barry

Lyricist Tim Rice

suggested that Rice come up with half a dozen potential song titles. "So I gave them six choices," Rice said, "and they chose 'All Time High.'" (Rice could not recall the other five, and has lost the original page that contained them.)

Barry wrote a melody that would incorporate those three syllables. Meanwhile, Rice received a script and visited the Pinewood studios during shooting in mid-December. "The scenes I saw, primarily, were a reconstruction of India, the downtown Indian markets and crowds and everything. And I remember meeting Roger Moore, who I'd met before on occasion."

Rice struggled a bit: "Conventional love songs are the hardest things to write and I remember thinking I wish I had a title like *Diamonds Are Forever*, which is a brilliant lyric by Don. It sets you off on a slightly more original approach to things." But Rice forged ahead, borrowing the phrase "we're two of a kind" from Octopussy's dialogue and adding lyrics like "we'll take on the world and win / so hold on tight, let the flight begin," which appear to refer to the climactic aerial scenes in the film.

As for the singer, 25-year-old Laura Branigan was everyone's first choice. Her high-energy song "Gloria" had hit the top 10 in both America and England in the fall of 1982. Rice recalled discussions with Broccoli about the choice, and in fact the producer was quoted in the British press in January

1983 as saying "we like her very much." Branigan herself said that she hadn't yet heard the song but that, "like everything else connected with 007, it's very mysterious."

"Laura Branigan was a big name at that moment," Barry recalled. "She was very hot at the time, she had a few hit records and a pretty powerful set of pipes," Rice added. But something happened; Branigan dropped out and Rita Coolidge entered the picture. Coolidge's top-10 hits ("Your Love Has Lifted Me Higher and Higher," "We're All Alone") were actually six years earlier, although she had had three others in the top 40 since then; she hadn't had even that much success in the U.K.

Asked about it some years later, Coolidge claimed that Barbara Broccoli, Cubby's daughter (who was billed on the film as "executive assistant") was a fan, and she had played Coolidge records during dinner one evening. Supposedly the elder Broccoli asked, "Who is that? That's the voice I want for the movie." Coolidge flew to London, met Barry and, she said, "had a lovely dinner at his house, but I didn't meet Tim Rice until the next day in the studio." United Artists announced the choice on March 29, 1983; Coolidge would not only record "All Time High" for *Octopussy* but be featured in the very first specifically produced music video from a Bond film.

According to Coolidge, Rice hadn't finished the lyrics when she arrived. "It was a little close, down to the wire," she later recalled. The recording session, she added, "was a bit tense."

Singer Rita Coolidge

Producer Phil Ramone, whose Bond history went back to *Casino Royale* and *On Her Majesty's Secret Service*, returned to produce "All Time High" for his old friend John Barry. Ramone had, in the intervening years, won Grammys producing pop albums for Paul Simon and Billy Joel and had recently produced the song sessions for Barry's *Svengali* (with Jodie Foster as a rock 'n' roll singer). "John and I had been friends all those years. He handpicked who he wanted; that was it," Ramone said. He flew to London, and their collaboration on the Coolidge vocal would result in another chart hit for Barry and Bond. "'All Time High' was an interesting record," Ramone said. "I don't think it went to the top as it should have."

Octopussy's complex plot—only marginally related to the original Ian Fleming novella and a short story, "The Property of a Lady"—involved stolen Fabergé eggs, a renegade Soviet general (Steven Berkoff), an exiled Afghan prince (Louis Jourdan) and a mysterious and wealthy woman named Octopussy (Maud Adams). The settings ranged from a banana-republic airbase to a circus in East Berlin to the colorful and lavish palaces of India.

Parts of the story also take place against a circus backdrop, requiring the odd snare-drum roll and trumpet fanfare, although the more traditional circus music ("Entry of the Gladiators," "Jubilee March," "Circus, Circus, Circus") was simply licensed from music libraries. The only real musical joke in the film occurs when Bond visits India and encounters a snake charmer (Vijay Amritraj) who is playing a tune on his pungi (gourd flute); when he sees Bond, he begins playing the "James Bond Theme" which immediately attracts 007's attention. "That's a charming tune," he says, thus making contact with a fellow agent. (That line, curiously, is not in the revised *Octopussy* script of July 9, 1982. It may have been improvised on location.)

Roger Moore and Maud Adams as Bond and Octopussy

While shooting was wrapping up in late January 1983, Barry was not only sorting out his tax problems with the British government but also attempting to schedule various scoring commitments. In November he had finished recording the music for a Tom Selleck adventure film, *High Road to China*, and had planned to score a family film, *The Golden Seal*, in December 1982 and

(SCORE HIGHLIGHTS, CONT.)

seeking missile's pursuit of Bond's minijet, so there is no score.

The Rita Coolidge vocal of "All Time High" (7½ minutes in) is set against Maurice Binder's cutting-edge laser effects and the usual bouncing naked-women silhouettes. When 009, escaping from knife-throwing circus thugs in East Berlin, is wounded (12 minutes), Barry dramatizes the moment with pounding timpani and urgent lower brass ("009 Gets the Knife," first half of the second band on the LP). A brief, Russian-flavored cue (19 minutes) and a longer, Indian-flavored one (25 minutes), the latter for shots of the Taj Mahal and 007's arrival in Udaipur, would have made delightful additions to the album. (The film's only musical joke, Indian agent Vijay's playing the "Bond Theme" to gain 007's attention, occurs at this point.)

Barry scored Bond and Vijay escaping Kamal Khan's assassin Gobinda, racing through the streets in three-wheeled vehicles (34 minutes, "Gobinda Attacks" on the LP), but only the ominous opening and the "Bond Theme" excerpt wound up in the film; much of it was reprised, however, in the next action sequence (37 minutes), as Bond battles Gobinda amid the hot-coals and sword-swallowing street entertainers. This is the film's main action theme, with the rat-a-tat brass of earlier Bond films, anxious strings and high flutes heightening the sense of danger.

"All Time High" makes its first post-titles appearance in a lightly jazzy source version as Bond meets Magda (42 minutes), and it is heard again in a more romantic vein (43 minutes, "That's My Little Octopussy" on the LP), with a beautiful alto flute

January 1983. Unfortunately, postproduction delays resulted in *Golden Seal* not being ready and thus potentially overlapping with *Octopussy*, which Barry needed to be writing by early March in order to record in mid-April.

Family friends came to the rescue. Barry's American contractor was Nathan Kaproff, and his first cellist was Nathan's brother Armand. Armand's son Dana was an experienced film composer (TV's *Once an Eagle*, Sam Fuller's *The Big Red One*) and agreed to collaborate; Barry would write the main themes and score key scenes, while Kaproff would do the rest (Barry had done this before, with Ken Thorne as his collaborator, on *They Might Be Giants* and *Murphy's War* in 1971). With Kaproff taking on most of *The Golden Seal* (recorded at CTS the last three days of March 1983), Barry was free to jump into *Octopussy*, which was recorded over five days during early April.

With *Never Say Never Again* looming as potentially serious competition, Barry—who had been approached by the filmmakers but turned it down out of loyalty to Broccoli and the original Bond team—made more frequent reference to the "James Bond Theme" as if to reinforce the notion that this 007 was the one, the only, James Bond. But Barry also wrote "All Time High" as the film's love theme and subsidiary themes for Octopussy, the danger and action moments.

Barry's music hints at the Indian locale, especially when Bond first arrives, but only in the subtlest way, without sitars or other Indian-music clichés. "If you dropped authentic music into these locales, they didn't work dramatically," he said later of *Octopussy*, adding that the subtlety was like "adding salt and pepper. All you could really do was keep the Bondian emphasis going, and then just give it a color."

Director John Glen was pleased to have the composer back. "We'd missed him badly," said Glen. "Although we'd had some really fine musicians come in and do our films, somehow John Barry was the originator. He gave some-

solo, as he beds her and she slips out with the Fabergé egg. Barry strikes a misterioso mood for Kamal Khan's boat trip to the Floating Palace (46 minutes, "Arrival at the Island of Octopussy" on the LP); bansuri flute offers a touch of Indian flavor. Barry follows Bond's stealth movements outside Khan's lavish home (53 minutes, "Bond at the Monsoon Palace" on the LP) with dark string suspense and military snare drums for the arrival of Gen. Orlov.

Most of Khan's *Most Dangerous Game*–style hunt of Bond through the Indian jungle is unscored, save for native drumming (not by Barry). Barry reprises his "Octopussy's Island" music for Bond's arrival and our first glimpse of the mysterious woman (1 hour, 7 minutes). Delicate textures underscore Bond and Octopussy's dialogue (1 hour, 13 minutes, "Bond Meets Octopussy" on the LP) and shift into "All Time High" as they argue and then make love.

The action motif dominates the 3½ minute sequence when Kamal's killers attack Bond with a particularly deadly buzzsaw (1 hour, 17 minutes, called "Yo Yo Fight and Death of Vijay"); a brief alto-flute variation on "All Time High" follows when Octopussy thinks Bond has been killed, and then comes another sad passage for the discovery of Vijay's body.

The most menacing music yet accompanies Bond's discovery that an atomic device is aboard a train car bound for West Germany (1 hour, 28 minutes, called "The Chase Bomb Theme" on the LP). He fights one of the red-shirted, knife-throwing circus thugs to Barry's pounding timpani and low

thing to the scenes that I don't think any other composer could possibly do. He shared the same excitement we all did for the Bond movies."

As happened six years earlier with *The Spy Who Loved Me*, the song became part of the advertising campaign, and in the case of *Octopussy* "All Time High" was ballyhooed long before the film itself was released: many film posters trumpeted the film as "James Bond's all time high."

Rita Coolidge attended the London royal premiere on June 6, 1983, although, as the press reported, the biggest cheers were reserved for Diana, Princess of Wales ("Sparkling Diana Outshines the Film Stars," reported the *Daily Express*). As Coolidge later reminisced, "Princess Diana came over to me and whispered, 'I do hope you've been paid.' I remember wondering if it was a British thing, or something about working with James Bond. I still don't know what she meant."

Few reviewers noticed the music. "A title song sung by Rita Coolidge seems, in the manner of 'For Your Eyes Only,' destined for the charts," opined *The Hollywood Reporter*. The *Washington Post* was downright mean, mentioning "the inane vocal version, its silly Tim Rice lyrics sung with deadly lethargy by Rita Coolidge, " although the same reviewer praised "Barry's penchant for inspiring romantic themes."

For the first time in Bond history, there was another outlet for the song, offering a new venue for promotion: a music video, which featured Coolidge lip-syncing to her vocal track (shot at the Royal Pavilion in Brighton, one of the film's locations) and extensive clips from the film. MTV (Music Television) had launched in August 1981, and the all-video cable channel was eager for product. The *Octopussy* video helped to promote the single, which was issued on Coolidge's label, A&M Records (run by Herb Alpert, who had had his own hit with a Bond theme 16 years earlier). The single charted on July 2, 1983,

(SCORE HIGHLIGHTS, CONT.)

brass action music (1 hour, 31 minutes). Bond's gun battle with the Soviet general's troops goes unscored, but when he steals a car and manages to drive it along the train tracks Barry launches into the "Bond Theme" again (1 hour, 35 minutes). More of Barry's "Chase Bomb Theme" accompanies Gen. Gogol's pursuit of the renegade Gen. Orlov (1 hour, 38 minutes) and the latter's death on the tracks.

The amazing Bond-atop-moving-train stuntwork goes unscored. Considerable circus-themed source music (including such traditional favorites as "Over the Waves," "Entry of the Gladiators" and "Dancing Plumes," all licensed) dominates the carnival scenes, as Bond races to reach the location before the bomb detonates. The "Chase Bomb" music returns for 007 saving the day (1 hour, 54 minutes).

Some of Barry's most interesting source music is heard during the scenes where Octopussy and her all-female team prepare to enter Khan's Monsoon Palace (1 hour, 56 minutes); it's Indian-style, with bansuri flute and plenty of ethnic percussion, all based on his mysterious theme for Octopussy's character. Barry underscores Octopussy's confrontation with Khan delicately at first but then applies the action motif throughout the battle between Khan's men and Octopussy's women (1 hour, 58 minutes, "The Palace Fight" on the LP) and liberally incorporates the "Bond Theme" for 007—who arrives with Q in a hot-air balloon—in action both at the Palace and then on horseback.

Again, there is no score for the sound-effects-dominated aerial stuntwork, as Bond and Gobinda

and reached number 36 on Billboard's Hot 100 chart. "All Time High" did even better on Billboard's Adult Contemporary chart, where it hit number 1 on August 6 and stayed there for four weeks. The soundtrack album reached only number 137 on Billboard's album charts and didn't chart at all in the U.K.; the Coolidge single managed to reach number 75 in England.

MGM/UA, which was now handling distribution, took out two full pages in the trade papers in January 1984 to call attention to possible Academy Award–worthy accomplishments in *Octopussy*, including the Barry score and Barry-Rice song. But although the song probably had the best chance, given its popularity during the second half of the year, no Oscar (or Grammy) nominations were forthcoming.

"It's not one of the most exciting Bond songs," Tim Rice conceded 28 years later. "It's just a nice, dreamy ballad. Looking back at it, I think it would have been more interesting had we tried to write a song called 'Octopussy.' It could have been quite clever. One's immediate thought was something rather salacious . . . but, in a funny way, that might have made it a more exciting song. It could even have been in the same tune: Da da da da da da Octo-pussy bum ba bum ba bum. . . ."

battle; only the climax, as Bond and Octopussy escape and Khan's plane crashes, is scored. "All Time High" variations greet the boating 007 and Octopussy (2 hours, 7 minutes) in a brief romantic prelude to Coolidge's vocal under the end titles.

". . . though I know there's danger there, I don't care . . ."

Never Say Never Again

Producer Kevin McClory, who gained control of *Thunderball* after Fleming's 1960 movie-script debacle and who co-produced the 1965 film with Broccoli and Saltzman, owned remake rights to *Thunderball*. In 1976 he persuaded Sean Connery and spy novelist Len Deighton to collaborate on a screenplay that was, for a while, called *Warhead*. It was eventually scrapped, however, when McClory gave the option to producer Jack Schwartzman in 1981. Connery agreed to the terms, which included complete creative control over the project, and would return as 007 in *Never Say Never Again* (a title coined by his wife Micheline, as Connery had long said he would never again do the role).

Just as, in 1966, the "battle of the Bonds" was on with *You Only Live Twice* and *Casino Royale* in production at the same time, it was "dueling Bonds" all over again, this time in 1982 with Moore starring in *Octopussy* and Connery in *Never Say Never Again*. Musically, the *Royale* and *Never* situations were similar: the composer would be contractually barred from using the "James Bond Theme" and would need to find a fresh way to illustrate the action and illuminate the characters.

Plotwise, it was close to *Thunderball*: an older, more seasoned Bond (Connery) is called back into service when SPECTRE, still headed by Blofeld (Max von Sydow), masterminds the theft of American nuclear warheads and holds NATO for ransom. Mad corporate magnate Largo (Klaus Maria Brandauer)

supervises the operation; Bond recruits Largo's lover Domino (Kim Basinger)
for help and tangles with his evil associate Fatima Blush (Barbara Carrera) in
both the Bahamas and the south of France.

No one seems to have given any thought to music during production of the
film, despite the inclusion of an elaborate tango performed by Connery and
Basinger in a Monte Carlo casino. Producer Schwartzman, director Irvin Kershner and star-producer Connery were all involved in the choice of composer
during post-production in the late spring of 1983.

James Horner, then an up-and-coming young American composer who had
already scored the hit films *48 Hrs.* and *Star Trek II: The Wrath of Khan*, was
high on both Schwartzman and Kershner's lists. He was in London for much
of the year, working on such films as *Krull*, *Brainstorm*, *The Dresser* and *Un-
common Valor*. According to Kershner, a schedule conflict precluded him from
doing the Bond film. Schwartzman later claimed that Connery rejected Horner,
although (if true) why is not clear.

One of cinema's leading composers happened to be in London in June
1983. Frenchman Michel Legrand was completing work on *Yentl*, one of his
most complex projects (for which he would win his third Academy Award) in
that it involved nine original songs as well as the dramatic underscore, for the
notoriously demanding producer-director-star Barbra Streisand. He had already won Oscars for writing "The Windmills of Your Mind" for *The Thomas
Crown Affair* and for the score of *Summer of '42*, and he was responsible for
some of the most enduring songs of the 1960s and 1970s, among them "I Will
Wait for You," "What Are You Doing the Rest of Your Life?" and "Pieces of
Dreams." He had also scored *Play Dirty*, the Michael Caine World War II
movie, for ex-Bond producer Harry Saltzman in 1968. But he was better
known for his romantic films; *Ice Station Zebra* was one of his few big-action-
movie credits.

Kershner and Streisand were friends; he had directed her a decade earlier
in *Up the Sandbox*. And since both their films happened to be in postproduction, "We used to meet and have dinner all the time," Kershner recalled. She
suggested Legrand for the job.

Legrand, however, was burned out after a particularly intense year-long
assignment. "I had promised myself that I would take a vacation at the completion of *Yentl*," Legrand said. "I had arrived at the end of a long adventure.
I was completely exhausted." He was mixing *Yentl* at Olympic Studios, his
favorite recording facility, when Connery himself telephoned, asked for his
services and invited him to a screening of the film the next day.

"Sean's warmth and his enthusiasm persuaded me," Legrand said. "And I
told myself, to attach a Bond to my filmography, it's not something to pass up!"
Connery attended the screening with Kershner and Schwartzman but was otherwise absent during the weeks to follow. Something else occurred to Legrand
at the time: "We were connected by the adventure of *Robin and Marian*, where
[director Richard] Lester threw out my score." (Legrand's daring, classically

styled music for the 1976 film, which starred Connery and Audrey Hepburn, was ultimately replaced by a John Barry score.)

"Sean knew it and, for me in a certain manner, it was a way of taking revenge on Lester's film. *Robin and Marian* and *Never Say Never Again* finally deal with the same subject: Can myths age?" It was a fascinating way to look at the new 007 film, which focused on a mature, possibly over-the-hill Bond, just as *Robin and Marian* dealt with the older Robin Hood and Maid Marian, who find each other again after many years.

Legrand wrote the score in Paris during June and July 1983. Well aware of the Barry imprint on the Connery years, Legrand had no intention of revisiting that. "It would have been artificial for me to re-create the Bond sound of the '60s," he said. "The idea of *Never Say Never Again* was to bring a distance, an irony, a second layer of connection to the official series, in relation to Connery's age. Immediately there was a distinction."

Connery's call to Legrand wasn't the only one the actor would make about the music. He also called lyricists Marilyn and Alan Bergman, who, like Legrand, were in London finishing their work on *Yentl* (which would earn them Oscars

(left to right) Alan Bergman, Michel Legrand and Marilyn Bergman in the early 1980s

too). "We had known him for years," Alan Bergman recalled. They had met in Connery's pre-007 days, while working on singer Jo Stafford's television series in London in 1961. Connery asked them to pen the words to the title song, and as longtime collaborators with Legrand they immediately agreed.

"They had a title, the title of the movie," Alan Bergman said. "Usually we don't use [the title of the film], but they wanted a title song. That was a given." The Bergmans added lyrics to Legrand's sensual, jazzy melody, written about Bond from a woman's point of view: "You walk in a room / a woman can feel the heat / One look is a guarantee / nights could be long and sweet. . . ."

Legrand thought of his main theme, especially "the slow version, for piano/ guitar or piano/vibraphone, [as] a little disillusioned, like a portrait of an older Bond."

The composer called the film a series of "luxurious and shimmering adventures, where everything was pulled toward the improbable and the spectacular." He was especially fond of the tango, which appeared in Lorenzo Semple Jr.'s original script ("a tango is being played by a small orchestra . . . music intensifies . . ."). Legrand pointed out that this was the first time a tango had been heard in a Bond film. Connery and Basinger danced to a temporary playback track on the set, Legrand said, "after which I composed 'Tango to Death' to correspond to the movements of the choreography, and to the orchestra on the screen. I would have orchestrated my tango for a small [ensemble], with solo bandoneón, but I was a prisoner of the image."

He also recalled writing the motorcycle chase scene, which included "a theme for big band, with a very fast tempo, curt and agitated, with horn punches that sound like razor blades." He also referred to the "suspense sequences for symphonic orchestra, in the neo-Stravinskian style, which correspond to SPECTRE's universe, with the atomic conspiracy."

Legrand recorded at Olympic Studios during the first week of August 1983. He usually composed and orchestrated all his own music, but in this case, music contractor Nat Peck recalled, he didn't orchestrate everything (occasional collaborator Armand Migiani did some cues). "Maybe he was exhausted after the tremendous effort of the Streisand film," Peck said. "He was just too tired to take on anything with the enthusiasm he usually could generate for any project he was working on. Unfortunately, it seeped through to the higher-ups and they weren't too thrilled with Michel's music."

Legrand conducted the London Symphony Orchestra one day, then freelance orchestras ranging from 88 to 93 players over three more days. "Michel is incredibly quick and English musicians are the fastest sight-readers in the world," engineer Keith Grant said, referring to musicians who can glance at a piece of music they've never seen before and play it from start to finish extremely well.

Actress Talia Shire, who was married to Schwartzman and attended some of the sessions, said: "When you have someone of the caliber of Michel Legrand, he brings an elegant score with something that sounds new, and very appropriate, for our Sean Connery. I thought he did a great job."

Kim Basinger and Sean Connery tango in *Never Say Never Again*

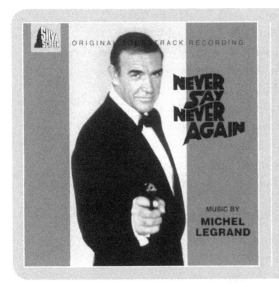

ORIGINAL SOUNDTRACK RECORDING

NEVER SAY NEVER AGAIN

MUSIC BY
MICHEL
LEGRAND

Michel Legrand's score for *Never Say Never Again* was criticized by the filmmakers and Bond fans alike; yet as a fundamentally jazz-based score, it has many fun moments and offers a very different slant on music for 007 even though it was far from what Connery fans were expecting.

Lani Hall's performance of the title song plays incongruously under the opening action sequence, as Bond fights his way through a Latin American jungle to rescue a kidnapped girl (which we soon learn was a training exercise). The opening phrase of the title theme recurs throughout the film, usually in short jazzy cues for Bond (the film's official cue sheet refers to these as "Bond Theme").

Legrand introduces SPECTRE assassin Fatima Blush with a stealthy-sounding string passage (7½

In the weeks after recording was finished, both Schwartzman and Kershner had concerns about what they had heard. "It wasn't the true James Bond score that I had envisioned," Kershner later said. "It just didn't work for me, and of course we couldn't redo the music, so I moved a lot of the music around. Something that was in one scene I moved to another scene." Schwartzman went so far as to cable Legrand in Paris on August 12, stating "there are serious problems with the score" and demanding that he return to London "for a solid period of at least two weeks to rewrite and/or remake the music score."

Legrand returned for one more day of recording, on August 20. In the meantime, questions arose about who would sing the title song. Schwartzman told Legrand in his August 12 cable: "I think we have Bonnie Tyler for the title song." But that didn't last long, because Tyler, whose "Total Eclipse of the Heart" was a number 1 hit that spring in the U.K., turned it down. "I was really, wow, a James Bond theme," she said in 2006. "I was so excited to be a part of this. And then I listened to it and I was really deflated. There wasn't anything you could do with that song. I really didn't like it."

Marilyn and Alan Bergman suggested Lani Hall for the song. Hall had once been part of Brasil '66 (singing "The Look of Love" at the Oscars) but embarked on a solo career in the 1970s; she was married to trumpeter Herb Alpert, another Bond veteran, having turned the *Casino Royale* theme into a 1967 hit. "She's a really great singer," Alan Bergman said, "and it was another way of making it different than what had preceded." Marilyn Bergman liked "the contrast between Lani and Shirley Bassey, who had been associated with these Bond movies."

Alpert produced the song with Hall's old Brasil '66 partner Sergio Mendes. "That was the first time that we had actually worked together since I had left the group in 1971," Hall said. "It was a lot of fun to be in the studio with Herb

---

minutes into the film), although considerably truncated (but it appears in its entirety as "Fatima Blush" on the LP); then it resurfaces (13 minutes) as Blush beats Jack Petachi in a room near Bond's, and it is heard again (16 minutes) when she spots Bond spying on them.

Bond's long fight with a health-club thug goes entirely unscored, while Petachi's replacement of dummy warheads with nuclear devices (24 minutes) receives a grim, chugging-strings and angry-brass treatment (the oddly titled "Plunder a Cruise Missile" on the LP). The first of several fun source pieces is a big-band chart on Blush's car radio as she prepares to murder Petachi (27 minutes, "Death of Jack Petachi" on the LP). A portion of Legrand's dramatic "Cruise Missile" music is heard again (30 minutes) as SPECTRE retrieves the nuclear missiles.

Another source cue, a jazz-rock piece, accompanies Largo watching Domino go through her dance routine (37 minutes, "Jealousy," although the LP has a different take); Bond's arrival in Nassau is greeted with authentic-sounding steel-band music (at 43 minutes, "Bahama Island" on the LP). The longest cue in the score, nearly five minutes, begins with a sexy saxophone for Bond's tryst with Blush (48 minutes) and then turns ominous with a dramatic drumbeat and suspenseful strings as she takes him scuba diving, leaving him to be devoured by electronically guided sharks. Legrand adds wordless voices for unusual colors, although the orchestra dominates in the film mix ("Fight to the Death with Tigersharks" on the LP).

Bond's arrival in Nice (56 minutes) is accompanied by a lovely French-flavored tune (the instrumen-

LANI HALL
PERFORMS THE
TITLE SONG FROM
THE NEW HIT
MOVIE STARRING

SEAN
CONNERY

NEVER
SAY
NEVER
AGAIN

Lani Hall as she appeared in the video for "Never Say Never Again"

tal midsection of "Une Chanson d'Amour" on the LP). Another jazzy source cue is the music heard on Largo's boat while Bond watches Domino dance (59 minutes, "Bond and Domino" on the CD). "Une Chanson d'Amour" recurs a minute later when Domino arrives on land and then, in a vocal version (1 hour) while Bond, posing as a masseur, works on Domino at the spa.

Largo's sadistic video game is also unscored, although his initial victory and Bond's determination to play one more game is acknowledged with a brass allusion to the "Never" theme (1 hour, 14 minutes, "Video Duel/Victory" on the CD). What follows is one of the film's musical highlights, as Bond and Domino tango on the casino dance floor (1 hour, 17 minutes, "Tango to Death" on the LP) and Blush prances down the long staircase. Bond discovers

Nicole's body, spots Blush leaving the villa and gives chase to a fast-tempo, brassy, bongo-driven jazz piece (1 hour, 22 minutes; "Chaser" on the LP). With the exception of a brief reprise at the end, the chase itself is not scored.

Bond and Domino talk over more of her funky dance music (1 hour, 35 minutes); Largo says goodbye to the chained Domino by playing a cassette recording of the tango (1 hour, 43 minutes). Then Bond rescues Domino on horseback (1 hour, 47 minutes) to a dancelike piece that once again features the brass section (strangely, Kershner declined to use Legrand's original music for this section, called "Escape from Palmyra" on the LP, which is filled with appropriate ethnic percussion touches for the North African setting and would have proven more effective).

and Sergio again. I remember Marilyn and Alan being there as well. It's a complicated song, melodically. It's not the kind of song that you could really walk away humming."

Legrand was not present at the August 19 and 23 sessions at A&M Records in Los Angeles. Veteran arranger-keyboardist Robbie Buchanan arranged the song, and for the end-title version Alpert added his distinctive solo trumpet. "Nobody asked me to play," Alpert said. "I kinda got inspired by that ending, and I wanted to see if I could have some fun fooling around with the trumpet. It was their choice to use it or not [in the film]." They did.

Hall also shot a video in which, attired in a classy black tuxedo, she sings in front of a giant blowup of Sean Connery as he appears in the film (intercut, of course, with scenes from the film). Hall and the Bergmans received equal treatment with the composer in newspaper ads for the film.

Legrand wrote a second song for the film, "Une Chanson d'Amour," with famed French lyricist Jean Drejac, the co-writer of "Sous le ciel de Paris (Under the Paris Sky)," which Edith Piaf made famous nearly 30 years earlier. Bulgarian singer Sophie Della auditioned in Paris with a Piaf song ("Non, je ne regrette rien") and won the job on condition that she sing the French lyric without an accent; she worked for a week with Drejac to perfect her pronunciation. The London recording was done in a single take. "I was living a dream," Della later recalled.

Never Say Never Again premiered in Los Angeles on October 7, 1983, but also enjoyed a lavish European premiere in Monte Carlo on November 17, with Monaco's entire royal family (Princes Rainier and Albert, Princesses Caroline and Stephanie) in attendance. Hall even sang the song live at the postscreening dinner. "I didn't really think about the glamour attached to the Bond films," she said. "I felt the excitement, getting caught up in all that energy,

Off Eritrea, Bond determines where the missing nuclear warhead is hidden and his military colleagues launch an underwater expedition from their submarine (1 hour, 52 minutes, "Tears of Allah" on the LP); Legrand's music is filled with dramatic portent. He applies stealthy music for Bond and Leiter in the underground cave (1 hour, 59 minutes, drawn from "A Last Blow to Largo" on the LP but truncated). The gun battle goes unscored, but Bond's climactic underwater fight with Largo (2 hours, 5 minutes, "Fight to the Death" on the CD) merits a big, often dissonant, orchestral treatment.

Herb Alpert's mellow trumpet is featured playing the title tune for a relaxing Domino and Bond (2 hours, 8 minutes); Lani Hall's vocal returns for the end titles, and Alpert's trumpet solo concludes the last minute and 20 seconds of the film.

when the film premiered in Monte Carlo. It was a big gala event, and that's when I went, 'Wow!'"

The reviews were mixed on the music. "A full-throated score by Michel Legrand," wrote *The Hollywood Reporter*; "title song is unimpressive, as is Michel Legrand's rather thin score," declared *Variety*. "Michel Legrand's French-accented ersatz jazz falls far short," added the *Hartford Courant*; "rarely supports the action properly and only distracts and clashes," complained a critic for the film-music quarterly *Soundtrack!*

Never Say Never became the first Bond film without a soundtrack album in the States or Europe. Alpert's A&M label issued the title-song single, which didn't quite make *Billboard*'s top 100 singles; it reached number 103 on October 22. Japan's Seven Seas label issued a 42-minute LP of highlights in 1983, but it wasn't until 1995 that England's Silva Screen issued a 62-minute CD containing several tracks not heard in the final cut of the film. The song did not chart in the U.K.

"I wrote this score," Legrand later said, "without taking into account the worldwide attention the return of Connery in the role of Bond would bring. It was only later that . . . I became aware of the passion, the aspiration that *Never Say Never Again* revived." In 2006 the composer added a symphonic arrangement of the title song to his concert programs.

"... until we dance into the fire ..."

A View to a Kill

t was now 1985. James Bond may not have changed much in the dozen years since Roger Moore took over the role, but rock 'n' roll had—and so had the movies' relationship with modern music.

When John Barry started with Bond in the 1960s, it was the heyday of the classic movie song, often written by score composers who were also great tunesmiths, such as Henry Mancini, Michel Legrand and Burt Bacharach. But a younger generation of filmmakers, in the late 1960s and early 1970s, began demanding a hipper, more contemporary sound; such recording artists as Isaac Hayes, Curtis Mayfield and Bob Dylan began contributing not just songs but also instrumental music to movies. By the late 1970s and early 1980s, with *Saturday Night Fever*, *Urban Cowboy* and other films, movie studios and record labels were partnering to maximize profit on both sides. And in 1984, for the first time, all five Best Song Oscar nominees were from the popular-music world, among them Phil Collins, Stevie Wonder and Kenny Loggins.

Music videos had also begun to force colossal changes in the record business. The popularity of MTV made an artist's image as important as his or her musical content, and by 1985 most had embraced the new medium, mostly for its promotional value but in some cases as a budding art form.

Although one Bond film had managed a huge chart hit by a rock 'n' rolling ex-Beatle, all of the other songs were written by established composers working in a more-or-less traditional movie songwriting form: music that related to the film and lyrics that could be easily understood and were (for the most part) specific to the story. As a result of the cultural shifts of the previous 20 years, all that would change with *A View to a Kill*.

Duran Duran was one of the hottest bands of the early 1980s: five handsome, twentysomething Englishmen whose looks made them as famous as the catchy, dance-oriented synth-pop they were playing. In just three years they had had 12 top-40 hits in England, notably "Hungry Like the Wolf," "Save a Prayer," "Is There Something I Should Know" and "The Reflex"; in the United States, eight of their singles had hit the top 20 and their videos were among the most popular on MTV.

"I had met Cubby Broccoli at a party in London," Duran Duran bassist John Taylor recalled in 2005. He brashly asked when Bond might have "a decent theme song again." A lunch meeting with Barry followed ("John Taylor knew everything imaginable about every Bond movie," the composer said), and the group was offered the opportunity to record the next Bond song. "I went back to the studio where we were recording 'Wild Boys,'" Taylor said in 1985. "I said, 'Hey guys, we're doing the James Bond theme.' Boom, that was it. Then we just had to write it."

The title was to have been *From a View to a Kill*, after Fleming's 1959 short story, but it was shortened to *A View to a Kill* before shooting began in August 1984. And even though the members of Duran Duran weren't thrilled about the title, they were excited about writing a Bond theme. By February, word was out that they were working on the song; Eon formally announced their signing on March 15.

Who wrote what has long been in dispute. Vocalist Simon Le Bon, in 1985, suggested that it began with keyboardist Nick Rhodes at the piano: "We were working for about a week before we really came up with the basic theme for the song. . . . We just happened across that, Nick and I did. We were at the piano, he was playing chords, and I just sang 'meeting you with a view to a kill,' and suddenly, ah, yes!" Guitarist Andy Taylor later attributed the beginnings to John Taylor, and then Le Bon working with Barry on that opening line: "[Drummer] Roger Taylor and I then developed a hybrid drum/electro sound that sounded great, and Simon added the chorus."

Le Bon's version: "[Barry] didn't really come with any of the basic musical ideas. He heard what we had done and knocked it into shape. And that's why it happened so quickly, because he was able to separate the good ideas from the bad ones. He has a great way of working brilliant chord arrangements. He was working with us as virtually a sixth member of the group, not really getting on our backs at all."

Barry later said he spent two weeks with the band in rehearsal rooms assembling the song piece by piece. "It was a totally alien way of working from the way I'd worked all my life," Barry said. "But I think we came up with a very strong song." Complicating matters was the fact that the stresses within the group were taking their toll. "It was a hard record to make," Rhodes said in 1986. "There was a lot of tension in the studio." Twenty years later, Rhodes added some perspective: "You've got five people in a band who pretty much thought they *were* James Bond. We weren't actually together in the studio that much, and there was a rift developing. I imagine it was quite difficult for John Barry. There were arguments about which bit was better than another bit, and we weren't really talking a lot at that time. We split into factions. Despite all the niggling little things going on personally between us, when we played 'A View to a Kill' together as a song for the first time, we knew that we'd nailed something again," Rhodes added. "And then we'd sort of unplug and go back to being miserable to each other."

Production was far more complicated than on any previous Bond song. The band recorded at Maison Rouge Studios in West London, with dance-music producer Bernard Edwards at the helm; Jason Corsaro then mixed it at New York's Power Station, and Barry, back in London, added orchestra on top of the band's track.

The lyrics made little sense, but various phrases seemed to hint at the world of espionage: "face to face in secret places . . . that fatal kiss is all we need . . . between the shades, assassination standing still. . . ."

That Duran Duran would also make a music video was never in question. On completion of the song, they approached former 10cc rockers Kevin Godley and Lol Creme, who shot the group's racy "Girls on Film" video as well as one for the Police's "Every Breath You Take." "We thought it would be fun to work on a piece for a Bond film," Creme said in 1985. "The trick was to get across the ideas for the song and do a promo for the movie at the same time. We saw the film early and decided the Eiffel Tower chase would be a good focus for the video." Their big hurdle: "We didn't like the song at first. It seemed silly."

Noted John Taylor, at the London premiere: "People associate us with very heavy conceptual videos, so it seemed nice to do a spoof this time around. We're kind of playing secret agents."

As with the much simpler video for "All Time High," the "View to a Kill" video (shot in early April) incorporated extensive clips from the film itself (and even opened with the traditional gun-barrel logo) while casting the Duran Duran boys as spies stationed strategically around and atop the Paris land-mark. This was a far more lavish affair, incorporating special video effects (airborne video cameras, presumably shooting those "views to a kill") and members of the band variously taking photographs, shooting people, or blow-ing things up. At the end, a pretty fan approaches the beret-wearing Le Bon, who turns to the camera and identifies himself as "Bon . . . Simon Le Bon."

Barry's collaboration with Duran Duran on the title song led to the composer being able to incorporate it into several moments in his dramatic underscore. He worked through March 1985 and began recording on April 1. And al-though he personally orchestrated all of the early Bond films himself, the pressure of shorter time schedules on American films in the late 1970s had

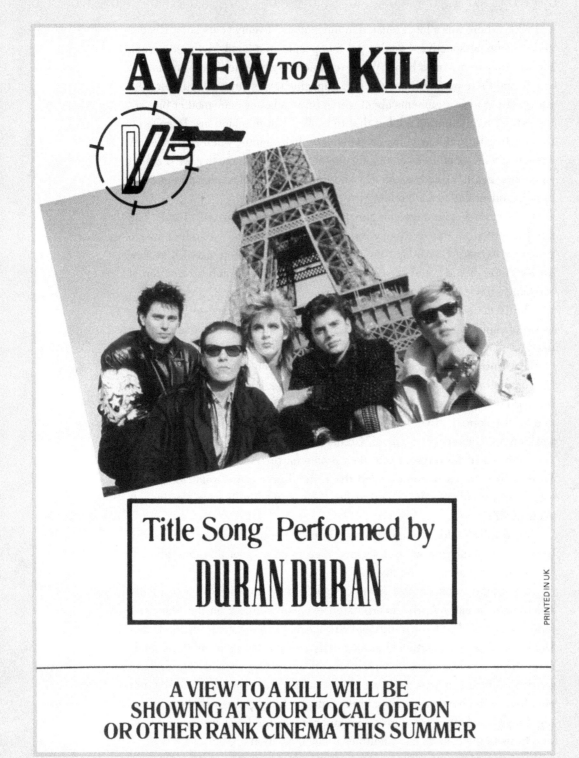

Duran Duran on location at the Eiffel Tower; advertising flyer that appeared in British cinemas during the summer of 1985

caused him to begin using orchestrators to assist in the time-consuming job of writing down literally every note played by every section in the orchestra.

Nic Raine orchestrated both *A View to a Kill* and *The Living Daylights* for Barry. "He was in a little mews house, not far from Hyde Park Corner," Raine recalled. "He'd hand me some sketches and say, 'Just make it loud, there's a lot of shooting going on.' He took it for granted that I'd do what I had to do. He didn't need to talk to me in any great detail about it."

Barry's sketches were sufficiently detailed, Raine said, that "there was nothing creatively for me to do. [He would write] two lines for woodwinds— seldom filled unless there was an alto flute solo or something—two for brass, two for strings and one for percussion. Essentially, it was all there apart from filling out the woodwinds, and maybe adding octaves or extra harmonies."

The composing and orchestrating took about four weeks, he recalled; the orchestra totaled about 70 players and they recorded at The Music Centre in Wembley, although with a new engineer, Dick Lewzey, because veteran Bond music mixer John Richards had moved to America. Unlike most composers, Raine said, "John wrote in film order, and he always recorded in film order. He thought it made sense, for all those attending the sessions from the production side, so they could feel the score grow and develop."

In each three-hour recording session, Barry would strive to record seven or eight minutes of music; with two sessions a day, an entire score was usually recorded in four or five days, Raine said (for *A View to a Kill*, April 1–4). "John was always very leisurely about recording. He would always come back [into the mixing booth, where Raine, Lewzey, and often Broccoli and director John Glen were listening] for playbacks. He'd listen to every take that was worth listening to, once with just orchestra and then once with dialogue. He was meticulous from that point of view."

Every day's work could be exhausting, however. Veteran ethnic-instrument player John Leach stayed late one evening to record the koto music for the

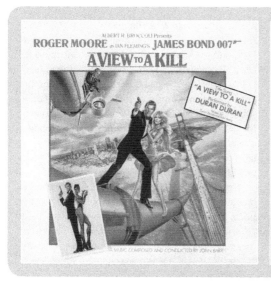

SCORE HIGHLIGHTS

After the practical necessity of frequent references to the "James Bond Theme" in *Octopussy* (nine, according to the official studio cue sheet)—because of the competition of a Sean Connery Bond movie in the marketplace at nearly the same time—it's interesting to note that, apart from the standard gunbarrel opening, the "Bond Theme" appears only once in the score for *A View to a Kill*.

Barry had plenty of musical material, beginning with the theme, which recurs frequently, most often in a lyrical fashion for love scenes; he contributes a majestic new theme for Zorin's grand plan, and a brass-and-percussion motif (with the surprising addition of wailing electric guitar) for the many action scenes.

After the traditional "Bond Theme," accompanying the gun-barrel logo, Bond's discovery of a body

John Barry working on the score for *A View to a Kill* in 1985

hot-tub scenes between Bond and Russian agent Pola Ivanova. "John was in a soundproofed room, and we told him to just start playing," Raine recalled. Leach began to improvise on the Japanese instrument. "We were knackered and dazed from the day's recording. Effectively, we just fell asleep while he was playing. And after about 20 minutes this little voice came over the intercom: 'Have you got enough now?'" (The film needed only about a minute and a half.)

The use of "Japanese music" in that scene is one of a handful of instances actually specified in the script. *A View to a Kill* deals with the mad industrial-

(SCORE HIGHLIGHTS, CONT.)

in the Siberian ice and his ambush by Soviet troops (called "Snow Job" on the LP) introduces Barry's action theme, which many observers have compared to the ski-action music in *On Her Majesty's Secret Service*, although there is something appropriately lighter about the tone of this one, perhaps befitting Roger Moore's tongue-in-cheek approach to the role. The jokey addition of "California Girls" to a supposedly snow-surfing Bond is a disastrous choice, interrupting and destroying the suspense of the scene. The British submarine scene, with its breathy-voiced blonde pilot (5 minutes into the film), offers the first use of "View" as a love theme, complete with sexy saxophone.

The Duran Duran song (6 minutes) is accompanied by Maurice Binder's amusing black-light titles (including a literal "dance into the fire," as Binder's

naked girls gyrate amid flames). Barry's brief transition to Paris (15 minutes) bears a decided resemblance to the theme from his then-recent score for *Until September*, a love story set in the City of Lights. May Day's escape, her shocking leap off the Eiffel Tower and Bond's taxicab pursuit (18 minutes, "May Day Jumps" on the LP) marks the sole use of the "Bond Theme" within the score. The wedding music ensemble on the boat sailing along the Seine (20 minutes) plays a Dixieland version of "View," one of Barry's more amusing musical asides.

Stacey's arrival at Zorin's chateau (28 minutes) is greeted with a curious alto saxophone solo; the party features strolling musicians playing Vivaldi (29 minutes). Bond introduces himself to Stacey (34 minutes, "Bond Meets Stacey" on the LP) to the strains of "View," a warm arrangement with a beau-

ist Zorin (Christopher Walken), who plots to corner the microchip market by destroying Silicon Valley; his lieutenant is a skydiving, kickboxing fiend named May Day (Grace Jones) and he is, briefly, assisted by a geologist named Stacey Sutton (Tanya Roberts). The script specifies that the strolling musicians at Zorin's lavish chateau reception "wear powdered wigs and 17th-century livery" while they play classical music (Vivaldi's *Four Seasons*, in a licensed performance by Trevor Pinnock and the English Concert). And Pola's love of Tchaikovsky, as mentioned in the script, is illustrated with excerpts from music-library performances of both *Romeo and Juliet* and *Swan Lake*.

Unmentioned in the script, and thus a choice that must have been made during post-production, was the widely criticized use of the Beach Boys' 1965 surf-music hit "California Girls" (actually a cover version by Gidea Park) while Bond is escaping Soviet killers in Siberia on skis during the pre-title sequence. Barry didn't like it: "Where you had a good action sequence it was like throwing a lame joke into the middle of something that was really working. Those things, I never agree with."

For the first time, a Bond movie premiered outside the U.K. As a way of thanking the city of San Francisco for its cooperation (a third of the film was shot there, its climax taking place over the Golden Gate Bridge), *A View to a Kill* received a splashy, star-studded premiere on May 22, 1985. But it was the appearance of Duran Duran's John Taylor and Andy Taylor that drew the biggest roar from the crowd, leaving the *San Francisco Chronicle* to headline its coverage "Rockers Outdraw 007."

The same thing happened in London on June 12. "Screaming pop fans brought chaos to the royal premiere," reported the *Daily Mail*. "A crowd of around 4,000, mostly teenage girls, packed the streets in and around London's Leicester Square hoping for a glimpse of Duran Duran. The group arrived in

tiful flute solo by Susan Milan, one of England's finest classical flutists. Bond and Tibbett investigate Zorin's hidden horse-doping lab (37 minutes, "Pegasus' Stable" on the LP) to a suspenseful flute-and-strings passage. "View" reappears as a love theme for Bond and May Day (43 minutes) but in a decidedly different form, with a tenor sax and then a trumpet signifying a more aggressive bed partner.

Bond and Zorin go riding while Tibbett is killed in the car wash, to a suspense cue dominated by timpani, strings and muted brass (47 minutes, "Tibbett Gets Washed Out"). There is no score for the steeplechase scene until the very end, when Bond discovers Tibbett dead. When May Day pushes their Rolls-Royce into a lake (53 minutes, "Bond Escapes Roller" on the LP), Barry uses repeating flutes with muted brass for Bond's survival underwater.

Barry introduces his Silicon Valley fanfare when Zorin reveals his plan (56 minutes) and then flies his blimp over the Golden Gate Bridge (58 minutes). Bond investigates Zorin's oil pumping station (1 hour, 2 minutes, "Bond Underwater" on the LP) to some of the score's most dramatic music yet. Bond meets old Soviet lover Pola Ivanova and they retreat together, winding up in a hot tub (1 hour, 7 minutes) to John Leach's improvised koto music.

Barry employs his action theme, incorporating an interesting variation on the Bond theme, for Bond's battle with Zorin's thugs at Stacey's house (1 hour, 15 minutes), and then he returns to a soft string version of "View" for Bond and Stacey's shared bottle of wine, again with an exquisite Susan Milan flute solo (1 hour, 19 minutes, "Wine with Stacey" on the LP).

James Bond pursuing May Day on the Eiffel Tower

A surprising 10 minutes goes by with no under-score; the murder of Stacey's boss Howe and Bond and Stacey's travails in the burning elevator shaft go without music. Only when they appear on the roof of San Francisco City Hall does music resume, and it's a heroic version of "View to a Kill" for horns and percussion (1 hour, 32 minutes). Much of the wild fire-truck chase is underscored with Barry's action theme (1 hour, 35 minutes, "He's Dangerous" on the LP).

Nearly a third of the 58 total minutes of original score is contained in the mine and climactic blimp scenes. Stacey and Bond deduce Zorin's plan to strings and flute (1 hour, 44 minutes, "Destroy Sili-con Valley" on the LP). And although the mine-flooding sequence is mostly without music, the in-flation and launch of Zorin's airship—intercut with Bond and May Day swimming through the mine—gets a dramatic, powerful orchestral musical treat-ment (1 hour, 53 minutes, "Airship to Silicon Valley" on the LP). A more suspenseful treatment of the same theme is used for Bond's attempt to stop the earthquake-inducing bomb and May Day's heroic sacrifice (1 hour, 56 minutes, "May Day Bombs Out" on the LP).

Barry returns to a brass-and-strings "View" for 007 hanging onto a rope below the Zorin blimp (2 hours, 1 minute), but the battle between Bond and Zorin atop the Golden Gate Bridge while Stacey hangs on for dear life (2 hours, 3 minutes, "Golden Gate Fight") gets the most thrilling treatment of the action theme in the entire score (although in the film

limousines to a crescendo of screams. . . ." Photographs of the rockers greeting Princess Diana appeared in the next day's papers (she was said to have called Duran Duran her favorite band).

The title song received its share of brickbats from the critics: "Low marks for Duran Duran's limp-disco title tune," sniffed the *Los Angeles Times*. "It's not really a song at all, it's the soundtrack for a rock video," contended the *Los Angeles Herald-Examiner*. "Opening credit sequence in MTV style is downright bizarre, and title song by Duran Duran will certainly not go down as one of the classic Bond tunes," insisted *Variety*. Reviewing the soundtrack album, *Billboard* offered a rare positive note: "Barry offers dependably stylish cues, but it's Duran Duran's main title song, a well-crafted if typical techno-pop piece, that will likely offer the main lure."

Duran Duran's music video helped to propel the song to the top of the charts, the first time ever for a Bond theme. It landed on Billboard's Hot 100 singles chart on May 18, and on July 13 it reached number 1—the very day Duran Duran performed the song as part of the Live Aid fundraising concerts for Ethiopian famine relief. Before 100,000 fans at JFK Stadium in Philadelphia, and an estimated worldwide television audience of 1.9 billion, "A View to a Kill" got the largest simultaneous hearing of any Bond theme in history (and, for singer Le Bon, an embarrassing moment when he hit a bad note late in the song). It was also the band's last live appearance for nearly two decades. In the U.K., it charted May 18 and reached number 2. The album charted June 29 in the United States and reached number 38, while in the U.K. it charted June 22 but reached only number 81.

A View to a Kill marked Roger Moore's final appearance as 007. Two years later, with a new actor in the role, it would also be time for a freshening of the James Bond sound.

the cue is slightly truncated). "View" returns in its love-theme guise (2 hours, 7 minutes) for Q's snooping on Bond and Stacey, just before the end credits and a reprise of the Duran Duran song (2 hours, 8 minutes).

"... the living's in the way we die ... "

The Living Daylights

When a new, younger man was signed to succeed middle-aged Roger Moore as James Bond, composer John Barry decided that the time was also right for a new, younger sound for 007.

Timothy Dalton was announced as the new Bond in August 1986, as production was about to begin on *The Living Daylights*. And, having scored a huge worldwide hit as co-writer of the theme for *A View to a Kill*, Barry agreed to come back an 11th time to help usher in a fresh face as the world's most famous "secret" agent.

Earlier that year, Barry won his fourth Academy Award for his romantic, symphonic score for *Out of Africa*. And recent scores such as *Until September* and *Frances* were cementing his reputation as a composer of lush, lyrical accompaniments to films of love and loss. On the other hand, he had recently been experimenting with the use of synthesizers as a different way of scoring pictures, especially suspenseful ones such as *Jagged Edge*.

So on *The Living Daylights* Barry was able to use all his musical wiles at once: pop songwriter, orchestral composer and forward-thinking applier of modern musical technology.

During the late summer of 1986, Barry was occupied with writing a lengthy, lavish and ultimately ill-fated score for the Eddie Murphy action-fantasy *The Golden Child*. (The 80-minute score, mostly discarded by the producers but eventually released on CD, was hailed as a "lost Bond score" by observers who considered it similar in tone to Barry's late 007 outings.) That assignment was completed in late September, allowing Barry to begin thinking about the Bond film that was about to begin shooting.

In the script, Bond is caught up in a complex plot involving high-ranking Soviet intelligence officer Koskov (Jeroen Krabbe) who is supposedly defecting to the West. Koskov's girlfriend, Czech cellist Kara Milovy (Maryam d'Abo), is duped into helping him escape his KGB guards. A Greek terrorist named Necros (Andreas Wisniewski) then supervises his "abduction" from England and transport to the Tangiers estate of an American arms dealer (Joe Don Baker). Eventually Bond and Kara find themselves at a Soviet airbase in Afghanistan, where they meet a Mujahidin leader (Art Malik) who helps 007 thwart the plot.

Because the early portions of the story take place in Czechoslovakia and Austria, *The Living Daylights* crew shot for two weeks in Vienna, including all of the scenes where Kara is performing on her cello. Director John Glen recalled conferring with Barry about the classical music that would be heard in the film. "We listened to various pieces before we chose what we were going to use," Glen said. "Obviously we needed something where the cello was featured strongly." (They ended up with Mozart, Borodin, Strauss, Dvořák and Tchaikovsky.) They recorded the classical selections with Gert Meditz conducting the Austrian Youth Orchestra and then filmed the ensemble, using the prerecorded music as playback on the set.

Maryam d'Abo was filmed "playing" the cello during several of these scenes. "I started taking private lessons a month prior to the film," she recalled. "I just learned the movements. They basically soaped the bow so there wasn't any sound [from the instrument]. It was hard work; I could have done with a couple more weeks of lessons. They demanded a lot of strength. No wonder cellists start when they are eight years old." The solo parts heard in the film were played by Austrian cellist Stefan Kropfitsch.

The actress, as Kara, "performs" with the orchestra in several scenes, notably at the end of the film when Barry himself is seen conducting Tchaikovsky's 1877 *Variations on a Rococo Theme* and Kara is the soloist. It was filmed on October 15, 1986, at Vienna's Schönbrunn Palace. Recalled Glen: "It was very unusual for John—unlike a lot of other people who liked to appear in movies, John had never asked before—but on that film, he asked if he could appear. At the time, it struck me as a bit strange. It was almost a premonition that this was going to be his last Bond. I was happy to accommodate him, and he was eminently qualified to do it."

In fact, Barry had done this once before, appearing on-screen as the conductor of a Madrid orchestra in Bryan Forbes's *Deadfall* (1968). On that occasion, he was conducting his own music (a single-movement guitar concerto that was ingeniously written to double as dramatic music for a jewel robbery occurring simultaneously with the concert). This time, he was supposed to be conducting the "Lenin's People's Conservatoire Orchestra."

Kara and Bond (Maryam d'Abo, Timothy Dalton) sail down a snow-covered hill in Kara's cello case

D'Abo socialized with Barry in London, when the unit was shooting at Pinewood. (She later realized that she had already appeared in two Barry films: *Until September* and *Out of Africa*.) "John was there, working on the music," she said. "He was just a joy to be around. I remember seeing him and having dinner with him and [his wife] Laurie, and John being so excited about writing the music. He was so adorable, saying 'Your love scenes inspire me to write this romantic music.' John was such a charmer with women."

In fact, Barry was so inspired that he wound up co-writing three songs for the film: the title song with Norwegian pop trio a-ha, and two additional songs with Chrissie Hynde of the Pretenders.

Warner Bros. Records executive Ray Still, who in his previous position at Parlophone Records had been involved with the Duran Duran song on the last film and thus already knew the Bond producers, suggested to Eon that they consider a-ha for the title tune. The group had had six straight top-10 hits in the U.K. in just over 15 months, including "Take on Me" and "The Sun Always Shines on TV." Like Duran Duran, they were handsome young guys whose videos were popular with teenagers. Both Barry and Glen went to see an a-ha concert. "I wasn't crazy about them," Glen later conceded. "The oldest person in the audience was about 15. There were all these screaming girls. I felt quite out of place. But we were trying to keep the series up-to-date and appeal to a younger audience."

So a-ha was signed in March 1987. At the press conference announcing their collaboration, Barry said, "I think we're going to have some fun with it." That feeling was apparently short-lived, however, as the trio refused even to screen the film. "I loved the title from the get-go and the tune popped in my head after a few days," a-ha's Pal Waaktaar later said. "John Barry added a wonderful dark and droning string score with heavy brass stabs that just reeked Bond."

Reaching that point, however, was not easy. Barry put a good face on the process in an interview conducted just after the April 23, 1987, session (where he added a 55-piece orchestra to the band): "We wanted a very strong number with a punchy opening sequence. They combine energy with a happy sound." But, reflecting years later, the composer likened the experience to "playing ping-pong with four balls. They had an attitude which I really didn't like at all. It was not a pleasant experience." A-ha's view was predictably different; as Magne Furuholmen later said, "It was great. We were working with John Barry. He just wasn't working with us." Ray Still of Warner Bros. chalked it

John Barry conducting, with Maryam d'Abo as the cellist, in the finale of *The Living Daylights*

John Barry (third from left) appears with Norwegian pop group a-ha at a press conference announcing their collaboration on *The Living Daylights*

John Barry's final score for the Bond series turned out to be one of the most melodically rich of all. *The Living Daylights* not only boasts a catchy title song, whose final version seems to owe a lot to Barry's arrangement and embellishment, but also two memorable themes that, when turned into songs with Chrissie Hynde's lyrics, rank among the composer's strongest of the decade.

The traditional gun-barrel opening segues into a brass fanfare for Gibraltar and a hint of the Bond bass line as the agents land. Barry launches into the Bond Theme for our first glimpse of Timothy Dalton as 007 (3½ minutes into the film). Barry's first use of the new synth-based rhythm occurs (4 minutes) as 007 chases down the killer, leaps atop his jeep and fights for control as they career down a hill, all to

up to "creative friction." Producer Michael G. Wilson, in a rare candid comment about the music of the Bond films, said, "We were somewhat disappointed with the result."

As with the Duran Duran track, the pop group enlisted Jason Corsaro as co-producer with them and Barry. The lyrics make only marginally more sense than those of "A View to a Kill" ("comes the morning and the headlights fade away / hundred thousand people, I'm the one they frame"). "You have to make it a bit abstract," Waaktaar told MTV.

In the meantime, Barry composed the score, which would ultimately require 57 minutes of music and demand two other main themes. But the most significant aspect of the *Living Daylights* score would be Barry's use, for the first time, of synthesizer-driven rhythm tracks. He worked with engineer-producer Paul Staveley O'Duffy, who ultimately received co-producing credit with Barry. "I've been wanting to put in these tracks, and they really cut through," Barry said at the time. "We've used them on about eight pieces, and when we get them mixed in with the orchestra, it is going to sound really terrific, with a lot of energy and impact, a slight freshness and more up-to-date sound."

The result was the most contemporary-sounding Bond score to date. "That was a new kind of rhythmic drive for the new Bond," orchestrator Nic Raine recalled. "The [synths] were all prerecorded, and the orchestra played along with that." The score was recorded the week of May 11, 1987, with an orchestra of about 70. Barry later said he had just four weeks to write it all, but he enjoyed the recording process at CTS Wembley with Dick Lewzey as engineer. "Studio 1 has got a lovely big movie sound," he said. "When this goes onto the large screen it really fills the theater."

the Bond Theme ("Exercise at Gibraltar" on the expanded 2003 CD). The a-ha song plays under the title sequence (7½ minutes), and designer Maurice Binder briefly acknowledges the lyrics ("the headlights fade away . . .") by adding car headlights at one point.

The Vienna sequence opens with Bond attending a performance of Mozart's Symphony no. 40, where he spots Kara and Koskov (10 minutes). Barry adds a layer of suspense as Kara appears to be the KGB sniper targeting Koskov (15 minutes, "The Sniper Was a Woman" on the LP) and Bond drives Koskov away. More of that string suspense, building to a climactic moment, accompanies Koskov's jet departure (20 minutes, "Koskov Escapes" on the LP).

"Where Has Every Body Gone?"—the song based on Barry's assassin theme—is first heard (24 minutes) playing on the Walkman portable music device worn by killer Necros as he runs through the English countryside and then impersonates a milkman to reach Koskov; an instrumental version (30 minutes, "Necros Attacks" on LP) follows as Necros kidnaps Koskov and they escape via helicopter.

In Bratislava, Bond watches Kara perform in a string quartet playing Borodin's Quartet no. 2 in D (36 minutes); Barry introduces his "Soviet" motif as she is taken off a bus by KGB agents (37 minutes, first half of "Approaching Kara" on the CD). She returns home to find Bond there and Barry introduces his love theme with an alto flute solo (40 minutes, "Kara Meets Bond" on LP).

Barry uses the synth-driven Bond Theme for the exciting Aston Martin car chase through the snow-covered countryside and on an icy lake, ending with

Barry incorporated the a-ha song into the score in a couple of places, but his villain theme and his love theme would also turn out to be the basis for songs heard in the film.

On May 17, Chrissie Hynde's involvement was announced. Singer-song-writer-guitarist and founder of the Pretenders, she was an Ohio-born rocker who had made her home in England for many years; her group had enjoyed 10 top-40 hits in the previous eight years, and her tough but lyrical way with a song was widely respected. Within a week, the titles of her two songs with Barry were announced: "Where Has Every Body Gone?" and "Where Have I Seen You?" The former title would be retained, but the latter (based on Barry's love theme) would be revamped as "If There Was a Man" and play over the film's end titles.

"I wouldn't even bother seeing a gung-ho sort of [movie]," Hynde said at the time of the film's premiere in 1987. "But this is just about a guy getting his job done."

Hynde admired Barry's previous work and managed to make time to collaborate despite having come off a grueling four months on the road. Her U.K. tour dates, in mid-to-late May 1987, enabled her to spend a few days working with Barry. "Chrissie Hynde was lovely; I adored working with her," the composer later said.

"I really like his cool reserve," Hynde said of Dalton's performance as Bond. "In the case of this James Bond film, when I heard John Barry's music, I just loved the music. It kind of inspired me, really, and I felt that I could sing something to it."

Added Barry: "The main villain walks around wearing a Walkman and strangles people with the headphone wire, so we use this ['Where Has Every Body Gone?'] as a signature. Every time you hear the Walkman song, which is

(SCORE HIGHLIGHTS, CONT.)

Bond and Kara careening downhill in her cello case (45 minutes, "Ice Chase" on LP). Their arrival in Vienna gets a warm love-theme treatment (at 54 minutes, much longer on LP as "Into Vienna"). Couples waltz outdoors to Strauss's "Tales from the Vienna Woods" (55 minutes), and Bond and Kara attend a performance of Mozart's *Marriage of Figaro* (59 minutes).

"Where Has Every Body Gone?" returns (1 hour, 3 minutes), signaling Necros's presence in Vienna; and the love theme returns just seconds later as Bond and Kara kiss for the first time (second half of "Approaching Kara" on CD). The first use of "Living Daylights" as an instrumental occurs when Bond spots Pushkin in Tangiers (1 hour, 8 minutes, last half of "Murder at the Fair" on CD). More is heard after Bond's faked "assassination" of Pushkin and

the chase across the rooftops (1 hour, 13 minutes, "Assassin and Drugged" on CD).

Kara is practicing the Dvořák cello concerto (1 hour, 18 minutes) when Bond returns. Their landing at a Soviet airbase in Afghanistan is met with Russian-sounding military music (1 hour, 24 minutes); Bond's subsequent fight with their jailor and their escape into the desert get an appropriate rhythmic treatment and a dramatic drumbeat (all three cues merged into "Airbase Jailbreak" on CD).

Kamran Shah leads them into their camp to a proud new theme for strings and brass (1 hour, 30 minutes, first half of "Mujahadin and Opium" on LP); they embark on a desert mission the next morning to a more dramatic treatment (1 hour, 37 minutes; second half). Barry interestingly intertwines his Mujahidin motif with that of Necros as Bond, disguised

a sinister, hard, biting piece, you know that the villain is in the vicinity. So that was already built into the plot.

"We also found that there was much more of a romantic feel this time, as opposed to any of the other Bond films," Barry said. "The love affair between Bond and the heroine is more sincere. I thought it would be lovely at the end of the movie, instead of going back to the main title song, to have a love ballad, which is the love theme that is used throughout the four or five love scenes in the picture, with lyrics by Chrissie. Both of these songs grew out of the material."

The lyrics for "Where Has Every Body Gone?" were clever ("because you're beautiful, and you'll soon be long gone / and the ashes of your memoirs will be strewn across the lawn"); those for "If There Was a Man" were yearning and poignant, about a woman whose men have failed her, while she still dreams of an ideal one, presumably 007 ("happy endings never find me / I put all my fantasies and hopes of love behind me"). Both were recorded at Paradise Studios in Chiswick in late May 1987.

Both a-ha and Hynde made music videos to promote the songs. For "The Living Daylights," the group chose director Steve Barron, who had made the innovative, animated video for their hit "Take On Me." He shot the trio on the 007 Stage at Pinewood and incorporated not only scenes from the movie but also video effects involving guns, cars and girls. Hynde's video for "If There Was a Man" was considerably simpler: just Hynde sitting on a stool and singing, against a plain backdrop, interspersed with shots of Dalton in the film.

The royal premiere of *The Living Daylights* took place June 29, 1987, at London's Odeon Leicester Square Cinema. Both Barry and Hynde attended and greeted the Prince and Princess of Wales; the event was a fundraiser for the Prince's Trust charity. In terms of the critics, few mentioned the music.

---

as an Afghan, returns to the Soviet base; tension builds as Bond is discovered (1 hour, 42 minutes, "Afghanistan Plan" on CD).

The Mujahidin attack on the Soviets is unscored. Bond takes off in the opium-filled plane to a synth-backed orchestral version of the title song (1 hour, 49 minutes, "Hercules Takes Off" on LP); then Barry reprises a similarly synth-plus-orchestra "Where Has Every Body Gone?" for the Necros-Bond fight, much of which takes place with them hanging thousands of feet in the air (1 hour, 52 minutes, "Inflight Fight" on LP). The plane nearly collides with a mountain, Bond and Kara come to the aid of the Mujahidin and they finally bail out in the jeep (1 hour, 57 minutes, "Air Bond" on CD).

A dramatic version of the Bond bass line finds Bond infiltrating Whitaker's compound (2 hours,

1 minute) and ultimately killing him ("Final Confrontation" on CD). Transitioning from Tangiers to Vienna, we see Kara performing in Tchaikovsky's *Variations on a Rococo Theme* with her valuable, now bullet-holed cello (2 hours, 5 minutes; John Barry is on the podium conducting). Bond greets Kara in her dressing room to a final, string-and-harp arrangement of the love theme (2 hours, 7 minutes), which leads into the vocal version of "If There Was a Man" for the end titles.

Barry recorded a more string-heavy, synth-less version of the song as well; it appears as "Alternate End Titles" on the CD.

"Once again composer John Barry . . . has graced 007's heroics with a full-throttled and sumptuous musical score, while the Norwegian supergroup a-ha catchily performed the stirring theme song," gushed *The Hollywood Reporter*; *Variety*'s critic was considerably cooler, referring to "John Barry's music score, unassertively enhancing." London's *Guardian* critic was less interested in Barry than in the profession of the new Bond girl: "a Czech classical cellist who opens her legs for Dvořák rather quicker than for Bond."

There was success on the pop charts, too, but not in America. The a-ha single charted in the U.K. on July 4 and zoomed to number 5, while Hynde's "If There Was a Man" charted on August 15 in the U.K. and reached number 49. The success of the singles helped drive sales of the album, which charted on August 1 and reached number 57 in the U.K. For the second time in Bond history, neither single nor album made the charts in the United States. (This also marked the first time that Bond music was commercially available in five formats: 7-inch and 12-inch singles, LP, cassette and compact disc.)

At awards time, there was a brief flurry of trade ads designed to remind voters of *Living Daylights* accomplishments, including the songs, but no such honors were forthcoming.

For Barry, it was the end of the line. He had musically introduced a fourth James Bond, but now he was finished. The headaches with a-ha were partially responsible; as he would later say, "I'm not going to go through this again. That was the end of it." To another interviewer, he added: "It lost its natural energy. It started to be just formula, and once that happens, the work gets really hard. The spontaneity and excitement of the original scores is gone, so you move on."

He said goodbye with a full-page ad in *Variety*'s salute to a quarter-century of Bond in the cinema: "Congratulations Cubby. It's been a great 25 years. Your friend, John Barry."

". . . and you know I'm going straight for your heart . . ."

Licence to Kill

As production geared up for *License Revoked*, which was to be the next film in the series, Bond producers found themselves dealing with several new realities: a need to trim costs to remain profitable; the AIDS epidemic, which would require that 007 be less promiscuous; and competition from other action thrillers whose premises were more strongly based in such real-world issues as terrorism and the drug trade. The result was a film that would be shot mostly in Mexico and find a single-minded Bond operating outside of his usual authority, determined to take revenge on a billionaire drug lord.

One other filmmaking reality would intrude: the rise of the music supervisor, an outside consultant who could find artists to perform songs and make record deals. By the late 1980s, the movie soundtrack business was booming. More and more films, especially those aimed at younger audiences, contained contemporary songs that could be marketed along with the movie and thus prove profitable for both record companies and movie studios.

Aside from Noel Rogers of United Artists recruiting John Barry as arranger for the original "James Bond Theme," musical decisions on all previous Bonds had been made in-house, with producers and composer choosing the artists and the score composer usually writing the title song. For *License Revoked* (which would eventually be retitled *Licence to Kill*) the MGM-UA marketing department exercised greater control over music than ever before.

Composer Michael Kamen

Studio marketing executive Gordon Weaver called a former colleague, Joel Sill, to oversee the music on the new Bond film. Sill had recently produced the music for such films as *La Bamba* and *Bright Lights, Big City*, and his ability to put together soundtrack deals was well known throughout the movie industry. Sill's first job was not about songs, however, but rather to suggest a possible composer.

John Barry had pretty much decided he was through with Bond, even before he suffered a life-threatening illness in early 1988: an esophagus rupture that required multiple surgeries and left him unable to eat or drink normally for months. Although *Variety* reported in April that he was "already noodling music for the next Bond epic," that was hardly the case. The Broccolis held out hope that he would return for one more film, but it was now out of the question.

Sill flew to Key West, Florida, where shooting was under way in early August 1988. There he met with the Broccolis and pitched American-born, London-based Michael Kamen as score composer. Kamen's credentials were impeccable: he had recently made a big splash as the composer of *Lethal Weapon* and *Die Hard*, two of the highest-grossing action movies of the previous 18 months. He was both Juilliard-trained as an orchestral composer and conversant with the pop and rock world, having worked with Pink Floyd, Queen and Eric Clapton.

Kamen had read many of the Fleming novels but not seen most of the films. Still, as he later recalled, "it was a real thrill" to be asked. He recalled meeting Cubby Broccoli and acknowledging his importance by telling him, "If I wore a hat, I'd take it off." As Kamen added, "the Broccoli crowd was very congenial and very close. I grew to be friendly with Timothy Dalton," Kamen said, and the actor later attended some of the scoring sessions.

In the story, Bond resigns from the Secret Service to track down wealthy drug dealer Sanchez (Robert Davi) who has murdered the new bride of pal Felix Leiter (David Hedison), who has himself been badly mauled by sharks. Bond helps Sanchez's lover (Talisa Soto) and finds a partner in American CIA contract pilot Pam (Carey Lowell) while tangling with Sanchez subordinates (Anthony Zerbe, Benicio del Toro) on a personal-vendetta mission that takes him from Key West to the Bahamas and South America.

Timothy Dalton and Carey Lowell as Bond and Pam in the climactic finale of *Licence to Kill*

Vic Flick, with his original "Bond Theme" guitar, performing on Michael Kamen's score for
Licence to Kill in early 1989

By early February 1989, Kamen had come up with a theme. As on *Lethal Weapon*, he brought in guitarist Clapton, and, at the suggestion of engineer Stephen McLaughlin, original Bond theme guitarist Vic Flick (who had not played on a Bond since the 1960s). Clapton and Flick joined Kamen, drummer Steve Ferrone and percussionist Ray Cooper at London's Townhouse Studios to record the music for a TV commercial that would also cross-promote the movie.

What actually happened that day depends on who's telling the story. "It was a disaster," recalled Sill. "Michael was completely unprepared. He was vamping, and this was the wrong time to do it." Remembered Flick: "It was kind of a bluesy, bendy tune, with Clapton fooling around from the outline of a theme on top of a basic backing track and me providing the dark-guitar countertheme in the bass end." Flick (who had brought his original 1960s guitar) recalled that "all day we worked on this composition and by the close it was sounding pretty good." McLaughlin recalled it as "a big Bond-y tune, and it also had a kind of quote of the Bond theme."

According to Flick, a video shoot for the commercial took place the next day "in the attic of a riverside wharf [in the] London dock area." Kamen summed it all up years later by saying that the session "didn't really bear any fruit." Sill dismissed it as "terrible," and together with the Broccolis a decision was made to shelve it. Issues involving payment for Clapton's participation further complicated matters, and as a result the track has never seen the light of day.

In addition, Kamen hoped to turn his main theme into a song, just as predecessors Barry, Hamlisch and Conti had done. Scottish songwriter B. A. Robertson, who had written hits for Cliff Richard and Mike & the Mechanics, was invited to pen the words. Kamen had not, however, had a hit film song at that point; that would come two years later, with the chart-topping Bryan Adams hit "(Everything I Do) I Do It for You" from Kamen's score for *Robin Hood: Prince of Thieves*. "I was very displeased to find that my tune and my melodies were not taken seriously," he later admitted. "I was sorry not to be able to write a Bond song. I thought I had written a really good one."

While the main-title song was still being debated, Sill had an idea for an end-title song to be done by Dave Stewart and Annie Lennox, who as the Eurythmics had enjoyed such 1980s hits as "Sweet Dreams (Are Made of This)" and "Here Comes the Rain Again." Sill set up a screening for them; Cubby Broccoli came by to greet them. But, Sill recalled, "the shark-biting scene completely turned Annie [Lennox] off. She just couldn't deal with the gore of it. So she passed."

Inspired by the notion that the film featured two strong female roles, Sill pushed the idea of different songs bookending the movie. He approached Irving Azoff, head of MCA Records, "because he had two of my favorite singers, Gladys Knight and Patti LaBelle." Azoff immediately approved the deal and won the soundtrack rights. Sill then convinced two major songwriters to write the opening and closing tunes for the film: Narada Michael Walden for the main title and Diane Warren for the end title. Together (Walden as producer, Warren as co-writer) they had made an Oscar-nominated, number-one hit of "Nothing's Gonna Stop Us Now," performed by Starship in the 1987 movie *Mannequin*.

The biggest challenge, Walden said many years later, was turning the phrase "license to kill" into a potential hit song. "I've got a license to kill anyone that would try to take you from me, anyone that would try to hurt you—that was the feeling," he said. "I know it's kind of bizarre, but that was the only way I could think of that could make it a hit." He wrote the chorus quickly and then brought in two favorite collaborators: Walter Afanasieff "to make sure that it had a nice flow" and Jeffrey Cohen to "help me write lyrics for the verses."

Walden, a former drummer with the Mahavishnu Orchestra and a two-time Grammy winner, most recently as Producer of the Year, went into the studio to create the backing track. He then approached Gladys Knight. "I knew we had to convince her that the song could be friendly enough that it wouldn't just be about killing," Walden recalled. Once she said yes, Walden flew to Las Vegas, where she lived, and recorded her vocal.

"She sang it down the octave a few times to get warm," Walden recalled, "then on the third, fourth and fifth take, she just sang the song flat-out. She wanted to do a verse and work on a few details. By that time, she'd already given me a record. But then she said, 'Let's do a performance of it.' What you're hearing [in the released version] is the whole last take, with little things here or there [tweaked in mixing]. The feeling and emotion is primarily that last take." Added Afanasieff: "That's a proud feather in my cap: in my life I got to be part of the James Bond theme-song tradition."

Reflecting back a decade later, Knight said: "I don't know if I'd do it again today. I'd do the project; it's just that particular thought [of a "license to kill"]. That bothered me for a long time. I don't advocate violence. Even though it's playacting, life's just too precious to me."

Walden never saw a script or any footage; nor did he converse with any of the Bond producers. Warren, however, screened the film, and—knowing that she was writing the end-title song—took her inspiration from the last two lines of dialogue in the film, as Bond kisses Pam in the pool. Echoing an earlier exchange in the film, she says, "Why don't you wait until you're asked?" and he responds, "So why don't you ask me?"

Warren wrote "If You Asked Me To" for Patti LaBelle. "I remember coming up with that chorus and that melody," Warren recalled. "Those chords reminded me of Bond, kind of weird, John Barry-ish things. There was something sexy and mysterious about it. It's one of my favorite songs. Diamonds are forever, and so are songs."

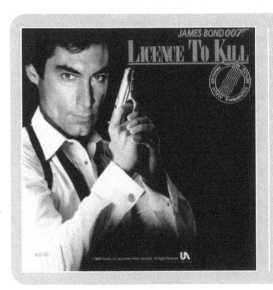

SCORE HIGHLIGHTS

Licence to Kill was more heavily scored than any other Bond film to that time. Michael Kamen supplied more than 76 minutes of original music, and counting the songs and source music the total exceeds 92 minutes of music.

Kamen was handed one of the toughest Bond films of all: grim, often unpleasant and at times brutally violent, where the music was often buried by sound effects and rarely given a chance to shine. Much of Kamen's score is atmospheric or textural, with few warm or melodic moments, although he invokes the "James Bond Theme" some 17 times (according to the film's official cue sheet) and offers fresh and compelling variations on it throughout.

He opens with a dramatic, timpani-fueled version of the theme, as played by original Bond-theme

Sill then hired Stewart Levine to produce the track; Levine had produced

Sill then hired Stewart Levine to produce the track; Levine had produced the Oscar-winning "Up Where We Belong" from *An Officer and a Gentleman,* and he in turn hired Aaron Zigman (later, the film composer of *Sex and the City* and *For Colored Girls*) to arrange it and play keyboards. Sill recalled Levine telling LaBelle not to "oversing" the song despite her reputation for big, belting, show-stopping performances; the song needed to build slowly, they felt. Before the song's release, Warren ran into LaBelle at a mutual friend's wedding. LaBelle happened to have a cassette tape of the performance, "so we sat in my car and listened to it about a hundred times. I missed my friend's wedding," Warren said with a laugh.

Kamen, although deprived of both the main-title and end-title songs, was formally announced as composer in early February 1989 and toiled on the underscore through March. (As the film's official press notes later stated, "the usual Bond composer, John Barry, was unable to take this assignment, thus opening the door for Kamen.") He had more than 75 minutes of orchestral music to write, and his initial encounters with Bond traditions did not go well.

He preferred not to record at CTS but was told this was not negotiable. "I remember bringing in a Kurzweil [music sampler-keyboard], which I had recently fallen in love with," he recalled in 2002. "My first experience at CTS was that the assistant engineer plugged this American Kurzweil into an English current and, when I walked in, this gray pall of smoke filled the room. The instrument blew up."

"They wanted him to do a very traditional, mainstream, serious action score," recalled McLaughlin, who received screen credit as "music programmer" and went on to engineer many of Kamen's subsequent scores. Kamen conducted the 70-member National Philharmonic Orchestra for a week in April 1989. Vic Flick returned to play the Bond theme on his original guitar.

guitarist Vic Flick under the gun-barrel logo; then the film intercuts the American Drug Enforcement Agency's surveillance of Sanchez's plane with a Rolls-Royce headed for Felix Leiter's wedding (first 1:09 of "James & Felix on Their Way to Church" on the soundtrack CD). Shifting to Sanchez discovering his lover Lupe in bed with another man, Kamen offers a Latin-sounding acoustic guitar over strings (1½ minutes into the film, first 1:18 of "His Funny Valentine" on the CD). Leiter and Bond go after Sanchez to a series of urgent Bond-theme variations (3 minutes, "Sanchez Is in the Bahamas" on CD) and his light plane is literally reeled into custody to Kamen's full-bore Bond Theme (5½ minutes, the 1:13–3:09 portion of "Licence Revoked" on the CD).

The Gladys Knight vocal plays under Maurice Binder's final main-title sequence (8½ minutes in),

although the song has been trimmed back from its original five-minute duration to under three minutes—and, in another Bond first, the singer and songwriters do not receive main-title credit. A steel band plays at Leiter's wedding reception (15 minutes, "Wedding Party" on CD, by Kamen friend Jimmy Duncan). Meanwhile, Sanchez escapes when his truck transport plunges into the ocean and he's rescued by divers (16 minutes, 1:10 to 2:59 of "James and Felix on Their Way to Church" on CD).

Acoustic guitar and eerie strings accompany the grisly shark torture of Leiter (20 minutes in, last half of "His Funny Valentine" on CD); Bond discovers the nearly dead Leiter and his late wife to Kamen's heart-rending strings and more guitar (23 minutes, last two minutes of "Ninja" on CD). A stealthy series of Bond Theme variations accompanies Bond's late-

Licence to Kill had its London premiere on June 13, 1989, and opened in America on July 14. There was scant mention of Kamen in the reviews, although a critic for *Film Monthly* singled him out: "Kamen has composed a score with sections of great originality . . . far more serious in content and in line with the new style of James Bond." A few noticed the Gladys Knight title song, which was the first time that a Bond tune had noticeable soul or R&B influences. "While the redoubtable Gladys Knight sings the theme . . . it's nowhere near 'Goldfinger,' 'From Russia with Love,' 'Live and Let Die' or 'The Spy Who Loved Me,'" opined *People* magazine. "A great title song performed by Gladys Knight," countered *L.A. Weekly*. "A few more vocal tracks than usual, and they're goodies . . . surefire success," noted *Billboard*. Knight later attended a star-studded, black-tie British Academy of Film and Television Arts (BAFTA) salute to Cubby Broccoli on July 10 in Los Angeles.

Videos of both songs made the rounds of MTV. British music-video director Daniel Kleinman helmed the "Licence to Kill" video, with a tuxedo-clad Knight, the usual scenes from the film and striking images of colorfully clad girls. Kleinman's visual choices led to his being chosen to succeed Maurice Binder as title designer for the next five Bond films. LaBelle's "If You Asked Me To" video—filled with artistic images of candles, flowers and elegant statuary—did not acknowledge its Bond origins at all.

Knight, who had not had a top-10 hit in the U.K. for over a decade, scored with her "Licence to Kill" single. It charted on June 10, 1989, and reached number 6; it never made the American pop charts but did manage to reach number 69 on the R&B charts. Similarly, sales of the single in the U.K. drove album sales; the soundtrack LP/CD charted on July 15 in the U.K. and reached number 17; it failed to chart in the United States.

On the other hand, the LaBelle single made it in the United States but not the U.K.; it charted in America on October 7 and reached number 79 (while

(SCORE HIGHLIGHTS, CONT.)

night surveillance of Sanchez henchman Krest's facility (27 minutes); string suspense, with interesting touches of marimba, follows (30 minutes) as they encounter the traitorous Killifer.

Bond meets M and resigns, done to a downbeat, Bond Theme-inspired string line (35 minutes, 0–1:12 of "Licence Revoked" on CD). More Bond Theme variations underscore Bond's underwater surveillance of Krest's boat and his encounter with Lupe (38 minutes). What follows is the longest single musical sequence of the film (44 minutes in), a six-minute-plus series of continuously exciting Bond Theme variations as Bond is attacked, waterskis away, hops a seaplane, commandeers it and escapes with millions in drug money (last six minutes of "Licence Revoked" on CD).

Bond meets Pam in a Bimini bar where Canadian singer-songwriter Tim Feehan's "Dirty Love" is playing on a jukebox (51 minutes); it plays throughout the bar brawl. Bond and Pam escape aboard a speedboat (54 minutes), negotiate a partnership and kiss to the warmest piece in the score, a theme for strings and Kamen's Kurzweil guitar sample (56 minutes, the two pieces combined on the "Pam" CD track, 0:59–3:49). Televangelist Joe Butcher appears on TV (1 hour, 2 minutes into the film) accompanied by the "Andantino for Organ," a production-music piece by Dick Walter.

Kamen applies more Bond Theme variations, augmented by more Latin guitar, for Bond's placement of plastic explosives outside Sanchez's drug-dealer summit (1 hour, 15 minutes). About to shoot

also scoring a top-10 hit on the R&B charts). But in a much later development that had no parallel in Bond-music history, the same song, covered by a different artist, hit the pop charts three years later. A conversation between Warren and an Epic Records executive led to Celine Dion recording a cover of "If You Asked Me To," and it went all the way to number 4 in the spring of 1992. "I knew the song was a hit when I recorded it," LaBelle later said, "and I was happy that Celine did it and did so well with it. But the arrangements are so close and we both have pretty powerful voices, so who knows why my version didn't take off?" (Surprisingly, Dion performed a medley of Bond songs in her 2011 Las Vegas act but failed to include "If You Asked Me To.")

One other postfilm curiosity occurred. Walden incorporated notes from "Goldfinger" into his "Licence to Kill" song and thus, some time after the release of the film (which cites only Walden, Afanasieff and Cohen as the songwriters), an agreement was reached to add the names of "Goldfinger" songwriters John Barry, Anthony Newley and Leslie Bricusse to the song so that the original songwriters or their estates would benefit from the songwriters' tip of the hat to that iconic brass line. "We took the horn line and incorporated it in our song," Walden conceded, "and had to pay the writers a handsome share for it."

For a variety of reasons—perhaps including the downbeat story, its more extreme violence (it was the first Bond film to receive a PG-13 rating), the lack of humor, the changing movie marketplace—*Licence to Kill* earned less at the American box office than any Bond of the previous 15 years and fared almost as poorly internationally. Studio turmoil in the months to come would result in no new Bond film for the next six years. And when the next film finally came around, 007's music would be very different from what had come before.

Sanchez, he is attacked by a pair of ninja fighters, prompting Kamen to unleash a battery of exotic percussion (1 hour, 22 minutes; first 3:56 of "Ninja" on CD) and then add a misterioso touch with piano as Bond awakes at Sanchez's palatial estate. Lupe helps Bond escape, to more Latin-flavored guitar and pizzicato strings (1 hour, 29 minutes; opening 59 seconds of "Pam" on the CD). Another rare, warm moment occurs when Lupe seduces Bond (1 hour, 40 minutes), to guitar and strings.

During Pam's encounter with Joe Butcher, Kamen plays a strange, synth-and-piano arrangement of Beethoven's "Für Elise" (1 hour, 48 minutes). Sanchez and his men escape the burning drug facility to urgent strings and high brass alarms (1 hour, 55 minutes), but the tanker chase that follows is largely unscored (although one trucker is playing the traditional "La Bamba" on his radio).

The climax begins with Latin trumpet and guitar flourishes, as Sanchez vows to win (2 hours, 2 minutes), and Kamen returns to the Bond Theme complete with screaming trumpets as 007 leaps aboard Sanchez's tanker and they battle it out mano a mano; the ending is downbeat, with harp and basses underscoring the reason for it all: Felix and his wife. A brief, lyrical, strings-with-Kurzweil interlude for Bond and Lupe, then Bond and Pam (2 hours, 9 minutes), precedes the end-title song, the Patti LaBelle vocal of "If You Asked Me To."

". . . time is not on your side . . ."

GoldenEye

Complex studio issues involving MGM-UA kept James Bond off the world's movie screens for six years. When 007 returned in 1995, he was played by a new actor: Pierce Brosnan, the Irish-born star of TV's *Remington Steele* and the man who would inhabit the role for the three films to follow.

As with *Licence to Kill*, the title was not one of Ian Fleming's originals but something that had emerged from the Fleming mystique: *GoldenEye* is the name of the author's Jamaican hideaway (although he spelled it "Goldeneye") and the place where he wrote all the Bond stories from 1952 until his death in 1964.

The arrival of Brosnan wasn't the only change on the horizon. Cubby Broccoli, now in declining health, had turned over the production reins to daughter Barbara Broccoli and stepson Michael Wilson; both Richard Maibaum, screenwriter on 13 of the films, and Maurice Binder, title designer on 14, had died; and John Glen, director of the last five Bonds, had moved on to other films. New director Martin Campbell was a TV veteran who had helmed the espionage classic *Reilly: Ace of Spies* and the modern thriller *Edge of Darkness* for the BBC. The filmmakers even decided to make M a woman.

This massive shift in the look and feel of the Bond world would also extend to the sound of 007.

In *GoldenEye*, Bond, regarded as "a sexist, misogynist dinosaur, a relic of the Cold War" by the new M (Judi Dench), looks into the theft of a space-based

Russian weapons system called GoldenEye. His investigation takes him to Monte Carlo, where he meets the dangerous Xenia Onatopp (Famke Janssen), then to Russia, where he discovers an old colleague (Sean Bean) has turned traitor and a computer programmer (Izabella Scorupco) may hold the key to stopping a plot to plunge England back into the Stone Age.

Shooting began in mid-January 1995, including scenes in the cheap bar run by Bond's old Soviet enemy Valentin Zukovsky (Robbie Coltrane), whose mistress Irina (Minnie Driver, in only her second feature film) is singing Tammy Wynette's country hit "Stand By Your Man" with a terrible accent. Scenes shot later in Monaco included a French military band playing the popular "Marche Lorraine."

As principal photography ended in early June 1995, the studio was already searching for a high-profile artist for the title song. They started at the top, asking the Rolling Stones to consider writing and recording a title song; the Stones turned them down. But the studio's subsequent concept, of a song penned by U2's Bono and the Edge and sung by Tina Turner, struck paydirt. Bono and the Edge, with Soul II Soul producer Nellee Hooper (who would reprise the role on this song) were at that moment enjoying top-20 status with their song "Hold Me, Thrill Me, Kiss Me, Kill Me" from *Batman Forever*.

"Bono and the Edge are neighbors of mine in the south of France," Turner later explained. "They came over and Edge played the song on my piano. Bono wanted to write the song because he spent his honeymoon at Ian Fleming's house in Jamaica."

Turner liked the song, even though its words (like most recent Bond tunes) had no relevance to the storyline. As she said at the time: "It sounds like the right track for the movie. Some soundtracks don't actually go with the movie somehow. This one sounds like it fits the movie."

The song offered a cool, sneaky Bond-like vibe and subtly incorporated the classic Bond bass line. The team of producer Hooper, arranger-conductor Craig Armstrong and programmer Marius De Vries (which had just finished "Hold Me, Thrill Me, Kiss Me, Kill Me" and would go on to do Baz Luhrmann's musical version of *Romeo + Juliet*) gave the final recording a lush and classic sound.

"The track was already quite Bond-like," Armstrong later said of the Bono-Turner demo he first heard. He conducted 70-plus musicians in the orchestral session on an afternoon in London's Olympic Studios and recalled Turner arriving that evening to put her final vocal on the track. The team, including De Vries doing all the drums and synth programming, had done so much together that there were no special instructions about what to do. "I just remember it being really un-tense," Armstrong said. "Bono was in a good mood. It was a really fun day."

As for the score, Barry, who was now fully healed and the possessor of a fifth Academy Award for his grand symphonic score for *Dances with Wolves*, was not returning to Bond, at least not yet. "I had commitments," he told an interviewer

Composer Eric Serra

the following year, specifically *Cry, the Beloved Country* and the IMAX 3D film *Across the Sea of Time*, "two projects I was really keen on, and I just had a newly born son, so I wanted to have time with him and enjoy that side of my life."

So a search ensued for a new composer. As MGM-UA Music President Marsha Gleeman said at the time: "When it became clear that John Barry would not be available . . . we decided to take the James Bond theme in an entirely new direction. We decided on Eric Serra."

Thirty-four-year-old Eric Serra was a French composer who had enjoyed huge success with his scores for the films of Luc Besson, notably *The Big Blue*, which won a 1988 Cesar award and reached the top of the French album charts; the spy thriller *La Femme Nikita* (1990); and *Leon: The Professional* (1994), about a professional assassin. Serra's use of synthesizers and his recent addition of orchestra, especially on the documentary *Atlantis* (1991), offered a very modern approach to film scoring. Film-composer agent Richard Kraft suggested Serra. "His scores for Besson were quite original and on the cutting edge of where the next generation of film music would eventually be heading," he later reflected.

Serra, who was in Spain at the time working on a solo album, reluctantly flew to London to meet with the Bond producers and see the mostly finished film. He initially turned it down. Remembered Kraft: "After fighting so hard to get Eric offered the film, I wanted to fly across the Atlantic to strangle him for not jumping at the opportunity." Serra was convinced to change his mind a few days later, after a conversation with the president of his record label, who effectively said, "Are you nuts?"

According to Serra, much of the film was temp-tracked ("scored" with temporary music tracks to eventually be replaced by original music) with his music from *The Professional*. The Bond producers "really liked the vibe and the atmosphere of *The Professional*, and they hired Eric to reproduce that in the Bond setting," recalled British composer John Altman, who orchestrated and conducted *Atlantis* and *Leon: The Professional* and would perform the same functions on *GoldenEye*.

"When they called me to score this movie, they said that they were big fans of my music," Serra said at the time, "so I thought the best thing was to write *my* music, and not to be influenced by the old James Bond. . . . So I just did what I wanted."

According to both participants and observers, this caused problems from the earliest screenings. Explained Kraft: "Eric's experience up to that point was pretty much working with Luc Besson, who was his best friend. This was the opposite end of the spectrum: walking into a very established series with really high stakes, strong producers and an unfamiliar director. There is a cultural difference between a European artistic film and the biggest franchise of all time."

Serra, at his studio in Paris, used his samples and synthesizers to create an electronic score, which he sent in digital form to orchestrator-conductor Altman. Altman, in London, would take Serra's synth demos for strings and woodwinds and translate those into parts to be played by real musicians. The end result was a mostly electronic score with real strings and the occasional flute or harp solo.

"I started with the very beginning of the movie," Serra said at the time. "The opening is all action, so the music is a little bit like *The Professional* with a lot of percussion and low sounds. . . . After that there is a sort of car chase on which I did a very funky, fast rhythm thing but much lighter than the beginning. . . . And then there was a sort of romantic sequence, completely orchestral. . . . There was the suspense, the tragic part, the romantic part, and the fun part."

Serra invited the producers, director and editor to his studio to preview his first 10 minutes of music, as it had "all the different colors" that would be featured in the score; Serra said they all approved, leaving him to continue and promising "complete freedom" apart from the occasional use of the Bond theme at appropriate moments.

Asked about the electronics, Serra said, "some of them I program, some of them I play. I use a lot of percussion all the time. . . . There is no rule; sometimes it is completely synthetic and completely programmed, sometimes it is played, sometimes it is looped. . . . I love to mix a lot of different things from totally different continents. I like, for example, to mix African percussion with symphony orchestra with synthesizers with vocals from ethnic records."

Composer-arranger John Altman, who reorchestrated the "James Bond Theme" for the tank chase

Serra estimated that he worked "six to seven weeks" on the score during the late summer of 1995. Altman conducted a large string section (60-plus players) and a few woodwind, brass and harp players over four days at London's Angel Studios in late August and mid-September.

Serra's industrial, sometimes metallic-sounding music was a radical new sound that began to unsettle the filmmakers. There were few allusions to the

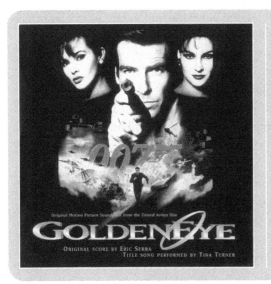

Original Motion Picture Soundtrack from the United Artists film
GOLDENEYE
ORIGINAL SCORE BY ERIC SERRA
TITLE SONG PERFORMED BY TINA TURNER

SCORE HIGHLIGHTS

Eric Serra announces the radical new sound of James Bond from the very beginning, scoring the gun-barrel logo with an electronica version of the "James Bond Theme" augmented with strings. (Serra later complained to producer Michael G. Wilson about how little of his score could be heard in the final version, and it is true that much was dubbed low and some pieces were eliminated in part or altogether.)

Bond's entry into the Soviet chemical facility is treated mostly with quiet textural sounds, although our first glimpse of Pierce Brosnan as Bond gets a surprising timpani-and-guitar arrangement of the Bond theme (3 minutes into the film, "Half of Everything Is Luck" in the "GoldenEye Overture" on CD). The pace picks up as Bond and ex–Secret Service

Pierce Brosnan as James Bond in the St. Petersburg tank chase

colleague Alec are beset by Soviet troops (5 minutes in, "The Other Half Is Fate") and Serra uses more of the Bond theme as 007 escapes via motorcycle and light plane (8 minutes, "For England, James," although the deep male voices audible in the album cannot be heard in the film).

Titles designer Daniel Kleinman's striking imagery plays over Tina Turner's vocal of "GoldenEye" (10½ minutes in, trimmed back by nearly two minutes from its full length), followed by a funky guitar-synth combo for Bond's road race with Xenia (14 minutes, "Ladies First" on CD). Serra introduces a romantic theme in a warm arrangement for strings as Bond and Xenia play baccarat (18½ minutes, "The Same Passions" on CD). A military band plays the "Marche Lorraine" (25 minutes) prior to the Tiger helicopter theft in the harbor and the cut to the

Severnaya control center, to more of Serra's industrial sounds (27 minutes, the misspelled "Xenya" in the "Little Surprise for You" suite on CD).

Natalya views her dead colleagues, to sad strings and flute, followed by a grim, more powerful statement for her emergence from the destroyed facility (41 minutes, "Among the Dead" and "Out of Hell" in "The Severnaya Suite" on CD) and a more intense string passage for her departure (45 minutes, "The Husky Tribe"). In St. Petersburg, a Russian military band plays the "Preobrajensky March" (48 minutes) as the Russian defense minister confronts Gen. Ourumov. Natalya's visit to a computer retailer merits synth chords plus jazzy bass (56 minutes, opening of "Boris and the Lethal Pen" in the "Scale to Hell" suite on CD).

Voices and bells greet Natalya as she meets Boris at a church (59 minutes, "Our Lady of Smolensk" on

"James Bond Theme," and the classic orchestral Bond sound certainly was missing. "For better or for worse," Richard Kraft reflected, "Eric Serra wrote an Eric Serra score for the movie. And no Bond movie had sounded like that. Film scoring was heading towards orchestral-synth hybrids, and *GoldenEye* was the first one that really did that. But there was a nervousness, throughout the whole scoring process, of 'Is this the right approach?'"

The concern reached a crisis point, late in the dubbing process (in which music, dialogue and sound effects are mixed), when editors balked at Serra's unorthodox take on the film's big set piece: Bond tearing up the streets of St. Petersburg in a Soviet tank. Serra played the Bond theme, mostly organ against a hard-rock beat, with what appeared to be eerie Middle Eastern-inspired vocal effects that had little relevance to the Russian locale.

"I think they were a bit afraid because it was too modern," Serra later said. "I was very naïve," explaining his refusal to change the music. Altman was asked to replace the cue with a more conventional orchestral arrangement of the Bond theme. Placed in a difficult position (he was working for Serra), Altman agreed to handle the rescore only if director Campbell phoned Serra, explained the situation and asked if it was all right.

"I got the call late on a Friday," Altman said. "I sat down and wrote and orchestrated the whole thing on Saturday and Sunday, it went for copying [to create parts for the individual musicians] on Monday and we recorded it on a Tuesday night," this time at CTS in order to accommodate an orchestra of more than 80. "What I did, basically, was a high-action thing with lots of brass and the Bond theme woven into it. Eric did what he felt was right; he chose to be eccentric with it. I tried to stay within the Bond tradition."

Serra was further upset when he heard the film's final mix at the opening in New York. "I was completely destroyed," he said. "Music was not a priority at all. You could hear only the loudest instruments, maybe 10 percent of the

CD) while the off-key Irina butchers "Stand By Your Man" when Bond visits Zukovsky's bar (1 hour in). Serra supplies eerie voices and suspenseful strings for the buildup to Bond's reunion with Alec (1 hour, 7 minutes; "Whispers" in "Whispering Statues" suite on CD); their conversation is underscored by melancholy piano (1 hour, 9 minutes, "Two Faced" in "Whispering Statues").

The escaping Bond and Natalya are hauled off by Russian troops to synth-driven military cadences and male voices (1 hour, 13 minutes, "D. M. Mychkine" in "A Little Surprise for You" on CD; the title refers to Defense Minister Mishkin). Natalya tells her story, to the sound of flute, strings and surprising violin solo (1 hour, 14 minutes). They manage to shoot their way out, to fast-paced rhythm and synth lines (1 hour, 18 minutes, "Run, Shoot and Jump" on CD).

John Altman's replacement scoring for Bond's destructive tank chase through St. Petersburg actually starts earlier, as Natalya is recaptured and Bond escapes into a yard filled with tanks (1 hour, 19 minutes). The rescore, for large conventional orchestra, explodes with the classic "Bond Theme" brass section but also follows the action as Bond tails Gen. Ourumov through the city for the next six minutes (Serra's original, unused version—which also uses the Bond theme, but more like a club mix, adding strange Eastern-sounding voices—is on the CD as "A Pleasant Drive in St. Petersburg").

The aftermath of the train-tank collision, Alec and Xenia's escape and Bond and Natalya's close call is scored with more strange noises and a heartbeat-like drum (1 hour, 31 minutes; "Fatal Weakness" on CD). A far more serene moment for strings, flute

orchestrations. Lots of little details were lost. For me it was a disaster; what you could hear did not make sense. It was one of the worst moments of my life."

Future Bond composer David Arnold later called Serra's score "quite bold, so unlike anything that had gone before . . . but it was one of those scores that I think perhaps the world wasn't really ready for." There was considerably less concern about Serra's sensuous end-title song, "The Experience of Love" (with lyrics by prolific English producer Rupert Hine).

The music credits were more complex than on any prior Bond film: "Synthesizer score recorded at X-Florians Studio, Paris, produced and performed by Eric Serra . . . Symphonic music recorded at Angel Recording Studios, London, by the London Studio Sessions Orchestra, conducted by John Altman, orchestrations by John Altman and David Arch."

GoldenEye premiered in New York City on November 13, 1995, and in London on November 21. Fewer reviewers than ever paid attention to the music, although *Variety* singled out the composer for criticism: "One disappointing note is the score by Luc Besson recruit Eric Serra." *Fanfare* went so far as to declare, "Serra's bizarre and spacey timbres will make you swear 007 is doing mushrooms." *Billboard*, however, raved about Tina Turner: "A tingly, feline performance. . . . Producer Nellee Hooper captures the essence of the movie, wrapping the track in sweeping strings and horns. . . . Bono and The Edge get in on the fun, writing a tune that's fraught with cryptic lyrical twists and romantic intrigue."

Turner participated in the promotion, making a classy video (directed by Jake Scott, son of filmmaker Ridley Scott) that was in rotation on cable's VH-1, and performing the song twice on TV: on December 3, as part of VH-1's *Fashion and Music Awards*, and on December 6, on the *Billboard Music Awards*

and harp accompanies Bond and Natalya's kiss and their trip to Cuba (1 hour, 34 minutes; "The Trip to Cuba," opening of "We Share the Same Passions" on CD). Their heart-to-heart talk on the beach is sensitively scored with strings, both melancholy and romantic (1 hour, 37 minutes; "That's What Keeps You Alone" on CD).

Bond and Natalya survive a plane crash, only to be menaced again by Xenia to more percussion and odd synth beats (1 hour, 42 minutes; "A Good Squeeze" in "Dish Out of Water" on CD). The massive dish antenna emerges from the water to portentous brass and military percussion (1 hour, 45 minutes; "The Antenna" in "Dish Out of Water" on CD). More of Serra's insistent drumbeats accompany Boris's attempts to undo Natalya's computer meddling (1 hour, 54 minutes; more of "Fatal Weak-

ness" on CD, although the album version lacks the strings that add considerably to the tension).

Serra reverts briefly to live musicians again for Alec's battle with Bond outside (1 hour, 57 minutes), but there is no score for much of their hand-to-hand combat. The orchestra returns (high strings, synth sounds and percussion) as they fight it out on the ladder (2 hours, 1 minute). Serra reprises his romantic theme as Bond and Natalya, safe at last, kiss (2 hours, 4 minutes; "For Ever, James" on CD). Serra sings his own "The Experience of Love" under the end titles.

televised by Fox. Virgin Records, which had the soundtrack, promoted it heavily, including ads in such movie magazines as *Premiere*. In the United States, the single charted on November 25 but managed to reach only number 102, while in the U.K. it reached number 7 on the singles charts. The album charted in the United States on December 2 but managed to reach only number 180.

The album featured most of Serra's score, including his original version of the tank-chase sequence (titled "A Pleasant Drive in St. Petersburg") but not Altman's orchestral interlude that replaced it. A modified version of the latter would appear five years later in a performance by ex-Barry orchestrator Nic Raine conducting the City of Prague Philharmonic.

Serra went on to score *The Fifth Element*, *Rollerball* and *Arthur and the Invisibles*. "Even with the frustration and disappointment, I'm very happy to be part of the James Bond legend," he said 16 years later. "Now, I would have composed something different to avoid the problems, plus I would have been a bit more professional instead of being so artistic." Orchestral-synth hybrids would soon become commonplace in film scoring. Altman would, five years later, win an Emmy for his own music for the television film *RKO 281*. And although Brosnan would continue as 007, there would now be a renewed debate over just how to support him musically.

". . . until the world falls away . . ."

Tomorrow Never Dies

*G*oldenEye was a critical and commercial success. It made $350 million worldwide and successfully reignited the Bond franchise with a new and well-liked actor. All the elements were in place for future installments, save one: music.

The studio deemed the Serra experiment unsuccessful. "When we decided to go with Eric Serra we knew that was a left turn," MGM Music Executive Vice President Michael Sandoval said, "but we were trying to bring some youthfulness and a modernness to the film. When it all came together, it didn't have the juice we were all hoping for."

So in late 1996—months before the start of production on the new film, titled *Tomorrow Never Dies*—John Barry was asked to consider returning. But it was now a very different Bond world than the one he had been instrumental in launching back in the 1960s. Since the mid-1980s, Bond title songs were considered as much a marketing tool as a creative aspect of the movies themselves. And even though MGM-UA and Eon remained partners in the Bond films, the songs had fallen more under the jurisdiction of the studio than the producers.

"We had various disagreements on how it would be done, how we would proceed essentially in terms of the song," Barry said in December 1997. "There were several areas that were non-negotiable. I wasn't going to regress." Without assurance that he would be at least co-writing the title song, Barry

Composer David Arnold

passed. (It didn't help that MGM-UA also refused to meet his minimum asking price for the score, offering him considerably less than other A-level composers were getting at the time.)

While the Barry negotiations were falling apart, composer David Arnold was finishing work on his new album, a collection of Bond-song covers titled *Shaken and Stirred*. The 35-year-old Luton native had burst onto the film-scoring scene with a hit Bjork song for *The Young Americans* in 1993, wrote a massive orchestral score for MGM-UA's science-fiction film *Stargate* in 1994 and then scored the biggest box-office hit of 1996, *Independence Day*.

Arnold met Barbara Broccoli in the wake of *Stargate*'s success and sent her the *Shaken and Stirred* songs during the two years it took to assemble the album (which included Propellerheads doing "On Her Majesty's Secret Service," David McAlmont singing "Diamonds Are Forever" and Iggy Pop singing "We Have All the Time in the World," among others). "They knew I was a huge Bond fan," Arnold said, recalling seeing *You Only Live Twice* as a boy and immediately falling for Barry's music. In the meantime, he had met Barry at George Martin's AIR Studios, played him his *Shaken and Stirred* songs and gotten an enthusiastic approval from "the guv'nor."

In early 1997, Barry and Arnold met again, "and he encouraged me [to do the Bond film]. He said, 'You are the rightful heir,' which is a bit of a trip," Arnold said. In fact, the *Shaken and Stirred* album demonstrated Arnold's respect for the Barry style while, as Barry said, "adding a whole other rhythmic freshness and interesting casting in terms of the artists chosen." Arnold won a Grammy for his *Independence Day* score in February and, after committing to an unorthodox writing and recording schedule, was given a shot at *Tomorrow Never Dies*.

Production didn't begin until April and wouldn't end until early September. With premiere dates already set for December, Arnold would need to score the film as it went along and not wait until fall for a cut of the entire film. "They knew I was totally committed," Arnold said in late 1997, "and I knew how I wanted it to sound. I wanted to do it with one foot in the '60s and one foot in the '90s. There are 35 years of musical heritage attached to this film, and audiences need to hear it. Without that music, you've got an action movie, you haven't got a Bond movie."

Arnold had spent, off and on, the previous two years dealing with Bond music for *Shaken and Stirred*. "I experimented with a lot of styles, trying to find ways of making the orchestra work with more high-tech rhythm loops, drum loops, synth stuff and guitars," he said. "So [the film score] felt like a classic sound but a modern approach, just as Pierce adopted for the characterization: he's got a classic feel, but it's also a contemporary approach to the character."

He read the script and started, in April, by writing a theme. He called singer-songwriter David McAlmont (with whom he had been working lately, and whose "Diamonds Are Forever" cover would hit Britain's top 40 in November) to help with the tune and veteran lyricist Don Black to pen the lyrics—just in case there could be a song, as in the Barry films where the title tune was also the main theme of the score. McAlmont helped with "the middle part" of the tune, Arnold said, and then brought in Black, who delivered "everything that a Bond song should be . . . that kind of entices you into the movie."

Tomorrow Never Dies concerns a media mogul named Elliot Carver (Jonathan Pryce) whose mad scheme to control the news and maximize television ratings involves orchestrating a naval war between Britain and China. It turns out that, in addition to allying with a techno-terrorist (Ricky Jay), Carver has married Bond's old flame Paris (Teri Hatcher), who meets a tragic end as a result. Bond joins forces with a Chinese agent (Hong Kong action star Michelle Yeoh) to thwart Carver's plot to start World War III.

Black hadn't written a Bond lyric since *The Man with the Golden Gun*, but he was delighted to be asked back. Unlike Black's work with Barry, in which Black would fit his words to a completed melody, "it's much more collaborative with David," Black said. "I would give him some random lines, four lines here, a disconnected couple of lines there. . . ." Within a day, Arnold said, Black had sent over "a bunch of ideas. They seemed so perfectly Bond-esque: 'Your life is a story I've already written. . . .' That's what Don is so amazing at, he has this reductive quality where he'll come up with a line or two that encompasses the whole story of the film."

Indeed, Black's grasp of the story was immediately apparent, incorporating clever references to Carver's newspaper "Tomorrow" and the news business generally: "tomorrow will arrive on time / I'll tease and tantalize with every line . . . trust me, I'll deliver. . . ." McAlmont sang the demo.

Pierce Brosnan and Michelle Yeoh

However, the studio wanted a major pop or rock name on the title song and, to that end, invited several major artists and songwriters to enter songs in what turned out to be a kind of under-the-radar song competition. "MGM invited a lot of people to submit," Arnold recalled. "I wasn't sure whether they knew that they were effectively being asked to join a band fight. Having spoken to Jarvis Cocker and Simon Le Bon, they certainly didn't know that they were up against other people. They were under the impression that they were being asked to write the song for the Bond movie."

Cocker's group Pulp ("Common People") and Le Bon's Duran Duran (whose "View to a Kill" topped the charts in 1985) were just two of the bands contacted; Saint Etienne ("Only Love Can Break Your Heart") submitted a song, as did Marc Almond ("Tears Run Rings"). So, reportedly, did producer-songwriter Glen Ballard. That all of the groups were in the dark about the "cattle call" was confirmed years later by Saint Etienne vocalist Sarah Cracknell: "Little did we know there were about a dozen other people who were presenting songs. I remember afterwards there were loads of bands with B sides called 'Tomorrow Never Lies' or 'Tomorrow Never Flies'. . . ."

In the end, studio executives chose Sheryl Crow, who was particularly hot at that moment. She had won five Grammy Awards in the previous two years, including Record of the Year, Best New Artist and Best Rock Album; she had placed three songs in the American top 20 within the previous eight months, and four in the British top 25 during the same period. Crow collaborated with songwriter-producer Mitchell Froom, who had helped with her recent second album.

"She was doing some pretty cool music, and didn't want to do something that was cheesy," Froom recalled. "She had a really nice tune that ended up being the melody of the song. My suggestion was that we make it much more epic. My musical reference was Gene Pitney's 'Town Without Pity'—exuberant but with an edge—using strings, but raw-sounding, not lush. The chords for the bridge were a tip of the hat to the kinds of harmonic progressions that John Barry used to use.

"We did it very quickly in, like, three days. We brought in a few string players and kept overdubbing them. We didn't have any horns. It wasn't optimal in terms of film sound; it was just rough and ready," Froom said. They recorded in late spring at the Magic Shop in New York City and then mixed at Sunset Sound Factory in Los Angeles. "A month after we turned it in, they called and asked for a 5.1 mix," Froom added, referring to modern five-channel surround-sound audio. "That's when I knew for sure that it was in the film."

Crow came up with an arresting opening line referring to Paris's murder ("darlin', I'm killed / I'm in a puddle on the floor . . ."), although her second verse was more generic ("martinis, girls and guns . . . you're not the only spy out there"). She was announced as the title-song performer in mid-June. "I'm a big Bond fan," she said at the time, "and I find all those hugely dramatic, highly suspenseful pieces fascinating." About her own song, she said "I'd really like to get back to the original feel of those '60s themes and do some-

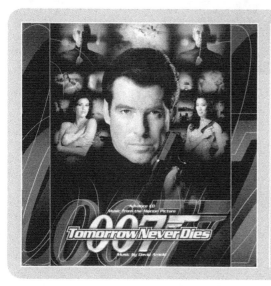

SCORE HIGHLIGHTS

Moviegoers who were missing the classic Bond sound in *GoldenEye* got it back in spades with David Arnold's score for *Tomorrow Never Dies*. And at more than 97 minutes of music, of which 88 was Arnold's, it contained by far the most music of any Bond film to date. Arnold correctly surmised what the film, and the series, needed: a reminder of the John Barry style but updated to the late 1990s with modern electronics and constant spurts of musical energy to drive the film along.

Arnold begins, naturally, with a classic, Barry-esque gun-barrel opening featuring the "Bond Theme" and a suspenseful orchestral buildup to the admiral's ill-timed missile launch (3 minutes into the film). Arnold expertly intertwines his own main theme (in vocal form, the "Surrender" song appearing at the

Singer Sheryl Crow around the time of her "Tomorrow Never Dies" single

thing that is part lounge and part what I do." Daniel Kleinman directed her music video.

Some who lost the song competition were critical of the winner: "I thought it was a bit rubbish, actually," said Sarah Cracknell. Don Black commented: "I do honestly think that ours was a better song; it tells the story of the film. With the Bond songs, it's changed a lot. They've gone very much for who's going to sing it as opposed to what it is. With John [Barry] and David [Arnold], it's always been: get the song right, then get the artist."

Arnold had already recorded the orchestral track for their song (along with the early portion of the score, May 31) and, after getting permission to use it as the end-title song, recruited k.d. lang as vocalist. "She has a gloriously understated delivery and when she opens up, she can take the roof off a house in the same way that Shirley Bassey can take the roof off," Arnold said later. The studio's adoption of the Crow song forced Arnold and Black to modify their song slightly from "Tomorrow Never Dies" to "Surrender."

"There really wasn't a title that worked," Arnold recalled, "[but] 'surrender' was a word that scanned: surrender, come and join me on my world-domination thing. It's about giving in to the inevitable." Lang's vocal was originally recorded in Los Angeles but, for complex tax reasons involving the film, had to be re-recorded in Toronto.

In the meantime, Arnold spent six months working on the score, an unusually long time for a composer on a single film. Because they were going to be scoring as the film came back from various locations around the world, Arnold wrote the music for the pre-title sequence first. "Roger [Spottiswoode, the director] wanted me to score something so he could get an idea of how it was going to be before we committed to it in its entirety," Arnold said. Synthesizer mockups, it was felt, would not be sufficient. The May 31 orchestral recording

(SCORE HIGHLIGHTS, CONT.) end of the film) and the "Bond Theme" as 007 steals a Russian fighter jet, done to some of the most energetic and authentically Barry-influenced music—with gestures borrowed from *From Russia with Love*, *Goldfinger* and *On Her Majesty's Secret Service*—in over a decade ("White Knight" on the original CD).

Sheryl Crow's title song (9½ minutes in) plays under Daniel Kleinman's inventive, high-tech-influenced titles filled with timepieces, circuit-covered women and guns firing. Military rhythms, low grim brass and drumbeats accompany the South China Sea action in which the HMS *Devonshire* is attacked and sinks; sampled choir and urgent, high brass for our first glimpse of Carver follow (12½ minutes, "The Sinking of the Devonshire" on CD).

Bond's dalliance with his language professor features a minute of Beethoven's Piano Concerto No. 5 (22 minutes). Bond's arrival in Hamburg, meeting Q and trying out his new BMW get the full "Bond Theme" treatment complete with sassy brass (27½ minutes and 30 minutes, "Company Car" on CD). The rock music for Carver's party is by Simon Greenaway and Sacha Collisson (later known as the electronica band Aurora) except for the reunion of Paris and Bond, which occurs to a cocktail piano version of the old standard "It Had to Be You" that Greenaway performs (32 minutes). Eerie strings, which relate to the *Devonshire* disaster, are heard as Carver makes his speech and Bond beats up Carver's goons (37 minutes, "Station Break" on the first CD, although the film version of the opening differs from that on the album).

Arnold introduces a new theme as Paris visits Bond's hotel room, a bittersweet tune for flute that

session at AIR Studios' Lyndhurst Hall thus became Arnold's very expensive audition.

Arnold scored the 9½ minute pre-title sequence with a combination of his own main theme and high-octane variations on the "James Bond Theme," with nods to classic Barry gestures including the machine-gun brass of *From Russia with Love*, the swirling strings of *On Her Majesty's Secret Service* and as much sassy, *Goldfinger*-style brass as he could manage. "It just rocked," Arnold recalled. "It had bits of the old stuff, bits of new stuff, big music for this huge opening. And he [Spottiswoode] loved it. From that point on, I was pretty much left alone to do what I wanted to do."

Recording sessions continued "about every five or six weeks" in an effort to keep on schedule. "What worried me more than anything was, I didn't know how the film was going to end," Arnold said in late 1997, "and you can't go back and change anything you've already done. But it worked, because as the film moves from location to location, the score changes gear and moves with it."

Arnold worked with his regular orchestrator and conductor, Nicholas Dodd. A graduate of London's Royal College of Music, Dodd was a veteran arranger-conductor whose symphonic credits ranged from "Mostly Mozart" to "An Evening with Procol Harum." They had met in the 1980s and collaborated on films dating back to *The Young Americans* and *Stargate*.

"I do really detailed sketches of the whole piece," Arnold explained, "mapping out the structure musically, getting a feeling for the tempo, the pulse, where the heart of it comes from. I'll run the picture a few times and try to respond to it purely emotionally. In the early days of the score, it's pretty detailed, so you've got string parts, percussion, woodwinds, brass. Nick's a genius anyway, and we've got a good shorthand going. Nick goes away and

swells to full orchestra (43 minutes, "Paris and Bond" on CD); they part to an acoustic-guitar version (45 minutes, "The Last Goodbye"). Bond breaks into Carver's secret lab (47½ minutes, "Hamburg Break In") to an interesting combination of orchestral and electronic sounds that turns into another high-energy piece as Bond is chased out (50 minutes, "Hamburg Break Out"). Arnold invokes the "Bond Theme" again, this time on guitar, as he escapes the building and takes Carver's call (53 minutes).

Bond finds Paris's body to the accompaniment of high strings and a guitar that briefly evokes her theme (55 minutes, "Doctor Kaufman") but uses his cell phone to disable the killer and escape to another fast-moving combination of Arnold's main theme and the Bond theme (at 58½ minutes, "*-3-Send" on CD). This leads to one of the highlights of

the score: Arnold's collaboration with Propeller-heads partner Alex Gifford, as Bond manages to retrieve his BMW and elude Carver's gang to an electronica-driven, high-energy medley of the Bond theme and Arnold's own (59½ minutes, "Backseat Driver" on CD).

Bond finds the missing *Devonshire* and explores it, to eerie string passages with electronic effects and finds Wai Lin there already; the two must escape the rapidly sinking ship (1 hour, 8 minutes, "Underwater Discovery" on CD). Arnold then uses a fascinating combination of electronics, orchestra and Eastern string and percussion instruments to evoke the sounds of Vietnam (1 hour, 12 minutes, "Helicopter Ride" on the second *TND* soundtrack, as with the remainder of the score). They escape Carver's headquarters via motorcycle and a seven-minute

does the orchestration, and I'll start working on the next piece. At the end of the picture, when you're panicking and there's no time to do anything, it gets down to two or three lines and, 'Remember what we did in that cue? Do that sort of thing here.' Nick's totally on top of it."

Recording, with an orchestra that ranged from 83 to 92 players, continued through late October 1997, including another cutting-edge musical sequence involving Alex Gifford of Propellerheads. Their earlier work together on the *On Her Majesty's Secret Service* cover turned out to be the perfect temporary music for the remote-controlled BMW car-chase sequence. "Alex is an enormous Bond fan," Arnold said. The composer did a rough synth version of the sequence—again alternating between his own theme and the "Bond Theme"— and then gave it to Gifford. "He did the drum programming, the piano solo, that synth bass through an amplifier. It was fabulous."

The final third of the film, which takes place in the Far East, included a vast number of authentic Chinese percussion instruments. "I kind of mapped it out using ethnic samples," Arnold explained, "and then we went into the studio with [London percussionist] Pete Lockett and replaced everything. Of course he brought all these new ideas and new sounds, but it was all one person playing it. We multitracked and built it up."

Spottiswoode was delighted with the result. "David made a fresh new score and yet still had those elements of the music that we really love from the past. He's a terrifically flexible, funny, wry collaborator. A smart man, very good musician, with tremendous confidence—and justified confidence—in what he does. Given that [the postproduction schedule] was totally impossible, David and I quickly shared the same attitude: we're going to have a good time doing it. The score went from an essential part of postproduction to an essential part of production."

chase that incorporates variations on the Bond theme and Arnold's own escalating, high-brass action motif as they are pursued by helicopter (1 hour, 17 minutes, "Bike Chase" on CD).

Chinese agents attack Wai Lin, to more furious, Eastern-percussion-dominated action music (1 hour, 25 minutes, "Bike Shop Fight" on CD). Another highlight occurs as Bond and Wai Lin sail to Ha Long Bay to Arnold's main theme, spiced with more Eastern sounds (1 hour, 30 minutes, mistitled "Kowloon Bay" on the CD). They discover and board the Stealth boat—which fires missiles toward British and Chinese ships—to dramatic orchestral material, augmented by Bond-theme variations as she is captured (1 hour, 33 minutes, "Boarding the Stealth" on CD).

Bond squares off with Carver, at first to tense strings, then to more brass- and electronics-driven Bond-theme variations as the action begins (1 hour, 40 minutes, "A Tricky Spot for 007" on CD). As the Stealth is on fire, Bond and Wai Lin are separated and things look bleak; Arnold invokes more Bond theme variations (1 hour, 48 minutes). Carver's death, interestingly, is unscored. For the finale, as a chained Wai Lin is dropped into the ocean and Bond squares off against Stamper, Arnold ratchets up the tension with constantly moving string and percussion figures, thrilling Bond-theme variations, touches of his own main theme and a powerful climax as Bond manages to save Wai Lin with an underwater kiss (1 hour, 50 minutes, "All in a Day's Work" on CD).

"Surrender," the k.d. lang vocal, is heard over the end titles (1 hour, 55 minutes).

The world premiere of *Tomorrow Never Dies* took place in London on December 9, 1997, and as usual there were a handful of notices about the music: The *Los Angeles Times* cited Arnold's use of "the way-familiar Monty Norman theme," while *The Times of London* complained of "enduring the silly title song, sung, just about, by Sheryl Crow." *The Hollywood Reporter*, however, liked both songs: "those Bond songs, which have been somewhat of a disappointment in recent installments, rediscover their groove this time out, with Sheryl Crow delivering an effective 'Tomorrow Never Dies' over the opening credits, while k.d. lang neatly captures the sultry essence of Shirley Bassey in the credit-closing 'Surrender.'"

Billboard raved about both Crow ("she wails with appropriate melodrama as an array of fluid guitar riffs and swooping strings and piano lines collide at the song's climax") and Arnold ("an excellent score . . . the best in recent memory") and noted the album addition (not in the film) of Moby's "dynamic reworking of the 'James Bond Theme.'" *L.A. Weekly* also liked the Arnold score, noting that he "brings a sly postmodern spin to the Bond franchise; he winks at the hokey conventions of spy music while respecting their endearing pop value." The *Village Voice* went even further: "It's this battle between the hypermasculine Bond ideal of cool perfection and the psychologically chaotic world he inhabits that Arnold manages to capture," then raving about the k.d. lang song at the expense of the Crow vocal ("sounds even more out of her shallow depths, incapable of hitting the notes or summoning Bondian authority and sophistication").

Despite the critical brickbats, Crow's "Tomorrow Never Dies" became the first Bond song since "For Your Eyes Only" to be nominated for a Golden Globe, while also receiving a 1998 Grammy nomination as Best Song Written for Visual Media. The single charted in the U.K. on December 13, peaking at number 12, but it didn't chart at all in the United States. Conversely, the A&M soundtrack album didn't make the British charts but just sneaked onto the American charts for one week, January 17, 1998, at number 197.

Not unlike what happened with the *Thunderball* album 32 years earlier, Arnold was still recording his score when the soundtrack album had to be assembled in order to make a November 25 release date. So the 12 score tracks on the 1997 A&M album reflected the first two-thirds of the score. Two years later, the enterprising American label Chapter III issued a second *Tomorrow Never Dies* soundtrack containing seven more tracks from the final reels of the movie (along with an 11-minute interview with the composer, a first for a Bond album).

John Barry was right: David Arnold was the heir apparent to the title of "James Bond composer." He would go on to score the next four films in the series.

21

"...no point in living if you can't feel alive ..."

The World Is Not Enough

The international success of *Tomorrow Never Dies* ($333 million world-wide) meant that planning soon began for *The World Is Not Enough*, another Fleming-related title (it was the motto on the Bond family crest, as revealed in the novel *On Her Majesty's Secret Service*) for an entirely original screenplay. David Arnold had done such a stellar job scoring *Tomorrow Never Dies*, and writing a song that the Bond producers liked, that they not only brought him back but offered him the plum job of title song composer as well.

Arnold thus became the only composer other than John Barry to score more than one Bond film, and once more he was following in Barry's footsteps: Barry's first Bond score, for *From Russia with Love*, saw someone else writing the title song. But on his second time out, *Goldfinger*, he got to do both. And as a full-fledged member of the Bond team, Arnold was signed early enough (in September 1998) that he met director Michael Apted during preproduction and then spent time on the set after production began in January 1999.

As they did on *Tomorrow Never Dies*, Arnold and lyricist Don Black wrote the title song first, in this case, in November and December, even before production had begun. "I made it clear to David ... the sort of tone I needed," Apted recalled, "that we wanted something romantic and haunting. And it was important to me that the song should be written and recorded early enough in the process ... at least a rough draft of the song, so that it could be incorporated into the score."

Arnold had a demo by early January 1999, getting approvals from Broccoli, Wilson and Apted before delivering it to his singer of choice: Scottish-born Shirley Manson of the alternative-rock band Garbage. "This opening title song is very much from Elektra's point of view," Arnold explained, referring to the duplicitous character played by Sophie Marceau. "It should be like a steel fist in a velvet glove. It beckons you in with its crooked finger, 'come on, come on,' and once it gets you in there, it strangles and stabs you in the back. Shirley's the only person I could think of in contemporary music who is the musical equivalent of Elektra. She's very confrontational as a performer, very up front and even though she's beautiful and very female, she has a lot of masculine energy," Arnold said. At the time, Garbage was very big in Britain: Eight top-20 hits and a number-one album in the previous three years. Once the studio approved the choice of artist, Arnold called Manson to tell her and, he recalled, "I've never heard anyone squeal quite as loud."

As Manson told the press in 1999: "We think our music has similarities with the whole Bond concept—something that you can enjoy on the surface but underneath there are lots of conflicting themes that you can get into, if you so wish."

Black's lyrics incorporated a key line from the script: "There's no point in living if you can't feel alive. . . ." "David sent us a rough demo with the synthesizer playing the string [parts] and we really loved it," drummer-producer Butch Vig said at the time. "Shirley wanted to change a few lyrics, which Don did really quickly. We were on tour so we went back and forth with David on the telephone . . . we'd play stuff over the phone and he'd play things back to us. Very crude, but it worked enough for us to bang out the arrangement."

Vig "came up with a track that is the record," Arnold said, "and I popped down to the studio when they were doing it. Shirley recorded the vocals, Don

Music from the MGM Motion Picture
Music by David Arnold
Title Song Performed by Garbage

The **World Is Not Enough**
007

Sophie Marceau and Pierce Brosnan as Elektra and Bond during the torture sequence in *The World Is Not Enough*

came down, and I put the orchestra on it." The song was recorded and mixed over the summer, with some work done in June at London's Metropolis Studios and more at Vancouver's Armoury Studios in August; word leaked in late June that Garbage was the chosen band. (Reports that Jamiroquai, Robbie Williams, Bjork and others had submitted potential themes were later dismissed; Garbage was the only band ever considered for the title song.)

The World Is Not Enough concerns the daughter (Marceau) of a murdered industrialist whose unfinished cross-Asia oil pipeline seems to be of intense interest to terrorist Renard (Robert Carlyle). As the action shifts from Spain to Azerbaijan, Turkey and Kazakhstan, Bond also encounters nuclear-weapons expert Christmas Jones (Denise Richards), runs into old Russian nemesis Zukovsky (Robbie Coltrane) and meets Q's successor (John Cleese).

A key plot point involves Bond falling for Elektra—the woman who would seduce and then betray him—and it required a kind of downbeat love theme. "We have to believe that not only is he protective of her, he actually falls in love with her," Arnold reflected a decade later. "We have to take their relationship at face value and not give anything away as to what might actually be going on. There's a very dark kind of perverted romance in the film."

The result was not only an equally memorable second theme but one that, Arnold thought, could also be a song. "Elektra's theme felt like a song without words. I wanted to use it at the end of the movie: he's had this love affair, he's been broken by it but he's got to pull himself back up." He told Don Black to think of it this way: "He's sitting on the beach, he's thinking about his life, about everything that's gone wrong and his part in it, and he's lost this person that might have been the one."

For "Only Myself to Blame," Black responded with an especially evocative lyric: "I've held other arms, but they don't feel the same / and I've only myself to blame. . . ." Arnold himself came up with one of the song's best lines: "there's no greater fool in the fool's hall of fame. . . ."

They recruited vocalist Scott Walker (of Walker Brothers and "The Sun Ain't Gonna Shine Anymore" fame) and Arnold arranged it for jazz combo (notably a very noirish muted trumpet and piano) plus strings. "Only Myself to Blame" was a candidate for end-title song, but as Arnold recalled, "Michael Apted felt that it was too much of a downer for the end of the movie. He

through it all, a combination of high-energy orchestral histrionics and variations on the Bond Theme (6½ minutes in, "Show Me the Money" and "Come in 007, Your Time Is Up" on the CD). Daniel Kleinman's inventive titles (petroleum-drenched nudes) play over Garbage's vocal of the main theme (14 minutes).

Bond's probe into Elektra King's kidnapping ordeal is underscored with an intriguing combination of electronic sounds and conventional strings (23 minutes, "Access Denied" on CD). Melancholy strings underline Bond's conversation with M about the ransom money for Elektra (25 minutes, "M's Confession" on CD, although only the first third is used in the film; presumably the dramatic sounds at its end were to introduce terrorist Renard).

Bond travels to Azerbaijan, to Arnold's intertwined main theme and Bond-theme variations, spiced with appropriate ethnic percussion (28 minutes, "Welcome to Baku" on CD, but again severely truncated and minus the ethnic vocals of Natacha Atlas). Bond and Elektra ski down a mountainside together to a very Barry-esque theme for horns and strings that points up the scenic beauty (34 minutes). The attack by skyborne ski vehicles again combines electronics and traditional orchestra, often in threatening variations on the main theme (36 minutes, "Ice Bandits" on CD).

Arnold wrote two source cues for Zukovsky's casino: the first, a jazzy sax piece; the second, a stunning jazz version of Elektra's theme for small combo featuring alto flute, muted trumpet and vibes

wanted to send people home on a high, which you can understand." It wound up on the soundtrack album but ranks with "Mr. Kiss Kiss Bang Bang" as one of the great songs written for a Bond film that failed to make it into the movie.

The schedule was somewhat less pressured this time, with the song finished early along with two main themes that would become the basis for key parts of the score. It also moved forward musically from *Tomorrow Never Dies* in the sense that Arnold used even more electronics. "I thought to [make] the whole thing a little more contemporary and use a lot of electronic rhythms to keep the thing jetting along," Arnold said. "I had a lot of conversations with Martin [Evans], the sound designer, about where the noise was going to be. I knew that it was pointless writing lots of tricky little bits and pieces if the world was going to be blowing up on top of it."

Again Nicholas Dodd orchestrated the entire score and conducted an 83-piece orchestra over six days at the end of September 1999. Dodd called *The World Is Not Enough* his favorite Bond score of the Arnold era: "Orchestra and electronics met perfectly in the middle. [Programmer and keyboard player] Steve Hilton did a fabulous job of the electronics. That was a perfect marriage: there is subtle electronics and subtle orchestration, and then there's bold electronics and bold orchestration. Lovely, sweeping, great fun."

As so much of the film takes place in the southwestern Asia region (including Azerbaijan, Turkey and Kazakhstan) Arnold once again asked Pete Lockett to handle most of the ethnic percussion and added two additional soloists for local flavor: qanun player Abdullah Chhadeh (Damascus-born, London-based soloist on the zither-like traditional Arabic instrument) and Chhadeh's then-wife, vocalist Natacha Atlas (Belgian-born, with Middle Eastern influences, who also sang "From Russia with Love" on Arnold's *Shaken and Stirred* album).

(46 minutes, "Casino" on CD). It's in this sequence that Elektra utters the line that became a key part of the title song lyric: "There's no point in living if you can't feel alive." We first meet the mad terrorist Renard to low sounds, both synth and strings, plus piano (49 minutes). Arnold plays Elektra's theme, strings and piano, for Bond and Elektra in bed (51 minutes, "Elektra's Theme" on CD).

Three minutes of quiet orchestral suspense, with electronic percussion and a touch of the Arabic instrument qanun, underscores Bond substituting himself for Elektra's traitorous security chief (53 minutes, "Body Double" on CD). In Kazakhstan, Bond meets Christmas Jones and descends to the weapons site; again low, grim sounds, especially as Bond confronts Renard, interestingly "in waltz time, for no particular reason," Arnold said (59 minutes, "Going Down" on CD). Arnold pulls out all the orchestral stops for the underground action as Bond and Jones escape while Renard steals the nuclear device (1 hour, 4 minutes, "The Bunker" on CD).

Bond and Jones locate and defuse Renard's nuclear device while on a speeding vehicle inside the oil pipeline, another powerful cue that uses both orchestra and electronics to constantly heighten the tension—as Arnold described it, "muscular and rhythmic, taut and tight" (1 hour, 14 minutes, "Pipeline" on CD). Renard threatens the imprisoned M and then visits Elektra, to a tortured version of her theme for alto flutes and low strings (1 hour, 24 minutes, "Remember Pleasure" on CD). On the Caspian Sea, Zukovsky's caviar factory comes

Nicholas Dodd conducts the orchestra at AIR studios, London

Shirley Manson as she appears in the Garbage video for "The World Is Not Enough"

The American commercial failure of both the Tina Turner and Sheryl Crow songs caused MGM to redouble its music-promotion efforts as a way of attracting young audiences to the film. The studio struck an unprecedented partnership with MTV to air 100 hours of Bond-related programming on its channels in the United States, Europe, Asia and Latin America, including a "Making of the Video" special partially funded by MTV, a behind-the-scenes movie special for MTV Europe, a week of 007-focused "Total Request Live" programs popular with American teenagers and appearances by Brosnan and Richards on the MTV Europe Music Awards.

under attack from Renard's men, prompting more fast-paced action music incorporating another series of screaming-brass Bond-theme variations, this time augmented by synth-percussion beats (1 hour, 27 minutes, "Caviar Factory" on CD).

Bond and Jones are abducted by Elektra's men, and Renard steals a Russian nuclear submarine, to a dark piano-and-strings line (1 hour, 40 minutes). Elektra tortures Bond, to another twisted version of her theme (1 hour, 44 minutes, "Torture Queen" on CD). With Zukovsky's help, Bond escapes, rescues M and confronts Elektra, to another fast-moving orchestral passage that concludes with a final, sad statement of her theme (1 hour, 47 minutes, "I Never Miss" on CD).

For the finale, in which Bond wreaks havoc aboard Renard's submarine and then battles him to stop the impending nuclear disaster, Arnold provides more than 10 minutes of nonstop suspense and action music that includes grand orchestral gestures, a driving electronic pulse and references to the "Bond Theme" and to his main theme (1 hour, 50 minutes, "Submarine" on CD). Arnold offers a romantic theme, actually based on the wonderful ski-sequence music, for Bond and Jones (2 hours, 3 minutes, "Christmas in Turkey" on CD). Arnold reprises the "James Bond Theme" in a big, exciting orchestral version, and then he works electronic variations on it and adds a bit of "The World Is Not Enough" for the end titles (2 hours, 4 minutes).

The Garbage video, directed by German Philipp Stolzl in late September 1999, was especially interesting for its plot (the first time a Bond music video had featured a story since Duran Duran's Eiffel Tower shot for *View to a Kill*). As Manson explained a few days later: "I play myself, but also an android version of me. The android sets out to cleanse the world of evil and it kills the real me—with the classic kiss of death, in true Bond style." Curiously, it's set in 1964 and she blows up both her own band and the Chicago theater where they're playing.

"Hopefully radio will understand [the song]," MGM Music Executive Vice President Michael Sandoval said at the time. "Going a little further to the left with the band, and then trying to create a coolness from the traditional sense of Bond, was the goal." *Billboard* raved about the single: "What an inspired choice to have those new-century techno-pop artisans of Garbage as the bearers of the latest Bond theme . . . rings of international intrigue, with the slinky gait, noirish guitar line, and grand chorus we have all come to expect. Yet the song's darkly sexy, electronic ambience is wholly in keeping with Garbage's distinctive soundprint . . . the best 007 theme in eons."

The single was released October 4, charted in the U.K. on November 27 and reached number 11; it failed, however, to chart in the United States, and the soundtrack album failed to chart on either side of the Atlantic. The film opened on November 9.

Arnold managed a rave from the *Los Angeles Times* ("a driving score that incorporates the familiar Bond theme") and a mention from *The Hollywood Reporter* ("the clarion call of the familiar Bond theme music still stirs the blood"). Six months later, Arnold won England's prestigious Ivor Novello Award for best original film score for *The World Is Not Enough*. And he got along so well with director Michael Apted that they went on to do three more films together.

For the next Bond film, however, there would be no David Arnold song; the studio would return to the concept of "major artist" for a title tune. Some, in fact, would contend it wasn't a "tune" at all.

"... it's not my time to go ..."

Die Another Day

*T*he World Is Not Enough made even more money than the previous two Brosnan films ($362 million worldwide), confirming that the moviegoing public still adored Fleming's creation. But the failure of the Garbage single in the United States led the new music management at MGM to look for an even-higher-profile artist to write and perform the title song for the next film.

Madonna topped their list. A chart-topping singer-songwriter for nearly two decades, she was one of the icons of the MTV generation and a five-time Grammy winner whose most recent award was for her song for a spy film (of sorts): the dance-pop track "Beautiful Stranger," from *Austin Powers: The Spy Who Shagged Me* and a top-20 hit in the summer of 1999.

"It was important for us to choose an artist that would creatively understand the relationship between the song and the film," Anita Camarata, executive vice president of MGM Music, said in 2002. "With every artist, you're taking a chance. But with Madonna, she has an extraordinary track record. She has written songs for films before and they were always perfect. She's just a very smart artist."

The first hint that a Madonna song for the new film (titled *Die Another Day*) was in the works was in mid-February, when "sources on the set" disclosed that she was in negotiations and might even make a cameo appearance in the film. The song deal was confirmed in mid-March, although her film appearance took longer to finalize. Some sources suggested that her deal was particularly complicated and may have cost the studio upwards of $1 million, including her fees for music and acting, participation in the music publishing, the album and single deal and a music video.

Work began on the song early in 2002, according to French composer Michel Colombier, who wrote and conducted the string arrangement. Colombier (a veteran composer whose credits included the pop symphony *Wings* and film scores for *White Nights* and *Against All Odds*) had recently worked with Madonna and her Paris-based producer Mirwais Ahmadzai on their album *Music*, supplying the string arrangement for the song "Don't Tell Me."

Madonna and Mirwais (as he was known professionally) were working on her next studio album when the call came from "the Bond people," Colombier said. One of the songs they were working on "could maybe work for it," Mirwais told Colombier; they sent a demo to the studio that was "this techno thing," an electronica piece rewritten to accommodate the film and the title. According to Colombier, the studio responded: "We love the song, but can you bridge it to the tradition of Bond in some way?" That's when Madonna and Mirwais called Colombier to help.

MGM sent Colombier (who was in Los Angeles) a rough edit of the opening of the film. "I knew that I had to do something film-score-esque," he said. Mirwais sent Colombier a long version of the Madonna-Mirwais track, Colombier wrote "a bunch of things to it" and then flew to London to conduct an ensemble of 60 string players at AIR Studios. From there, Mirwais took the track back to Paris and then did "a complete production job," Colombier said. "What you hear is not what I wrote. The way that it came out is completely Mirwais. He is a master manipulator. Sixty real strings, played live, became audio files in his computer. They can be chopped like pieces of fabric. He's amazingly brilliant with that."

Colombier also designed an instrumental version of the theme for possible use over the end titles. Madonna attended the recording session in London, he noted. "In the instrumental version, there is a moment when I went into almost a tango feeling. At the rehearsal, they did it extremely well, instinctively. When we started doing the take, it just lost the 'fire.' Madonna, in the booth, grabbed the talkback mic and told them, 'It's not sexy enough, think about sex!' She really participates."

Colombier's rich string arrangement provided the drama, especially in the opening measures before Madonna's vocal enters. Her cryptic lyrics were a curiosity ("I'm gonna keep this secret / I'm gonna close my body now . . .") but Mirwais's electronica sounds, which dominate the track, made "Die Another Day" the most sonically edgy Bond theme ever. (Soon afterward, Madonna asked Colombier to score her film *Swept Away*, which would be released later in 2002, a month before the Bond film.)

The track apparently went through various incarnations. "We went through several interpolations of it," producer Michael G. Wilson later said, "but I think when she saw the rough material we were going to use, she sort of adapted the song and changed the title to 'Die Another Day.'" Added director

(left to right) Toby Stephens, Rosamund Pike, Madonna and Pierce Brosnan as the fencing is about to begin in *Die Another Day*

Lee Tamahori: "When I first heard it, I was a little concerned because it seemed to have stops and starts and didn't seem to be that evocative. But she rewrote—the chorus was written for the movie, and I think it's made quite a profound difference."

As Madonna herself said before the film's release: "I hemmed and hawed about it for a while. Everybody wants to do the theme song of a James Bond movie, and I never like to do what everybody else likes to do. It's just some perverse thing in me. But then I thought about it and I said, you know what? James Bond needs to get techno."

Years later, she praised Colombier's contribution: "Mirwais brought Michel to me. That song is so cinematic; I'm so excited when I get to work with a live orchestra. Those strings in 'Die Another Day' are chilling and, because of that, it's one of my favorite songs."

Acknowledging the challenge of scoring *Die Another Day*'s opening title sequence, in which Bond is imprisoned and tortured for over a year in North Korea, MGM's Camarata felt that Madonna "nailed the essence of the film. It is a much more difficult main-title sequence to write for than in the past. She helped set up the story with her song," adding that Madonna's strange psychology references ("I'm gonna destroy my ego . . . Sigmund Freud . . . analyze this . . .") were "her take on what's going on in the movie." Titles designer Daniel Kleinman later confessed that the track posed creative problems:

"The images and the music were quite difficult to reconcile. If I had a decision about what music track would have gone with a sequence of Bond being tortured, I probably wouldn't have chosen that particular song."

Madonna's two-minute cameo appearance as Verity, Bond's fencing instructor, was filmed at Pinewood on July 9, 2002, the next-to-last day of principal photography. It would mark the first and only time that a Bond theme performer would also take on an acting role in the movie. "She was a little reluctant," producer Wilson said, "but we had a part that we thought would be fun for her to play, and I think it works well."

The story picks up after 007 is exchanged for disfigured North Korean terrorist Zao (Rick Yune). M suspends Bond's "00" status, and he strikes out on his own to track Zao to Cuba, where he meets American spy Jinx Johnson (Halle Berry) and discovers a connection to British billionaire Gustav Graves (Toby Stephens). Returning to London, he meets Graves's assistant Miranda Frost (Rosamund Pike) and travels to Iceland, where he finds Graves in league with Zao and must stop a powerful space-based weapon; ultimately the story takes both Bond and Jinx back to Korea.

The early decision to use a Madonna song as the movie's theme left composer David Arnold to focus on the score itself. (He and Don Black had started a song, "I Will Return," but they never finished it after Madonna was signed.) Once again, the colors of the exotic locations of a Bond movie offered some of the most interesting musical opportunities. "I spent a few weeks researching traditional Cuban rhythms," Arnold said, "and found out ultimately that most of it sounds like traditional African rhythms. When I tried that, everyone said, 'this doesn't feel Cuban.' Your audience expects all those signature licks and rhythms that we know and love from holiday programs. If there's one thing I've learned, it's that you can't be too 'on the nail' with a Bond movie."

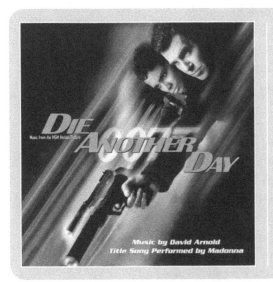

Music by David Arnold
Title Song Performed by Madonna

SCORE HIGHLIGHTS

The 105-plus minutes of music in *Die Another Day* set another record for most music ever in a Bond film. Nearly 96 minutes of that was David Arnold's original score, also using more musical technology than ever before. Paralleling the Madonna techno title track, the Arnold score relied heavily on electronics and even high-tech manipulation of traditionally recorded orchestral tracks.

This up-to-date sound is apparent from the very start of the film, with the gun-barrel "Bond Theme" augmented with electronic sounds, just prior to the surfing sequence as 007 and friends reach North Korea's Pukch'ong Coast, to Bond-theme variations that continue, with the addition of glittering electronic sounds for the conflict diamonds (called "On the Beach" on CD, although it's missing the surfing

Halle Berry as Jinx in Cuba, backed by Arnold's colorful music

So Arnold gathered some of his favorite musicians at AIR's Studio 1 one evening. "I got a few bottles of tequila, made margaritas, and I said, 'We're in Cuba.' It was brilliant. We had about six percussionists, two guitarists, a beaten-up old piano and a rag-tag sounding brass section. You just have to tell them, 'that Buena Vista [Social Club] trumpet thing, play it like that.' It was the most fun I think I had on that movie."

Bond's presence in Korea, at the start and end of the film, demanded authentic-sounding ethnic percussion and, for the third Bond film in a row Arnold turned to top London percussionist Pete Lockett. "He played most of it himself," Arnold recalled. "We spent a couple of nights bashing out rhythms and getting all the traditional Korean sounds together."

The high quantity of action in the new film also posed a challenge. "The first one [*Tomorrow Never Dies*] was more orchestra, with a couple of electronic things, and the last one [*World Is Not Enough*] was very electronic. This is an extension of both of those. There are action cues where we use a lot of electronics with a lot of orchestra." But, he added, "it's good to share the responsibility for some of the rhythmic propulsion with ethnic-based instruments rather than completely electronic."

Arnold also used the rapidly advancing musical technology of the time. "So where we've been doing things electronically with drums and guitars and percussive elements, I thought it would be interesting to try and make the orchestra perform in the same way. So we rehearse in an orchestral style, but then I'll record the woodwinds, brass and strings separately—maintaining the dynamics that they had in rehearsal—which enables me to have the brass section play backwards and forwards and throw it around the surrounds, while the rest of the orchestra apparently carries on playing.

"So you go from a normal orchestral performance to find that the brass are playing backwards, or the strings have been chopped up into tiny pieces and

music). Bond steals a hovercraft, over more wild, electronically manipulated orchestral Bond-theme variations with incredible brass highs (9 minutes into the film, "Hovercraft Chase" on CD).

In a departure from the standard title sequence, the imprisonment and torture of Bond over the next 14 months, along with images of scorpions and the usual women, both aflame and icy, plays over the incongruous Madonna dance track (13 minutes in). Eastern percussion spices the opening of a highly dramatic moment as Bond is exchanged for Zao on a foggy bridge, then sedated and finally examined (18 minutes, "Some Kind of Hero?" on CD).

Bond's determination to learn the truth, over M's objections, is underscored by strong horns and strings, followed by another electronic-percussion-driven Bond theme as he escapes the Hong Kong hospital (23 minutes in). A warm, strings-and-piano theme accompanies masseuse Peaceful Fountains of Desire at the hotel (28 minutes), but it's Bond's next port of call that presents a more colorful musical moment: Havana, with delightful Latin jazz (31 minutes, "Welcome to Cuba" on CD). Orange-bikinied Jinx emerges from the ocean, in one of the most memorable entrances since Ursula Andress in *Dr. No*, to a new motif for strings and flute (36 minutes, "Jinx Jordan" on CD). They make love to a more passionate version of this music (at 38 minutes, "Jinx & James" on CD).

Bond and Jinx, working separately, infiltrate the gene therapy clinic, blow it up and pursue the escaping Zao to a five-minute action-music cue (43

they're traveling around the cinema. Things like that are making use of the technology in a way which is interesting sonically. It's mainly to try and do something unusual, something that hasn't been heard before." This was particularly true of the early hovercraft chase and the later car chase on the ice, Arnold said.

However, it also heightened the complexity of the composer's job overall. With more electronics to deal with—and the fact that, for the first time, Arnold needed to "demo" each cue (that is, prepare a synthesizer version to preview it for the director and receive approval to go ahead), he needed an early start. He "spotted" the film with director Lee Tamahori (that is, went methodically through the entire rough cut, choosing where music would start and stop and what the music needed to accomplish in every scene) in late June 2002 and then wrote through July, August and September. "It takes a lot longer to build electronic elements than it does to write the orchestral parts," he said.

Nicholas Dodd conducted an 85-piece orchestra over five days during the last week of September. There was never any plan to adapt the Madonna song into the score; Arnold's work was two-thirds completed before he ever heard the final version.

The presence of Madonna, not only as theme composer and performer but briefly as actress in the film, naturally resulted in more media coverage of the music than usual. Little of it was positive. "Madonna shrieking a tuneless theme song," griped London's *Sunday Times*. "The techno thump of Madonna's cheerless title song," noted the *Los Angeles Times*. "Madonna contributes a dumb cameo along with a tinny theme song," complained the *Wall Street Journal*. "Madonna, who co-wrote and sings the banal title song, does an unbilled cameo," wrote *Variety*. The *New York Times* referred to "Madonna's electronically enhanced chirps emanat[ing] from the soundtrack."

minutes). Bond, on a plane back to London, reads about Gustav Graves, to the Clash's "London Calling" (50 minutes). After an unscored introduction to Madonna as his fencing instructor, Bond's swordfight with Graves gets an exciting, ever-building orchestral treatment (56 minutes). More Bond-theme and fast-paced string-suspense treatment accompany Bond's "virtual reality" test (1 hour, 3 minutes). A hard-hitting, rock-oriented "Bond Theme" accompanies 007's Aston Martin en route to Graves's Iceland installation (1 hour, 8 minutes).

The "Dirty Vegas Mix" of Madonna's title theme is heard in the background at Graves's Ice Palace party (1 hour, 11 minutes), while Graves introduces his satellite Icarus, to the sounds of curiously ominous fanfares and choral chants (1 hour, 14 min-

utes, "Icarus" on CD; Arnold called the text "cod Latin," dealing with the unveiling of the device in space). Bond activates his invisible Aston Martin over quiet synth percussion and a stealthy orchestral passage (1 hour, 16 minutes), but it's the next cue that's especially interesting for its synth-pulse-driven suspense for Jinx in action, followed by a cool romantic piano for Bond and Miranda (1 hour, 19 minutes, "A Touch of Frost" on CD). Bond dives beneath Graves's laboratory and then fights a henchman while high-powered lasers are flashing around, to more electronica-over-orchestra (1 hour, 21 minutes, "Laser Fight" on CD).

Bond learns that Miranda is the traitor. He then manages to escape from Graves and Zao to a five-minute action cue that incorporates synth backbeats,

The music press was slightly more positive, although far from unanimous. "It's an odd number," wrote *Billboard*, "somewhat disjointed, a bit nonsensical, and not so much melodic as a highly stylized jam. . . . With repeated listening, there are enough clever goings-on and a hook that sinks into the consciousness to make this a captivating journey." *Spin* referred to "that brilliant, melodramatic song . . . sounds like a stoic response to a world gone mad." *Entertainment Weekly* dismissed it as "the flat James Bond theme, neither Madonna Classic nor Diet Madonna With Lemon: no buzz, not tangy." In London, the *Times* said "Madonna has turned the movie's title track into a rather unsuitable vehicle for her current obsession with the cold, vocodorised melodic contours of European electro." The rock critic for England's *Telegraph*, however, placed it among the top-five all-time Bond themes: "Madonna's electro-R&B workout is expressively weird, brutally modern, satisfyingly original and evocative of the dark heart of Bond." The controversy even played out in the tabloid press, where Sir Elton John dismissed the Madonna song as "the worst Bond tune of all time."

Madonna's four-minute music video took its cue from the movie's torture scenes but also finds her swordfighting against herself (one dressed in white, the other black). Shot in Hollywood in late August 2002, it reportedly cost an estimated $6 million, making it among the most expensive videos of its time. It got a splashy MTV debut on October 10.

All the attention, promotion and Madonna's name paid off: "Die Another Day" became the highest-debuting song of 2002 on *Billboard*'s Hot 100 charts, landing at number 41 on October 19 and rocketing to number 8 four weeks later, making it the most successful Bond song since "A View to a Kill" in 1985. It also went to number 1 on the Club Play and Singles Sales charts. In the U.K., it did even better, charting November 9 and reaching number 3. An additional inducement to buying the soundtrack album was the presence

(SCORE HIGHLIGHTS, CONT.)

choir for the activated Icarus and a screaming-brass "Bond Theme" for 007's race across the ice and ingenious tidal-wave surfing survival (1 hour, 30 minutes, "Whiteout" on CD). Arnold's synths, wah-wah brass and driving beat power the Aston-versus-Jaguar car chase on the ice while Jinx desperately tries to escape when Icarus is activated again (1 hour, 37 minutes, "Iced Inc." on CD). Arnold heightens the stakes with more intense Bond-theme variations as the car chase continues inside the crumbling Ice Palace and he saves Jinx (1 hour, 40 minutes).

The crisis escalates as Bond and Jinx parachute into North Korea and Icarus destroys a missile. Arnold reprises his high-brass Bond-theme as 007 and Jinx dash aboard the plane (1 hour, 47 minutes). Ar-nold then embarks on a nearly 12-minute orchestral-and-choral tour de force—constantly heightening the tension and incorporating a jeopardy-infused "Bond Theme"—as Graves kills his father, Icarus begins incinerating the Korean demilitarized zone, Bond battles Graves and Miranda fights Jinx (1 hour, 50 minutes, "Antonov" on CD). Eastern sounds, notably Andy Findon's bamboo flute and Natacha Atlas's wordless vocal, flavor the mix.

As their plane goes down in flames, Bond and Jinx escape in a helicopter, to ever-escalating, fast-moving orchestral figures climaxing in another high-brass, tension-relieving Bond-theme quote (2 hours, 2 minutes). An amusing postscript involving Bond and Moneypenny gets a romantic string treatment (2 hours, 5 minutes), but the real finale for Bond and

of a Paul Oakenfold remix of the "James Bond Theme" that was not in the
movie; the album managed to reach number 156 in the United States but did
not chart in the U.K.

The song was nominated for a Golden Globe and for two Grammy Awards
(Best Dance Recording and Short Form Music Video). MGM promoted it for
the Best Song Oscar, too, but this was one award that eluded the Material Girl.
(She did, however, curtsy for Queen Elizabeth II at the royal premiere of *Die
Another Day* on November 18, 2002, at London's Royal Albert Hall, which
was also attended by fellow Bond-song performer Shirley Bassey.) On the flip
side, she was nominated for Hollywood's Golden Raspberry Award (the so-
called "Razzie") for Worst Original Song, and she won the not-so-coveted
award as Worst Supporting Actress for her role in the film.

The film made an astounding $432 million worldwide and marked Pierce
Brosnan's final appearance as 007. It would take four more years to find a new
Bond and "reboot the franchise," as observers put it in the 21st-century ver-
nacular. For the producers, however, musical consistency would be a priority.

Jinx takes place in the Far East, as Arnold reprises,
with lush strings and strong horns, the Bond-Jinx
love theme (2 hours, 7 minutes, "Going Down Together" on CD), which, notably, has just a hint of
John Barry's "You Only Live Twice" theme (a film
also set in the Far East).

Madonna's "Dirty Vegas Mix" techno track plays
under the end titles (2 hours, 8 minutes).

". . . the coldest blood runs through my veins . . ."

Casino Royale (2006)

In the 44 years since James Bond first appeared on movie screens, he had undergone many changes, including five actors, tonal shifts from serious to camp and back, growing reliance on tricks and gadgetry and a constant reach for the most earth-shaking plots imaginable.

In 2006, however, Ian Fleming's seemingly timeless hero underwent the biggest makeover of all, one that would return to the very first novel, *Casino Royale*, recast the role and start the saga all over again. This time, Eon was dealing with Sony Pictures Entertainment, which had inherited distribution rights as part of its role in the 2005 buyout of MGM (MGM and Eon had, in 1999, retrieved the rights to *Casino Royale* from Sony, which in turn had controlled the 1967 Columbia film).

"We felt the last film was too fantastical, so we decided to go back to the basics and update," producer Michael G. Wilson told the *Los Angeles Times*. "For years, my father wanted to make *Casino Royale*—it's the Holy Grail," producer Barbara Broccoli added. "We wanted to make a tougher film, the way it should have been made years ago."

So they cast British actor Daniel Craig in a 007 "origin story" that harkened back to Bond's beginnings in British Intelligence and retold the Fleming story of Bond falling for Vesper Lynd (French actress Eva Green) and the scheme to beat terrorists' banker Le Chiffre (Mads Mikkelsen) in a high-stakes poker game in the tiny country of Montenegro.

James Bond (Daniel Craig) comforts a shaken Vesper Lynd (Eva Green) in *Casino Royale*

Surprisingly, the composer was in place long before Craig was cast as Bond. In the aftermath of the success of *Die Another Day*, David Arnold was asked to remain on the Bond team. So as the field was narrowing to the final three actors (Craig, Henry Cavill and Sam Worthington), Arnold assisted the casting process by scoring their *From Russia with Love*–inspired screen tests (using music from earlier Bond films and other Arnold projects). The producers even asked his opinion. "It's a rare privilege to be involved in anything like that," Arnold said a few years later. "I'm sure they were talking to a lot of people." He recalled Craig's test: "It was the way he moved, with such purpose and confidence, that sold it for me. If there was any trouble, he was the guy you wanted to go to."

Chris Cornell working on the title song, "You Know My Name"

Craig was announced as Bond in October 2005, and even before shooting began on *Casino Royale* in January Arnold was thinking about the song and discussing possibilities with Broccoli, Wilson and Lia Vollack, president of worldwide music for Sony. "I realized early on that it had to be a male vocalist," Arnold said in 2006. "Daniel's is a very physical, masculine, rugged reading of the character. There is a kind of confrontational aspect to Daniel. So we knew we probably didn't want a slinky, velvet-curtained record; a come-hither kind of song; or a who-is-that-dangerous-stranger kind of song."

It was Vollack who suggested Chris Cornell as a possible singer. Former guitarist and lead singer for the Seattle grunge band Soundgarden and the hard-rock band Audioslave, Cornell was then embarking on a solo career. "They were looking to redefine Bond with a different look and feel, a tougher, grittier Bond," Vollack recalled. So we wanted something more in the Paul McCartney 'Live and Let Die' epic-rock [style], something that had a little bit of an edge. Chris is a spectacularly good writer and also has one of the best voices in rock. It was a good combination."

Arnold visited the Prague locations in March 2006 and talked with Craig about his approach to the character. Craig expressed interest in the music, Arnold said, "because he knew it was a big part of [the entire Bond experience]. I think he appreciated the curiosity that I had about him and what he was going to do; the whole point of this is to make him look as good as we possibly could." The casino scenes were being shot at the time, Arnold recalled.

"Chris [Cornell] came on the third day I was there. We watched some cut footage and spoke with [director] Martin Campbell about ideas for the music," he added. Meetings with Craig, Broccoli, Wilson and Campbell followed, including screening a rough cut of the African chase footage.

Cornell returned to his home in Paris, Arnold to London, and they began working separately. A few weeks later they got together and shared ideas. "We sat down with a couple of guitars; he played me his stuff, I played him mine, and it was almost like we'd written two parts of the same song," Arnold later reflected. Back home in Chichester, Arnold came up with a hard-hitting intro and mulled over the idea that the new Bond song should be "built out of the DNA of the Bond theme." So the final song, Arnold later said, "shares a lot of the same genetic material as the Bond Theme but in a different order and in a different shape."

The title, "You Know My Name," was Arnold's idea, and intriguingly similar to one of the advertising lines used when Pierce Brosnan was introduced as Bond in 1995 ("you know the name; you know the number"). The preceding line of the song, "the coldest blood runs through my veins," was Cornell's (along with most of the lyrics). Other lines derive directly from the film's gambling motif: "the odds will betray you . . . try to hide your hand . . . life is gone

David Arnold with his score for the title song, "You Know My Name"

with just a spin of the wheel. . . ." Cornell later said that he had read the Fleming novel but was relieved that the song didn't need to be titled "Casino Royale" (something Arnold said was never seriously considered). "I was very lucky with the fact that there's emotional depth to the character, to the performance, to the script, and so there was something to relate to, emotionally."

At the recording, Cornell and Arnold played all of the guitars and the bass; they brought in a studio drummer. The song was finished by the time principal photography was completed on July 21; Arnold played it at the wrap party and added orchestra to the track later (one mix for the film that was more brass-heavy, another for the single). Noted Cornell: "I was given a lot of time from first seeing the edit to negotiating the deal and then writing the song, demo'ing it . . . then actually recording the song, doing the mixes; it was all very comfortable. We had plenty of time to do it." He topped off the experience by shooting a compelling video (which, like most Bond music videos, was heavily intercut with scenes from the film).

At 144 minutes, *Casino Royale* would turn out to be the longest Bond film ever (beating *On Her Majesty's Secret Service* by four minutes). The length was just one of several gambles that the filmmakers were taking on a movie that was, in part, about gambling. One of the biggest was the overall concept of the score: that the "James Bond Theme," the music most associated with the character, the signature piece of the entire series for over more than four decades, would never be played until the very end of the film.

The idea originated in the script, which ended with the character identifying himself with the classic line "The name is Bond, James Bond," followed by a script direction that "we hear, for the first time, the guitar strains of the famous Bond theme. Cut to black. Credits roll. The end."

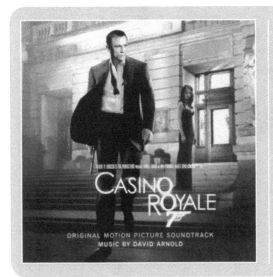

SCORE HIGHLIGHTS

For *Casino Royale*, Arnold composed more than 91 minutes of music and—because of the score's notable conceit, that the "Bond Theme" will be only hinted at from time to time until the very end of the movie—only five minutes of that involve quotations from Monty Norman's original. And for this reason, *Casino Royale* was the first Eon Bond film not to open with the standard gun-barrel logo and thus no "Bond Theme" (although the logo is cleverly interpolated into the opening titles).

The bedrock of the score is the Arnold-Cornell song "You Know My Name" (especially its powerful intro), and its presence throughout the score gives the film a thematic consistency that harks back to the classic John Barry scores of decades past. In addition, his touching theme for Vesper and her trou-

Arnold concurred with the concept. "As soon as you play that theme, somehow there is no more danger," he said in 2006. "When you play that theme with Bond in action, there seems to be a sense of inevitability that he will prevail. It gives you, as an audience member, a very comfortable place to be. You relax and think, 'How's he going to do it this time?' [But] there are moments in this film where he doesn't win. In fact, he loses more than he wins." Arnold tested it for himself, playing the theme against specific scenes in the film, "and it dissolved any danger, any sense that there really was anything going wrong. The other argument was, he's not 'James Bond' yet, so why are we playing the theme?"

It was a topic of considerable debate, Arnold recalled, especially after test screenings took place. "We discussed the whole idea," he said. "Is this whole thing—not playing the Bond Theme—just a kind of neat intellectual trick which pays off for some people but may alienate other people from the character?" There was particular concern on the part of the studio, Arnold remembered, "a couple of panicked calls, saying 'We're not sure if this is a good idea.'"

So even though Arnold's original version of the score applied the Bond-theme bass line here and there in a subtle way, the final version hints somewhat more strongly at it in several places. "My thinking was, as long as it sounded like Bond music in the rest of the film, we'd be OK. I gave him elements, like he was earning his stripes: as he won his first game of cards, when he wins the DB5, when he puts on his tux for the first time. As he straps on these elements that form the man, we, the audience is kind of rewarded; 'here's a bit more, we're not quite there yet.' I think that's why it had such a huge impact at the end of the film."

It wasn't a universally loved idea. Sean Connery later admitted to being disappointed by the choice: "I did have one reservation," he said in 2008.

bled relationship with Bond adds depth and substance to the entire score. This is the only Bond score to become commercially available in its entirety (in the references below, DL stands for the "download" version of the album, which has 13 more tracks than the CD).

The black-and-white opening in Prague alternates between suspenseful string harmonics and pounding percussion plus angry brass (½ minute into the film, "License: 2 Kills" DL). This leads directly into the Chris Cornell vocal under the colorful, playing-card-inspired title sequence (3½ minutes in, "You Know My Name"). Arnold spices the Uganda sequence with African percussion and ominous basses for Le Chiffre (7½ minutes in, "Reveal Le Chiffre" DL). Still more tribal drumming accompanies the early Madagascar scenes (9½ minutes, "Mongoose vs. Snake" DL).

The film's first big chase, in which Bond pursues a bomber through the streets of Antananarivo, onto a construction site and into an embassy earns Arnold's first high-energy orchestral sequence, more than seven minutes long, with driving percussion (10½ minutes in, "Bombers Away" DL and "African Rundown" on CD). Calmer moments follow, as Le Chiffre plays cards on his yacht (19 minutes, "Nothing Sinister" on CD; 21 minutes, "Push Them Overboard" DL). Quiet strings and percussion accompany Bond's investigation using M's own computer (22 minutes, "Unauthorized Access" on CD).

Bond's arrival in Nassau earns a hint of the Bond theme and a sassy-brass version of the main theme

"They sort of diluted the Bond musical theme, which you hear only at the very end. When I heard it, I thought, 'Oh, that's what I've been missing.'" "Bond Theme" composer Monty Norman said he thought Arnold "did an excellent job of teasing the theme throughout the film and finally arranging a terrific version as a climax." However, he noted, "the subtlety of the idea eluded quite a few people. I was asked many times why the theme was only played at the end and found myself explaining the reasoning. Nevertheless, I believe it was worth doing that way."

Arnold, again, played guitar on the Bond theme as the end titles rolled. "These projects take anywhere from six weeks to three months to do," he explained in 2006. "You've been largely isolated by yourself in a dark room. It's not an awful lot of fun. I've done it on the last three [*World Is Not Enough*, *Die Another Day*, *Casino Royale*], experimenting with different guitars and amps. It's like a reward I give myself at the end of this process."

It was also a reward for the 78 musicians that Nicholas Dodd conducted over five days in the last week of September 2006. "We made it the last thing that we played, on a Friday afternoon," Arnold said. "We'd been through the whole week playing this score, which was some fairly heavy going. We'd recorded 90 minutes of music, and it had been four years since we'd played [the theme], so everyone was revved up for it and ready."

It had been a pressure-packed time, especially for the composer. "Our downbeat [the start of recording] was eight weeks after the end of principal photography," he said, and editor Stuart Baird was still cutting while Arnold was writing music. "About nine or 10 days before downbeat, they cut 10 or 15 minutes out of the film. It hit a couple of sequences quite hard," requiring last-minute musical rewrites. Ultimately a final recording session was scheduled for October 9 to make final musical fixes, including those "Bond Theme" hints at critical points in the narrative.

(SCORE HIGHLIGHTS, CONT.)

(24 minutes, "Blunt Instrument" on CD). Bond tracks Le Chiffre associate Dimitrios's recent movements to the sound of quiet flute and harp (28 minutes, "CCTV" on CD), catches the eye of his wife Solange during a lovely Barry-esque melody for strings (30 minutes, "Solange" on CD) and connects Dimitrios to Le Chiffre, with a variation on the main theme (31 minutes, "Bedside Computer" DL). Bond's arrival at the casino is accompanied by Gary Trotman's steel-drum version of the traditional Jamaican folk song "Linstead Market" (32 minutes).

Bond's beating Dimitrios at cards and winning his Aston Martin is bookended with a flute version of Solange's motif, his win punctuated by the Bond-theme bass line (33 minutes, "Trip Aces" on CD). Bond follows Dimitrios to Miami, kills him and stops a terrorist from destroying a new jet, all to an in-tense, nearly 13-minute long, brass-and-electronic-percussion-driven action sequence based partly on the main theme (40 minutes, "Miami International" on CD). The postscript is a brief brass buildup to the terrorist's demise (53 minutes, "Beep Beep Beep Bang" DL).

Bond meets Vesper en route via train to Montenegro, a brief but gorgeous scene-setter (58 minutes, "I'm the Money" on CD); it's reprised, along with a main-theme variation, when Bond gets his new Aston Martin (1 hour, 5 minutes in, "Aston Montenegro" on CD). A lighter touch, counterpointing the Bond-theme bass line and the main theme, is heard for Bond and Vesper's hotel-room banter (1 hour, 7 minutes, "Dinner Jackets" on CD).

Arnold scores the first card game delicately with strings and hints of danger for Vesper and Le Chiffre

The composer's touching, tender music for Vesper underwent a rewrite too. "She appears to be very together and strong, but then you realize that she's extraordinarily vulnerable," Arnold said. "They have a real resonant, grownup kind of relationship. It's witty and beautiful, and I scored that scene [Vesper and Bond in the shower] much more fractured and exposed, very delicate. It's a dangerous thing they're getting into; she's deeply disturbed by what she's seen, and I think she's really scared. Barbara [Broccoli] made a very interesting point: she felt that that was the moment where they cemented their relationship . . . a burgeoning sense of togetherness was starting to blossom, and she wanted that to be more beautiful—there is some beauty in this awful thing that's happened." Arnold returned to the scene and wrote a warmer piece, still delicate, but more about the romance than the danger.

The "Bond music" to which Arnold referred was still, in many ways, the sound of John Barry. Arnold and Cornell's strong, tough theme with its powerful intro became the foundation of the *Casino Royale* score; and although some electronic elements remained, many of the quirky, unusual synth sounds of the previous three scores were gone. A more timeless orchestral approach was called for. Yet the minor keys, the alto flutes, the string voicings were all reminiscent of classic Barry (who, since his last brush with the Bond world a decade earlier, had scored the period spy film *Enigma*, written the London musical *Brighton Rock*, penned two concept albums and enjoyed a triumphant return to the concert hall in 1998).

"He is the sound of James Bond," Arnold said at the time. "There's no point in getting away from it. John casts an enormous shadow. You ignore it at your peril. It's inescapably entwined with the character."

Added Barbara Broccoli: "David is an extraordinary composer in his own right, but I think his reverence for John and his understanding of John's achievements, particularly in relation to the Bond films, is what really made

(1 hour, 11 minutes, "The Tell" on CD), with another ominous postscript for Bond examining Le Chiffre's inhaler (1 hour, 16 minutes, "Inhaler" DL). Le Chiffre is attacked in his room and Bond battles the killers in the hotel stairwell to echoing ethnic flutes and furious, ever-building strings and percussion (1 hour, 17 minutes, "Stairwell Fight" on CD). Bond comforts Vesper to her theme, a beautiful passage for piano and strings (1 hour, 23 minutes, "Vesper" on CD). Arnold subtly builds suspense throughout the climactic card game (1 hour, 26 minutes, "Bond Loses It All" on CD).

Felix Leiter introduces himself (1 hour, 31 minutes, "Brother From Langley" DL). Bond realizes he's been poisoned, to dissonant strings and brass, then races to save his own life, this with another fast-paced, orchestra-racing passage having a Bond-theme bass line at the end (1 hour, 34 minutes, "Dirty Martini" on CD). The final game is treated even more suspensefully, with eerie strings and a clever counterpoint of the main theme and Bond Theme after his victory (1 hour, 39 minutes, "Bond Wins It All" on CD).

Bond races after the kidnapped Vesper, and then nearly runs her over, to an urgent, percussion-driven variation on the main theme (1 hour, 45 minutes, "The End of an Aston Martin" on CD). Eerie sounds, some electronic and some orchestral, portend evil as Le Chiffre prepares to torture a naked Bond (1 hour, 48 minutes, "Prelude to a Beating" DL). The torture itself goes unscored. More strange and unnerving sounds accompany Le Chiffre's killing (1 hour, 52 minutes, "The Bad Die Young" on CD) and Bond's awakening (1 hour, 53 minutes, "Coming Round" DL).

him the right person to take over. They have a very close relationship. To him, it was very important that he carry on John's tradition because he feels it's such an integral part of the James Bond film franchise."

Casino Royale was a resounding success, both as a film and a score (which director Campbell later praised as "terrific"). Queen Elizabeth II attended the royal premiere in London on November 14, 2006. At over $594 million worldwide, it earned the biggest worldwide gross of any Bond film to date. Only the trade critics seemed to notice the music: "David Arnold's superb score chooses to mirror the rise and fall of tensions and emotions," noted *The Hollywood Reporter*; "the score by David Arnold, in his fourth Bond outing, is very good . . . the title song sung by Chris Cornell . . . is a dud," griped *Variety*. *Billboard*, however, disagreed, calling "You Know My Name" the best Bond theme since "A View to a Kill": "Chris Cornell's gritty voice . . . jerk[s] the 007 franchise back to life with a dose of straight-ahead rock. . . . It's a rough diamond of a rock tune, earthy yet elegant."

The song scored big in the U.K., charting on December 16 and reaching number 7; it disappointed in the United States, charting a week earlier but reaching only number 79. The soundtrack album, for the first time ever in the Bond series, did not include the title song (Cornell issued a single on his own label) and thus failed to chart on either side of the Atlantic. That was not the only surprise based on changing music-industry practices; the soundtrack CD contained 74 minutes of Arnold's score, but another 14 minutes was available via download from the internet; as a result, the 88 minutes of score (plus the four-minute title song, available as a single or via download) was the most Bond music ever made commercially available to the public from a single film.

Bond and Vesper kiss and vacation together to a beautiful flute-and-strings rendition of her theme (2 hours in, "I'm Yours" DL). They sail off together to a swelling-strings arrangement of her theme, and they reach Venice to mostly warm romantic music (2 hours, 2 minutes, "City of Lovers" on CD). Bond learns he's been tricked and races after Vesper to a five-minute combination of orchestral suspense and furious action based on the main theme (2 hour, 6 minutes, "The Switch" on CD).

The Venetian palazzo begins to collapse, to a highly dramatic piece based on the main theme, again intertwined with the Bond bass line (2 hours, 11 minutes, "Fall of a House in Venice" on CD, then "Running to the Elevator" DL). Bond desperately attempts to save Vesper, during a tortured and finally tender version of her theme (2 hours, 14 minutes,

"Death of Vesper" on CD). M and Bond discuss Vesper, to an intriguing counterpoint of her theme with the Bond-theme bass line (2 hours, 18 minutes, "The Bitch Is Dead" on CD). Bond catches up with the ultimate villain and introduces himself as we hear the film's only complete statement of the "James Bond Theme" (2 hours, 20 minutes, "The Name's Bond . . . James Bond" on CD), which begins the end titles; they conclude with the Cornell vocal of "You Know My Name."

Arnold was nominated for the Anthony Asquith Award for Film Music by the British Academy of Film and Television Arts, and Arnold and Cornell were jointly nominated for a Grammy as Best Song Written for a Motion Picture (they later won the World Soundtrack Award for the song).

James Bond was back—and would return, with the same composer, one more time.

24

". . . a door left open, a woman walking by . . ."

Quantum of Solace

asino Royale was such a hit, both critically and commercially, that it would be a hard act to follow. The producers began with another daring choice: the new film would be a direct sequel to Daniel Craig's Bond debut, titled *Quantum of Solace*, after one of the five short stories in Ian Fleming's 1960 collection *For Your Eyes Only*.

Composer David Arnold, on his fifth assignment as 007's composer, was already at work. He was discussing music with director Marc Forster as early as October 2007, months before the start of production. Forster's idea (a departure from Bond tradition) was that Arnold should compose themes for characters and situations based on montages that would be sent back from the various locations. "I was to write not to film, but to the concept, the idea, the philosophy of the characters," Arnold remembered. "It was quite liberating, in a way."

But the big news was the possibility that Amy Winehouse, the 24-year-old British jazz/soul singer with the beehive hairdo who had just won five Grammys including Record of the Year, Song of the Year and Best New Artist, might record the new Bond theme. "We had a good meeting with her," Sony president of worldwide music Lia Vollack recalled. "[Her producer] Mark Ronson was there. We were hopeful that something would work out."

Many observers met the news with excitement: "To compare her with a former Bond songstress, Winehouse is Shirley Bassey with a rebel's streak,"

Composer David Arnold accepting his Richard Kirk Award from BMI, May 18, 2011

said one American critic, adding that much of Winehouse's *Back to Black* album "sounded like a riff on Bassey's version of 'Diamonds Are Forever.'" Added a British critic: "With her sexy, retro style and dangerous, contemporary edge, she seemed a perfect fit."

Arnold and Ronson worked on song ideas in early March 2008 and, two weeks later, got together with the Dap-Kings (who played on *Back to Black*) to record a rough backing track. Winehouse, who was to have written the lyrics and come up with a title, didn't show up to sing the next day as expected. Or the day after that; or any time over the next three weeks. And while she promised to come up with a title and lyrics, she never did.

In late April, Ronson confirmed to the BBC that he and Winehouse were "working on it. They asked Amy. . . . So hopefully something will come of it. The demo sounds like a James Bond theme," he said. Five days later, he told the Associated Press that Winehouse was "not ready to record any music" and that it would take "some miracle of science" to finish the track. Winehouse's much-publicized battles with drugs and alcohol took their toll on the singer-songwriter, who tragically died at the age of 27 on July 23, 2011.

"I think she wanted to do it, but at that particular point she was not in good shape," Vollack said. They waited for several weeks, hoping that she could contribute, but eventually gave up and abandoned the effort. Added Arnold: "There was no melody or lyric, just a chord pattern and groove that Amy was meant to write alongside. None of these were ever presented to the producers of the movie, as there was nothing really of substance to play anyone."

Enter Jack White, guitarist, producer and leader of the White Stripes rock band. "Jack White is a huge Bond fan," Vollack said. "He does such a variety of projects with such a variety of artists. He and Alicia [Keys] had been talking about collaborating. We were actually approached by them. We thought it would be interesting; when an artist is really passionate, you often get something that's really good. I am very fond of that song."

The song was "Another Way to Die," written by White and performed by White and Keys, the soul singer and pianist; between them they had collected 19 Grammys in the previous seven years. Announced July 29, 2008, theirs was the first duet in Bond-song history. White penned it after reading the script and recorded a basic track in Nashville with his Raconteurs bassist Jack Lawrence (White played guitar and drums). Keys later added her vocal, and although she was originally engaged as a solo artist, White ended up joining her on vocals.

"Alicia put some electric energy into her breath that cemented itself into the magnetic tape," White later said. "Very inspiring to watch. It gave me a new voice, and I wasn't myself anymore. I drummed for her voice and she mimicked the guitar tones, then we joined our voices and screamed and moaned about these characters in the film and their isolation, having no one to trust, not even themselves. Maybe we became them for a few minutes," White added, noting that he insisted on recording it with analog equipment, not the standard digital machines. "The Memphis Horns were there to help us out, along with some of Nashville's finest. We wanted to push soul into those tapes," he said, "and join the family of Barry, Bassey, Connery and Craig." As he told another interviewer: "I didn't want to imitate anything or be retro. It just had to feel like Bond." (White told Arnold that the guitar riff for his 2003 song "Seven Nation Army" was Bond-inspired.)

For her part, Keys said, "[White's] sound is very raw. I thought that by combining that style with my voice, we could do something really interesting that mixes rock and soul," adding on another occasion that "the thing we worked on was elevating the energy of the song, so each part is a bit different than the last one."

Like Madonna, however, White was not interested in a collaboration with the score composer. Arnold did incorporate "little bits and pieces" of the song into his score, however.

In *Quantum of Solace*, Bond seeks revenge for the murder of Vesper and unearths a global conspiracy—Quantum, so secret that it's unknown even to MI6—headed by environmentalist Dominic Greene (Mathieu Amalric), whose lover Camille Montes (Olga Kurylenko) turns out to have a revenge agenda of her own: killing a Bolivian general who murdered her parents. The mission takes Bond to Italy, Haiti, Austria, Bolivia and Russia. Along the way he links up with old allies Leiter (Jeffrey Wright) and Mathis (Giancarlo Giannini).

In early May, Forster filmed a contemporary staging of Puccini's *Tosca* at the Bregenz Festival in Austria with Karine Babajanyan as Tosca and Sebastien Soules as Scarpia. Its "Te Deum" (the finale of Act I) would serve as the backdrop for a key expository sequence in which Bond learns of Quantum's plans and its many high-profile members. Forster shot over nine days at the Seebuhne floating stage on the shores of Lake Constance. "Having two stories told simultaneously in the same time frame, reflecting one another, is a gift I've been given with Tosca in Bregenz," Forster said at the time. "*Tosca* is a terrific metaphor for Bond on so many levels," likely referring to deception and revenge in the opera's libretto.

The director asked Arnold to create key themes while the film was in production between January and June. Forster's editors would create "character and mood reels," such as villain Greene ("no dialogue, just the way he looked, the way he moved, sitting in a chair," Arnold recalled) as well as Camille, Bond and the various locales. "I was writing themes inspired by the characters

SCORE HIGHLIGHTS

David Arnold's score for *Quantum of Solace*, though the shortest in duration of his five Bonds (61 minutes), is actually among the most complex in terms of his use of themes. He not only supplies new motives for the characters but reprises Vesper's theme from the earlier film, occasionally drops in hints of the White song and offers new sonic twists on the classic Bond Theme.

That this will be a very different Bond film is signaled at the start with Arnold's ominous strings, which lead directly into a sound-effects-filled Aston Martin vs. Alfa Romeo car chase. But Arnold rejoins the action with electronics and orchestra and, in Siena, Italy, a recurring six-note theme for horns counterpointed with the Bond bass line ("Time to Get Out" on the CD). A three-minute version of

Bond and Camille (Daniel Craig, Olga Kurylenko) trudge through the desert to one of David Arnold's most evocative cues in *Quantum of Solace*

and places in the film, rather than the story," Arnold explained. The idea was that "the story takes care of itself, and music will inform you emotionally about people. For me, it was very exciting and very different"—although it also meant committing to a full eight months on the film for what would amount to about 60 minutes of score.

The early creation of themes, demos created in Arnold's studio, allowed Forster's editors to temp-track the film as it was edited. "That 'Night at the Opera' cue is one of those pieces," he noted. "It wasn't written for that scene. It was the Quantum theme, a creepy kind of tentacled thing, this headless organization that kept getting closer and closer. The whole of that opera sequence was done with a chopped-up demo of that original idea. I might not have done it like that. It was like temping it with original work, and then restructuring it by the time you get to record the orchestra. There are four or five moments in the film where that worked really well."

Arnold described the score generally as having a "much more introspective and somewhat ambiguous sound. I've used very organic-sounding synthetic elements, where normally you might have cellos and basses; deep, dark, throbbing electronic sound with real strings and woodwinds over the top. On other occasions, we have the orchestra providing the bottom end and uncomfortable, ugly top-end stuff going on. So it's a much more ambiguous score, and unsettling in some places."

Once again, Nicholas Dodd was Arnold's collaborator, orchestrating and conducting. He explained the process: "Once Dave has given me the scaffolding, the bare bones if you will, I come and sit down with him. He plays the cue for me, I look at the picture and I take all his comments on board. [Arnold's music] is pretty well thought out in the sense of structure, where the rhythm is, what melody is going to be used. I will sometimes add a countermelody, although not so much in the last three [Bonds]. Anything that needs to be added to make it orchestrally sensible, for whatever mood, I will do.

"We sort of hear music in the same way. If he raises his eyebrow and looks at me, I know exactly what he means. I'll ask him for the electronics separately, so I can hear exactly what I'm playing with; then I'll write [orchestrate] it. My score is read by a synth player, who demos it up for the director and David. They

---

"Another Way to Die" accompanies the title sequence (four minutes into the film).

Bond's pursuit of the MI6 traitor, across Siena rooftops and into a church being restored, employs the same theme with variations, again mostly orchestra (10 minutes in, "The Palio" on CD). Bond's trip back to London earns a new sound, an echoing electric guitar over the classic Bond bass line (15 minutes, "Inside Man" on CD), and his trip to Haiti is accompanied by one of the most unusual versions of the Bond Theme ever, with Caribbean percussion almost drowning out the guitar (18 minutes, "Bond in Haiti" on CD).

Bond's hotel-room fight is unscored, but for his initial encounter with Camille and her attempt to kill him Arnold supplies acoustic guitars, orchestra and a bit of electronics; Bond's motorcycle ride gets even more rhythmic treatment (21 minutes, "Somebody Wants to Kill You" on CD). Greene and Camille talk, to grim sounds, featuring the panpipes for her and the low-brass Quantum theme (24 minutes, "Greene and Camille" on CD). Bond's rescue of Camille in a Haitian-harbor boat chase adds rock guitar and drums to the usual strong brass and rhythm elements, ending with the Bond Theme (27 minutes, "Pursuit at Port au Prince" on CD). The background source music is authentic, including tracks by Haitian artists Nickenson Prud'homme ("Zamni," for Bond at the hotel desk) and Wyclef Jean ("24 e tan pou viv," for security-guard talk at the wharf).

Greene heads to a meeting with CIA officers to more ominous sounds, both electronic and orches-

Overhead shot of Nicholas Dodd conducting the orchestra at AIR

make their comments and corrections are made if necessary. My score goes to the copyist and then to the recording session. That's it for every single cue."

As on *Casino Royale*, Dodd conducted a 78-piece orchestra. Recording took place over seven days in early-to-mid-September 2008. "We usually re-

(SCORE HIGHLIGHTS, CONT.)

tral (32 minutes, "No Interest in Dominic Greene" on CD). One of the most intriguing and evocative pieces of the entire score is heard as Bond, Greene and members of the Quantum group arrive at a performance of *Tosca* in Bregenz, Austria; Arnold builds and builds the tension with the Quantum theme (39 minutes, "Night at the Opera" on CD). Bond overhears the Quantum plan during the Puccini performance (42 minutes) and then finds himself suspended by M, to more ominous sounds (46 minutes, "Restrict Bond's Movements" on CD).

That six-note theme returns in a short but beautiful passage as Bond visits Mathis (48 minutes, "Talamone" on CD). Vesper's descending-piano motif from *Casino Royale* returns in a tender arrangement as Bond gets quietly drunk (51 minutes, "What's

Keeping You Awake" on CD). Arnold flavors the Bond Theme with wonderful Latin guitars and percussion for their arrival in La Paz (53 minutes, "Bolivian Taxi Ride" on CD); he then reprises it in a softer, more conventional form as he propositions his English-consulate colleague Fields (55 minutes, "Field Trip" on CD).

Jaime Cuadra's "Regresa" and "Cholo Soy" are heard as background source pieces at Greene's party (56 minutes). Melancholy strings and piano, echoing Vesper's theme, accompany Mathis' death (1 hour, 2 minutes in, "Forgive Yourself" on CD). Ethnic flutes and timpani beats accompany Bond's acquisition of an old plane (1 hour, 5 minutes; "DC3" on CD). Bond and Camille's plane is attacked from above, to high-energy rhythm and powerful brass

cord eight minutes per [three-hour] session, or 16 minutes a day," Dodd said. "The red light goes on, your pulse goes up and it's a performance. But I've never thought of the Bond scores as anything other than fun. I'm like a kid in a candy store."

Ethnic instruments were again called for, with the various Latin American locations: Pete Lockett supplied the ethnic percussion, with acoustic guitars, mandolin, charango and pan pipes also used. An even more authentic Latin American sound was provided by Peruvian singer-arranger Jaime Cuadra, whose modern versions of period folk songs "Regresa," "Cholo Soy" and "El Provinciano" were licensed for background music during scenes in Bolivia; similarly, Haitian artists Wyclef Jean and Nickenson Prud'homme can be heard in the Port-au-Prince scenes.

As for the end title, there was at first some thought of repeating the title song. "But then," Arnold recalled, "Marc wanted to end his movie with something very different, a little more left-field and intriguing." Editor Matt Chesse suggested they consider remix artist Kieran Hebden (known professionally as Four Tet). "So we got Kieran in to show him some of the movie and talk about the piece. I sent Kieran away with sections of the score that might be interesting to reconstruct an end title with. He came back a couple weeks later with a version that sounded pretty cool." The piece, nicknamed "Crawl, End Crawl," came too late to add to the soundtrack album but was eventually released on iTunes.

Quantum of Solace premiered in London on October 29, 2008. Critics were mostly unkind, and even savage in their dismissal of the Jack White–Alicia Keys song: "An abysmal cacophony of incompatible musical idioms," declared the *New York Times*; "ghastly theme song . . . an anti-fusion of Jack White's caterwauls and Alicia Keys' breathy soul stylings. . . . Worst Bond theme ever?

figures (1 hour, 7 minutes, "Target Terminated" on CD), although their daring leap with a single parachute goes unscored.

Camille explains her vendetta to Bond, and they walk out of the desert to another of Arnold's most evocative cues, for strings, pan flutes and Latin guitars (1 hour, 13 minutes, "Camille's Story" on CD). Fields's oil-covered body is found and Bond departs the hotel, to angry drums and high-tension Bond Theme variations (1 hour, 19 minutes, "Oil Fields" on CD). Another Jaime Cuadra track ("El Provinciano") and one by Brazilian composer Antonio Pinto ("10") can barely be heard during Bond and Leiter's bar rendezvous (1 hour, 21 minutes).

Massive percussion, guitar and a dramatic orchestral buildup accompany Greene's arrival at the general's desert compound (1 hour, 26 minutes, "Have You Ever Killed Someone?" on CD). Bond's assault on the place, Camille's attack on her quarry and Bond's fight with Greene—all of which take place as the compound explodes and goes up in flames—is the subject of an eight-minute cue (at 1 hour, 28 minutes, "Perla de Las Dunas" on CD) that propels the action with fast-paced electronics and orchestra, pauses briefly for Camille's echoing pan flute and then resumes with a powerful Bond Theme bass line as Greene is left in the desert to die.

Bond and Camille part, and he heads for Russia, to the sound of delicate strings, an echoing electric guitar and metallic sounds (1 hour, 37 minutes, "The Dead Don't Care About Vengeance" on CD). A final reference to the six-note main theme and a touch-

Let's just say Madonna is now off the hook for 'Die Another Day,'" added *New York* magazine. *Rolling Stone* put it simply: "even the new theme song, 'Another Way to Die,' sung by Jack White and Alicia Keys, sucks." *The Hollywood Reporter* praised the score, however: "Jack White's title song passes without notice, but composer David Arnold provides a top-flight action score, keeping the familiar themes to a minimum."

The music press was mixed on the song: "a sparse, low-slung, mid-tempo, distorted, dirty Delta blues-rock wail, short on melody and high on attitude," said London's *Telegraph*; "if the aim was to match the edgier, darker side of the agent, the song succeeds," noted London's *Independent*; the *New Musical Express* remained unconvinced, complaining that it "just falls between doing something radical and not being retro enough."

White and Keys shot a video in Toronto in September, although it lacked the usual collection of Bond movie clips. The song charted in the U.K. on October 4 and reached all the way to number 9; in the United States it charted on November 29, 2008, but hit only number 81; the album, on Keys's label J Records, didn't chart on either side of the Atlantic. The video, however, was nominated for a 2008 Grammy.

A six-note phrase that Arnold originally penned for the unfinished Winehouse song and that pops up occasionally in the film was later spun off into a song of its own. In 2009, Arnold produced a new album for Dame Shirley Bassey. Black penned a lyric that uses the word "solace" several times, leading Bond fans to speculate that it may have been intended for *Quantum of Solace*; but it was actually written months later.

"It basically contains the string riff and feel [from the aborted Winehouse tune] but is melodically and chordally different from the original idea. I liked the string line, especially, [and] decided to write the song with Don when I

(SCORE HIGHLIGHTS, CONT.)

ing counterpoint of Vesper's piano theme with the Bond bass line, as he drops Vesper's necklace into the snow, concludes the story (1 hour, 41 minutes; "I Never Left" on CD). Arnold starts the end titles with the "James Bond Theme" (1 hour, 42 minutes) and then segues to an electronica mash-up of Arnold's themes by Four Tet (1 hour, 43 minutes, "Crawl, End Crawl," not on the CD but later made available for download).

knew I was going to do the Bassey record," Arnold said. The song, "No Good
About Goodbye," appeared on Bassey's album *The Performance*, released in
November 2009 (which also included "Our Time Is Now," another new song
penned by Black and John Barry). Its downbeat vibe and haunting lyrics ("no
solace in a kiss / no comfort in a sigh / no good about goodbye") might easily
have pertained to *Quantum*, making it another Arnold-Black composition that
many Bond fans understandably consider a lost, or would-be, Bond song.

The album's reunion of John Barry, Don Black, David Arnold and Dame
Shirley (along with arranger-conductor Nicholas Dodd), who collectively had
created the sound of 17 of the 24 Bond films, would never happen again. The
next time that Black, Arnold and Bassey got together was less than two years
later, for John Barry's memorial service at London's Royal Albert Hall.

25

"... where worlds collide and days are dark ..."

Skyfall

ueen Elizabeth II turned from her writing table, looked up at Daniel Craig and said, "Good evening, Mr. Bond."

"Good evening, your majesty," he replied, and soon an actor playing 007 was escorting the real queen down a hallway to a waiting helicopter on the Buckingham Palace lawn.

It was July 27, 2012, the night of the opening ceremonies of the summer Olympic Games, being watched live by an estimated 900 million viewers around the world. Just after 8:30 P.M. London time, the two appeared to parachute into the Olympic Stadium to the strains of the original 1962 recording of the "James Bond Theme."

In what may have been the most extraordinary moment in the history of the franchise, the British monarch acknowledged the immense popularity of Ian Fleming's creation and its place as one of Great Britain's best-known cultural assets. And, even though its world premiere was over two months away, *Skyfall*, the 23rd official film in the series, got the biggest plug imaginable.

The year 2012 marked the 50th anniversary of the Bond films, so celebrations were in order. And the disappointing reception for *Quantum of Solace* meant greater pressure on the Bond producers to deliver a film that not only met higher expectations, but also paid homage to aspects of the Bond mythology that had helped make the franchise so successful.

Daniel Craig with his Aston Martin DB5 near Bond's childhood home of Skyfall in Scotland

To that end, Wilson and Broccoli hired Sam Mendes, the Oscar-winning director of *American Beauty* and an acclaimed stage director of such London productions as *Cabaret* and *Oliver!* He would be working from a script by veteran Bond writers Neal Purvis and Robert Wade, polished by Oscar-nominated Hollywood veteran John Logan (*Gladiator*).

The idea was risky, the potential payoff great: the film would open with Bond (Craig, in his third outing as 007) nearly killed in Istanbul after an assignment goes wildly wrong. He decides to return to London after an explosion at MI6's headquarters and it becomes clear that M herself (Judi Dench) is the target of a vengeful adversary (Javier Bardem as the eccentric, dangerous Silva). Bond's assignment takes him to Shanghai and Macau, where he meets the mysterious Severine (Bérénice Marlohe), then back to London and ultimately to his childhood home in Scotland. Along the way he encounters fellow agent Eve (Naomie Harris), an influential politician (Ralph Fiennes), the new Q (Ben Whishaw) and an old family friend (Albert Finney).

Skyfall would contain several references to earlier films (notably the surprise appearance of the Aston Martin DB5 from *Goldfinger*), but a special one quietly honored longtime Bond composer John Barry, who died in January 2011. Barry's last London apartment was at 82 Cadogan Square in the Knightsbridge district, and in *Skyfall* it turns out to be M's residence, at least in exterior views.

The new, high-profile director would mean a change in musical direction too. Four of his films featured music by American composer Thomas Newman, whose 10 Academy Award nominations included two for Mendes films (*American Beauty* and *Road to Perdition*) along with nods for Pixar films (*Finding Nemo*, *WALL-E*) and a modern classic (*The Shawshank Redemption*).

Widely considered one of the most thoughtful and talented composers working in films, Newman is the son of legendary film composer Alfred Newman but with his own distinctive voice. Able to work in traditional orchestral terms, he is equally comfortable in the more modern electronic milieu and loves creating unusual sonic landscapes. His nearly 70 films include collaborations with such diverse directors as Robert Altman (*The Player*), Steven Soderbergh (*Erin Brockovich*) and Ron Howard (*Cinderella Man*). When he learned that Mendes had won the Bond assignment in early 2010, he emailed to offer his services and discovered that Mendes already had him in mind for the music.

"I've known Sam since 1998, and he has always taken me to the extremes of the best work I've done," Newman said. "So it was an opportunity to sit in a room with him and be creative, and I don't think I'd want to miss that chance."

At the request of the producers, Mendes took a courtesy meeting with David Arnold, composer of the five previous Bonds. But, as Arnold later reported, "Sam wanted to continue his working relationship with Thomas Newman. I would hate to be a composer foisted upon a director if the director would rather have someone else. I've never expected to be asked back just because I'd done the previous films." Arnold eventually wound up as musical director for closing ceremonies of the 2012 Olympics, which by coincidence came during the summer months, when the film would be in post-production anyway.

Newman met with Wilson and Broccoli at his Los Angeles studio in late 2010, then flew to London in January 2011 for further discussions. He wouldn't be formally announced as *Skyfall*'s composer until January 2012.

Meanwhile, the search had begun for a title song performer. Sony music head Lia Vollack had become friends with Broccoli and Wilson over the previous two films and started the discussions several months before the November 2011 start of production on *Skyfall*. "We very much wanted to go with a sultry, chanteuse-style female vocalist, something that was quintessentially Bond," Vollack explained, "and outside of the hip-hop world, there are a finite number of female stars who fit that bill."

Topping Vollack's list was the new superstar Adele. Her album *21* was already a smash, and the single "Rolling in the Deep" hit the top of the American charts in May 2011 (no. 2 in the U.K.). Vollack and her colleague Rob Stringer, chairman of Sony Music's Columbia Records label, went to see her perform at Los Angeles' Greek Theatre on August 15, and began talking to her manager Jonathan Dickins and songwriter-producer Paul Epworth about the possibility of engaging her for the Bond film.

The process actually evolved over eight months. "We wanted a bit of the flavor, the feel, to express the history of the franchise," Vollack said. Adele, she felt, had all the right qualities: she was British, an immediately recognizable name and voice, and a fine (soon to be multi-Grammy-winning) songwriter. "She's got this soulful, haunting, evocative quality. It just felt right to bring [the franchise] back to that classic Shirley Bassey feel that you associate with those early Bond films."

Epworth—who at the age of 11 had a wristwatch that played the Bond theme—agreed: "I don't think there are many singers who could convey the mood and the moment the song is supposed to reflect, with the necessary drama, without overdoing it." He met with Vollack and Broccoli, then read the script. "They had very clear ideas of what was necessary. Obviously the script dictated everything, really, but they definitely knew what they were after," Epworth recalled. "Because it was the 50th anniversary, they were keen to do something that fitted into the historical side of it. It had to be a ballad and, from my perspective, modern in a way that had a timeless quality."

Adele was, at first, reluctant to commit to writing and singing the new Bond theme. "It's a big responsibility doing a Bond song: Paul McCartney's done it, Shirley Bassey's the queen of them," she said later. "I was worried I was going to let everyone down by doing it. But I got convinced and I loved the script," she added. Adding to the pressure, she acknowledged, she was just coming off the biggest album of the year. And she was only 24 years old.

But she was intrigued, met with the filmmakers and began mulling ideas. On September 3, she nearly gave away the secret during an appearance on ITV's *Jonathan Ross Show* when she said she was "going back in the studio in November, fingers crossed." When Ross pressed her for more details, she let slip that "this is actually a theme." Ross immediately guessed and began humming the "James Bond Theme," but Adele would only say "it's a concept, it's one song," blushed and changed the subject.

Epworth "spent a lot of time loosely working on ideas," he said. In January 2012, he added, "I had a day free and decided to put it all together. I had the basic part of the melody ready to go as a backing track, without a vocal. I wasn't sure whether what I'd done was any good, so I called Adele up and said, 'Remember those lyrics you told me you had? What are they like and what ideas have you got? Can we have a talk about it?' It just so happened that she was able to meet me the following day. She listened to what I'd done, grinned, and went, 'Give me a microphone.' And she sang most of the first chorus. We came back about a month later and finished off the rest of the song."

What followed were months of slight changes and improvements. "Up until May, when we actually cut the backing track at Abbey Road, I spent a lot of time trying to see if there was anything better I could do. I went back and changed a couple of chords, changed the harmony, just to make it more interesting." And he continued to talk with director Mendes, "a good creative dialogue," as Epworth put it. "He was very specific about details. But really, from the very first version, I had a feeling that they knew the song captured what they were looking for."

By May, parts of Adele's vocals had been recorded. "She came in and cut the second half of the track," Epworth recalled. "We changed a few lyrics in that recording session." Metro Voices, London's leading choral group specializing in film music, was called to provide the backup vocals. These were recorded May 11 at Abbey Road, director Jenny O'Grady said: "There were four singers who multitracked to make a bigger sound and to add the extra harmonies needed. I was there to choirmaster the session, and to work on the arrangement with Paul and Adele, as nothing was written apart from the lyrics. It was all very secretive," she added, "I didn't even know it was for Adele until I got there." Nor was she told that it would be for a Bond film. "When I was listening to the track, I looked at her and Paul and said, 'This sounds like a Bond theme,' and they went, 'Yes, it's *Skyfall*,'" she added with a laugh.

And from the May 2012 Abbey Road sessions emerged the finished song "Skyfall"—at least the version sung by Adele and played by her backup band. Executives from Eon and Sony, and Mendes, all approved—and heaved a sigh of relief that Adele and Epworth had come through. "My part was nothing without what Adele brought to it," Epworth later said. "Without her lyric, her turn of phrase, and her melody, it's just a bunch of chords. I feel very lucky to have been able to collaborate with her once again."

Mendes first heard the demo while he was shooting in England. He claimed to have listened to it "over and over again for like two hours," then shared it with both Broccoli and Daniel Craig, "who both shed a tear," he said. He later called it "perfect, really—atmospherically, the mood, everything, just bang on."

Thomas Newman has always been a Bond fan. When he got the assignment, he watched *Goldfinger* and *Thunderball*, he said, "just to immerse myself in a Bond place. You can say to yourself, 'it's just a movie,' but in the end, no, you're scoring *a James Bond* movie."

He left for London on June 18. Production had finished in late May and Mendes was then deep in the editing process. Newman had been reading the script, looking at footage (including the stunningly photographed silhouette fight in the Shanghai highrise) and had even written what Newman's longtime music editor Bill Bernstein called "a beautiful, lush theme" that, sadly, never found its way into the film.

Newman shipped the key elements of his Los Angeles studio to London so that he could work on familiar gear. They saw a rough, completed film in late July; Newman began writing, "feverishly," he said, what was originally anticipated as 75 minutes of music eventually ballooned to more than 95 minutes. The time pressure was tremendous. Newman later estimated that he had somewhere between four and six weeks, and he worked seven days a week until the final recording session.

(left to right) Orchestrator J.A.C. Redford, composer Thomas Newman and contractor Isobel Griffiths on the scoring stage at London's Abbey Road

Mendes was a frequent visitor to Newman's writing room at Abbey Road, listening to and commenting on synthesizer mockups (those "demo" versions designed to sound similar to what would later be recorded with orchestra). "He's very musical," Newman pointed out. "His leadership, which I've always thought was amazing, was particularly amazing on Bond. He understands color. 'This needs more support in brass,' he might say. He was so specific, and enthusiastic."

A hybrid score incorporating both traditional orchestral and more contemporary electronic sounds was always indicated, Newman said. "I knew there was an obligation for big orchestra because that is 'tuxedo' in a way, the idea of strings and lushness. And at the same time, electronic, sequential writing feels like the music of today, music that I can relate to as well. So there was a sense of expectation and obligation. Sam wanted to reinvent a little bit, but at the same time harken back. It probably was why he hired me: at my best, I could bring a freshness of approach and, hopefully, still acknowledge what's classic about Bond."

Assisting in that task were guitarist George Doering and keyboardist John Beasley, two longtime Newman collaborators who flew over from Los Angeles in early August. "Tom having taken over two rooms right outside Abbey Road

Studio One," Doering recalled, "Beasley and I set up a little studio in one of the rooms. Tom would give us a cue he'd written, talk it over with us about the direction (and the important hit points), and then Beas and I would layer it up with rhythms and other noises into Beasley's laptop.

"Tom would listen back and mold it into the sound he was going for. Then, a couple of days each week, we'd go up to Studio Three and work long days doing even more layers. I played quite a lot of hammered rhythms on dulcimers and stringdrum and other acoustic instruments, and did a lot of rough bowing noises—all stuff that hopefully blends into the score and just helps push it along without intruding. I also did the normal electric-guitar stuff (like the Bond Theme) as well as ambient electric noises. Beasley was amazingly inventive with new sounds, as were the two percussionists from London [Paul Clarvis, Frank Ricotti] that did quite a lot of layers on the Studio Three days."

Newman felt the music "needed to be exciting, compelling, thrusting forward. It needed energy and muscularity and all the things you would expect from Bond." And although he had recently done a pair of thrillers (*The Debt* and *The Adjustment Bureau*, both released in 2011), they weren't really comparable, he said: "There's more sustained action in a Bond movie. There is repose and reflection, and style over action, but most of the time I'd get comments from Sam like 'Bigger! Louder! Fortissimo!'"

The biggest challenge turned out to be the opening 15 minutes, which went through multiple rewrites. But, he added, "when you invoke the Bond Theme, everyone—everyone!—is going to have an opinion about what the guitar should sound like, what bongo drums should sound like, and the bark of brass. People are going to weigh in, all the way down to passive audience members. And the same is true with the opening of a Bond movie. It just has to be incredibly exciting."

Newman's orchestrator J.A.C. Redford arrived from Los Angeles on August 10. Redford—who is himself an accomplished composer for film (*The Trip to Bountiful*), television (*St. Elsewhere*) and the concert world—had been Newman's orchestrator since *WALL-E*. He took Newman's detailed sketches and mockups and translated them into full orchestral scores ready for performance by the orchestra. Equally important, he also wrote the orchestral arrangement for the title song.

Newman already had his hands full with the score, so he asked Redford to handle the song. It was an ideal way to assure that the song would have a classy orchestral treatment, and to allow song and score to blend together nicely.

He met with Epworth, who already had a complete mockup of the song including his ideas for the strings and brass: "Some of the Bond-like elements in the arrangement were there from the beginning, in his conception," Redford said. He added the Bondian techniques of stopped horns, trombones in unison and other gestures. He even transcribed the rhythm tracks (guitars, bass, drums, piano) that had already been laid down in the studio, "knowing that someday the Academy might want to play it," he added with a laugh.

Newman added some ideas as well, and Redford conducted the track on the evening of August 29, at the end of the second day of recording at Abbey Road. There were 77 musicians in the orchestra, and the booth was crowded with onlookers: Adele (with her dachshund Louie), Epworth, Broccoli, Wilson and Mendes all attended. It was a three-hour session, with Epworth and Redford consulting between every take. "J.A.C. ran with it and turned it into the beautiful, lush and classic centerpiece it is," Epworth said, adding that "it was quite a powerful moment. Between everybody in the room, there were some moist eyes."

Adele's vocals were already finalized, so she did not emerge to greet the orchestra, probably because her involvement in the film had not yet been formally announced. But, Redford said, "She could not have been nicer. She was so courteous, down-to-earth, helpful and complimentary. She responded very open-heartedly to the whole process." And, Redford noted, "it was more like a record session than a film session" because the title sequence was still unfinished. The full, four minute and 40-second song was recorded and would be trimmed later to match the opening titles.

The score itself was recorded over six days at Abbey Road—the first time that a Bond score was recorded in its entirety at the fabled London studio, best known for the Beatles records but also, in earlier decades as EMI Studios, the site of recordings by Sir Edward Elgar and Pablo Casals. Money became an issue as the postproduction budget was squeezed in those final weeks, so woodwinds were eliminated from the orchestra. The 79-piece orchestra that recorded on August 28 and 29 consisted mostly of strings and brass, and that number was further reduced to 69 players for the final four days on September 5-6 and 20-21. Flutist Phil Todd's occasional solos were recorded separately at Sphere Studios in central London.

Newman conducted the entire score, with Redford and Mendes listening to everything in the booth alongside mixer Simon Rhodes, offering comments

SCORE HIGHLIGHTS

Among dyed-in-the-wool Bond fans, Thomas Newman's *Skyfall* score was polarizing: some liked Newman's fresh approach, others missed David Arnold's touch, still others questioned Newman's penchant for energy, mood and atmosphere over easily discernable melody.

The music critic for Slate.com perhaps best articulated why this new voice succeeded: "It's Thomas Newman's fresh, inventive work that really gives a new sonic sheen to our beloved secret agent. . . . Newman is clearly an aesthetic stranger to Bond-land, but this unfamiliarity allows him to hear it fresh and pull out new ideas. For example, his feline approach to action sequences—sleeker, more poised and restrained than the bravado that previous scores trafficked in—better suits a Bond

and occasionally asking for rewrites when something didn't sound quite right to the director. "Very positive, but incredibly demanding at the same time," Newman said of Mendes. "He calls it brinksmanship."

Added music editor Bernstein, who participated in the dubbing process later: "Mendes, more than any other director, understands what music brings to a film. Sound effects are fine, but if you want feeling, excitement and drive, music is where you're getting it. And he likes to put it forward." Mendes later praised Newman for "a great, great job on this score, weaving in the new and the traditional."

On Monday, October 1, Adele used the social-networking service Twitter to confirm the rumors with a photograph of her hand on the orchestral chart for the "Skyfall" song; in a press statement later that day, she admitted being "a little hesitant" because of the pressure associated with a Bond film but added that the recording session for the orchestra was "one of the proudest moments of my life. I'll be back combing my hair when I'm 60 telling people I was a Bond girl back in the day."

About 90 seconds of the song leaked online October 2, bringing about a rush of premature reviews. The full version made its official debut just after midnight London time (0:07) on Friday, October 5, Global James Bond Day, marking the 50th anniversary to the day of the London release of *Dr. No*.

A descending series of piano chords precedes Adele's opening lines, which allude to the possibility that Bond—who has been wounded and is falling into a river as the film begins—is facing death ("this is the end / hold your breath and count to 10"). But then, as the chorus begins, the song soars with renewed confidence ("we will stand tall, face it all together, at skyfall"). The second verse alludes to Bond's home, where the entire film will climax ("skyfall is where we start") and to 007 himself ("you may have my number, you can take

(SCORE HIGHLIGHTS, CONT.)

hemmed in by bureaucracies and reliant on technology that has little to do with brute force. Newman applies a surgical touch to the classic Bond theme, extracting the uncertainty and even sadness of those tangy chords while leaving behind all the brash posturing. We know we are in a new era when the iconic two-chord punch violently drops into a much more tentative, roiling texture in Newman's opening cue."

More than 77 minutes of Newman's score were included on the Sony Classical soundtrack album. Oscar voters were treated to a 2-CD "for your consideration" promotional package that contained more music (over 82 minutes) but omitted any overt reference to the Bond Theme. Titles listed below are those given on the commercially available album;

those that only appear on the promotional Oscar discs are noted as "FYC."

Newman opens the film with a two-note brass reference to the Bond Theme (on which, veteran trumpet player Derek Watkins later said, Mendes asked him to "hold back a bit" and not blast it out as he might have for Barry or Arnold). Most of the 12-minute pre-credits action sequence is scored, mixing vaguely ethnic sounds for the Turkish setting and urgent, driving string figures for Bond chasing assassin Patrice through the streets ("Grand Bazaar, Istanbul" on the album). Their fight atop the moving train incorporates intriguing snippets of the Bond Theme and an ever-heightening tension in the strings and brass as Eve prepares to fire (7 minutes into the film, "The Bloody Shot").

Adele and Paul Epworth, moments after winning the Academy Award for their "Skyfall" song at the Oscar ceremonies February 24, 2013

my name / but you'll never have my heart"). The familiar four-note Bond bass line appears, a linking device to classic Bond songs of the past.

The script informed the song both musically and lyrically, Epworth said: "The song is so much about death and rebirth. It's almost like two people having each other's back when the world ends, when everything comes down

The Adele song begins (13 minutes in) as the wounded Bond falls into a river and slowly descends. Daniel Kleinman's title sequence is another visual delight, alluding to past Bond titles (the girls, guns and knives) while also hinting at scenes to come; the song is slightly abridged from the single version.

Newman's stoic, brass-choir "M" motif is first heard as Mallory suggests that she step down (just under 19 minutes, "Voluntary Retirement"); the subsequent explosion at MI6 headquarters is unscored. We learn that 007 is alive to quiet guitar and exotic flute sounds (21 minutes, "Enjoying Death"); M's theme is reprised (24 minutes, "Coffins," FYC). Bond visits the new MI6 (27 minutes, "New Digs") to a blend of modern rhythm sounds with more tradi-

tional, and dignified, strings and brass. The Bond Theme bass line returns during the painful extraction of shrapnel from his shoulder (32 minutes, "Day Wasted").

An alto-flute Bond Theme reference plays during 007's meeting with Q at the National Gallery, which segues directly into a grand orchestral statement—incorporating Asian percussion and exotic flute sounds—for stunning shots of the Shanghai skyline (40 minutes, "Brave New World"). Patrice's arrival is greeted with the most modern-sounding music yet, mostly electronic and industrial sounds with a backbeat (42 1/2 minutes, "Shanghai Drive"). Newman shifts back into more dramatic orchestral mode for Bond's elevator ride—which, according to Mendes, intentionally evokes Bernard Herrmann's classic

around your ears. If you've got each other, you can conquer anything, you can get over it, you can get it through it. That's where the music came from for me.

"There was only one thing it could be," he said. "It's trying to find a way to make Bond's apparent demise into something that wasn't necessarily final. It felt melancholy, sad and full of loss, but it didn't feel like it was truly the end. I had this idea that the chords descend as the sky falling, so it comes crashing down after the second chorus. The section after that was like these green pastoral shoots of rebirth, the cycle of life, from death to triumph. That was definitely something we set out to try and capture. I guess that's why it's four and a half minutes long," he said with a laugh.

Entertainment Weekly praised its "lush cinematic sweep . . . a classically composed torch song," while the New York *Daily News* called Adele "the biggest voice to grace this spy-thriller realm since Dame Shirley Bassey." The *Los Angeles Times* felt that it "hints at the classic, more traditional Bond themes of yore," while the *London Telegraph* decided it "reeks of pastiche . . . although it is certainly one of the better efforts to try to capture that classic torch-song, femme-fatale vibe." The *Wall Street Journal* liked its "sweep and drama . . . the orchestral support gives it a classical timelessness that sets it apart from typical pop songs," while *The Hollywood Reporter* declared it "every inch a classic Bond theme."

Billboard's review summarized the majority of reactions: "Not only is it a gorgeously cinematic opus featuring a 77-piece orchestra and pristine production, its lyrics aren't spy nonsense.... Considering that Adele's established sound is rooted in blue-eyed soul, her sophisticated channeling of Bassey will likely work in her favor."

It did. The song debuted at no. 8 on *Billboard's* Hot 100 chart, shot to no. 1 on iTunes in 48 countries, and debuted at no. 4 as a single in the U.K. The Adele single, on her XL/Columbia label, became only the second Bond theme to be omitted from the film's soundtrack (following Chris Cornell's *Ca-*

Vertigo score—as the assassin prepares for another hit (45 minutes, "Jellyfish"). Bond's brutal fight with Patrice is played mostly with brass and percussion (49 minutes, "Silhouette").

Newman's evocative theme for the beautiful Severine is first heard when she spots Bond (50 minutes, "Modigliani"). Eve's arrival is treated lightly and delicately: sexy flute and vibes with a pizzicato-string edge (53 minutes, "Close Shave"). (Newman's first try at this scene, lush strings, guitar and brushes on drums, called "Old Dog, New Tricks," was recorded but later rejected by Mendes as too romantic and became a bonus track on the iTunes *Skyfall* release.)

Newman reprises the Adele theme melody as Bond sails into Macau, then transitions into exotic

percussion, shakuhachi-like flute, a brief reference to Severine, and ominous hints of the villainy about (55 minutes, "Komodo Dragon"). Newman elevates the tension in Bond's conversation with Severine with guitar, strings and another hint of the Bond Theme (1 hour, "Someone Usually Dies"). Aggressive strings, muted brass and a valedictory Bond Theme playing the original guitar riff underscore his fight with the bodyguards (1 hour, 3 minutes, "Komodo Dragons," FYC).

The most complete version of Newman's string-drenched Severine theme occurs when Bond joins her in the shower (1 hour, 6 minutes, "Severine"), while the exterior shots of the yacht sailing to a nearby abandoned island get a rich orchestral treatment (1 hour, 8 minutes, "The Chimera"). Interestingly, Bond's initial

sino Royale song). Nearly 78 minutes of Thomas Newman's score was on the "official" *Skyfall* album, released by Sony Classical on November 6, and it became the highest-charting Bond album since 1985 (arriving at no. 100 on the album chart, having sold 5,000 copies, according to Nielsen SoundScan).

Skyfall's star-studded royal premiere was October 23 and it opened in the U.K. on October 26; it debuted on American screens November 9. Critical reaction was overwhelmingly positive, proving that Daniel Craig and the Bond team had topped themselves once again. The London *Times* even mentioned the song in its opening paragraph: "From the moment the orchestral sound of Adele belts out, sending a nostalgic shiver down the audience's collective spine . . ." The New York *Daily News*, too, said "Adele's soaring theme ranks with the Bond films' best," while *Variety* added "Adele's sultry cabaret-style theme song echoes the throaty Shirley Bassey tunes of old."

Few mentioned Newman's score, perhaps because the Adele song had been so widely publicized that the rest of the film's music took an inevitable back seat. One of the rare instances was in *The Hollywood Reporter*: "Thomas Newman's score is far from generic, finding many moods while delightfully allowing room for Monty Norman's immortal Bond Theme when the moment calls for it." Later music critics enthused, however: "The entire Shanghai and Macau sequences are classics of James Bond lore, filled with exotic color and emotional dread, the tone set precisely by Newman's score," noted *Film Score Monthly*.

As awards season began a few weeks later, both song and score were cited again and again. On January 13, 2013, "Skyfall" became the first Bond theme to win a Golden Globe award from the Hollywood Foreign Press Association (Adele, afterwards, called it "very surreal and quite hilarious"). Then on February 10, Newman accepted the British Academy of Film and Television Arts' original-music award at a televised ceremony in London, offering "a

meeting with Silva goes unscored. The music playing on Silva's outside loudspeakers is French singer-songwriter Charles Trenet's 1938 recording of "Boum!" Newman invokes the Bond Theme on guitar again when Bond apprehends Silva (1 hour, 20 minutes, "Fight / Capture Silva," not on CD).

Strange, atonal sounds for Silva's display of his deformity (1 hour, 23 minutes, "Cyanide," FYC) are followed by one of the score's longest cues. It's a fast-paced, five-minute piece in which Mendes intercuts Silva's escape with M's public grilling and Q's decoding of Silva's computer, then—with the addition of more traditional orchestra—jumps to 007 as the chase in London's tube system begins (1 hour, 26 minutes, "Quartermaster"). He catches the train, then searches for Silva to more suspense, mostly via strings (1 hour, 34 minutes, "Health & Safety"). He spots and chases Silva into darkened tunnels (1 hour, 35 minutes, "Granborough Road"); Newman adds brass to heighten the suspense and support M's powerful testimony as Silva nears the conference room (1 hour, 38 1/2 minutes, "Tennyson").

Brass and lots of percussion take center stage as Mallory is wounded during the subsequent shootout and Bond rescues M (1 hour, 41 minutes, "Enquiry"). Then, as Bond unveils his old Aston Martin DB5 and they drive off, Newman quite appropriately defers to the Bond Theme, including guitar and bongos, in its most complete form yet (1 hour, 44 minutes, "Bread-crumbs"). A highly atmospheric cue accompanies them en route to Bond's childhood home (1 hour, 47 minutes, "Skyfall") and a more propulsive one un-

Thomas Newman accepting his BAFTA award for original film music on February 10, 2013

big shout-out to Monty Norman and the late John Barry for that iconic theme which always makes everyone get up and smile"—and, directing his remarks to longtime collaborator Sam Mendes, added one word: "brinksmanship," a reference to Mendes' own push-everyone-to-the-creative-edge credo.

The Academy Award nominations were announced January 10, and both the Adele song (formally credited to "Adele Adkins and Paul Epworth") and

Newman's score were among the Oscar nominees (as were the film's gorgeous Roger Deakins cinematography, its sound editing and sound mixing).

The Oscar ceremonies on February 24 turned out to be an unexpected bonanza for Bond fans. Not only would Adele perform "Skyfall" for the first and only time since recording it nine months earlier, but ex-Bond girl Halle Berry introduced a film tribute to the 007 films and Dame Shirley Bassey flew in to reprise her greatest Bond hit, "Goldfinger."

Berry reminded the audience that "in film after film, moviegoers have been treated to songs reflective of the moment and scores as cool as 007 himself. Bond music is a genre all its own, guaranteed to make your heart beat faster and take your breath away." Oscar music director William Ross led a 60-piece orchestra in a two-minute medley of the "James Bond Theme" and "Live and Let Die" to accompany the clip montage. Bassey then wowed the Dolby Theater crowd with her matchless rendition of the 1964 John Barry classic, earning the evening's first standing ovation.

Adele sang "Skyfall" live, with her own four-man band, four backup singers, a 32-voice male choir and 19 onstage musicians who were playing along with a track recorded a few days earlier by Ross's orchestra. Interestingly, Ross later said, Bassey and Adele were the only performers who did not pre-record their vocals (a common practice with live, high-pressure shows like the Oscars). Sally Stevens, who organized the choir, later spoke of Adele's "darling, sweet, unaffected personality. She was very friendly with everyone, and brought her new little baby with her from the U.K., and a nanny. Adele had had serious vocal problems a couple of years earlier, but everything returned in full force. She sounded wonderful, in rehearsal and at the show."

When it came time for the awards themselves, Newman lost the original-score Oscar to *Life of Pi*, but Adele and Epworth won for their "Skyfall" song. Both thanked Broccoli and Wilson, and Adele began to cry when she thanked her

<hr />

(SCORE HIGHLIGHTS, CONT.)

derlines their preparations (1 hour, 51 minutes, "Kill Them First").

Silva's advance unit arrives to weird, pitch-bending brass and percussion, then more decisive orchestral gestures as the initial attack is repelled (1 hour, 54 minutes, "Welcome to Scotland"). Silva plays The Animals' 1965 recording of John Lee Hooker's "Boom Boom" as his helicopter attacks the ancient edifice to a fast-moving, building series of Bond Theme variations (2 hours, "She's Mine"). Newman adds more of his chugging, rhythm-section suspense as Bond leaves the burning wreck of his old homestead (2 hours, 5 minutes, "The Moors"). He then applies an explosive variation on the Bond Theme for Bond's underwater battle with one of Silva's minions, along with eerie, increasingly in-

tense sounds as Silva confronts M (2 hours, 8 minutes, "Deep Water").

M's theme returns, now at its most solemn (2 hours, 13 minutes, "Mother") as she dies in the chapel and we cut to Bond on the rooftop of MI6. And, as 007 meets Moneypenny and the new M, Newman concludes with the Bond Theme as arranged by David Arnold for the finale of *Casino Royale* (2 hours, 17 minutes, not on CD). It opens the end credits, then segues into "Adrenaline" ("a groove with Middle Eastern strings," Newman said, intended for but unused in an earlier scene) plus excerpts from "The Bloody Shot" and "Komodo Dragon."

producer and co-writer Epworth ("who believed in me all the time"), and Epworth returned the compliment by calling her "the best person I've ever worked with."

The final honors to come their way were the Grammy Awards, nearly a year later because of the later eligibility period of the National Academy of Recording Arts and Sciences. Both song and score were nominated and, on January 26, 2014, both won. Newman was present to accept his award.

Skyfall had been a worldwide sensation: it became the highest-grossing film ever in Great Britain, taking in over £94 million in just six weeks. It eventually earned more than $304 million in the U.S. to rank as the fourth highest-grossing film of 2012. Its final worldwide box-office tally of $1.1 billion propelled it to the no. 8 spot among all-time box-office leaders.

Its title song had become the first Bond music ever to win an Academy Award, its score only the second ever nominated. By the end of 2013, the Adele single had gone platinum, selling over 2 million units, while Newman's score album had sold over 30,000. Sam Mendes was signed to direct the next Bond film, set for release in October 2015. Bond, and Bond music, was bigger than ever.

Afterword

On June 20, 2011, 5,000 people leapt to their feet to cheer Welsh singer Shirley Bassey in London's Royal Albert Hall.

She had just electrified the audience by singing two of her signature tunes, "Diamonds Are Forever" and "Goldfinger," in tribute to a favorite colleague: composer John Barry, who had died on January 30 and who was eulogized throughout the evening by some of England's most famous actors, songwriters and television personalities.

Her performance came on the heels of a thrilling performance by the Royal Philharmonic Orchestra of the "James Bond Suite," a 15-minute arrangement of themes from the first seven films in the series. It too had the audience on its collective feet.

And when composer David Arnold played guitar as Nicholas Dodd conducted the "James Bond Theme" as an encore, the crowd could not contain its enthusiasm. It all added up to proof positive that James Bond music—as launched by Monty Norman, reimagined by Barry and carried forth by multiple composers thereafter—resonates more than ever with filmgoers and music lovers alike.

Fifty years after *Dr. No*, Bond songs and Bond themes still seem timeless, and they even fill concert halls. Carl Davis, who travels the world conducting concerts of Bond music (and who scored the TV-movie *The Secret Life of Ian Fleming* in 1990), sums it up this way: "The character of Bond is very

David Arnold performs the "James Bond Theme" with Nicholas Dodd conducting the Royal Philharmonic Orchestra at John Barry's memorial service June 20, 2011, at London's Royal Albert Hall

inspiring. He is sort of the British Superman. We are talking about a subject that is dangerous and sexy, with a lifestyle that's very glamorous. Music can convey all these qualities. It's very potent."

And, he points out, a survey of 50 years of Bond music is, in some ways, a grand overview of the directions that pop music has gone: from the ballads of the 1960s to the disco of the '70s, the harder-edged rock of the '80s, rhythm-and-blues, electronica and the postmodern realm of the early 21st century.

That Bond music not only is of its time but has been hugely influential is evidenced by the many homages and parodies that have surfaced in recent years, notably Michael Giacchino's music for *The Incredibles* and George S. Clinton's for the *Austin Powers* spy spoofs. "Analyzing it, finding out what the elements are, you realize the genius of what Barry did," says Clinton. And the sly use of the Bond Theme's ominous, repeating four-note bass line is now universally recognized as Bond-like, or at least spylike, in everything from

The Simpsons to *Family Guy* cartoons. Bond videogames carry on the same musical ideas.

The legacy of 007 themes and scores is more than just great tunes. Think back to the military cadences of the raid on Fort Knox in *Goldfinger*; the threatening, even terrifying, music of the space sequences in *You Only Live Twice*; the thrilling ski-chase music of *On Her Majesty's Secret Service*; or the many occasions when ethnic instruments flavored an exotic locale, from the Jamaican scenes of *Dr. No* to the Egyptian colors of *The Spy Who Loved Me* and the Cuban sounds of *Die Another Day*.

"To this day, I cannot fail to cry when I hear 'We Have All the Time in the World,'" says Bond producer Barbara Broccoli, who was only nine when Louis Armstrong sang it for her father's production of *On Her Majesty's Secret Service*. "It's a tragic song, but it's filled with so much hope, because it's so much about love, and love surviving even death." Broccoli's memories are shared by millions who recall the emotions attached to key Bond moments that were driven, and often created, by the score.

John Barry was honored with an O.B.E. in 1999, and he should have been knighted during his lifetime. He never received an Oscar nomination for any of his Bond scores or songs (although he ultimately won five Oscars and four Grammys for his other film music). But his influence is enormous. "The main reason I wanted to get into this business," says his successor David Arnold, "was my early experience of watching John Barry films in the cinema. I've thought about it often ever since. The elegant simplicity of the arrangement, and yet the chordal complexity, and the unusual jazz-inflected changes—you feel like it's going to go somewhere, then it goes somewhere else, so you're feeling exhilarated and slightly uneasy at the same time. And then his brilliant, elegant way with melody. . . ."

Half a century later, the Bond phenomenon shows no signs of abating. The next 007 epic, again starring Daniel Craig, is already in pre-production. Expect more musical excitement, perhaps even a compelling new theme or two. But one thing is certain: "James Bond will return" . . . accompanied by music that will touch us, enthrall us and excite us. Ian Fleming would surely be astounded.

Music written for the Bond films, as most of the composers will tell you, is best heard as a part of the films for which they were written. At the same time, the best film music is that which not only serves the film but also proves to be a compelling listening experience on its own—and many Bond scores are just that.

This is a listener's guide to the original soundtrack albums. For historical and informational purposes we have listed the original LPs (issued at the time of the film release, between 1962 and 1989 in the United States and U.K.). Numbers indicate the stereo releases (although the monaural American *Thunderball* has an interesting history, and we have noted that). Because so many of the compact disc releases of these films have been expanded to include more music, we have listed only the most recent, expanded editions. CD listings for films released from 1995 to 2008 are the original soundtrack releases. All except two (*Casino Royale*, 2006, and *Skyfall*) contain the title songs; in those cases we have also noted the CD single that featured the song.

Dr. No (Monty Norman)
LP: United Artists SULP 1097 (U.K.), UAS 5108 (U.S.)
CD: EMI-Capitol 72435-80890-2-8

From Russia with Love (Lionel Bart, John Barry)
LP: United Artists SULP 1052 (U.K.), UAS 5116 (U.S.)
CD: EMI-Capitol 72435-80588-2-6

Goldfinger (John Barry)
LP: United Artists SULP 1076 (U.K., four more score tracks than U.S. release), UAS 5117 (U.S., has instrumental version of theme missing from U.K. version)
CD: EMI-Capitol 72435-80891-2-7

Thunderball (John Barry)
LP: United Artists SULP 1110 (U.K.), UAS 5132 (U.S., although the monaural album, UAL 4132, has a different "Mr. Kiss Kiss Bang Bang" than the stereo version)
CD: EMI-Capitol 72435-80589-2-5

Casino Royale (1967, Burt Bacharach)
LP: RCA Victor RD 7874 (U.K.), Colgems COSO 5005 (U.S.)
CD: Kritzerland KR 20017-6; Quartet QRSCE 037 (expanded)

You Only Live Twice (John Barry)
LP: United Artists SULP 1171 (U.K.), UAS 5155 (U.S.)
CD: EMI-Capitol 72435-41418-2-9

On Her Majesty's Secret Service (John Barry)
LP: United Artists UAS 29020 (U.K.), UAS 5204 (U.S.)
CD: EMI-Capitol 72435-41419-2-8

Diamonds Are Forever (John Barry)
LP: United Artists UAS 29216 (U.K.), UAS 5220 (U.S.)
CD: EMI-Capitol 72435-41420-2-4

Live and Let Die (Paul McCartney, George Martin)
LP: United Artists UAS 29475 (U.K.), UA-LA100G (U.S.)
CD: EMI-Capitol 72435-41421-2-3

The Man with the Golden Gun (John Barry)
LP: United Artists UAS 29671 (U.K.), UA-LA358-G (U.S.)
CD: EMI-Capitol 72435-41424-2-0

The Spy Who Loved Me (Marvin Hamlisch)
LP: United Artists UAG 30098 (U.K.), UA-LA774-H (U.S.)
CD: EMI-Capitol 72435-41469-2-3

Moonraker (John Barry)
LP: United Artists UAG 30247 (U.K.), UA-LA971-1 (U.S.)
CD: EMI-Capitol 72435-41469-2-3

For Your Eyes Only (Bill Conti)
LP: Liberty LBG 30337 (U.K.), LOO-1109 (U.S.)
CD: EMI-Capitol 72435-41449-2-9

Octopussy (John Barry)
LP: A&M AMLX 64967 (U.K.), SP 4967 (U.S.)
CD: EMI-Capitol 72435-41450-2-5

Never Say Never Again (Michel Legrand)
LP: Seven Seas K28P 4122 (Japan)
CD: Silva Screen FILMCD 145

A View to a Kill (John Barry)
LP: Parlophone EJ 24 0349 1 (U.K.), Capitol SJ 14123 (U.S.)
CD: EMI-Capitol 72435-41448-2-0

The Living Daylights (John Barry)
LP: Warner Bros. WX 111 (U.K.), 25616-1 (U.S.)
CD: EMI-Capitol 72435-41451-2-4

Licence to Kill (Michael Kamen)
LP: MCA 6307 (U.K. and U.S.)
CD: MCA MCAD 6307

GoldenEye (Eric Serra)
CD: Virgin 7243 8 41048 2 5

Tomorrow Never Dies (David Arnold)
CD: A&M 31454 0830 2 (contains Sheryl Crow, k.d. lang vocals but less score);
    Chapter III CHA 0125 (missing the vocals but contains more score and
    composer interview)

The World Is Not Enough (David Arnold)
CD: MCA 088 112101-2

Die Another Day (David Arnold)
CD: Warner Bros. 48348-2

Casino Royale (2006, David Arnold)
CD: Chris Cornell song, Suretone/Interscope 060251718880; score, Sony
    Classical 88697-02369-2; additional score excerpts on iTunes

Quantum of Solace (David Arnold)
CD: J Records 88697-37089-2

Skyfall (Thomas Newman)
CD: Adele song XL/Columbia XLS593CD; score, Sony Classical 8876540
    1402; one additional cut on iTunes.

Other notable Bond-related albums:

Great Movie Sounds of John Barry (1966)
LP: CBS SBPG 62402 (U.K.), Columbia CS 9293 (U.S)
    Barry recorded several collections that included Bond themes, but this—
with "From Russia with Love," "Goldfinger" and "Thunderball"—features
what may be his most powerful arrangement of the "James Bond Theme." It

was reissued on several CD collections including *The Music of John Barry* (Sony 476750 2), which contains generous excerpts from all three of his 1960s Columbia collections and their many new arrangements of Bond themes, among them "007" and "Mr. Kiss Kiss Bang Bang."

The Concert John Barry (1972)
LP: Polydor 2383 156. CD: Universal France 532 720 2
This album preserved the symphonic arrangements that Barry created for a London concert with the Royal Philharmonic Orchestra. Included is his 18-minute "James Bond Suite," with "Goldfinger," the "Bond Theme," "From Russia with Love," "Thunderball," "007," "You Only Live Twice," "On Her Majesty's Secret Service" and "Diamonds Are Forever."

The Best of James Bond 30th Anniversary Limited Edition (1992)
CDs: EMI Records USA 0777-7-98560-2 2
A must-have for Bond fans, this two-CD set contains the usual collection of Bond title songs (through "Licence to Kill") but adds a second disc of previously unavailable music, including the four U.K. *Goldfinger* tracks, an extra 21 minutes from the *Thunderball* score, early demos of "Goldfinger" and "You Only Live Twice," and especially the unused "Mr. Kiss Kiss Bang Bang" vocals from *Thunderball* by Dionne Warwick and Shirley Bassey.

Moviola (1992) and *Moviola II: Action and Adventure* (1995)
CDs: Epic EK 52985, 66401.
Barry revisited "We Have All the Time in the World" on the first disc and "All Time High" on the second, both with the Royal Philharmonic Orchestra. On the second, he also performed a new version of the "James Bond Suite."

Bond Back in Action (1999) and *Bond Back in Action 2* (2000)
CDs: Silva Screen SSD 1100, 1119.
Veteran Barry orchestrator Nic Raine conducted the City of Prague Philharmonic in these two albums that offered re-recordings of memorable score highlights throughout the Bond series. One of the attractions for Bond music buffs is his re-creation of excerpts not available on the original movie soundtracks, notably some of Norman's dramatic music from *Dr. No*; portions of *Diamonds Are Forever*, *The Man with the Golden Gun* and *Moonraker*; and John Altman's St. Petersburg tank chase from *GoldenEye*.

Completing the Circle (Monty Norman, 2005)
CD: Bronze Records GBRCD 1007
For this song collection, Norman retrieved his original "Bad Sign, Good Sign" (which he eventually developed into the "James Bond Theme") and sang it himself.

Over the years, many songwriters and artists jumped on the Bondwagon, offering songs for consideration as title tunes for various 007 films. And in one case, a Hollywood songwriting team actually penned a score for an Ian Fleming-based film that had nothing to do with 007. Some of the notable—and a few notorious—attempts:

"Thunderball" (Johnny Cash, 1965).

One of the biggest musical mysteries in Bond history, this May 1965 Nashville recording is clearly about 007 and the plot of the film then in production ("the power of her engines now is drowned in the sea . . . somewhere there is a man who could the stop the thing in time . . . he's feared by all in crime"). Johnny Cash had enjoyed a long string of hits on the country charts for a decade, but it's hard to imagine Broccoli and Saltzman accepting a country-flavored theme for a British Secret Service agent on a mission to retrieve stolen nuclear warheads in the Bahamas. If it was submitted as a "spec" theme, it went nowhere.

"Thunderball" (Lionel Bart, 1965).

The *From Russia With Love* songwriter penned a proposed theme for the fourth Bond film during the late summer of 1965, although why remains a mystery. His "Thunderball" was a hard-rocking love song with no connection to the film's plot ("does she want me back / Thunderball / if that's what you're trying to say . . .") and an odd combination of surf guitar, whistling and male choir. A vocal version and three instrumentals (romantic piano, bossa nova and jazz trio) were recorded on September 10, 1965 in New York City. Bart's archivist reports that Broccoli and Saltzman heard the recordings but turned them down (in the midst of the turmoil between "Mr. Kiss Kiss Bang Bang" and the Barry-Black "Thunderball" then being written). The Bart tapes were discovered and released in 2012.

"You Only Live Twice" (Lorraine Chandler, 1967).

This track from Detroit-born soul singer Lorraine Chandler sports the Bond bass line and a Japanese-flavored guitar-trumpet lick; it was apparently discovered in the RCA vaults in the 1990s. Once again, however, the producers were unlikely to forgo a John Barry title song for a little-known American artist who had never had a hit record.

Chitty Chitty Bang Bang (Richard and Robert Sherman, 1968).

Only peripherally related to Bond, this children's movie musical was based on Ian Fleming's 1964 novel and was produced by Albert R. Broccoli. Although the stars are Dick Van Dyke and Sally Ann Howes, Bond veterans Desmond Llewelyn ("Q") and Gert Frobe (the villain in *Goldfinger*) appear, and Bond art director Ken Adam designed the sets. The Sherman brothers (of *Mary Poppins* fame) penned a delightful score including the infectious title song and the touching lullaby "Hushabye Mountain." There's nothing especially Bondian about the score, but the Fleming connection and the film's magical car, which remains a favorite of children everywhere, merited mention.

"The Man with the Golden Gun" (Alice Cooper, 1973).

The shock-rock performer wrote and recorded a demo for a possible *Man with the Golden Gun* title song; it was part of his *Muscle of Love* album released in late 1973. "It was such a sure bet," he declared in 2006. "Everybody in the movie business heard it and went, that's so dead-on. Ours was so much more James Bond [than the song ultimately used]. We gave the song balls." The reality was different: middle-aged, conservative producers Broccoli and Saltzman were hardly likely to adopt a theme by an artist who staged mock executions on stage, used live boa constrictors and was once reputed to have bitten off the head of a chicken during his act.

"For Your Eyes Only" (Blondie, 1981).

The New York-based rock group was briefly under consideration to perform the movie theme before Sheena Easton was chosen. The group had had three number-one hits in the previous year (including "Call Me" from *American Gigolo*). Lead singer Debbie Harry said years later that "they just wanted me to sing on their track. We actually wrote a song, our own version, and submitted it." Their rejected "For Your Eyes Only" (with lyrics including "we both have our orders and a trick up the sleeve") appeared on the group's 1982 album *The Hunter*.

"Never Say Never Again" (Phyllis Hyman, 1983).

Of all the Bond songs that "might have been," this one has the most intriguing backstory. Canadian actor-songwriter Stephen Forsyth (who played a spy in the Italian-produced 1966 film *Fury in Marrakesh*) knew *Never Say Never Again* director Irvin Kershner and, along with partner Jim Ryan, penned a proposed title song for the film. Soul singer Phyllis Hyman (a Tony nominee for *Sophisticated Ladies*) sang the demo but Kershner declined to listen, citing potential legal concerns. Forsyth's attorney sent it to the Warner Bros. music department, where according to Forsyth it was played and liked. But Michel

Legrand was, by now, in place as composer, and his clout as an Oscar-winning composer trumped the work of a more obscure artist; the song went nowhere.

"This Must Be the Place I Waited Years to Leave" (Pet Shop Boys, 1986).

Band member Neil Tennant once said this song was penned as a "musical exercise" in case they were asked to pen the theme for *The Living Daylights* (which, "it had been intimated," he said, they might). At the time, they were coming off their first number-one hit in the U.K., "West End Girls." The offer from Eon never came. It was ultimately released as part of the synthpop group's 1990 album *Behaviour*.

"GoldenEye" (Ace of Base, 1995).

The Swedish pop group submitted a memorable tune (later reworked into the song "The Juvenile"). The story goes that its label Arista worried about the possibility of this hot band being dragged down by a possible Bond-movie failure and thus withdrew the song; whether that's actually true, or whether the prospect of a song by U2's Bono and the Edge won out in terms of sheer publicity value, is unknown.

"Tomorrow Never Dies" (Saint Etienne, Pulp, Swan Lee, Dot Allison, the Fixx, 1997).

These are just a few of the many artists who submitted potential themes to MGM's music department. It was the biggest "cattle call" in the history of the franchise; it irritated many when they later learned that they were part of a massive competition; and it was a stunt that was never repeated again. In terms of hit potential, Pulp's rocking number and Saint Etienne's softer pop approach may have had the edge, although Scottish singer Dot Allison (recently of One Dove) supplied an intriguing song. Danish band Swan Lee and veteran English rockers The Fixx would seem to have had little chance given the competition.

"The World Is Not Enough" (Straw, 1999).

This is another instance of a decent song that its creators may have hoped had a chance but in reality had none; David Arnold had the gig from the start, and his choice of Garbage was backed by the studio. Just because the British group added "kiss kiss, bang bang" to the lyrics was hardly going to convince the filmmakers to alter their course.

"Beyond the Ice" (Red Flag, 2002).

The synthpop/industrial-music duo created a demo for *Die Another Day* that incorporated such phrases as "license to thrill" and "you only live twice." But Madonna was already in the mix in early 2002, and once she committed to write and perform the title song, no one else stood a chance.

Unraveling the largely untold saga of 50 years of Bond music was an extraordinary challenge that required a huge amount of research; many new interviews (those conducted by me are denoted "JB" in the list below); access to music-business insiders in London, New York and Los Angeles; and, frankly, a veteran reporter's sense of where previous writers went wrong, placing too much trust in faulty memories or simply failing to do their homework.

Books consulted are listed in the bibliography; newspaper and magazine pieces are cited below. Those most frequently cited are abbreviated as follows: *Daily Variety* (DV), *Weekly Variety* (WV), *New York Times* (NYT), *Los Angeles Times* (LAT) and *The Hollywood Reporter* (HR).

Complementing my own interviews were those of author and documentary filmmaker John Cork, whose 1999–2000 talks with composers and filmmakers can be heard (sometimes as commentaries, sometimes in featurettes) on the Bond DVDs issued by MGM-UA between 2000 and 2009. The John Barry biographies by Geoff Leonard et al. and Eddi Fiegel also provided useful background information and, occasionally, quotes, cited below as well.

Also immensely helpful were the interviews done by documentary filmmaker Stephen Franklin for the 2006 television special *James Bond's Greatest Hits* (referred to as JBGH), in which I was privileged to participate. These are all specifically noted, as are interviews done by other writers. In a few cases, highly credible sources asked to remain anonymous, and I respected those wishes.

Background on the films, their production and the plots was drawn from several sources, notably the books cited in the bibliography and the (mostly) Cork-produced "making of" featurettes on the "special edition" Bond DVDs. Bond scripts and call sheets (the daily guides to production on every film), along with hundreds of vital press clippings and publicity materials, were happily discovered in the John Cork Collection at the University of Southern California's Cinematic Arts Library.

The comings and goings of many of the people discussed in this book were detailed in the pages of *Variety* (via the *Variety* Archives and my own clipping files). Chart statistics are from *Billboard* in the United States and the Guinness and Virgin guides in the U.K., all cited in the bibliography. Cue sheets detailing every piece of music in every film were provided by colleagues at ASCAP and BMI.

Grammy statistics were furnished by the National Academy of Recording Arts and Sciences. All Oscar-related segments were viewed at the Academy of Motion Picture Arts and Sciences Pickford Center for Motion Picture Study in Hollywood. Recording dates were assembled from several primary sources, especially the EMI logbook entries obtained by Scott Shea for the 30th-anniversary Bond music collection; database entries for current holdings at Abbey Road; London orchestra contractor Isobel Griffiths; and musicians union representatives in London and Los Angeles.

Introduction
John Barry interviews by JB 3/9/96, 10/11/08. David Arnold interview by JB 10/9/08. Sean Connery quote from interview in *Hemispheres* magazine, April 2008.

1 Dr. No
Background includes *Belle* stories WV 5/17/61, 6/14/61. Also Gerry Bron notes in *Completing the Circle* CD 2005; and Norman info at http://www.montynorman.com and http://www.musical-theatre.net/html/composers/montynorman.html.

All Monty Norman quotes from interviews by JB 6/10/11, 7/10/11 unless otherwise stated.

Also considerable background from chapters 17 and 18 of Norman's unpublished autobiography, *A Walking Stick Full of Bagels*, kindly furnished by the author.

Daily Gleaner stories 1/16/62, 2/23/62. Saltzman quote from Norman interview in *007 Magazine* no. 46. "Lotus life" quote from Norman interview by Cork 1999. Byron Lee: *Reggae and Caribbean Music*. Norman press release: Blue Island, Ill., *Sun-Standard* 7/4/63.

Fleming's interest in calypso: from Lycett bio.

"West Indian music" from Cork interview. Malcolm/Ranglin lawsuit and settlement: *Daily Gleaner* 2/27/62, 3/10/62, 1/12/63, 9/17/63; also 2011-12 Ranglin emails with English musician Mike Collins.

Also consulted: Pierot Corsini, "Monty Norman: Portrait of the Theme Maker," *Ear* magazine, July–August 1987; Tomas Hedman, "The Full Monty," *007 Magazine*, no. 46, 2005; and letter from Norman to Geoff Leonard, 1989.

UA memos dated 1/9/62, 3/23/62 from United Artists Collection at University of Wisconsin. Peter Hunt interview: *From Silents to Satellite* no. 16; Terence Young interview, *From Silents to Satellite* no. 15.

Barry on Bond theme: Karlin, *On the Track*; Brown, *Overtones and Undertones*. Earliest known interview with Barry on the subject: Bruce Charlton, "John Barry Put Bond to Music," *New Musical Express*, Nov. 2, 1962.

Vic Flick interview with JB 6/8/11; also his autobiography *Vic Flick: Guitarman*.

Burt Rhodes background from http://www.jazzprofessional.com; also information from trial testimony.

Hunt rumor about guitar: Robert Short interview by JB 7/11/11.

Barry "If I didn't I don't know why . . ." *From Silents to Satellite* no. 15.

Flick quote about Bond movies from Cork 1999.

Broccoli and Young issues with score, from *When the Snow Melts*.

Norman-Maurice Binder disagreement, letter of 8/22/62 courtesy of Norman.

EMI stats, David Toop notes from *John Barry: The EMI Years* Vol. 3.

Reviews: LAT 4/28/63, HR 3/15/63, *Film Daily* 3/19/63, *Daily Mirror* 9/20/62. *Billboard* 10/20/62, 4/27/63, 6/22/63.

Barry on seeing film: from *On the Track, Overtones and Undertones*. Broccoli from *When the Snow Melts*.

Novello award to Norman, *Billboard* 5/28/77.

Score Highlights

Barry quote from *Film Music Screencraft*. Hunt quote from Cork documentary.

Andress voice dubbing: Nikki van der Zyl email 4/14/12.

Lawsuit

David Arnold, "The Man with the Midas Touch," *Mojo*, November 1997.

John Harlow, "Theme Tune Wrangle Has 007 Shaken and Stirred," *Sunday Times of London*, 10/12/97.

Also consulted: Norman's website (re: the *Melody Maker* and *Vox* actions). Emails detailing issues in the case from Simon Smith (representing Norman) and Wayne De Nicolo (representing the Times), September–October 2002. Also detailed and extensive notes on testimony from two industry professionals present throughout the trial.

Further coverage of the trial and outcome: *Times of London* 3/6, 15, 20/01. Also London *Daily Telegraph* 3/6, 7, 15, 20/01.

2 From Russia with Love

Barry quotes, Cork 1999. Young interview by editor (not the composer) John Williams, *From Silents to Satellite* no. 15. Bart title song deal DV 4/17/63. *Russia* press party info: Graham Rye, *007 Magazine* no. 52.

Barry in Istanbul, from Cork 1999; *Overtones and Undertones*; Fiegel (chicken story).

Ember Records: from liner notes *The Ember Years* Vol. 1 (Pete Walker, Geoff Leonard) and Vol. 2 (David Toop). Also *Billboard* 7/13/63, 8/24/63.

Elizabeth Taylor in London: *Ember Years* Vol. 1; DV 10/8/63, 4/29/64.

Barry on score, Fleming, "007": from Cork 1999. Vic Flick interview by JB 6/8/11, plus his book *Vic Flick: Guitarman*.

Young: from *Russia* DVD.

Bart writing song: *Billboard* 7/6/63, Don Black interview by JB 5/6/11. George Martin: from JBGH. Also *The Singer's Singer* Monro bio.

Details on Martin, the tack piano, etc., from Richard Moore's "sessionography" in the "Special Reserve" limited edition of *The Singer's Singer*.

Zulu / Winston Affair: WV 7/17/63, 8/7/63, 10/16/63; also Fiegel.

Russia press release: UA Collection at Univ. of Wisconsin.

Reviews: DV 10/14/63, WV 3/18/64. *Billboard* 4/25/64, 8/22/64; Monro album review 5/9/64. Music publishing issues WV 5/6/64.

David Picker interview by JB 7/20/11.

Box office: from Tino Balio *United Artists* book.

Score Highlights

Alan Haven background from Leonard/Walker notes in *The Knack* CD (Rykodisc 1988). Barry on xylophone: from Royal S. Brown interview in *Overtones & Undertones*.

Noise during Monro vocal track: from producer Richard Moore's notes in *Matt Monro: The Complete Singles Collection* (EMI 2010).

3 Goldfinger

Caine/Stamp: JB interviews with Caine 10/17/08, Barry 10/11/08; also Fiegel.

Hamilton: DVD commentary.

Barry on "Russia," "Goldfinger" songs: Cork 1999.

Peacock: Liverpool *Echo* 3/9/64. Peacock quotes from Fiegel.

Newley/Bricusse: Bricusse interview by JB 3/19/11; also his autobiography. Newley interview by Scott Shea 12/23/91; Shea also discovered the Newley demo recordings during his research for the 30th-anniversary Bond CDs. Barry on Newley: Cork 1999.

Bassey/Barry affair: Fiegel; *Miss Shirley Bassey*.

Bricusse on Bassey from JB interview. Barry conducting concert tour, WV 12/25/63.

Barry on "conviction": Fiegel.

Bassey performance and wardrobe incident: Cork 1999, JBGH; Flick quotes from *Miss Shirley Bassey*, also JB interviews with Flick 6/8/11, Eric Tomlinson 7/24/11, Derek Watkins 6/7/11.

Barry, song integral to score, *Film Music: Screencraft*.

Barry on keeping tension: Dick Tatham, *Showtime*, November 1965. AP story by Mary Campbell from *Baltimore Sun* 7/28/66.

John Scott interview by JB 4/10/96.

Finger cymbals, etc.: *Film Music: Screencraft*. Flick on banjo, JB interview 6/8/11. Jimmy Page, *When Giants Walked the Earth*.

Hamilton story about reorchestrating from Fiegel.

Saltzman quote about song: from JBGH. Reviews WV 9/23/64, WV 11/18/64, *Billboard* 11/14/64.

Barry signing CBS deal: WV 3/17/65.

Bricusse, gold record, *Billboard* photo 7/10/65.

Barry on "thank you" from Saltzman, JB 10/11/08, also JBGH and Fiegel.

Score Highlights

Barry interview with JB 10/11/08.

4 Thunderball

Backstory of the Kevin McClory affair well told in *The Battle for Bond*.

Barry profiles *Billboard* 1/16/65, WV 2/3/65. CBS deal *Billboard* 3/13/65, WV 3/17/65.

Barry to Nassau WV 4/21/65. "Kiss Kiss Bang Bang" anecdote from Fiegel.

Newley quote, Barry comment on redefining Bond: Cork 1999.

King Errisson interview by JB 8/2/11. Also *Nassau Guardian* 12/22/03.

Barry on Nassau visit: Cork 1999. Bricusse from JB interview 3/19/11.

Barry on underwater cues: Cork 1999.

Barry on Warwick: JB interview 8/21/90, Bricusse quote from his autobiography.

"Thunderball" song: Cork 1999; Black interview by JB 5/6/11; also *Wrestling with Elephants*. Tom Jones announcement *New Musical Express* 9/24/65.

Recording dates courtesy of Scott Shea's research for the 30th anniv. Bond CD set.

Jones: *Daily Mail* 2/6/11; Jeff Bond interview 8/15/10. Barry on Jones: Cork 1999.

Bassey lawsuit: *Billboard* 10/30/65, WV 11/3/65; *Times of London* 11/18,19,23/65; *Daily Express* 11/23/65, *Daily Mirror* 11/18/65. Also correspondence in UA Collection at Univ. of Wisconsin dated 11/12/65. Bricusse interview in *Ear* magazine, July–August 1987.

Reviews: LAT 12/20/65, HR 12/21/65. *Billboard* 11/27/65, 12/4/65.

"Great Movie Sounds of John Barry": *Billboard* 5/14/66.

"Million dollar Mickey Mouse music": *Showtime* mag. 11/65; *Time* 1/14/66. Barry explanation of the phrase from Fiegel.

Score Highlights

Lukas Kendall, *Film Score Monthly*, April–May 2003.

5 Casino Royale (1967)

Backstory of film well told by Graham Rye in *007 Magazine* no. 40; original TV adaptation of *Casino Royale*, DV 10/26/54.

The chronology of Feldman's interaction with Bacharach and David, and the ups and downs of scoring and finding artists to perform, is drawn from Feldman's own highly detailed datebooks, diaries and financial documents in the Charles K. Feldman Collection at the American Film Institute's Louis B. Mayer Library in Los Angeles.

Hal David interview by JB 5/24/11. Bacharach as composer DV 9/28/65. Reference to multiple songs being written: DV 4/5/66. *Luv* story DV 11/23/66.

Mike Redway interview by JB 10/25/11. Joseph McGrath interview by JB 7/18/11.

Bacharach on "Look of Love": "As You Remember Them: Some Notes on the Music," Vol. 2, 1972; and BB interview on "Dusty Springfield: Once Upon a Time 1964–1969" DVD. Also *Songwriters on Songwriting*.

Ramone interview by JB 5/4/11; also his book *Making Records*.

Johnny Rivers: DV 1/18/67, HR 1/20/67, DV 2/17/67, UPI story in Altoona, Pa., *Mirror* 2/21/67. Rivers quote from Dominic, *Bacharach Song by Song*.

Herb Alpert interview by JB 10/21/11; also liner notes in *Sounds Like . . .* CD 2005. Also Rosen, *Billboard Book of #1 Albums*. Bob Edmondson of Tijuana Brass interview by JB 6/29/11.

Feldman quote from film's press notes.

Premiere info: WV 4/19, 26/67. Reviews: LAT 5/1/67, HR 5/1/67, DV 4/17/67. Music reviews: *Billboard* 4/22/67, WV 3/29/67, 4/19/67, 6/21/67. Shani Wallis: *Billboard* 4/8/67, 6/3/67, 6/10/67.

Bacharach on A&M: WV 3/29/67, *Billboard* 4/8/67.

LP audiophile obsession: NYT 7/28/91.

Oscar coverage: Dusty Springfield and Sergio Mendes WV 3/13/68, 4/3/68. Also *Chicago Tribune* 4/11/68, DV 4/11/68. Bricusse interview by JB 3/19/11.

Score Highlights

Bacharach's complete sketches and all of the Shuken and Hayes orchestrations for the London recordings were examined at Sony music library in Culver City, 10/4/11.

6 You Only Live Twice

Great Movie Sounds of John Barry reviews: LAT 10/23/66, *Billboard* 5/14/66.

Story about Bond music WV 11/23/66.

Bricusse interview by JB 3/19/11; also his autobiography *The Music Man*.

Julie Rogers demo: "Best of James Bond 30th Anniversary" album; Rogers interview 6/27/07 from http://www.mi6-hq.com; also final quote from JBGH, 2006. (Rogers recording made 1/1/67, contrary to reports it had been done a year earlier; tape mislabeled.)

Barry working in L.A. January 1967: DV 1/24/67, 2/2/67.

Barry on music supervision, "lyrical style": from Cork 1999. Aretha Franklin idea: from Fiegel. Walker Brothers report: *New Musical Express* 9/2/66.

Sinatra and Barry on the recording session: Cork 1999; also coverage in *Melody Maker* 5/13/67; *Daily Express* 5/5/67; "Look at London," from unidentified English weekly, early May 1967 (in Cork Collection at USC).

John Richards interview by JB 5/27/11; John Leach interview by JB 10/19/08.

Musicians on session: article by Geoff Leonard and Pete Walker in *007 Magazine* no. 36.

Barry on Japan and space: Cork 1999. Also DV 4/19/67.

Crawford calling Barry: from Leonard et al., *John Barry: Man with the Midas Touch*.

Reviews: DV 6/14/67, HR 6/15/67.

Final quote about Barry: WV 4/26/67.

Score Highlights

Barry quote about Hunt and "Bond Theme" from Steven Jay Rubin interview with JB 1978.

7 On Her Majesty's Secret Service

Barry's 8/69 start: DV 7/18/69, WV 8/13/69.

Hunt and Barry quotes on approach: from Fiegel. Lazenby: Philip Masheter interview 1/24/95.

Hunt on "OHMSS" song: from DVD commentary. Barry: Cork 1999. Bricusse: from *Ear* magazine July–August 1987.

Moog synthesizer: *Analog Days*. Also helpful background from NYT 2/16/69 and LAT 3/2/69. Phil Ramone interview by JB 5/4/11. John Glen interview by JB 10/21/11.

Third marriage for Barry: WV 12/3/69.

Hal David interview by JB 5/24/11. Barry quotes from Leonard interview in *Music from the Movies*, Winter 1994–95; Philip Masheter interview 10/26/94.

Armstrong in New York: David interview by JB; Ramone interview by JB; Barry from Cork 1999. Also *Down Beat* 12/25/69.

Armstrong biographer quote from *What a Wonderful World*; also background on session from photographer Jack Bradley, by JB 7/9/11. Armstrong recorded the song on Oct. 23, 1969, not the 28th as claimed in the Armstrong discography; two EMI records substantiate this.

Barry reminiscing: from Steven Jay Rubin interview, 1978.

Reviews: LAT 12/18/69, DV 12/17/69, *Films & Filming* February 1970.

Guinness commercial: MGM master use license dated 5/16/94. Barry quote from *Music from the Movies* no. 7, winter 1994–95.

8 Diamonds Are Forever

Barry quote: from Cork 1999. Don Black quotes from *Wrestling with Elephants*; Cork 1999; and JB interview with Black 5/6/11. Saltzman anecdote: from BBC Radio 2 "The Real John Barry" part 4 (1/19/01).

Bassey announced: WV 8/25/71. Extra lyrics: Black email 6/10/11.

Mary, Queen of Scots crunch: WV 8/18/71, DV 8/27/71, 9/3/71.

Stephen Pickard interview by JB 7/7/11.

Cary Bates: "Cary Bates on John Barry," *File Forty* no. 8, April 1974. Also Bates interview by JB 7/8/11.

Disagreements with Hamilton: Bates piece in *File Forty*; "Inside John Barry" in *RTS Music Gazette* by Michael Perilstein 10/76.

Reviews: LAT 12/16/71, DV 12/15/71. Music campaign in trades: DV 12/15/71.

Oscar song nominations: *Film Score Monthly* online: "The Oscar Finalists: Best Song" by Scott Bettencourt, 6/12/03, 6/19/03.

UA Records story *Billboard* 12/4/71. Also soundtrack issues: *Film Score Monthly* vol. 8 no. 5, June 2003.

Army Archerd on McCartney: DV 1/27/72.

Score Highlights

John Richards by JB 5/27/11.

9 Live and Let Die

Michael Perilstein quote: *RTS Music Gazette* 10/76, from 1971 interview. Cary Bates, from JB interview 7/8/11.

Moore playing Bond DV 8/2/72.

Kass background: WV 5/7/69, WV 6/18/69, WV 5/6/70, DV 8/25/71, WV 3/1/72.

McCartney quotes: *Wingspan*, Capitol DVD, 2001; *Mojo* magazine October 2010.

Family Way background: Chip Madinger notes from Varese Sarabande CD 2011.

George Martin interview by JB via email 6/14/11, 8/14/11. Also Martin's book *All You Need Is Ears*.

Guy Hamilton, from Cork DVD commentary. (Hamilton remembered hearing the song in New Orleans, not Jamaica, but memory was faulty on other things: he thought Paul was just forming Wings, for example, and that the Bond picture might help launch this "new group"; *Music from the Movies*, spring 1995.)

New Orleans background: *Keeping the Beat on the Street: The New Orleans Brass Band Renaissance*. Also, *New Orleans Jazz Funerals From the Inside* DVD, 1996.

Kass-Saltzman memo: UA Collection at Univ. of Wisconsin.

B. J. Arnau: *Newsweek* 8/27/73. (RCA contract: *Billboard* 9/16/72.) Broccoli memo to UA's Fred Goldberg 5/7/73 in UA Collection at Univ. of Wisconsin. Also "For Brenda, Adjective Orgy," AP story in *Hartford Courant* 8/26/73.

Kass vacation with Moore: DV 3/22/73. WB position: DV 10/31/73, *Billboard* 11/3/73.

James Paul McCartney special: *TV Guide* 4/14/73, HR 4/17/73, *Daily Mirror* 5/10/73.

Lyrics: *Washington Post* 7/30/09 "Paul Farhi Interviews Former Beatle on Past and Future Music."

Reviews: DV 6/27/73, HR 6/27/73, L.A. *Herald-Examiner* 6/29/73, *Washington Post* 6/27/73, *Billboard* 6/30/73.

Broccoli and Oscar ads: Memos dated 12/26/73 in UA Collection at Univ. of Wisconsin.

Oscar night: DV 4/3/74, WV 4/10/74.

McCartney on Oscars: "McCartney on Beatles Breakup: Let It Be," Robert Hilburn, LAT 4/21/74.

10 The Man with the Golden Gun

Barry's Bond suite: Leonard et al., *John Barry: A Life in Music*. Also Hollywood Bowl program for 8/18/73.

Barry interview by Martyn Crosthwaite in *RTS Music Gazette* 10/79; also, Barry from Cork 1999.

Black quotes: from Cork 1999; from JBGH; and from JB interview 5/6/11.

Broccoli quote from *Daily Express* 10/8/74. Also coverage in *Daily Mirror* 10/8/74, *Daily Mail* 10/8/74.

Lulu quotes: *East Anglian Daily Times* 7/13/11. Also *Entertainment Weekly* 12/3/99 and JBGH.

John Richards by JB 5/27/11. Barry on score's tone: from Cork 1999. Lulu BBC series DV 11/11/74.

Reviews: DV 12/10/74, HR 12/10/74, *Billboard* 12/26/74, *Daily Mirror* 11/26/74, WV 1/15/74.

11 The Spy Who Loved Me

Barry tax exile: Leonard et al., Fiegel bios. Broccoli and Barry at fundraiser: DV 6/2/76 (script no. 241 in Cork Collection at USC).

Most of the Hamlisch quotes in this chapter from interview by JB 4/12/11. Some from Cork interview 1999. Quote on Oscar night from *Inside Oscar*.

Sager interview by JB 8/10/11. Carly Simon interview from Cork 1999; also from *Bond: The Legacy*. Simon "tongue-in-cheek" quote from AP story in *Lakeland* (Florida) *Ledger*, 5/24/78.

Wilson and Gilbert quotes from Cork's DVD commentary track.

Paul Buckmaster interview by JB 9/22/11; also 2009 interview by Christian Dublin at http://www.xecutives.net.

Time frame for writing and recording: *Hartford Courant* 12/2/76, *Baltimore Sun* 2/7/77. Hamlisch formally announced as composer WV 2/16/77, LAT 2/21/77 (and AP stories). Liz Smith column 3/18/77, in *Evening Capital*, Annapolis, Md., indicated three months in London.

Washington concerts: *Washington Post* 6/27/77.

Reviews: HR 7/7/77, DV 7/7/77, LAT 7/31/77, *High Fidelity* 12/77, NYT 7/28/77, *Billboard* 10/8/77.

"Nobody Does it Better than Bond" ad LAT 8/28/77. DV ads 11/9/77, 11/30/77; HR ads 1/9/78, 3/3/78, 3/15/78.

Oscars: reviews DV 4/4/78, WV 4/5/78. *Inside Oscar* (Hula Hoop quote).

12 Moonraker

Tax exiles: Moore's *My Word Is My Bond*. Broccoli reference HR 7/19/77.

Barry: Steven Jay Rubin interview late 1978.

Paul Williams interview by JB 5/22/11. Lyrics (c) 2012 Paul Williams, used by permission and with grateful thanks.

Sinatra background: from *Sessions with Sinatra*, also *NY Post* 6/29/79, *NY Daily News* 6/29/79 (with pix of Sinatra at premiere in New York).

Barry planning score, from Crosthwaite interview in *RTS Music Gazette* 11/79. Barry on "symphonic" score from *Moonraker* magazine October 1979.

Dan Wallin, Gay Goodwin Wallin interview by JB 7/13/11.

Barry on Mathis: *Soundtrack* no. 58, June 1996. Confirmation of Mathis recording: Mathis email 7/15/11.

Kate Bush offer: *Daily Express* 5/23/79, *Billboard* 7/7/79.

Polo Lounge story: from both *Soundtrack* no. 58, *Entertainment Weekly* 12/3/99.

Hal David interview by JB 5/24/11. Bassey interview from JBGH.

New York premiere: Eon press release 6/27/79. Reviews: *New Yorker* 7/9/79, HR 6/27/79, LAT 6/29/79, *Time* 7/2/79, *Billboard* 7/21/79, 7/28/79.

Barry complaints: HR 7/6/79.

13 For Your Eyes Only

Bill Conti interviews: with JB 10/3/02 and 9/28/11; also Archive of American Television interview (also by JB) 9/20/10. Conti announced WV 2/18/81.

Conti schedule in London: interview by Barrie Waugh, "Bill's Backing Bond," *A Fistful of Soundtracks* no. 3, July 1981. Also 1986 BBC radio interview; Cork 1999.

Sheena Easton, from Cork interview (on both *FYEO* and the Maurice Binder minidoc on *You Only Live Twice* DVD).

Easton records song, DV 4/16/81. Easton on keeping others out: *Entertainment Weekly* 12/3/99.

Conti on the score itself: interviews by JB 10/3/02 and JB 9/28/11 for synths; Cork for "country" music.

Peter Myers interview by JB 10/3/11. Also John Richards interview by JB 5/27/11.

Easton promotion: WV 6/10/81, 6/17/81. Reviews HR 6/24/81, NYT 6/26/81.

Song trade ads: HR 1/13/82, 1/21/82.

Oscars: *Inside Oscar*. Also DV 2/11/82, 3/30/82. Also consulted "Oscar's Greatest Moments" VHS. Walter Painter interview by JB 10/25/11.

14 Octopussy

Barry tax issues: *Daily Mail* 3/4/83.

Tim Rice: JB interview 6/9/11. Barry: Cork 2000.

Branigan reports: *Daily Mirror* 1/21/83, *Daily Express* 2/1/83, DV 1/26/83.

Coolidge to sing: UA press release 3/29/83. DV 3/30/83.

Coolidge quotes: interview by Spencer Leigh in *Country Music People* magazine, October 2006. Also story in *Billboard Book of #1 Adult Contemporary Hits*. Coolidge appearance in JBGH; *Entertainment Weekly* 12/3/99.

Phil Ramone interview by JB 5/4/11.

John Glen quote from *Octopussy* DVD.

Dana Kaproff and *Golden Seal*: Kaproff interview by JB 10/12/11.

Coolidge at London premiere, etc.: *Daily Express* 6/7/83.

Reviews: HR 6/8/83, *Washington Post* 7/24/83. Trade ad DV 1/9/84.

15 Never Say Never Again

Background from *The Battle for Bond* and *NSNA* DVD.

Kershner interview by Matthew Field from *007 Magazine* no. 40. Also Schwartzman comment from Graham Rye intro; Ford Thaxton conversation with Schwartzman ca. 1993.

Legrand interview 10/7/11 in French by Stephane Lerouge, English translation by Michelle Guy. Also, details on Legrand dates of writing and scoring courtesy of Lerouge; further details from Legrand manager Jim DiGiovanni, and Warner Bros. music files.

Marilyn and Alan Bergman interview by JB 5/25/11. Nat Peck interview by JB 10/8/11. Keith Grant interview by JB 9/28/11. Talia Shire interview by JB 10/7/11.

Bergman signing: WV 7/20/83.

Bonnie Tyler interview JBGH 2006.

Lani Hall and Herb Alpert interview by JB 10/21/11. Robbie Buchanan emails 10/30/11, 11/2/11.

Sophie Della (now known as Sofia Margo) emails from Paris 11/7/11, 11/8/11; she confirmed the early August 1983 recording date (her song was recorded August 2).

Premiere info and reviews: WV 11/30/83, DV 10/4/83, HR 10/5/83. *Hartford Courant* 10/10/83. *Soundtrack!* December 1983.

16 A View to a Kill

Taylor: London party quote from *Duran Duran Live from London* DVD, 2005. Also from on-video-set interview. Barry comments from Cork 2000.

More details on Duran Duran song from *Billboard* 2/2/85, 5/18/85, 6/1/85; Eon press release 3/15/85. Also DV 3/21/85, 4/26/85, 4/29/85.

LeBon: from on-video-set interview. Andy Taylor: from *Wild Boy: My Life in Duran Duran*. Rhodes: "Duran Duran Takes a Stab at Respectability," LAT 12/7/86. 2006 quotes from JBGH.

Le Bon quotes about songwriting: from Leonard, 2nd ed.

John Taylor detailed production info in the 2005 DVD (also credits from the single). Video: Lol Creme interview in LAT 7/28/85.

Taylor at royal premiere: video clip of telecast (ITV 6/12/85).

Nic Raine interview by JB 8/10/11. Premiere coverage: LAT 5/25/85, *Daily Mail* 6/13/85. Reviews: LAT 5/24/85, L.A. *Herald-Examiner* 5/24/85, DV 5/23/85. *Billboard* 6/1/85.

17 The Living Daylights

Golden Child info from my own liner notes, La-La Land CD 2010. Also "lost Bond score" quote from http://www.johnbarry.org.uk/news.php.

Name of the orchestra Barry is conducting is from the film's press notes.

Maryam d'Abo interview by JB 9/23/11; John Glen interview by JB 10/21/11. Also consulted: Glen's memoir *For My Eyes Only*.

a-ha doing theme: *Screen International* 3/14/87, *New Musical Express* 4/11/87, DV 4/10/87, WV 4/1/87.

Barry on a-ha press conference quote from JBGH. Waaktaar quote from a-ha.com website. Later Waaktaar quote from MTV 7/29/87.

Barry on a-ha: WV 5/13/87; later from *Soundtrack!* no. 58; "ping pong" quote from David Toop interview, *The Face* July 1987. Magne: from JBGH. Still and Wilson quotes: from *Empire* June–July 1989.

Barry quotes about the songs, synthesizer rhythm tracks, scoring, all from "Soundtracks" by Kevin Hilton in *Pro Sound News*, June–July 1987. Raine interview by JB 8/10/11.

Hynde involvement: DV 5/18/87, 5/27/87. L.A. *Herald-Examiner* 5/21/87. Song titles from DV 5/27/87 and David Toop article in *The Face*, July 1987.

Hynde: *USA Today* 7/31/87; MTV interviews 7/29/87; emails with Hynde's manager Andrea Mills September–October 2011. Barry quote from Cork 2000.

Royal premiere: DV 6/30/87. Reviews: DV 6/30/87, HR 7/31/87, *Guardian* quote from Glen's *For My Eyes Only*. Oscar 2-page "for your consideration" ad DV 1/22/88.

Final Barry quote from Cork interview 2000; also from Fiegel. *Variety* ad from Barry to Broccoli WV 5/13/87.

18 Licence to Kill

Barry info: DV 3/22/88, 4/11/88; also Fiegel and Leonard books.

Michael Kamen interview by JB 10/10/02.

Joel Sill interview by JB 10/17/11. Vic Flick book, plus Flick interview by JB 6/8/11; email 10/20/11. Stephen McLaughlin interview by JB 10/26/11.

Clapton session date from *Eric Clapton: The Complete Recording Sessions 1963–1992*.

Narada Michael Walden interview by JB 7/20/11, Diane Warren interview by JB 6/14/11; also *Billboard* 8/1/92. Aaron Zigman emails 11/14/11. Afanasieff quote: *Billboard* 12/12/98. Knight quote: *Entertainment Weekly* 12/3/99.

Kamen announced: *Screen International* 2/11/89, DV 2/16/89.

Info on film opening: DV 1/13/89, 7/12/89. Reviews: *Film Monthly* 10/89, *People* 7/17/89, *LA Weekly* 7/28/89. *Billboard* 7/22/89. Song on R&B charts from *Billboard* 2/7/04.

LaBelle quote from David Nathan notes to "Patti LaBelle: Greatest Hits" CD, MCA 1996.

Walden on "Goldfinger" quote: from JBGH.

19 GoldenEye

Brosnan/film background: DV 4/12/94, 6/8/94.

Rolling Stones: LAT 6/1/95 and 6/8/95, DV 6/2/95. Bono and Turner: DV 8/17/95, HR 10/30/95. Turner quotes from *Entertainment Weekly* 12/3/99, *Jet* magazine 11/20/95.

Craig Armstrong interview by JB 11/25/11.

Turner and Barry quotes from TV special *The World of 007*, aired 10/24/95 in United States.

Barry quote from Daniel Mangodt interview in *Soundtrack!* no. 58, 1996.

Gleeman from HR 8/29/95.

Richard Kraft interview by JB 5/24/11, John Altman interview by JB 8/30/11. Other Altman interviews: *Music from the Movies* no. 10, autumn–winter 1995–96; JBGH.

Eric Serra interview by JB 11/25/11; also Serra interview by Lukas Kendall in *Film Score Monthly* no. 63, November 1995. Also *Billboard* 11/25/95. Arnold quote from JBGH.

Reviews: DV 11/15/95, *Billboard* 11/4/95. *Fanfare* 3/96. *Premiere* ad December 1995 issue.

20 Tomorrow Never Dies

Grosses: HR 3/6/98. MGM's Sandoval "handling music direction": DV 4/3/97. Sandoval interview: *007 Magazine* no. 44.

Barry interview by JB 12/9/97. Richard Kraft interview by JB 5/24/11. (Two other sources with direct knowledge of the Barry negotiations confirmed the story about the studio's position.)

David Arnold interviews by JB 6/11/97, 12/4/97, 12/7/97, 6/23/99, 6/21/11. Don Black interview by JB 5/6/11.

Sheryl Crow announced: HR 6/16/97. Mitchell Froom interview by JB 9/22/11. Quotes from *Goldeneye* magazine no. 6, summer 1997. Also *Billboard* 9/6/97. Cracknell quote from JBGH.

Roger Spottiswoode interview by JB 12/5/97.

Articles by JB on Arnold: *For Your Eyes Only* no. 37, summer 1997; LAT 12/18/97.

Reviews: HR 12/15/97, LAT 12/19/97, *Times of London* 12/11/97. *Billboard* reviews 11/15/97, 12/6/97. *LA Weekly* 12/26/97, *Village Voice* 12/23/97.

21 The World Is Not Enough

Arnold interview by JB 6/21/11; Don Black interview by JB 5/6/11. Also Arnold and Apted commentary tracks on DVD.

Some dates and background from Fogerty and Crow vs. MGM, Universal and Eon Productions lawsuit (http://caselaw.findlaw.com/us-6th-circuit/1380062.html).

Butch Vig interview from James Rumley, "Garbage Exclusive Interview" at http://www.ianfleming.org, 1999. Garbage announcements: *Music Week* 6/26/99, HR 7/8/99.

Manson: from *Sunday Times of London* 10/10/99.

Dodd interview by JB 11/3/11.

MGM-MTV partnership: *Wall Street Journal* 9/29/99, WV 10/4/99, MTV press release 9/29/99. Radioactive/MCA press release on single and album 11/8/99.

Sandoval quote from interview by Greg Bechtloff in *007 Magazine* no. 44. *Billboard* review 10/30/99. Reviews LAT 11/19/99, HR 11/15/99. Ivor Novello story: *Billboard* 6/10/2000.

22 Die Another Day

Anita Camarata interview by JB 10/10/02. Madonna reports: *Us* 2/18/02, LAT 3/16/02, *Screen International* 3/22/02, LAT 3/25/02 and 7/10/02, HR 7/10/02.

Michel Colombier interview by JB 10/9/02; JB story on the song WV 11/11/02.

Michael Wilson and Lee Tamahori comments from DVD. Madonna interview from CNN's "Larry King Live" 10/10/02. Madonna quote on Colombier: JB interview with Madonna 12/2/11. Kleinman interview from JBGH. Michael Wilson comment from JBGH.

David Arnold interviews by JB 10/4/02, 6/21/11. Also consulted: *Music from the Movies* no. 35–36; Arnold interview on DVD. "I Will Return" from Dan Goldwasser interview 11/06 for http://www.soundtrack.net.

Reviews: *Sunday Times of London* 11/17/02. LAT 11/23/02. *Wall Street Journal* 11/22/02. DV 11/18/02. NYT 11/22/02. *Billboard* 10/19/02. *Spin* 4/24/03. *Entertainment Weekly* 4/25/03. *Times of London* 11/15/02. *Daily Telegraph* 10/23/08. Elton John comment from *London Sun* 11/29/02.

Video: *Vanity Fair* 10/02. Chart success: *Billboard* 10/19/02, 11/9/02, 12/27/03. Madonna at royal premiere: *People* 12/2/02. *Variety* ad promoting song WV 12/9/02.

Additional chart info from detailed week-by-week analysis at http://www.madonnanation.com/chartsarchive.

Razzie reference: *Madonna: Like an Icon*.

23 Casino Royale (2006)

Background: LAT 11/10/06 (including Wilson and Broccoli quotes).

David Arnold interviews by JB 11/30/06, 6/21/11, 12/1/11. Lia Vollack interview by JB 11/7/11. Cornell quotes from Chowdhury interview in *Kiss Kiss Bang Bang* no. 5.

Connery quote from *Hemispheres* magazine 4/08. Norman quote to JB via email 12/4/11.

Barbara Broccoli interview by JB 10/15/08. Campbell quote from DVD commentary.

Reviews: HR 11/10/06, DV 11/10/06, *Billboard* 12/16/06. Premiere coverage DV 11/16/06.

ENDNOTES
295

24 Quantum of Solace

David Arnold interviews by JB 10/9/08, 6/21/11, 8/16/11, 12/5/11, 12/12/11; Lia Vollack by JB 11/7/11. Also background interviews with those involved behind the scenes with the early Winehouse material. Early critic appraisals: LAT 5/11/08, *London Telegraph* 9/24/08.

Ronson quotes: *BBC News* 4/28/08, AP story 5/3/08. Winehouse obituaries *London Telegraph* 7/23/11, DV 7/25/11.

Jack White: announcements *Billboard* 7/29/08, LAT 7/30/08, *Rolling Stone* 7/29/08. White quotes from *Us* 8/21/08, *Rolling Stone* 10/2/08. Keys quotes from *New Musical Express* 10/25/08, *Wall Street Journal* 11/14/08.

Forster on opera sequence: from *Bond On Set: Filming Quantum of Solace*.

Arnold on the score: JB interview 6/21/11 plus Tommy Pearson's September 2008 interview from http://www.stageandscreenonline.com.

Nicholas Dodd interview by JB 11/3/11. Jaime Cuadra background from Steve Oxenrider's profile in *007 Magazine*, November 2009.

Premiere: WV 11/3/08. Reviews: NYT 11/19/08, *New York* 11/17/08, *Rolling Stone* 11/27/08, HR 10/27/08. *London Telegraph* 9/24/08 (*New Musical Express* quote in same story).

Arnold on "No Good About Goodbye": JB interviews 6/21/11, 12/5/11.

25 Skyfall

Olympics stunt: BBC News 7/27/12, *Sun* 11/13/12, *Daily Mail* 3/23/13.

Barry flat as M's residence: *007 Magazine* review 10/14/12.

David Arnold quote: www.cultbox.co.uk 1/18/12.

Thomas Newman interviews by JB 11/23/12, 1/25/13. Lia Vollack interviews by JB 10/29/12, 11/15/12. Paul Epworth interview by JB 11/15/12. Jenny O'Grady interview by JB 1/20/14. George Doering interview by JB 1/12/14. JAC Redford interview by JB 11/29/12.

Adele with Jonathan Ross: *Daily Mail* 9/3/11. Adele on the song: Interviews with Ryan Seacrest at the Golden Globe Awards, then backstage in Globe pressroom 1/13/13.

Mendes on Adele song: *Thompson on Hollywood* blog, 11/15/12, also *Skyfall* Blu-Ray commentary track. Mendes on Newman, also from commentary track.

Recording dates courtesy of Isobel Griffiths 11/26/12.

Adele and the song: LAT 10/1/12, London *Telegraph* 10/1/12, BBC Newsbeat 10/2/12.

Song reviews: *Entertainment Weekly* 10/4/12, New York *Daily News* 10/4/12, *Telegraph* 10/5/12, *Wall Street Journal* 10/5/12, HR 10/4/12, *Billboard* 10/20/12.

Music stats: Billboard.com reports 10/4,5,6,10,19/12, 11/16/12. Soundtrack album: *Billboard* 11/24/12.

Box-office stats from boxofficemojo.com.

Film and score reviews: *Times of London* 10/13/12, New York *Daily News* 10/20/12, *Variety* 10/15/12, HR 10/13/12. *Film Score Monthly* January 2013.

Adele remarks at Golden Globe Awards (backstage) 1/13/13; Newman remarks at BAFTA honors 2/10/13.

Oscars: JB interviews with Chris Walden 2/19/13, Mark Graham 2/25/13, William Ross 8/2/13, Sally Stevens 12/7/13.

Score Highlights

Newman score review www.slate.com 1/15/13. Derek Watkins interview by special correspondent 10/23/12.

Vertigo reference: Mendes commentary track on *Skyfall* Blu-Ray.

Also consulted: Newman comments in Chris Hewitt interview at www.empireonline .com, November 2012; also, Newman interviews by JB.

Afterword

Carl Davis interview by JB 11//24/11. George S. Clinton interview by JB 3/25/07. Barbara Broccoli interview by JB 10/15/08.

Appendix 2

Lionel Bart "Thunderball": Bart archivist Brenda Evans letter to Geoff Leonard 10/8/13.

Alice Cooper at Moore/Barry party: WV 3/27/74 (song issued on his *Muscle of Love* album). Quotes from JBGH.

Blondie/Debbie Harry quotes: JBGH. Conti confirmed Blondie was in the mix.

"Never Say Never Again": Stephen Forsyth interview 6/15/11; Hyman vocal on YouTube.

Bibliography

Alvarez, Max Joseph. *Index to Motion Pictures Reviewed by Variety, 1907–1980*. Metuchen, N.J.: Scarecrow Press, 1982.

Balio, Tino. *United Artists: The Company That Changed the Film Industry, Volume 2, 1951–1978*. Madison: University of Wisconsin Press, 2009.

Barnes, Alan, and Marcus Hearn. *Kiss Kiss, Bang! Bang! The Unofficial James Bond Film Companion*. London: BT Batsford, 1997.

Benson, Raymond. *The James Bond Bedside Companion*. New York: Dodd, Mead, 1984.

Biederman, Danny. *James Bond 007 Collection*. Van Nuys, Calif.: Alfred, 2001.

Bouzereau, Laurent. *The Art of Bond*. New York: Abrams, 2006.

Bricusse, Leslie. *The Music Man: The Life and Good Times of a Songwriter*. London: Metro, 2006.

———. *The Leslie Bricusse Songbook*. New York: Cherry Lane Music, 2007.

Broccoli, Albert R., with Donald Zec. *When the Snow Melts: The Autobiography of Cubby Broccoli*. London: Boxtree, 1998.

Bronson, Fred. *The Billboard Book of Number One Hits*. New York: Billboard, 1988.

Brosnan, John. *James Bond in the Cinema*, 2nd ed. La Jolla, Calif.: Barnes, 1981.

Brown, Royal S. *Overtones and Undertones: Reading Film Music*. Berkeley: University of California Press, 1994.

Burlingame, Jon. *Sound and Vision: 60 Years of Motion Picture Soundtracks*. New York: Billboard Books, 2000.

Burns, Mick. *Keeping the Beat on the Street: The New Orleans Brass Band Renaissance*. Baton Rouge: Louisiana State University Press, 2006.

Cork, John, and Collin Stutz. *James Bond Encyclopedia*. New York: DK, 2007.

Cork, John, and Bruce Scivally. *James Bond: The Legacy*. New York: Abrams, 2002.

Daniels, George G., ed. *As You Remember Them: The Men and the Music*. New York: Time-Life Records, 1972.

Dominic, Serene. *Burt Bacharach: Song by Song*. New York: Schirmer, 2003.

Fiegel, Eddi. *John Barry: A Sixties Theme*. London: Constable , 1998.

Flick, Vic. *Vic Flick: Guitarman*. Albany, Ga.: Bear Manor Media, 2008.

Gambaccini, Paul, Tim Rice and Jonathan Rice. *The Guinness Book of British Hit Albums*, 7th ed. Middlesex: Guinness, 1996.

Gambaccini, Paul, Tim Rice and Jonathan Rice. *The Guinness Book of British Hit Singles*, 8th ed. Middlesex: Guinness, 1991.

Glen, John, with Marcus Hearn. *For My Eyes Only*. Dulles, Va.: Brassey's, 2001.

Granata, Charles L. *Sessions with Sinatra: Frank Sinatra and the Art of Recording*. Chicago: A Capella Books, 1999.

Hamlisch, Marvin, with Gerald Gardner. *The Way I Was*. New York: Scribner, 1992.

Hardy, Phil, and Dave Laing. *The Faber Companion to 20th-Century Popular Music*. London: Faber and Faber, 1990.

Helfenstein, Charles. *The Making of* On Her Majesty's Secret Service. Baltimore, Md.: Spies, 2009.

Inverne, James. *Wrestling with Elephants: The Authorised Biography of Don Black*. London: Sanctuary, 2003.

Karlin, Fred, and Rayburn Wright. *On the Track: A Guide to Contemporary Film Scoring*, 2nd ed. New York: Routledge, 2004.

Larson, Randall D. *Music from the House of Hammer: Music in the Hammer Horror Films, 1950–1980*. Lanham, Md.: Scarecrow Press, 1996.

Leonard, Geoff, Pete Walker, and Gareth Bramley. *John Barry: A Life in Music*. Bristol, England: Sansom, 1998.

Leonard, Geoff, Pete Walker, and Gareth Bramley. *John Barry: The Man with the Midas Touch*. Bristol, England: Redcliffe Press, 2008.

Lycett, Andrew. *Ian Fleming: The Man Behind James Bond*. Atlanta: Turner, 1995.

Martin, George, with Jeremy Hornsby. *All You Need Is Ears*. New York: St. Martin's Press, 1979.

Monro, Michele. *The Singer's Singer: The Life and Music of Matt Monro*. London: Titan Books, 2010.

Moore, Roger, with Gareth Owen. *My Word Is My Bond*. New York: It Books, 2009.

O'Brien, Lucy. *Madonna: Like an Icon*. New York: Harper Entertainment, 2007.

O'Neil, Thomas. *The Grammys*. New York: Perigee, 1993.

Parish, James Robert, and Michael R. Pitts. *The Great Spy Pictures*. Metuchen, N.J.: Scarecrow Press, 1974.

Pfeiffer, Lee, and Dave Worrall. *The Essential Bond: The Authorized Guide to the World of 007*. New York: Harper Paperbacks, 2002.

Pfeiffer, Lee, and Philip Lisa. *The Incredible World of 007*. New York: Citadel Press, 1995.

Pinch, Trevor, and Frank Trocco. *Analog Days: The Invention and Impact of the Moog Synthesizer*. Cambridge, Mass.: Harvard University Press, 2002.

Platts, Robin. *Burt Bacharach & Hal David: What the World Needs Now*. Burlington, Ont., Can.: CG Publishing, 2003.

Ramone, Phil, with Charles L. Granata. *Making Records: The Scenes Behind the Music*. New York: Hyperion, 2007.

Ricciardi, Ricky. *What a Wonderful World: The Magic of Louis Armstrong's Later Years*. New York: Pantheon Books, 2011.

Roach, Martin, ed. *The Virgin Book of British Hit Albums*. London: Virgin Books, 2009.

Roberty, Marc. *Eric Clapton: The Complete Recording Sessions, 1963–1992*. New York: St. Martin's Press, 1999.

Rosen, Craig. *The Billboard Book of Number One Albums*. New York: Billboard Books, 1996.

Rubin, Steven Jay. *The Complete James Bond Movie Encyclopedia*. Chicago: Contemporary Books, 1995.

Rubin, Steven Jay. *The James Bond Films*. Westport, Conn.: Arlington House, 1981.

Russell, Barry. *John Barry's Goldfinger in Focus*. London: Rhinegold, 2007.

Russell, Mark, and James Young. *Film Music: Screencraft*. Boston: Focal Press, 2000.

Sellers, Robert. *The Battle for Bond*. Sheffield, England: Tomahawk Press, 2008.

Smith, Jeff. *The Sounds of Commerce: Marketing Popular Film Music*. New York: Columbia University Press, 1998.

Sherk, Warren. *Film and Television Music*. Lanham, Md.: Scarecrow Press, 2011.

Stafford, David and Caroline. *Fings Ain't Wot They Used T'Be: The Lionel Bart Story*. London: Omnibus Press, 2011.

Taylor, Andy. *Wild Boy: My Life in Duran Duran*. New York: Grand Central Publishing, 2008.

Thompson, Dave. *Reggae & Caribbean Music*. San Francisco: Backbeat Books, 2002.

Turner, Adrian. *Goldfinger*. New York: Bloomsbury, 1998.

Variety's Directory of Major U.S. Show Business Awards. New York: Bowker, 1989.

The Virgin Book of British Hit Singles. London: Virgin Books, 2010.

Wall, Mick. *When Giants Walked the Earth: A Biography of Led Zeppelin*. New York: St. Martin's Press, 2009.

Williams, Greg. *Bond on Set: Filming Quantum of Solace*. New York: DK, 2008.

Whitburn, Joel. *The Billboard Book of Top 40 Hits*, 3rd ed. New York: Billboard, 1987.

———. *The Billboard Hot 100 Charts: The Sixties*. Menomonee Falls, Wis.: Record Research, 1990.

———. *Top Adult Contemporary 1961–2001*. Menomonee Falls, Wis.: Record Research, 2002.

———. *Top Pop Albums*, 7th ed. Menomonee Falls, Wis.: Record Research, 2010.

———. *Top Pop Singles*, 13th ed. Menomonee Falls, Wis.: Record Research, 2011.

Wiley, Mason, and Damien Bona. *Inside Oscar: The Unofficial History of the Academy Awards*, 10th ed. New York: Ballantine Books, 1993.

Williams, John L. *Miss Shirley Bassey*. London: Quercus, 2010.

Zollo, Paul. *Songwriters on Songwriting*. New York: Da Capo Press, 1997.

Photo Credits

p. 3: Rex Features.

pp. 7, 13: Monty Norman.

pp. 9, 27, 38, 49, 73, 76, 83, 99, 107, 116, 129, 136, 148, 149: United Artists / Photofest.

pp. 14, 36, 54, 72, 86, 101, 106, 110, 118, 119, 132, 138, 157, 158, 170, 178, 186, 192, 210, 214: The Film Music Society.

p. 24: Graham Rye / *007 Magazine*.

pp. 30, 52, 95: Don Black.

p. 32: Eric Tomlinson.

p. 37: United Artists / Photofest / Springer.

p. 40: Leslie Bricusse.

p. 60: Columbia Pictures / Photofest.

p. 62: Photofest.

p. 63: Mike Redway.

p. 88: Photo by Jack Bradley, courtesy The Film Music Society.

pp. 105, 146, 153, 265: Academy of Motion Picture Arts and Sciences.

p. 125: Bison Archives / Marc Wanamaker.

p. 140: Photo by Gay Goodwin Wallin.

pp. 160, 180, 184, 185, 193, 205, 212: MGM-UA / Photofest.

p. 166. Photo by Spike Nannarello, courtesy of Alan and Marilyn Bergman.

p. 168: Warner Bros. / Photofest.

p. 176: *Cinema Retro* magazine.

p. 194: Vic Flick.

p. 202: Eric Serra.

p. 204: Photo by Danny Clifford, courtesy John Altman.

pp. 221, 229, 231: MGM / Photofest.

pp. 224, 252: Nicholas Dodd.

pp. 237, 238: MGM / Columbia Pictures / Photofest.

p. 239: Photo by Julie Edwards.

p. 247: BMI / Getty Images.

p. 250, 257: Sony Pictures / Photofest.

p. 261: Bill Bernstein.

p. 268: British Academy of Film and Television Arts.

p. 272: Photo by Marilee Bradford.

Index

CPSIA information can be obtained
at www.ICGtesting.com
Printed in the USA
LVHW101355110920
665709LV00017B/670